# Making Sense of Education in Post-Handover Hong Kong

Since 1997, when Hong Kong became a Special Administrative Region of the People's Republic of China, a string of education reforms have been introduced to improve the quality of education and maintain Hong Kong's economic competitiveness in the age of globalisation. This book provides a comprehensive and critical analysis of major issues and challenges faced by the education system, ranging from preschool to higher education. It analyses the prospects for educational development in Hong Kong. It further addresses how Hong Kong's government has responded to the perceived challenges of the external environment and internal forces and explains the rationales for the actions taken. Not only does it review how the reform initiative challenges have been dealt with, but it also reviews how effective these initiatives are and its implications on future directions.

**Thomas Kwan-Choi Tse** received his PhD degree with a focus on sociology of education at the University of Warwick, United Kingdom, in 1997. He is currently an associate professor of the Department of Educational Administration and Policy, the Chinese University of Hong Kong. He teaches and publishes in the fields of civic education, moral education, educational policy and sociology of education.

**Michael H. Lee** received his doctorate in the field of higher education studies at the University of Hong Kong, is a lecturer in the Department of History of the Chinese University of Hong Kong, teaching and researching in the area of educational history, development and policy in Hong Kong, Malaysia and Singapore.

# Routledge Critical Studies in Asian Education

Series Editors:
S. Gopinathan and Wing On Lee

For a full list of titles in this series, please visit www.routledge.com

**Multicultural Education in South Korea**
Language, Ideology and Culture
*Kang Mi Ok*

**Asia as Method in Education Studies**
*Edited by Hongzhi Zhang, Philip Wing Keung Chan and Jane Kenway*

**Secondary School English Education in Asia**
From Policy to Practice
*Edited by Bernard Spolsky and Kiwan Sung*

**A Critical Study of Thailand's Higher Education Reforms**
The culture of borrowing
*Rattana Lao*

**Mapping the Terrain of Education Reform**
Global Trends and Local Responses in the Philippines
*Vicente Chua Reyes, Jr.*

**Non-formal Education and Civil Society in Japan**
*Edited by Kaori H. Okano*

**Knowledge, Control and Critical Thinking in Singapore**
State ideology and the politics of pedagogic recontextualization
*Leonel Lim*

**Languages in the Malaysian Education System**
Monolingual strands in multilingual settings
*Edited by Asmah Haji Omar*

**Policy Discourses in Malaysian Education**
A nation in the making
*Edited by Suseela Malakolunthu and Nagappan C. Rengasamy*

**Making Sense of Education in Post-Handover Hong Kong**
Achievements and challenges
*Edited by Thomas Kwan-Choi Tse and Michael H. Lee*

# Making Sense of Education in Post-Handover Hong Kong

Achievements and challenges

Edited by Thomas Kwan-Choi Tse and Michael H. Lee

LONDON AND NEW YORK

First published 2017 by Routledge

2 Park Square, Milton Park, Abingdon, Oxfordshire OX14 4RN
711 Third Avenue, New York, NY 10017

*Routledge is an imprint of the Taylor & Francis Group, an informa business*

First issued in paperback 2018

Copyright © 2017 selection and editorial matter, Thomas Kwan-Choi Tse and Michael H. Lee; individual chapters, the contributors

The right of Thomas Kwan-Choi Tse and Michael H. Lee to be identified as the authors of the editorial material, and of the authors for their individual chapters, has been asserted in accordance with sections 77 and 78 of the Copyright, Designs and Patents Act 1988.

All rights reserved. No part of this book may be reprinted or reproduced or utilised in any form or by any electronic, mechanical, or other means, now known or hereafter invented, including photocopying and recording, or in any information storage or retrieval system, without permission in writing from the publishers.

Notice:
Product or corporate names may be trademarks or registered trademarks, and are used only for identification and explanation without intent to infringe.

*British Library Cataloguing in Publication Data*
A catalogue record for this book is available from the British Library

*Library of Congress Cataloging-in-Publication Data*
A catalogue record for this book has been requested

ISBN: 978-1-138-90851-2 (hbk)
ISBN: 978-1-138-60463-6 (pbk)

Typeset in Galliard
by Apex CoVantage, LLC

# Contents

*Acknowledgements* — vii
*Contributors* — viii

1 Introduction: setting and issues — 1
   MICHAEL H. LEE AND THOMAS KWAN-CHOI TSE

2 Vouchers in early childhood education: market still?
   What to choose next? — 21
   GAIL WAI-KWAN YUEN

3 Parental choice in the new education market:
   aided-turn-direct subsidy scheme schools in focus — 40
   JACQUELINE CHAK-KEI WOO

4 Unlocking the dilemma of language policy in the
   post-1997 era — 54
   ANITA YUK-KANG POON

5 In search of equal and excellent basic education in
   Hong Kong: insights from programme for
   international student assessment — 73
   ESTHER SUI-CHU HO

6 Shadow education: features, expansion and implications — 95
   KEVIN WAI-HO YUNG AND MARK BRAY

7 Curriculum reform: why, how, what and where it is
   headed for — 112
   CHI-CHUNG LAM AND NGAI-YING WONG

## Contents

8 Civic education in Hong Kong: from the colonial
era to the post-occupy movement era 127
YAN-WING LEUNG, ERIC KING-MAN CHONG,
AND TIMOTHY WAI-WA YUEN

9 Changing governance, accountability and leadership:
Hong Kong education meets neo-liberalism 145
NICHOLAS SUN-KEUNG PANG

10 Should there be public reporting of school performance?:
the lessons from the school inspection reports disputes 161
THOMAS KWAN-CHOI TSE

11 Parent and home-school relationships: issues and challenges 180
SHUN-WING NG

12 Changing student diversity, changing cultures and changing
education policies: cross-boundary students, Chinese
immigrant students and non-Chinese speaking
students in focus 200
CELESTE YUET-MUI YUEN

13 Excellence without a soul?: higher education in
post-1997 Hong Kong 215
MICHAEL H. LEE

*Index* 233

# Acknowledgements

The editors sincerely thank the Routledge Critical Studies in Asian Education Series Editors, Professor S. Gopinathan and Professor Wing On Lee for their encouragement, support and invaluable advice. We are thankful for the support we received from all contributors who make this inter-institutional collaborative book project possible. We also thank those at Routledge and Apex CoVantage who have assisted in the production of this book.

We would like to dedicate this edited volume to Professor Tsang Wing Kwong (Adjunct Professor, Department of Educational Administration and Policy, The Chinese University of Hong Kong), in recognition of his contributions to educational policy discourse that have inspired so many followers.

Chapter 13 is a revised and updated version of M. H. Lee (2014), "Hong Kong Higher Education in the 21st Century", *Hong Kong Teachers' Centre Journal*, 13, 15–34, by permission of Hong Kong Teachers' Centre.

Thomas Kwan-Choi Tse and Michael H. Lee<br>
The Chinese University of Hong Kong<br>
September 2016

# Contributors

**Mark Bray** is UNESCO chair professor in comparative education at the University of Hong Kong. He has worked at that university since 1986, prior to which he taught in secondary schools in Kenya and Nigeria and at the Universities of Edinburgh, Papua New Guinea and London. His work has included focus on the administration and financing of education systems. His 1999 book on shadow education published by UNESCO's International Institute for Educational Planning (IIEP) was the first substantial international review of this topic and has been followed up by empirical work in a number of locations, including Hong Kong. His work on shadow education has been translated into 20 languages.

**Eric King-Man Chong** is an assistant professor in the Department of Social Sciences, The Education University of Hong Kong. Having developed an interest in citizenship education since he joined the HKIEd in 2000, he served in research and curriculum development positions in the Centre for Citizenship Education (2000–2005), including teaching fellow (2005–2008), senior teaching fellow (2009–2011), lecturer (2011–2015) and assistant professor (2016 to present). He had also served in the Moral and Civic Education Section of EDB in 2008. Dr. Chong teaches general studies, civic education, and liberal studies in undergraduate, PGDE and in-service teachers' PDP programmes in which pedagogy and subject knowledge about local, national and global issues are covered. He is also working on internship arrangement of BSocSc (Global & Environmental Studies) and BA (LSE) programmes. His main research interests are citizenship education, politics and national identity. He has worked on school-based development projects on topics of citizenship education, liberal studies, general studies, rule of law, human rights, basic law education and global citizenship education.

**Esther Sui-Chu Ho** received her PhD from University of British Columbia, is professor of Department of Education Administration and Policy and director of Hong Kong Centre for International Student Assessment, The Chinese University of Hong Kong. Her working experiences include teaching in Hong Kong primary and secondary schools; project manager of HKPISA-2000 to HKPISA-2015, and Macau-PISA-2003; professional consultant of China-PISA 2006 Trial Study and Shanghai-PISA 2009; Fulbright scholar at

Pennsylvania State University (2004) and Johns Hopkins University (2010); and teaching consultant of the World Bank in the District Primary Educational Programme, India. Her research interests include: parental involvement in children's education, home-school community collaboration, school effectiveness and school reform, decentralisation and school-based management, research methodology in education, multilevel analysis in educational research.

**Chi-Chung Lam** is an adjunct professor at the Department of Curriculum and Instruction, The Chinese University of Hong Kong. He received his master's degree on geographical education and doctoral degree in curriculum studies from the Institute of Education, University of London. He has extensive working experience in secondary schools and the university sector. In the past two decades, Professor Lam has been active in research work on the curriculum change and reform in Hong Kong. He has published over 80 refereed journal papers, mostly on curriculum reform and implementation, geographical curriculum changes, mathematics curriculum and teachers' beliefs.

**Michael H. Lee**, who received his doctorate in the field of higher education studies at the University of Hong Kong, is a lecturer in the Department of History of the Chinese University of Hong Kong, teaching and researching in the area of educational history, development and policy in Hong Kong, Malaysia and Singapore. Some of his journal articles were published in *Asia-Pacific Education Review*, *Australian Journal of Education*, *Higher Education Research and Development*, and *Journal of Higher Education Policy and Management*; as well as book chapters in *Changing Governance and Public Policy in East Asia*, *Crossing Borders in East Asian Higher Education*, *Globalization and Higher Education in India*, *Globalization and the Singapore Curriculum: From Policy to Classroom*, and *International Handbook on Globalization, Education and Policy Research*.

**Yan-Wing Leung** is an adjunct associate professor of the Educational Policy and Leadership Department and was the co-director of the Centre for Governance and Citizenship, The Education University of Hong Kong. Dr. Leung teaches and researches mainly on civic missions of schools, civic education, human rights education, national education, values education, political socialisation and educational policies. He has published in international and regional journals, made public speeches and been involved in policies debates in various local and international media. Engaging actively in civil society in Hong Kong, Dr. Leung is the coordinator of the Hong Kong Alliance for Civic Education.

**Shun-Wing Ng** is professor and head of Department of Education Policy and Leadership at The Education University of Hong Kong. He is presently the programme leader of the training programmes for aspiring principals, newly appointed principals and serving principals. Dr. Ng has published books, book chapters and refereed articles in international journals regarding education policies, home-school relations, international education, educational change and reform and citizenship education. Dr. Ng has recently been awarded the Annual IISE Best Article 2013 for his article, entitled "Rethinking the Mission of Internationalisation of Higher Education in Asia-Pacific Region", by the University of Pittsburgh Institute for International Studies in Education (IISE).

**Nicholas Sun-Keung Pang** is the professor and chairman of the Department of Educational Administration and Policy at the Chinese University of Hong Kong, the director of the Hong Kong Centre for the Development of Educational Leadership and was former chairman of Hong Kong Educational Research Association. Prof. Pang specialises in educational administration, management and leadership, as well as school effectiveness and improvement, and he has been publishing widely, locally and internationally.

**Anita Yuk-Kang Poon** is an associate professor in the Department of Education Studies at Hong Kong Baptist University. She obtained her PhD from Queensland University of Technology in Australia. She has published a book, a number of book chapters and journal articles on medium of instruction, language policy and planning, language use in Hong Kong, English-language teaching, English-language education and education policies. She has contributed articles to journals like: *Current Issues in Language Planning, International Journal of Bilingual Education and Bilingualism, International Review of Education, The Asia-Pacific Education Researcher*, etc.

**Thomas Kwan-Choi Tse** received his PhD degree with a focus on sociology of education at the University of Warwick, United Kingdom, in 1997. He is currently an associate professor of the Department of Educational Administration and Policy, the Chinese University of Hong Kong. He teaches and publishes in the fields of civic education, moral education, educational policy and sociology of education. His works on education reforms in Hong Kong appear in the journals like *Education and Society, Education and Urban Society, International Journal of Education Reform*, and *International Studies in Sociology of Education*; as well as the books such as *Education and Society in Hong Kong and Macau* (2nd ed.), *Globalization and Education, Education Reform and the Quest for Excellence, Remaking Citizenship in Hong Kong*, and *Globalisation, the Nation-state and the Citizen*.

**Ngai-Ying Wong** is honorary professor, Department of Curriculum and Instruction, The Education University of Hong Kong. Before he retired from the Faculty of Education, the Chinese University of Hong Kong, he was the chair of the Board of Undergraduate Studies and the programme director of the Master of Science in Mathematics Education. He is also the founding president of the Hong Kong Association for Mathematics Education. His research interests include classroom environment, mathematics curriculum reform, beliefs about mathematics, bianshi teaching, Confucian Cultural Heritage Learner's phenomena and student activities.

**Jacqueline Chak-Kei Woo** received her PhD degree in the field of education policy, with a focus on sociology of education at the Chinese University of Hong Kong in 2011. She received her master's degree in international education in New York University. Her working experiences include working as a senior programme manager of sub-degree and Yi Jin programmes in Hong Kong; coordinated relief programme in New York City. She had also taught in a secondary school in Hong Kong and in universities in both Hong Kong and mainland China. Dr. Woo is currently an instructor at the Open University of Hong Kong.

**Gail Wai-Kwan Yuen** is assistant professor in the Department of Education Policy and Leadership at The Education University of Hong Kong. Her work focuses on policy and advocacy for young children, as well as teacher professionalism. Dr. Yuen has conducted a number of research projects on education vouchers for kindergartens in Hong Kong. She is also active in working with advocates to influence the policy agenda and public discourse on early childhood education.

**Celeste Yuet-Mui Yuen** is an associate professor in the Department of Education Policy and Leadership at The Education University of Hong Kong. Her PhD degree was on curriculum studies and awarded by the University of London, United Kingdom, in 1995. Her research areas are focused on ethnic minority, immigrant education and intercultural education. She has led over 10 territory-wide consultancy studies and large-scale projects. On the subject relating to this manuscript, for example, she has recently secured funding from the Research Grant Council in Hong Kong to conduct one public policy and one general research fund research projects. Some of her papers on immigrant and minority student education appear in international journals such as *Journal of Youth Studies, Australian Educational Researcher, Compare, Teaching and Teacher Education, Journal of Education, Citizenship and Social Justice, Intercultural Education, Pacific-Asian Education*, etc.

**Timothy Wai-Wa Yuen** serves as an assistant professor in the Education Policy and Leadership Department of The Education University of Hong Kong. His research interest is on citizenship/political education and education policies. Dr Yuen's recent publications can be found in *Intercultural Education, International Journal of Educational Management, Compare, Citizenship Teaching and Learning, International Studies in Educational Administration,* and *Citizenship, Social and Economics Education: An International Journal*.

**Kevin Wai-Ho Yung** received his PhD degree at the Faculty of Education, The University of Hong Kong. His study focused on Hong Kong secondary school students' English learning experiences in shadow education. He had worked as an English instructor at tutorial institutes in Hong Kong prior to teaching English for Academic and Specific Purposes at the Centre for Applied English Studies, The University of Hong Kong. His research interests include shadow education, English learning motivation, autonomy and out-of-class language learning.

# 1 Introduction

## Setting and issues

*Michael H. Lee and Thomas Kwan-Choi Tse*

"Those who stand on tiptoe will not stand firm.
Those who walk with long step will not walk well."

— Laotze

"Striving to better, oft we mar what's well."

— William Shakespeare

## Preamble

The year 1997 is undoubtedly one with historical significance for Hong Kong, mainly because it marked the end of the over 150-year British colonial rule with the transfer of sovereignty to the People's Republic of China. Hong Kong then became a Special Administrative Region (hereafter, HKSAR) entitled to a high degree of autonomy in governance in all areas but foreign affairs and national defence in line with the "one country, two systems" framework as stipulated in the Basic Law. The HKSAR government was enthusiastic to demonstrate its strong determination, commitment and ability to bring about sustainable social progress and developments in order to convince the general public that Hong Kong would be governed more effectively and efficiently than under the colonial administration. Therefore, the first chief executive, Tung Chee-Hwa, pledged to launch a series of reforms covering a range of public policy areas, such as health care, public housing, social welfare and also education (Scott, 2005; Tung, 1997). A comprehensive review of the education system in Hong Kong was carried out subsequently in 1999–2000 with the aim to identify development strategies and reform measures to be adopted to deal with changes and challenges arising from globalisation and the emergence of a knowledge-based economy (Education Commission, 1999).

A string of education reforms have been introduced since the handover of sovereignty to improve the quality of education and maintain Hong Kong's economic competitiveness in the age of globalisation. While the Hong Kong education system has experienced some changes and challenges subject to effects of globalisation, it is internationally recognised as among the most successful for its outstanding performance in international comparisons and rankings, as validated by top rankings achieved by Hong Kong in international comparative studies like the Trends in International Mathematics and Science Study (TIMSS) and the Programme for International Student Assessment (PISA) for primary and secondary education, and the ones conducted by *Times Higher Education Supplement* and QS *World University Rankings* for university education (Information Services Department, 2012, 2013; OECD, 2011).

What happened in Hong Kong is very similar to other countries which have been actively learning and borrowing policies and practices being widely promoted by such international institutions as the World Bank, the Organisation for Economic Co-Operation and Development (OECD) and UNESCO in order to maintain and strengthen the competitiveness of the education system across the globe (Cheng, 2009, 2015; Taylor, Rizvi, Lingard, & Henry, 1997).

Moreover, a strong and competent education system has been widely considered as indispensable to achieving competitiveness for national economies, as both innovation and creativity are viewed as the keys of economic success. Therefore, it is not surprising for Hong Kong to be internationally perceived as having one of the most successful education systems. However, while there has been a consensus that education should be a priority of public policy in Hong Kong, there have been inevitable controversies over what and how reforms should be proposed and implemented because it is difficult to have the interests of diverse stakeholders being well taken care of or even compromised as similar as most of other countries. This edited volume provides a comprehensive and critical analysis of major issues and challenges facing the education system in Hong Kong since 1997.

In the subsequent twelve chapters in this volume, each will review a particular sector or issue of the Hong Kong education system, addressing respectively: 1) the background or development of the particular policy initiative or educational problem; 2) the roles and reactions of different stakeholders involved; 3) the outcome or emerging issues and problems related to the policy implementation; as well as 4) reflections on the implications or future directions of education reforms and developments.

Contributors to the volume focus on various aspects of the Hong Kong education system, ranging from preschool education to higher education, and the various domains including curriculum, civic education and national identity, medium of instruction, school management, parents and home-school relationships, students of marginal groups, shadow education and student performance.

Together we examine how effective the education policies have been implemented to respond to problems and challenges arising from globalisation and to changing local political, social and economic contexts. Controversies over the issues such as voucher system in kindergartens, medium of instruction policy, direct subsidy scheme schools, public reporting of school performance, national education and inclusive education have been our foci. In view of the new scenario, we need a more comprehensive account that critically analyses the impacts of the reforms on educational development and also explores how the education system in Hong Kong should tackle the problems that inhibit the effective implementation of education reforms and policies and cope with the emerging challenges arising from globalisation and the ever-changing socio-economic environment.

Moreover, at a time when it has passed the first twenty years of the new regime under the Hong Kong SAR government, it is appropriate to "take stock and look forward" on Hong Kong education by providing critical and analytical accounts more systematically in this edited volume.

The overall concern of this volume is threefold. First of all is the perceived challenges of external environment, like globalisation and national re-integration, and internal forces, such as changing demographic composition driving the government to undertake education reforms, and the effectiveness of reforms addressing those challenges. Second, it concerns the consequences and impacts of education reforms on stakeholders and their acceptance or resistance to the implementation of education policies and reforms. Finally, it probes into major factors affecting the future directions of education reforms and development in Hong Kong, with special reference to the role of the government as well as the relationship and possible tension between the government and stakeholders. This volume not only serves as an up-to-date reference on the development of education reforms and policies in Hong Kong but also contributes to the wider academic literature and systematic analysis of the territory's educational development strategies (Cheng, 2009, 2015; Ho, Morris, & Chung, 2005; Marsh & Lee, 2014; Postiglione & Lee, 1997; Sharma, 2013; Sweeting, 2004; Tsang, 1998, 2006, 2011).

## Internal and external contexts of changes

Providing an overview of the Hong Kong education system, Table 1.1 lists the total population of Hong Kong, the numbers of education institutions and student enrollments at different educational levels, and the total government expenditure on education respectively in 1997 and 2014.

Table 1.1 shows that the total Hong Kong population grew from 6.5 million in 1997 to 7.2 million in 2014. In terms of the number of education institutions, the number of primary and secondary schools decreased slightly whereas that of kindergartens increased more significantly between 1997 and 2014. The number of students enrolled in the early childhood, primary and secondary levels dropped, with a more significant decrease for both the primary and secondary sectors, amounting to a quarter of the original size of school population. This coincides with the phenomenon of low birth rate in Hong Kong during the same period of time. While the number of UGC-funded institutions remained intact, there has been an increase in that of privately-funded higher education institutions, which reached 11 in 2014. This denotes the expansion of the privately-run or self-financed higher education sector in Hong Kong, together with a more significant growth of students enrolled in self-financed programmes offered by the UGC-funded institutions at the same time. Moreover, the HKSAR government has kept increasing expenditures on education over years, with an increase of about 57 per cent from HK$47 billion in 1997 to HK$74 billion in 2014. Nevertheless, both the ratios of total government expenditure on education to the total government expenditure and to Gross Domestic Product (GDP) decreased from 24.2 per cent to 18.7 per cent and from 3.5 per cent to 3.3 per cent

4  *Michael H. Lee and Thomas Kwan-Choi Tse*

*Table 1.1* Hong Kong education at a glance

| Year | 1997 | 2014 |
|---|---|---|
| **Hong Kong population** | | |
| Total Population | 6,502,100 | 7,241,700 |
| **Education institutions** | | |
| Number of kindergartens | 740 | 978 |
| Number of primary schools | 606 | 571 |
| Number of secondary schools | 523 | 509 |
| Number of UGC-funded institutions | 8 | 8 |
| Number of privately-funded higher education institutions | n.a. | 11 |
| **Student enrollments** | | |
| Kindergarten students | 177,462 | 176,397 |
| Primary education students | 461,911 | 329,300 |
| Secondary education students | 458,118 | 375,603 |
| UGC-funded institutions students | 86,202 | 190,573 |
| **Government expenditure** | | |
| Total government expenditure on education | HK$47 billion | HK$74 billion |
| Ratio of total government expenditure on education to total government expenditure | 24.2% | 18.7% |
| Ratio of total government expenditure on education to Gross Domestic Product (GDP) | 3.5% | 3.3% |

Sources: (Census & Statistics Department, 1998, 2015; Education Commission, 2004).

between 1997 and 2014 respectively. This probably points to growing competition between education and other policy areas, such as health care, housing and social welfare for larger shares of public financial resources in face of social problems related to poverty and ageing society in Hong Kong.

The education reform programme launched by the HKSAR government after 1997 was unprecedented in a sense that it covered all aspects of the education system simultaneously with the introduction of a huge number of policy recommendations and reform measures to be carried out at a rapid rate within a short period of time (Law, 2007; Morris & Scott, 2005). The education reform blueprint, which was released in September 2000 by the Education Commission (2000a), embraces a wide range of critical issues, including academic system for secondary and university education, curriculum reform and development, student assessment mechanisms and public examinations, medium of instruction and language education, teacher professionalism, school admission system, school-based management, private education, civic and national education, and post-secondary educational opportunities.

In order to grasp a better understanding about education reforms in Hong Kong, Table 1.2 summarises major reform policies across different stages of

Table 1.2 Education reforms in Hong Kong since 2000

| Stage of education | Academic structure | Allocation mechanism & interface between different stages | Curriculum reform | Assessment mechanism | Complementary measures |
|---|---|---|---|---|---|
| Early childhood education | Have one government department to regulate all kindergartens & child care centres | Primary one allocation mechanism: Based on the principle of "vicinity", school places are allocated according to school nets and parental choice. Applicants with siblings/parents studying/working in the school must be admitted. 20 percent of places are allocated by schools at their own discretion. Remaining places are allocated centrally according to school nets & parental choices, one-tenth of which not subject to any restrictions on school nets. | Strengthen the interface between early childhood & primary education. Should not use curriculum which is too advanced for the children's developmental stage. | | Raise the professional standards of principals & teachers (including duly raising the entry requirements & providing the necessary training) Strengthen the quality assurance mechanism Promote parent education & participation |
| Nine-year basic education (primary & junior secondary levels) | | Reform of secondary school places allocation system: Transition: Abolish Academic Aptitude Tests (AAT) & use the school's average results of the AAT over the past three years for scaling purpose. Reduce the number of bands from five to three & increase the percentage of discretionary places from 10 per cent to 20 per cent & eventually to 30 per cent five years later. | Re-group all subjects into 8 key learning areas. Provide students with 5 types of learning experiences for whole-person development. | Introduce Basic Competency Assessment in Chinese, English and mathematics comprising two parts: | Implement more effective remedial & enhancement measures. Promote school-based management. Enhance the professional standards & commitment of principals & teachers. Provide professional support to principals & schools. |

(*Continued*)

Table 1.2 (Continued)

| Stage of education | Academic structure | Allocation mechanism & interface between different stages | Curriculum reform | Assessment mechanism | Complementary measures |
|---|---|---|---|---|---|
| | | Long-term: The students' school internal results used for allocating S1 places. Encourage the development of "linked schools" (or "through-train schools"). Interface between S3 & S4: Provide learning opportunities for all willing & able students. Implement the new interface mechanism. | Eliminate the obsolete elements of the curriculum & update the content. Promote moral & civic education, foster a reading culture, encourage the use of project learning & the use of information technology in education. | Student assessment used to assess the students' basic competencies in Chinese, English & mathematics from P1 to S3 & to facilitate the provision of guidance & support to students in need; System assessment used to monitor the basic standards of all schools at P3, P6 & S3, & to facilitate schools in formatting improvement measures for effective teaching & learning. | Establish district education support network. Promote parent education & participation. Make good use of talents & resources in the community to support education. Implement effective quality assurance mechanism for schools. |

| | | | |
|---|---|---|---|
| Senior secondary education | Implement the proposed 3-year academic structure & formulate detailed proposals & implementation time table (Note: The 3-year academic system has been implemented since 2009). | Reform the university admission system: Universities should consider the students' overall performance for the purpose of admission, such as internal assessment reports prepared by secondary schools, portfolios prepared by students, interviews & results in public examinations. | Provide five types of key learning experiences. Provide choices of different combinations. Provide more work-related experiences. | Extend the teacher assessment scheme by phases. Adopt the "core competence approach" in public examinations. |
| Higher education | Develop a transferable credit unit system among institutions & faculties. Encourage the development of different types of higher education institutions, including community colleges & private universities. | | Provide inter-disciplinary learning opportunities & strengthen general education. Increase postgraduate places. | Strengthen quality assurance mechanisms so as to ensure the standard of university graduates. | UGC to explore an appropriate funding mechanism together with the universities, so as to tie in with the reform of the university admission system & the implementation of the credit unit system. Enrich campus life. |

*(Continued)*

Table 1.2 (Continued)

| Stage of education | Academic structure | Allocation mechanism & interface between different stages | Curriculum reform | Assessment mechanism | Complementary measures |
|---|---|---|---|---|---|
| Continuing education | Provide diversified learning opportunities. | A flexible admission system which provides different entry/exit points. | Cover a wide range of learning areas including academic, professional, vocational education & personal development. | Develop a flexible & transferable qualifications recognition system. Establish a quality assurance mechanism. | Promote a life-long learning culture. Establish a website on continuing education. Promote co-operation among different sectors of the community. Promote the use of the existing community resources to set up life-long learning centres. |

Sources: (Curriculum Development Council, 2000; Education Commission, 2000a, 2000b)

education implemented since 2000, when the education reform blueprint was formally launched by the HKSAR government.

In the subsequent years, different measures of the education reform blueprint have been put in place accordingly, together with other important new initiatives like the voucher scheme for kindergartens, prioritising education services as one of the six local major industries and facilitating the internationalisation of the education sector, the 12 years of free education policy, a formal introduction of the Qualifications Framework and strengthening of national education with a number of financial and curricular support (Tse, 2013).

Among many factors involved, this volume highlights two pressures on policy-making and practice, namely external forces as represented by globalisation and Hong Kong's re-integration into mainland China, and internal forces pointing to the changing demographic and socio-economic changes and needs in society, on shaping the development of education reforms in Hong Kong since 1997.

In the tide of intense global competition, many countries wanted to provide a ready supply of skilled labour and to enhance their competitive edge through the development of the knowledge-producing institutions and industries. Education reform also becomes a derivative of labour and economic policy. As examined by Lam and Wong in Chapter 7, the major curriculum reform initiatives, such as the emphasis of generic skill development, learning to learn, information technology in education, life-long and life-wide learning, have been strongly influenced by the trend of curriculum changes in other developed countries. This package of reform was a reaction of the HKSAR government in the new political arena, to strengthen economic competitiveness, fix social problems and enhance educational quality.

Being a crucial aspect of cultural capital, language acquisition is another important aspect of education reform. Medium of instruction and language enhancement continue to be the foci of curriculum concern for the HKSAR government. Two language policies, namely the compulsory Chinese-medium instruction policy and the "biliterate/trilingual policy", were put forward right after the handover. The former is meant to rectify the previous English-dominant medium of instruction policies with a view to enhance the quality of learning through using the first language of most students. The latter aims at raising the standard of two written languages (Chinese and English) and three spoken languages (Cantonese, English and Putonghua) in order to enhance the global competiveness of Hong Kong.

As for the development of higher education, which is more concerned about the process of internationalisation, the notion of developing Hong Kong as a regional education hub has been put forward by the government in line with its notion of promoting Hong Kong as Asia's world city. It also implies the need for strengthening Hong Kong's higher education institutions' international competitiveness and also their enrolment of more non-local students.

Since 1978 when the policy of nine-year compulsory education was implemented, the development of the Hong Kong education system, which is still predominantly financed by the government, has been under the profound influence of the philosophy of neo-liberalism and the ethos of marketization in tandem with the notion of "quality education" (Cheng, 2007; Goodstadt, 2013; Mok & Chan, 2002; Tse, 2005). The potential effects of neoliberalism-led globalisation on education are far-reaching as it has brought a paradigm shift in educational management, administration and governance in many countries. Education systems nowadays put more stress on the short-term, the symbolic and expedient achievements than those of the past, which focused on the long-term, the real and substantive goals and objectives, discretion and reserving judgement, and character. Likewise, the old-fashioned values of wisdom, trust, empathy, compassion, grace, and honesty in managing education have changed into the so-called values of contracts, markets, choice, and competition in educational management, administration and governance, as shown in Chapter 9. Besides subsidies to enhance choice and quality and voucher schemes, quality improvement is achieved through a number of strategies, like professional upgrading for principals and teachers, school-based management, launching of a quality assurance mechanism and a compulsory requirement of operation transparency. Principals are given more autonomy and flexibility in the deployment of resources, curriculum development, staff development and other professional managerial matters in return for greater accountability. Schools have institutionalised a self-evaluation framework in daily practice for continuous improvement.

Nowadays many industrialised regions have adopted an educational market, and a canon of this market is choice. How parental choice unfolds in the new education market has become a crucial issue. The practice of neo-liberalism in education is far more intensive after 1997 and the neo-liberal notions of choice and quality embedded in the policy discourse have constructed education in an imaginary of a vibrant market. Concerning the themes of parental choice and education market and their impacts on education development in Hong Kong, they are discussed in the relevant chapters covering the voucher scheme for kindergartens (Chapter 2), the extension of the Direct Subsidy Scheme (DSS) schools (Chapter 3) and public reporting of school performance (Chapter 10).

Globalisation has also affected the ways higher education operates. "Entrepreneurial universities" have become the new model, and the local higher education system also adopted global practices in the process of policy borrowing and learning since the 1990s. The higher education sector in Hong Kong has been increasingly subject to the influence of fiscal constraints, market forces, and public sector management and reforms with market forces and competitions as the core values. These new ideas of governance and management adhere to the business-oriented culture and practices prevailing in the private sector, in response to the extended influence of the on-going process of public sector reforms spreading across countries. In this aspect, in Chapter 13, Lee addresses major developments and changes of higher education, which comprises degree-awarding public and private universities as well as self-financed community colleges that are dedicated to associate degree programmes. Comprehensive reviews and reforms on higher education have been carried out in Hong Kong since the 1990s, when it witnessed the processes of both quantitative expansion and qualitative consolidation, which led to several remarkable issues and changes, such as the institutionalisation of quality assurance mechanisms, the reorientation of the government-university relationship, the growth of private or self-financed higher education institutions and the internationalisation of higher education to cater for Hong Kong's aspiration to become a regional education hub.

Apart from neo-liberalism, it is also noteworthy that the education system in Hong Kong has encountered new challenges arising from the seriousness of social inequalities, low birth rate of local people and a shrinking student population, along with the growth of immigrant students from the Chinese mainland and ethnic minority students.

With special reference to the demographic change, Hong Kong has witnessed unprecedented developments in the demography of its student population since the handover in 1997. First, the fertility rate in Hong Kong has greatly decreased over the past three decades, and now Hong Kong is one of places with the lowest birth rates in the world that is substantially below the replacement level. Second, there has been a noticeable increase in Hong Kong and mainland Chinese intermarriages, and subsequently, the numbers of cross-boundary and Chinese immigrant students from mainland China has increased. Third, a quota of 150 permits per day for mainland Chinese residents migrating to Hong Kong to join their spouses, children and relatives means Hong Kong accommodates nearly 55,000 new immigrants from mainland China each year. Fourth, currently there are around 40,000 South Asian children in Hong Kong either born locally or overseas. The changing student diversity has presented the local educational system and mainstream schools with challenges and problems. The aspirations of promoting Hong Kong itself as a cosmopolitan area are reflected in the curriculum reform that underlines a global outlook. Facing the student population with diverse cultural backgrounds such as immigrant and minority students, there has been a growing awareness of the need to equalise opportunities for these socially disadvantaged student groups and improve their education outcomes. Whilst the government has introduced some policy initiatives to address this issue, accommodating the needs of increasingly diverse student bodies remains a concern.

Last but not the least, the changing political environment, such as national reintegration, governance crisis and a quest for further democratisation, also have repercussions on the educational system, as reflected in the controversy over the policy of making Moral and National Education (MNE) a compulsory subject for all primary and secondary schools in 2012, as well as the Occupy Movement in 2014 arising from the controversy over the political reform concerning the universal suffrage methods of the chief executive in 2017.

## Responses

These reforms implemented since the early 2000s were not all accepted by educational practitioners and other stakeholders in the society although most of those initiatives were considered to be good for the Hong Kong education system in the long run. The major problem lies in how these reforms were implemented by the government, which neglected the importance of building mutual trust relationships with the stakeholders of the education sector for effective policy implementation. This refers to the acute tension between policy implementation and facilitation procedures in the education system (Dale, 1989; Ip & Lee, 2007). Trust, government capacity and political credibility turn out to be among the most critical issues determining whether reform initiatives can be implemented properly, especially during the time when the HKSAR government encounters an unprecedented crisis of governance. Moreover, apart from the factors of marketization and a concern with global competitiveness, mainland China's influences on local education policy and curriculum since 1997 also deserve greater attention. Controversies related to national integration abound in the areas like civic and national education, the use of Putonghua as a medium of instruction and a dramatic increase of cross-boundary students from mainland China. Therefore, education policy-making and implementation in Hong Kong have become more contested and challengeable during the post-handover period.

Analysing the relationship of the government to the formulation and implementation of education policy in Hong Kong, this volume delves into implementation theory, addressing the gap between the street-level bureaucrats (or teachers) and central policy-makers. While the top-down approach of policy implementation may not be able to achieve policy goals, effective implementation requires transaction between policy proponents, implementers and other stakeholders whose support is necessary for action to happen. In Hong Kong, the problem of education policy implementation also lies in the translation of policy intents into specific policy actions, which generate more debate and concern among the relevant stakeholders. This scenario is closely related to such factors as the legitimacy of the regime, the disarticulated political system and the destructive political culture (Morris & Scott, 2005). Many cases of tensions are in part linked to inadequate public discussion and transparent engagement of key stakeholders in the policy production process, even for polices with goodwill. The hasty announcement of Pre-primary Education Voucher Scheme by then–Chief Executive Donald Tsang in 2007 is a case in point. Many implementation issues with the voucher scheme can be attributed to its particular design in terms of rate, stringent criteria of fee remission and cost recovery, coupled with the conceptual challenges, as shown in Chapter 2. These have also inevitably dampened the policy impact, which allow only a small number of families to receive extra support on tuition payments. But disadvantaged groups have not been adequately attended by the voucher scheme.

Another policy disaster was the MNE proposal released by former Chief Executive Donald Tsang in 2010. As part of the on-going education and curriculum reforms, there have been widespread concerns in the local and international communities over the future development of civic and national education in Hong Kong during the post-handover era. In 2012, there was large-scale resistance against the government policy of mandating 'national education' as a compulsory school subject. Under tremendous pressure the HKSAR government was forced to shelve the proposal and reverted to the original practice of school-based civic education. Leung, Chong and Yuen point out in Chapter 8 that controversies arising from the national education issue are closely related to the much-heightened level of political awareness of the citizenry during the much-debated process of democratisation, which demands a democratic political reform and the outcry for a more socially just society, as what was demonstrated in the Occupy Movement in 2014.

Concerning the changing role of the government in education, there is a dilemma facing the Hong Kong SAR government. On the one hand, in line with neo-liberal ideas addressing the importance of choice and market competition, the government intends to allow individual schools and education institutions greater autonomy in exchange for accountability, efficiency, responsiveness and responsibility (Whitty, 2002). On the other hand, there is a growing intention for the government to be more interventionist in some particular areas of education, like the policy of teachers' professional development as shown in the cases of imposing teachers' language benchmark tests and the MNE programme in schools, both of which aroused controversies in the education sector and society at large. This reflects the government's attempt to increase rather than decrease central control over education (Scott, 2005). In the case of Hong Kong, this re-regulation is reflected in a more intensified practice of managerialism, which facilitated the tightening of government control of education from a distance. The concerns with efficiency and quality control of public services in the name of accountability and transparency have caused new demands for the prevalence of systematic assessments in many instances. Upgrading professional qualifications, strengthening the quality assurance mechanism (annual school development plan, internal review and external evaluation based on performance standards), increasing operation transparency (releasing school details and review reports online) and linking performance with funding are common technocratic measures to tighten control. As detailed in a number of chapters, for the last two decades, the local education sector has been changing quickly in response to the imperative of accountability, including reforms related to measure the performance of schools and the concerns about school accountability to various stakeholders.

As shown in Chapter 3 about DSS, the new emphasis on competition, choice, accountability and performativity of schools in the education market also generated many controversies. Different stakeholders have different considerations behind the scene of DSS. Elite school principals felt dissatisfied with the quality of the students via the government-run school allocation system, and they wanted to remain elitist by having more autonomy in student admission. Parents were deeply dissatisfied with government policies, and they found the selective aided-turn-DSS schools as a sanctuary to quality education, where they could escape with policy of school places central allocation and the medium of instruction policy. The educated, assertive middle-class parents also associated themselves together and preferred a selected and exclusive community, in which only parents with similar backgrounds were welcome.

Closely related to the notions of parental choice and education market is managerialism. Several chapters also turn to address the impacts of managerialism on schools and higher education institutions and its stakeholders, including school leaders, teachers and parents. Chapter 9 by Pang argues that under the impacts of neo-liberalism, the education system in Hong Kong has adapted those values of contract, market, choice, competition, efficiency, flexibility, managerialism and accountability.

The new accountability orientation also conveys the notion that parents play a significant role in school-based management. Home-school co-operation and partnerships have been developed when parent representatives have eventually been allowed to participate in managing schools through legislation in July 2004. By 2012, most of the schools in Hong Kong have already had their Incorporated Management Committees in place, and parents, teachers and alumni are included as school governors. Nevertheless, there are tensions among parents, teachers and principals at the school-level and between the Education Bureau and school sponsoring bodies during this process. There are inevitably micro- and macro-politics arising from parents' involvement in school operation. This Incorporated Management Committee arrangement has met continuous resistance and criticisms from the Catholic Church. Although the relevant ordinance was passed by the government, there has still been a long and heated debate between school sponsoring bodies and the government, and their relationships have so far been heavily hampered. Furthermore, as analysed by Ng in Chapter 11, while parents have been encouraged to get involved school management, they have been sometimes marginalised by the school body, and the notion of "parents-as-school-governors" is, to some extent, policy rhetoric because of the imbalance of power between parents and schools.

Likewise, public reporting on individual schools' performance is becoming more and more common in Hong Kong from the 1990s onwards. This demand for information has been addressed by intensive and comprehensive assessments coupled with information disclosure to the public so as to satisfy parents' right of access to information, in tandem with the promotion of a "consumer-centred culture" which defines the roles of parents and students as customers or clients. While disclosing information to the public was justified in terms of information accessibility, parental choice, accountability and school improvement, this is a very complex and contested affair as different stakeholders may have different views on the necessity, availability and dissemination of school data, as shown by Tse in Chapter 10. The controversies over the disclosure of school inspection reports also touch upon the issues such as legitimacy and fairness of assessment mechanisms, fullness and accuracy of reporting and proper dissemination and uses of such information.

As explicated by Lam and Wong in Chapter 7, the curriculum reform since the early 2000s has been large in scale and radical in nature. Not surprisingly, many stakeholders, including school teachers, did not agree with or support it. However, the present wave of reform has attained a higher level of adoption and implementation because school management and teachers could not resist the performativity measures like school review and territory-wide systematic assessment. The shrinking student population has also intensified the competition among schools. Many schools have had to adopt the many reform initiatives simply for survival. The increasing complexities and rising expectations of education have also made teachers' work much more demanding than before. The deterioration of working conditions in the school sector and an intensification of the teaching load as well as non-teaching duties in schools have led to a series of protests from the teachers. Such a strong reaction from the school sector also indicates the inadequate capacity of the education system to support large-scale radical changes.

## Consequences, intended and unintended, positive and negative

Apart from demonstrating the educational achievements of Hong Kong system in various domains, this volume also critically analyses major issues and challenges facing the education system in Hong Kong since 1997. Various chapters examine how the education policies were implemented to respond to problems and challenges arising from globalisation and the changing political, social and economic contexts. In addition, we critically analyse the prospects for educational development in Hong Kong and evaluate which strategies can be adopted to cope with the on-going processes of social and economic restructuring and national identity formation in the twenty-first century. Several contributors also call for a reflection on the benefits and the hazards education reform has brought to us.

Education is seen as transformational force for social equity and excellence in its outcome. Achieving high quality and fostering equal education opportunity are two major goals for basic education. The two goals are often in conflict and not easily achieved. Chapter 5 by Ho offers an in-depth analysis of Hong Kong students' performance in scientific, reading and mathematical literacy in PISA over the years 2000–2012 from an international perspective. The achievement gap between students from different social backgrounds is assessed in terms of gender, immigration status, family structure, parent occupation, parent education and family's economic, social and cultural status. Ho suggests that Hong Kong's education system has achieved both excellence and equality of opportunity when compared with other participating countries. The achievement gap between boys versus girls and high versus low socio-economic status (SES) students are relatively small when compared with that of the OECD international average. However, the achievement gap between the first-generation students and local students in Hong Kong is substantial. The academic and social segregation among schools is still a significant and strong factor affecting student performance which needs to be addressed through social and educational policies and practices.

Education has traditionally been viewed as a level-playing field, and it played an important role in social mobility to individuals in Hong Kong. But class differentiation also becomes more salient as middle-class families have appropriated school choices in the new rules of the game in view of a significant increase of DSS schools, as shown in Woo's chapter. DSS schools favour these families in the contesting field of school choice as the admission procedures and relatively high tuition fees of DSS schools require resources, including time, cultural resources and personal network. Elite schools have also become rather exclusive for middle-class and other well-to-do families, resulting in social closure. With a growing number of top aided-schools leaving the public school sector to the private sector, the location of social capitals has been transferred and redistributed. Similarly, private supplementary tutoring, de facto a hidden form of education privatisation, also calls into question the global norm of fee-free education. While shadow education may compensate for shortcomings in mainstream schooling, it can undermine educational reforms and exacerbate social inequalities.

As for the further expansion of higher education, the government has been highly cautious about the quota of publicly-funded university education, and there has been more emphasis on the provision of privately-funded or self-financed programmes in the form of community colleges. And that educational access to higher education, whilst expanded, has also become more unequal in quality. This growth of private higher education institutions also implies a fundamental change of the character of higher education – which is not just a public good funded by the government but also a commodity for economic exchange.

In Hong Kong, immigrant and minority students are still under-represented in the higher education sectors, and their access to quality education is also disabled by low SES. Interwoven with class factors, immigrant and ethnic minority children could not get enough financial or educational support from their parents due to their low income and educational level. The declared policy of 12 years of free education for all in 2008 is still an illusion. The selective nature of Hong Kong schooling means that the current school curriculum mainly serves academically able pupils; and schools are very subtly promoting segregated, if not exclusive, education for immigrant and minority students.

As mentioned earlier, the education system in Hong Kong is restructured on those neo-liberal values of contract, market, choice, competition, efficiency, flexibility, decentralisation, privatisation and accountability, which involves also further infiltration by business forces into education. A strong emphasis placed on the quality of education is translated into many quantifiable and measurable performance assessments and indicators. The adoption of quality assurance and performance indicators often comes with intra- and inter-institutional competition for resources and the application of business principles and practices in administration. And there are seriously unintended and sometimes negative consequences related to that, as indicated in Chapter 10. It might also lead to increased commoditization of education and making quality education only accessible to elites, leading to greater economic and social inequality.

That language policy issues are circumscribed by political, economic, social and cultural factors, particularly Hong Kong's people's changing language attitudes, language identity and national identity, declining quality of education, equity in education, and restricted mobility. However, Poon in Chapter 4 contends that the compulsory Chinese-medium-instruction policy and the biliterate/trilingual policy are driven by two opposite forces that underpin the education reform, and thus ironically producing contrasting outcomes. And one of the unintended consequences of the post-1997 language policy is segregation between schools and students.

There is also heavy hidden cost of a high-performance system like Hong Kong, which ranks among societies with particularly high incidence of shadow education. Particularly popular are classes in English, Chinese and mathematics, since these are core subjects needed for progression from one level to the next. Ironic enough, as shown in Chapter 6 by Yung and Bray, a surge of demand for private supplementary tutoring is due to education reform, including changes of language policy, expansion of post-secondary education, the reduction of the number of public examinations to one from two, the implementation of school-based assessment as a high-stakes one. Faced with an increase in academic and social competition, many students seek additional support from shadow education, particularly for the core examination subjects. Meanwhile, the authors remind us of the backwash effect of shadow education on regular schooling. Despite its contribution to human capital and remedial learning, shadow education may create tensions with mainstream education and also conflict with the initiatives of education reforms.

## Implications

Concerning the implications this volume has for our thinking about changes and challenges facing the education system in Hong Kong and the future directions of education reforms and developments in Hong Kong, our colleagues also show that while the neo-liberal strategy is effective in inducing the implementation of reform initiatives, there is a heavy price to pay. And many contributors call for a reflection on the benefits and the costs when formulating and implementing the relevant education policies. As is shown in many chapters, the conflicts, tensions and dilemmas which arose from the current reform are valuable lessons for policy-makers and practitioners. They could also inspire those involved on how education reform should proceed in other educational systems.

Policy choices and designs in education mirror ways of thinking and valuing education for children. Education, local and global alike, is confronting the hegemonic influence of neo-liberalism which favours privatisation, decentralisation, marketization, enhancing choice and flexibility and managerialism. Competitiveness- or finance-driven reforms are emphasised while equity-driven reforms are often neglected (Carnoy, 2002).

Education is more than a labour and economic policy, and a multi-dimensional and holistic quality perspective means a commitment to democracy, social justice and care. The holistic perspective requires a willingness to commit substantial public investment in the next generation and building an equitable and quality education system for all children. Despite an increase in public expenditure on education, Hong Kong still falls far below the OECD's recommended level of public investment for education. The public spending on education, particularly at early childhood level, remains relatively low. Meanwhile, the government needs to offer assistance to students with special needs. The very presence of student groups with different needs creates a need for promoting equality of education in mainstream schools. Authentic integration cannot be achieved simply by physical integration. There needs to be a change from a mono-cultural deficit perspective on educating immigrant and minority students to an affirming perspective in which all cultures are equally valued, as pointed out by Celeste Yuen in Chapter 12. While they came a bit late, some measures to facilitate schools to create an inclusive learning environment for accommodating ethnic diversity in school, and promoting respect to cultural and religious differences after the *2014 Policy Address,* are steps on the right track.

It is time for policy-makers to seriously reflect upon the social inequality that educational policies have indirectly created, and to revise the relevant measures. Taking DSS as an example, we need to review their current admission procedures and scholarship arrangement so that all families can enjoy fair opportunities for quality education. Similarly, although there are now piece-meal policies and initiatives to offer support for language learning, nonetheless there are still no systematic policies advocating equality of education opportunities for all.

Since 1997, the government has had strained relationships with various stakeholders, like school sponsoring bodies, teachers and parents. Re-building a partnership of mutual trust and respect between the government and various stakeholders is a difficult process that requires much effort. And in the process of democratisation and an upheaval of civic consciousness of the citizenry for social justice, Hong Kong education has to be reconstructed, both in conceptual and political aspects, in order to address the concerns raised in the society. Likewise, if the reform is to achieve sustainable development in education, the HKSAR government needs to enhance teachers' professional competency and autonomy through capacity building and lessen the pressure for public accountability. It is more important to uphold the core values of integrity and professional autonomy in education. Apart from competition, collaboration among educational institutions and practitioners is also a viable option.

# References

Carnoy, M. (2002). Foreword. In H. Daun (Ed.), *Educational restructuring in the context of globalization and national policy* (xv–xviii). New York: Routledge.

Census and Statistics Department. (1998). *Hong Kong annual digest of statistics 1998 edition*. Hong Kong: Printing Department.

Census and Statistics Department. (2015). *Hong Kong annual digest of statistics 2015 edition*. Hong Kong: Census and Statistics Department.

Cheng, K. M. (2007). Reforming education beyond education. In Y. M. Yeung (Ed.), *The first decade of the HKSAR* (pp. 251–272). Hong Kong: The Chinese University Press.

Cheng, Y. C. (2009). Educational reforms in Hong Kong in the last decade: Reform syndrome and new developments. *International Journal of Educational Management, 23*(1), 65–86.

Cheng, Y. C. (2015). Globalization and Hong Kong educational reforms. In J. Zajda (Ed.), *Second international handbook on globalization, education and policy research* (pp. 219–241). Dordrecht: Springer.

Dale, R. (1989). *The state and education policy*. Milton Keynes: Open University Press.

Education Commission. (1999). *Review of academic system, aims of education: Consultation document*. Hong Kong: Government Printer.

Education Commission. (2000a). *Learning for life, learning through life: Reform proposals for the education system in Hong Kong*. Hong Kong: Government Printer.

Education Commission. (2000b). *Review of education system reform proposals: Consultation document*. Hong Kong: Government Printer.

Education Commission. (2004). *Education statistics*. Hong Kong: Education Commission.

Goodstadt, L. (2013). *Poverty in the midst of affluence: How Hong Kong mismanaged its prosperity.* Hong Kong: Hong Kong University Press.
Ho, L. S., Morris, P., & Chung, Y. P. Eds. (2005). *Education reform and the quest for excellence: The Hong Kong story.* Hong Kong: Hong Kong University Press.
Information Services Department. (2012). *International study shows Hong Kong students' outstanding performance in reading literacy, mathematics and science.* (Press release on December 12, 2012). Retrieved from http://www.info.gov.hk/gia/general/201212/12/P201212120332.htm
Information Services Department. (2013). *International study shows Hong Kong students' reading, mathematical and scientific literacy continue to rank among the world's best.* (Press release on December 3, 2013). Retrieved from http://www.info.gov.hk/gia/general/201312/03/P201312030421.htm
Ip, K. Y., & Lee, M. (2007). From excitement to disillusionment: The lessons of education reform in Hong Kong, 1997–2007. In J. Y. S. Cheng (Ed.), *The Hong Kong special administrative region in its first decade* (pp. 667–698). Hong Kong: City University of Hong Kong Press.
Law, W. W. (2007). Schooling in Hong Kong. In G. Postiglione & J. Tan (Eds.), *Going to school in East Asia* (pp. 86–121). Westport, CT: Greenwood Publishing.
Marsh, C., & Lee, J. C. K. Eds. (2014). *Asia's high performing education system: The case of Hong Kong.* New York: Routledge.
Mok, J. K. H., & Chan, D. K. K. Eds. (2002). *Globalization and education: The quest for quality education in Hong Kong.* Hong Kong: Hong Kong University Press.
Morris, P., & Scott, I. (2005). Education reform and policy implementation in Hong Kong. In L. Ho, P. Morris & Y. Chung (Eds.), *Education reform and the quest for excellence: The Hong Kong story* (pp. 83–97). Hong Kong: Hong Kong University Press.
OECD. (2011). *Strong performers and successful reformers in education: Lessons from PISA for the United States.* Paris: OECD. Retrieved from http://www.oecd.org/pisa/46623978.pdf
Postiglione, G., & Lee, W. O. Eds. (1997). *Schooling in Hong Kong: Organization, teaching and social context.* Hong Kong: Hong Kong University Press.
Scott, I. (2005). Education policymaking in a disarticulated system. In L. Ho, P. Morris & Y. Chung (Eds.), *Education reform and the quest for excellence: The Hong Kong story* (pp. 23–36). Hong Kong: Hong Kong University Press.
Sharma, A. (2013). Hong Kong: Structuring the education system for a diversified society. In P. Hsieh (Ed.), *Education in East Asia* (pp. 49–77). London: Bloomsbury.
Sweeting, A. (2004). *Education in Hong Kong 1941–2001: Visions and revisions.* Hong Kong: Hong Kong University Press.
Taylor, S., Rizvi, F., Lingard, B., & Henry, M. (1997). *Educational policy and the politics of change.* London: Routledge.
Tsang, W. K. (1998). *Analysis of educational policy in Hong Kong: Sociological perspectives.* Hong Kong: Joint Publishing (in Chinese).
Tsang, W. K. Ed. (2006). *Educational blueprint in 21st century: The discourses on educational reform in HKSAR.* Hong Kong: The Chinese University Press (in Chinese).
Tsang, W. K. (2011). *Analysis of educational policy in HKSAR.* Hong Kong: Joint Publishing (in Chinese).
Tse, T. K. C. (2005). Quality education in Hong Kong: The anomalies of managerialism and marketization. In L. S. Ho, P. Morris & Y. P. Chung (Eds.), *Education*

reform and the quest for excellence: The Hong Kong story (pp. 99–123). Hong Kong: Hong Kong University Press.

Tse, T. K. C. (2013). Endless controversies over education reforms. In K. Law & J. Cheng (Eds.), *On the chessboard: Donald Tsang's legacy for C.Y. Leung* (pp. 163–193). Hong Kong: City University of Hong Kong Press (in Chinese).

Tung, C. H. (1997). *Building Hong Kong for a new era*. Hong Kong: Printing Department.

Whitty, G. (2002). *Making sense of education policy*. London: Paul Chapman Publishing.

# 2 Vouchers in early childhood education

## Market still? What to choose next?

*Gail Wai-Kwan Yuen*

## Introduction

Early childhood education in Hong Kong is situated in a peripheral position, reflecting a policy trajectory of neo-liberalism that vividly connects to the active interplay of global-local politics. The British colonial legacy has a significant role to play in justifying this peripheral position in a liberal market economy. Developed alongside the public education system, early childhood education is fully operational in a market context. In spite of sharing a similar historical start as primary and secondary education and being highly valued by parents, early childhood education has remained in the private sector while its counterparts have become aided provisions. As such, the notions of equity, choice and quality embedded in the neo-liberal policy discourse have resulted in a specific construction of early childhood education that continues to manifest in the local imaginary of a "vibrant" market.

Under the British governance, early childhood education received minimal attention. Since the late 1970s, local advocates have begun to press the colonial government to address issues concerning cost, quality, equity and the welfare of the teaching profession. Not only local advocates but also international experts (Llewellyn, 1982) recommended an aided early childhood education sector. At the time, official support rendered to the sector was very much limited to three financial schemes, including the means-tested fee remission scheme, rent and rates reimbursement scheme, as well as kindergarten subsidy scheme (associated with recommended master pay scales for teachers and later renamed as the kindergarten and child care centre subsidy scheme). The first scheme targeted parents, and the other two schemes applied to non-profit-making operators. The colonial government, in response to public pressure, reiterated continuously that full subsidy for early childhood education involved too much money and resources were limited. It often resorted to a pattern of measures to deflate the pressure (i.e., increasing the kindergarten subsidy scheme and at the same time relaxing the tuition fee control, modifying the pay scales and changing the eligibility of the fee remission scheme) (Yuen, 2010). Although providing teachers with initial professional training became a momentous effort in the mid-1990s, the official position of promoting quality early childhood education in the private sector was clearly maintained by the last governor

(Patten, 1996). This laissez-faire or market approach to early childhood education was strikingly the same as the one noted in the 1960s: "For the time being, it will be necessary to rely on voluntary organisations and private enterprise to provide education at this level" (Hong Kong Government, 1965, 2). But the policy inertia further revealed the growing influence of neo-liberalism in the qualitative development of the local education system in the 1990s (Yuen, 2010).

The practice of neo-liberalism in early childhood education was far more intensive after the change of sovereignty in 1997. Two major waves of education reform were initiated by the Hong Kong SAR government. The first wave of reform recommended providing more parent subsidies to enhance choice and quality while rejecting full subsidies for the sector (Education Commission, 2000). Although there were no major initiatives on parent subsidies, the first wave of reform did set the tone for introducing the Pre-primary Education Voucher Scheme (thereafter voucher scheme) in the second wave of reform. The voucher scheme envisions children aged 3 to 6 to have access to affordable and quality education. It is positioned as a form of family support to reduce financial burden (Tsang, 2006). Parents receive a flat-rate voucher per child for the use of half-day or full-day services. Non-profit-making kindergartens providing a local curriculum and charging tuitions within the maximum caps can join the scheme. To realise a full-fledged market mechanism, the direct subsidy to operators and recommended master pay scales were removed. Quality improvement is achieved through professional upgrading, a quality assurance mechanism and a compulsory requirement of operation transparency. Only kindergartens with satisfactory performance can stay in the scheme (Education and Manpower Bureau, 2006). Implemented since 2007, the voucher scheme has met continuous challenges.

This chapter examines the prevalence of neo-liberalism in early childhood education in Hong Kong, highlighting the voucher scheme as a technology of control. The discussion will begin with a conceptual perspective on vouchers as a policy tool, followed by a review of policy tensions and impact in terms of equity, choice and quality, then the pertinent issues to be addressed and finally the implications for the next possible policy choice.

## Vouchers as a policy tool

Vouchers are highly contested due to the competing values underpinning different ideological orientations about the roles of education and government. Parent subsidy in the form of vouchers is a demand-side policy to enhance choice and stimulate competition. With choice and competition as the key tenets of neo-liberalism, markets are said to be able to meet diverse needs and preferences, drive production costs down and improve quality (Moss, 2009). Assumed as most efficient for allocating resources, markets give choice to individuals who are motivated by self-interests to make the best decisions through rational thinking (e.g., weighting cost and quality, measuring personal satisfaction) (Stein, 2001). Compared with a publicly-funded provision, vouchers cost much less (OECD, 2006). It is no surprise why neo-liberalism looks so appealing to governments. The neo-liberal discourse changes education policy from being an ideological commitment to social justice to having a sole focus on performativity (Luke, 1997). It reduces education policy to a mere audit of measureable results (Apple, 2004), emphasising "evidence" or "what works" that characterises corporate managerialism (Rizvi & Lingard, 2010). Policy as discourse thereby produces regimes of truth to govern thought and action (Ball, 1994).

There is no compelling evidence in support of the effectiveness of vouchers (Penn, 2012). Most often limited to conceptual debates, vouchers have not been widely adopted by governments, even in the United States where the idea was first conceived by Milton Friedman (Nelson, Palonsky, & McCarthy, 2010). Hong Kong has also undergone debates about vouchers for school education (Hung, 2006). In a local review of voucher programmes around the world, inconclusive results, including those at early childhood level, were reported (Lee & Wong, 2002). Current research on vouchers for the early years reveals two key issues. One concerns whether the voucher value is high enough to make significant impact on improving access in the market. The other concerns whether vouchers can ensure equitable access for all families because they tend to give a comparative advantage to those already having more market access (Chen, 2008; Granell, 2002; Lee, 2006; Sparkes & West, 1998). As informed by research on parent choice in early childhood markets, cost is a major practical concern, and parent backgrounds (e.g. family income, education, maternal employment) tend to influence access to services (e.g., Davis & Connelly, 2005; Kim & Fram, 2009; Peyton, Jacob, O'Brien, & Roy, 2001; Vincent, Braun, & Ball, 2010). Early childhood services serve the dual goals of meeting children's educational needs and parents' employment needs. This means access is about having an appropriate choice of service for not only the child but also the parent(s) (OECD, 2006).

The conscious choice of vouchers as a policy tool, regardless of their contested nature, limited application and questionable impact, points to the exercise of authoritative power to privilege some values over others. As Rizvi and Lingard (2010) explain, policy is a value-laden representation of both means and ends for steering thought and action to construct a collective imaginary. It involves the appropriation of competing values originating from ideological differences. Since policy needs to be presented as the desired future working in the public interest, values may not be made explicit. Through masking whose interests are actually represented, policy appropriates specific values with authority and seeks to demand public consent on the collective imaginary as "inevitable, timeless and natural, territorially bounded and entirely legitimate" (Rizvi & Lingard, 2010, 13).

The voucher scheme in Hong Kong attempts to construct a collective imaginary of market efficiency sustained by individuals taking responsibility to maximise personal satisfaction. Neoliberals have re-articulated the notion of choice as the right to choice rather than the freedom to choose. This notion of choice neutralises the different values that are inherent to choice itself and displaces the role of education in building individual capacity for the freedom to choose in order to ensure social justice for all, including the historically disadvantaged groups (e.g., low income, ethnic minorities, immigrants, women) (Stein, 2001). In this connexion, the neoliberal notion of equity has come to mean access to institutions only. It leaves out outcomes that are achieved through such process measures as diverse provisions and treatments to facilitate social inclusion and participation (Rizvi & Lingard, 2010). Policy as discourse in effect constructs "the subjectivities, the voices, the knowledge, the power relations" of individuals (Ball, 1994, 22). "The ideal citizen . . . [is]: an autonomous subject, in no way dependent, with rights but also matching responsibilities, self-governing and responsible for managing his or her risks through making market choices" (Dahlberg & Moss, 2005, 44).

In Rizvi and Lingard's term (2010), the voucher scheme is a distributive policy. Through distributing resources to individual parents, the scheme seems to give everyone an equal start. Moss (2014) criticises the neglect of historical injustice by this kind of proclamation. It effectively ratifies "social regularities rooted in asymmetrical power relationships" (as cited in Paquette, 2007, 338). In today's global age, equity concerns whether students have equitable access to quality education. As was in the past, it requires tampering with the existing economic pie to redistribute resources to address historical injustice (Paquette, 2007). Yet, the voucher scheme in Hong Kong focuses on making early childhood education more affordable and not more equitable in the traditional sense. According to Paull (2012), providing universal subsidy without meticulous attention on equitable access to quality education can further widen the rich-poor gap.

The voucher scheme presents a notion of quality very much from a managerial perspective. Strengthening the quality assurance mechanism (annual school development plan, internal review and external evaluation based on pre-determined performance standards), increasing the transparency of operation (publishing operation details and quality review results on-line) and linking performance with continuous participation in the scheme (Education and Manpower Bureau, 2006) are technocratic measures to tighten control and produce measurable results to ensure certainty in sustaining the collective imaginary of market efficiency. The voucher scheme follows the same policy pattern of the first wave of reform (Education Commission, 2000). Apart from the technocratic measures, the scheme has raised the entry professional qualifications for teachers and principals from initial to sub-degree level and from sub-degree to degree level, respectively. Subsidy for professional upgrading to the required levels was included in the voucher value of the first five-year policy cycle (Education and Manpower Bureau, 2006). Although a new level of professional competence is expected, it came with the withdrawal of the recommended master pay scales and direct subsidy to operators, as well as the condition of "the voucher goes with the parent." These additional measures have worked to perfect the performance of a full-fledged market mechanism, extending the official rhetoric beyond preserving market responsiveness (Education and Manpower Bureau, 2006). As assumed, quality is self-evident in the early childhood market.

The technocratic measures of the voucher scheme are necessary but not sufficient enough to offer quality early childhood education in Hong Kong. Similar to choice, quality is a contested concept shaped by competing values. It requires children and adults alike to engage in reflections and dialogues to make sense of the cultural specific notion of quality (Dahlberg, Moss, & Pence, 2007). On a different note, the quality of early childhood education is multi-dimensional, involving a wide range of inter-related aspects: orientation quality (type and level of government attention given to the sector); structural quality (e.g., physical environment, staff qualification and compensation, work condition, child-staff ratio); educational philosophy and practice; process quality (pedagogical relationship and interaction); operational quality (leadership and management); child outcome quality (achievement of pedagogical goals through centre evaluation); and standards relating to parent/community outreach and involvement (e.g., in disadvantaged communities) (OECD, 2006). Without taking a multi-dimensional perspective, it would be hard to conceive ways to achieve equitable access to quality early childhood education. For young children and the historically disadvantaged groups in particular, high-quality educational processes and outcomes matter tremendously if they are to build individual capacity for the freedom to choose in life, amidst the rapid and unstable changes of the local and global contexts.

## The voucher scheme: Tensions and impact

Facing conceptual challenges concerning the issues of equity, choice and quality, the voucher scheme in Hong Kong has encountered on-going tensions. These tensions are in part linked to inadequate public and transparent engagement of key stakeholders in the policy production process. The scheme was first announced by then Chief Executive Donald Tsang in the year before his election for the second term in 2007. It was presented as a bundled package to legislators, who found little room for negotiation (Forestier, 2006). While parents generally welcomed the new financial support, the sudden announcement took the sector by surprise. The hasty announcement and implementation, as well as the particular design of the voucher scheme, coupled with the conceptual challenges, have inevitably dampened the policy impact.

Three on-going tensions have emerged given the particular design of the voucher scheme. One major tension is related to the flat-rate value based on half-day operation (Education and Manpower, 2006). The design is premised on the long-standing policy positions that half-day education is good enough for young children and that parents should spend more time with their children (Education Bureau, 2010). The half-day and full-day binary reflects the dichotomized views on education and care (anything beyond half-day education) and paternalistic views on gender roles. It fails to acknowledge the unique pedagogical practice in working with young children and a broader concept of education. This binary affects parents, more seriously mothers who work or want to work. It also affects full-day operation, particularly full-day kindergartens which offer an integrated curriculum and special needs services in support of children's well-being and learning. The effects of the historical and gendered policy positions go as far as provision planning of different operation modes (Yuen, 2015).

The second tension concerns the means-tested fee remission scheme which was the only form of parent subsidy before the voucher scheme. It is still made available to those in need of extra financial assistance under the voucher scheme. The fee remission scheme currently in use for early childhood education is same as the one adopted for the aided sector of primary and secondary education. The scheme has stringent criteria, including low family income thresholds for eligibility. It does not take note of the private nature of early childhood education, having to charge high tuitions and add-on fees. This means many families with genuine financial needs may not be eligible for additional subsidies. To those who are qualified to receive additional subsidies, the voucher scheme may not make a significant difference to them because they could have received similar coverage from the fee remission scheme alone.

The third tension involves the fact that the voucher value makes no reference to a unit cost for sustaining different operation modes and more importantly, quality provision. Annual cost adjustments impose continuous pressure on participating kindergartens to increase tuitions and yet not to exceed the maximum caps. The Audit Commission (2013) has noted a continuous decline in the participation rate of kindergartens. Rising operating costs and the tuition cap requirements may have contributed to such decline. In brief, the three major tensions have affected the extent of effectiveness of the voucher scheme, which will be discussed next in terms of equity, choice and quality.

## *Equity*

The voucher scheme has made early childhood education relatively more affordable, especially for better resourced families. Three local studies consistently show a high level of agreement among parents with regard to the effects of reducing financial burden and saving money (Li, Wong, & Wang, 2010; Yuen & Lam, 2016; Yuen & Yu, 2010). Parents of higher socio-economic status (SES) are significantly more positive towards these effects (Yuen & Lam, 2016; Yuen & Yu, 2010). There is also a high level of agreement on weakened policy effectiveness by tuition increases, with significantly more parents of lower SES agreeing to this effect. Tuition increases have produced cancel-out effects on the annual increase of the voucher value (Yuen & Lam, 2016). Regarding family financial burden, it is important to note that parents have to pay other fees (e.g., meals, learning materials, school bus) in addition to tuitions. Half-day services, usually preferred by parents of higher SES, charge more add-on fees. The tuitions of full-day services are higher and generally preferred by parents of lower SES and working mothers (Yuen, 2015). As reported by another study (Yuen & Yu, 2010), full-day kindergartens serve mostly families with fewer resources and both parents working. Over half of these families have to seek additional subsidies through the fee remission scheme. Understandably, the stringent eligibility criteria of this scheme can allow only a small number of families to receive extra support on tuition payment.

The needs of the historically disadvantaged groups have not been adequately attended by the voucher scheme. Yuen and Lam (2016) reveal a significant relation between the affordability of the current choice option and SES (i.e., the choice option becoming less affordable with the lowering of SES). In spite of the voucher scheme and other forms of subsidies, like fee remission, if applicable, parents of lower SES continue to struggle to afford early childhood education. There are profound between-group differences in relation to the total sum of monthly school expenses (tuition and other fees) as a percentage of monthly family income; generally speaking, the lower the SES, the higher the monthly school expenses as a percentage of monthly family income. Furthermore, the extra money saved from the voucher scheme means new opportunities to some families. While higher SES groups tend to spend the saving on interest classes and learning materials, lower SES groups are more likely to use the extra money to cover general expenses of the family. In light of the keen education race that constantly reminds local parents to give their children a head start (Lui, 2011), this unintended policy outcome, together with the comparative advantage given to better resourced families by the voucher scheme to access services in the market, is likely to have widened the rich-poor gap at early childhood level. Similar to other places with voucher experiences (Granell, 2002; Ho, 2006), parents express an overwhelming preference for free early childhood education in Hong Kong (Li, Wong, & Wang, 2010; Yuen & Lam, 2016; Yuen & Yu, 2010). Their preference for a public provision over the voucher scheme reflects clear concerns about financial burden, equity, choice and quality (Yuen, 2015; Yuen & Lam, 2016).

## *Choice*

When compared with the effect of reducing financial burden, the impact made by the voucher scheme on enhancing choice is considerably weaker. There is a lower level of agreement among parents that the voucher scheme has increased their kindergarten options (Yuen, 2015; Yuen & Yu, 2010). The new options brought forth by the scheme are mostly in the form of enrolling the child in interest classes after kindergarten. The scheme has simulated a new demand for full-day services, especially among parents of lower SES. Unable to access full-day services, some families have to compromise by choosing half-day services instead. Significantly more parents of lower SES have problems finding full-day services in their neighbourhood (Yuen, 2015). Under the voucher scheme, parents and children in need of full-day services experience double disadvantages in terms of access to affordable and appropriate services. Apparently, less resourced families are not in a favourable position to find a choice option that can serve both child and adult needs. This in turn affects their likelihood of having a desirable start to enable social inclusion and participation. As observed by Paull (2012), the dichotomized practice of governments to attend to one of the two goals of early childhood services (i.e., either children's educational needs or parents' employment needs) is prominent. Hong Kong offers an obvious example.

The voucher scheme, which promotes the right to choice and focuses on financial assistance only to facilitate access to services, has left out the market situations (e.g., distribution, type and supply of services) that parents face in real life. It is common for families with fewer resources and working mothers to be underserved by markets (OECD, 2006). In Hong Kong, the closing and opening of kindergartens is left largely to the market. Irregularities in provision exist. The voucher scheme privileges half-day services, thus producing a market composition of choice options that work more advantageously for some but not all families. The per-head calculation method provides no incentives to voucher kindergartens to offer full-day services. Regardless of the strong demand for full-day services over an extended period of time, the market has not demonstrated an effective strategy switch by turning the extra supply of half-day places into full-day places (Yuen, 2015). Overall, there is no clear sign of a responsive market that can generate the best possible mixture of options to meet diverse needs and preferences, as assumed by neo-liberals (Moss, 2009).

In a similar vein, the relatively weaker impact of the intended policy outcome on choice has to do with inadequate understanding of choice practice in the early years. Effectively speaking, the extra subsidy that parents receive from the voucher scheme does not change much of their choice practice. Research on parent choice of early childhood services has widely confirmed the considerations of both pragmatic and educational factors (e.g., Braun, Vincent, & Ball, 2008; Johansen, Leibowitz, & Waite, 1996; Kim & Fram, 2009; Peyton et al., 2001). Heavily involved in care responsibilities, mothers most often rely on the convenience of the material context (distance and time) to manage these responsibilities (Yuen, 2015). Their preference for convenience reflects the complexities (e.g., family resources, work schedules, home situations) that mothers face in choice-making. They consider not only the child's well-being (e.g., physical health, strength, safety) but also household resource management (e.g., arranging the child's drop-off and pick-up). The latter is a particular concern among working mothers. While those with higher SES can enjoy greater capacity to mobilise a range of resources like school buses, domestic helpers or relatives to take care of the child or choose a cross-district option, mothers of lower SES are significantly bounded by kindergartens that fall within walking distance and short travel time. As shown, mothers are emotionally and morally engaged in choice-making (Yuen, 2015). Their choice practice is not in congruence with the neo-liberal assumption which reduces choice to abstract reasoning (Stein, 2001). Ertas and Shields (2012) argue that the choice practice of families with limited resources requires more thorough understanding and attention if the issue of access is to be dealt with effectively.

## *Quality*

Under the voucher scheme, parents are pivotal because their decisions about choice of service have been placed in what amounts to a de facto relationship with both the market and quality (Yuen & Grieshaber, 2009). What parents look for in choice of service and whether they consider the selected service to be the best choice, or at least a good quality service, is closely connected to what they expect the child to learn and how they want the child to develop in the early years. Parents are full of ambiguities and ambivalence when thinking about the learning and development of young children. While showing an awareness of the official stance on happy learning and child-centred pedagogy (see Guide to the Pre-primary Curriculum of Curriculum Development Council, 2006, for details), parents still struggle to cope with the cultural fear of what losing an academic curriculum might mean for the child's future. The relatively strong child orientation displayed among parents with middle-income and high education reveals the conscious "making" of a particular image of the child based on middle-class values. These parents are more ready to appropriate the official stance and yet wrestle with the competing discourses when choosing and defining quality of service (Yuen & Grieshaber, 2009). In general, parents tend to speak highly of the quality of their choice of service if they think that the early childhood institution is able to meet the criteria they most value, a phenomenon also found in other research (Cryer, Tietze, & Wessels, 2002; Long, Wilson, Kutnick, & Telford, 1996; Noble, 2007).

A market notion of quality is evident as early childhood institutions and parents interact with the voucher scheme in the market. Quality is understood by parents as having loving and specifically trained early childhood teachers to guide children to learn the basics and become happy learners through an exciting curriculum packed with active, diverse activities (Yuen & Grieshaber, 2009). Previous research (Chan & Chan, 2003; Hong Kong Christian Service, 2002; Weikart, 1999) indicates a high tendency for early childhood institutions to perform in accordance with what they think parents want. The market notion of quality is problematic in a number of ways. First, it reproduces the technical image that early childhood education is capable of doing just the basics (i.e., character, life skills, cognitive abilities [academic knowledge] and languages [English and Chinese]). Second, for a curriculum to be considered one of quality, it must include all sorts of experiences (in and beyond the classroom). While early childhood institutions stretch themselves to expand the breadth of the curriculum to meet the expected demands of parents, the space for teachers and children to engage in deeper learning or intellectually challenging work may also be narrowed. Early childhood teachers seem to be positioned more as managers of activities than as curriculum planners and thinkers. The voucher scheme has set the entry qualification at sub-degree level, rendering little help to change the dominant image of early childhood teachers as technicians delivering pre-determined child outcomes (Yuen & Grieshaber, 2009).

The specific notion of quality produced by combining policy and market function may have limited rather than expanded the possibilities for transforming the early childhood education sector into something even more desirable (Yuen & Grieshaber, 2009). The voucher scheme, as previously explained, intends to control and improve quality largely through a number of technocratic measures and a full-fledged market mechanism. It is supposed to realise the reform ideal of students as protagonists in the educational process to achieve holistic development, life-long learning and life-wide learning (Education Commission, 2000). Unfortunately, the "vibrant" early childhood market emphasises measurable results and not processes; it focuses on parents and not children. Through intensifying the governing of the self and sector by means of universal truths about choice and quality, the voucher scheme expects parents to bear the responsibility and risk of educating the young child. It is pure irony that the scheme is used to perfect the market in order to produce the desirable notion of quality in a sector that has already been intensely governed by market forces (Yuen & Grieshaber, 2009).

In sum, the local research points to the fact that the voucher scheme has made some impact, specifically in terms of reducing financial burden and enhancing choice. The common issues of vouchers, namely inadequate value and inequitable access, remain unresolved. The empirical evidence consistently highlights that parents of lower SES and working mothers are being disadvantaged by the voucher scheme. The collective imaginary constructed by the scheme has masked the privileging of parents who are more able to take up private responsibility. The voucher scheme appropriates values associated with class and gender in addition to the neo-liberal ones. Its mere focus on access to institutions fails to attend to the potential outcomes that private responsibility may have on the socially and economically disadvantaged groups (Tronto, 2013). As a technology of control, the voucher scheme looks promising with regard to constructing parents as the ideal consumers and the sector as an efficient market. However, the local research reveals that making choices and defining quality in early childhood education are filled with emotions, moral considerations, ambiguities and complexities. The early childhood market has not met the needs but has succeeded in constructing a specific notion of quality that reproduces the technical images of early childhood education and teachers.

## Pertinent issues of the voucher scheme

The issues of vouchers with equity, choice and quality reflect the larger problems of the market approach to early childhood education. In contrast to the neo-liberal emphasis on "evidence" or "what works," there is insufficient empirical evidence to show how markets work in practise and how well they work in education. It is also doubtful if the universal assumptions about market efficiency can work across contexts (Moss, 2009, 2014). Market failure has already been noted for early childhood services. Nonetheless, governments continue to rely on markets and incremental measures to support services for young children. One major market failure is caused by the fact that educating and caring for young children is different from a typical commodity (Paull, 2012). It is not naturally good, as argued by neoliberals (Tronto, 2013). Parents do not necessarily enjoy consumer sovereignty (Paull, 2012), due to the nature of care responsibilities, market situations and other factors like parent backgrounds being highlighted before (Yuen, 2015). Besides, markets are inherently inequitable. They set out to serve the interests of those who can help sustain competition. Markets do so by supporting their needs at the expense of others (Tronto, 2013). From Tronto's (2013) feminist perspective, the political construction of private responsibility enables governments to avoid taking full responsibility to deal with the problems created by markets and maintain paternal power to allocate care responsibilities, which in turn exacerbates historical injustice.

Markets, often presented by governments as an inevitable solution to educational issues, justify minimal involvement in the lives of young children. As is the case in Hong Kong, the voucher scheme has led to a significant increase of resources, from HK$1,290 million (2.7 per cent of the total education expenses) in 2006/07 (Education Bureau, 2008) to HK$3,486 million (4.7 per cent) in 2014/15 (Education Bureau, 2015). Spending on early childhood education (ages 3–6), however, remains relatively low, amounting to 23 per cent and 14 per cent of the revised budget estimates of primary and secondary education, respectively, in 2014/15 (Education Bureau, 2015). Hong Kong spends significantly less on education for children aged 3 to 6 in comparison with other countries. For example, in 2012, only 0.14 per cent of the GDP in Hong Kong as opposed to 0.5 per cent and 0.7 per cent of the GDP in Sweden and the United Kingdom, respectively (Yuen & Yu, 2014). Local research reveals a strong demand for more government involvement, notably in the form of public provision (Li, Wong, & Wang, 2010; Yuen, 2015; Yuen & Yu, 2010). The resistance demonstrated by parents towards the neo-liberal imaginary of market efficiency goes in tandem with the international call for increased government effort and direct funding to ensure equitable access to quality provision and achieve the dual goals of early childhood services. Unfortunately, Hong Kong falls far below the recommended level of public investment for quality provision (i.e., at least 1 per cent of the GDP) (OECD, 2006).

The predominant non-profit-making nature of the early childhood market in Hong Kong has made market efficiency less attainable. This characteristic is less common in other countries, for example, Taiwan, the United Kingdom and the United States, where the private sector is composed of mostly for-profit-making operators. Research shows that non-profit-making operators are more likely to provide higher quality services than for-profit-making operators (Cleveland, Forer, Hyatt, Japel, & Krashinsky, 2007). In 2014/15, 87 per cent (760 out of 874) of local kindergartens were run by non-profit-making operators (School Education Statistics Section, 2015). Non-profit-making kindergartens are subject to 5 per cent profit control and have to rely on tuitions and other add-on fees for survival. With escalating operating costs contributed by such factors as inflation, professional upgrading and rent hikes in a cosmopolitan setting, the overcharging problem reported by the Audit Commission (2013) reflects the difficulty that voucher kindergartens are facing. Competition has not brought the production costs down as expected (Moss, 2009). Actually, cost reduction would mean a compromise of quality (e.g., paying less for qualified or experienced teachers). In the market, large resource and quality gaps exist between non-profit-making kindergartens. The per-head calculation method of the voucher scheme has further widened these gaps by favouring half-day operation which has two daily sessions and kindergartens bigger in size. The scheme intensifies problems in full-day operation which serves only one group of students and kindergartens smaller in capacity. In the absence of a unit cost calculation that contributes to quality provision, the work environment of teachers is less than satisfactory. A local study found serious concerns among early childhood teachers over their remuneration, work pressure, stability and morale following the implementation of the voucher scheme. As revealed by the study, over 80 per cent of the teachers indicated that they felt "less valued as a teacher when compared with primary or secondary school teachers" (Yuen, Lai, & Law, 2010). High teacher turnover (44 per cent of 751 voucher kindergartens with a turnover rate ranging from 20 per cent to 80 per cent) is a grave concern (Audit Commission, 2013).

The neo-liberal policy discourse decontextualises educational issues, the consequence of which is the missed opportunity to ensure equitable access to quality provision and achieve the dual goals of early childhood services. In a quick glance at the social and economic situations, Hong Kong has been experiencing stagnant real earnings and continuous decline in the ability to repay mortgages (Center for Quality of Life, 2014), as well as prolonged poverty with a Gini-coefficient at 0.5-level (Economic Analysis Division, 2012). Over 50 per cent of mothers with children under the age of 6 work full-time (Census and Statistics Department, 2012). Government statistics show a significant proportion of women working long hours. The situation is worst among low-pay occupations (Census and Statistics Department, 2014). The difficulty in balancing work and family responsibilities has created lots of stressful parenthood and childhood experiences. In terms of children's well-being and learning, they suffer from anxiety or depression resulting from the highly competitive school system (United Nations Committee on the Rights of the Child, 2013). While insufficient resources for special education have been reported at primary and secondary education levels (Equal Opportunities Commission, 2012a), young children with potential special educational needs have to wait for a lengthy period to receive assessment and rehabilitation services, thus missing the prime time for effective assistance (Panel on Education, Legislative Council, 2014). There is also minimal effort to integrate ethnic minority students into the mainstream at all levels (Equal Opportunities Commission, 2012b). The significant increase of cross-border marriages, contributing to almost half of all marriages in 2013, has led to a continual flow of young children holding a single entry permit to Hong Kong (Lau, 2015). New immigrant parents encounter more difficulty in parenting than local parents (Leung, Leung, & Chan, 2007). According to the United Nations Committee on the Rights of the Child (2013), Hong Kong still lacks "a comprehensive policy and strategy on children in their respective jurisprudence to guide, in a holistic and integrated manner, all laws, policies, plans and programmes affecting children" (para. 10). In this light, the essential role that early childhood education can play in facing challenges emerged from the changing social and economic landscapes in Hong Kong has not been examined. Neither has its relation to primary and secondary education been revisited to smooth transitions and continuities for building an equitable and quality education system for all children.

## Market still? What to choose next?

A major change of early childhood education policy will take place with the recent release of a report by the Committee on Free Kindergarten Education (2015) in support of 15-year free education (12-year free primary and secondary education plus 3-year free kindergarten education) in Hong Kong. One key recommendation of the report is to provide free half-day education for children aged 3 to 6 enrolled in non-profit-making kindergartens; additional subsidies are recommended for those attending and operating full-day services (Committee on Free Kindergarten Education, 2015). What is worth noting in the report is the repeating emphasis on the importance of maintaining the vibrancy and flexibility of kindergarten operation. Unlike the voucher scheme which gives a subsidy to parents, the report recommends subsidising basic teaching-related expenses with reference to half-day operation and per-head calculation (Committee on Free Kindergarten Education, 2015). The direct funding of operation is notably a step towards the right direction. But it still adheres strongly to the market orientation in practice. The pattern of resource allocation and positioning of early childhood education in the private market remain unchanged. Since its release, the report has attracted criticisms in terms of policy coherence, long-term directions and the effectiveness of the new recommendations in attending to the issues of quality, inequity and instability associated with student intake and number, the size and mode of operation, as well as the absence of compulsory master pay scales and systematic assistance for students with special educational needs (e.g., Alliance on the Fight for 15-Year Free Education, 2015; Council of Non-profit-making Organisations for Pre-primary Education, 2015). As concrete measures are still in the process of finalisation, some questions deserve ardent attention when considering the next policy choice: What constitutes basic operation that is crucial to offering high-quality provision? To what extent can the new funding mode help narrow the resource and quality gaps between kindergartens? How far can it go to ensure quality and inclusive learning processes, and in turn better outcomes for all children? In what ways can it sustain the diverse modes of operation, especially full-day kindergartens?

Policy choices and designs in early childhood education mirror how problems and target groups are understood. They legitimatize particular socio-political constructions of the sector and all those involved as well as the extent of government involvement in children's lives (Rigby, Tarrant, & Newman, 2007). How ready the Hong Kong government is to move away from the market approach will depend on its ways of thinking and valuing education for young children.

Taking a critical turn on future policy directions would require openness to alternative perspectives. Early childhood education, local and global alike, is confronting the hegemonic influence of neo-liberalism, which favours privatisation, marketisation and corporate managerialism. There is an enormous gap between evidence and action. On the one hand, the significance of early childhood education to children, families, vulnerable groups and society as a whole has been strongly argued and widely communicated. On the other hand, there are lots of delayed actions. Policy tools like vouchers, which rely on universal market assumptions and do not attend to local contexts wholeheartedly, cannot be expected to make a significant impact. They would continue to take social justice for granted and curtail the possibility of a "(re)commitment to democracy, equality and sustainability" (Moss, 2014, 49). Education has a fundamental role to play in shaping a caring and democratic society. "But it can only do so if it is protected from those who see it as one more product to be consumed as we measure it" (Apple, 2004, 620).

A holistic quality perspective is imperative to making policy choices. As discussed earlier, quality in early childhood education is multi-dimensional, requiring a genuine recognition of the interconnectedness of various aspects of quality (OECD, 2006). High importance should be given to process quality (pedagogical relationship and interaction), which is pivotal to learning progress in the early years (Sammons, 2010). Process quality is subject to the presence of a coherently built quality structure and high professional competence. The latter hinges on the development of teacher professionalism at degree level (Barnett, 2004; Burchinal, Cryer, Clifford, & Howes, 2002; Sammons, 2010). Siraj-Blatchford (2010) reveals that "sustained shared thinking" (e.g., solving problems, clarifying concepts, extending thinking) characterises the pedagogical interactions of excellent centres. The increasing complexities and rising expectations of early childhood education have also made teachers' work intellectually, emotionally and ethically more demanding than before. A sub-degree qualification can no longer meet the professional challenges in early childhood settings.

The holistic quality perspective requires a willingness to commit substantial public investment or as Paquette (2007) suggests, tamper with the existing economic pie to redistribute resources. Based on the key observations of a cross-national study of early childhood systems (ages 0–6) in 20 countries, OECD (2006) recommends that direct funding of operation is far more effective than parent or indirect subsidy for developing and sustaining quality provision. Only high-quality provision can maximise the well-established personal and social benefits (e.g., social inclusion, gender equality, poverty eradication) of early childhood services. The direct funding mode in the form of public provision brings advantages in the areas of effective control, economy of scale, achievement of more even quality, professional improvement and equitable access and participation. Furthermore, the institutionalisation of early childhood education in Hong Kong enables a more efficient construction of a systemic structure with primary and secondary education. Reconceptualising the relation between early childhood and other levels of education is a relatively new international endeavour (Moss, 2013). The benefits of building strong and equal partnerships across levels of education can help improve system accountability and responsiveness, especially when primary and secondary schools experience tensions in support of students with special educational needs. It is in this direction that equitable access to institutions, processes and outcomes, hence the development of individual capacity for the freedom to choose, can be realised.

## Acknowledgement

The work described in this chapter was supported by a grant from the Central Policy Unit of the Government of the Hong Kong Special Administrative Region and the Research Grants Council of the Hong Kong Special Administrative Region, China (HKIEd 8013-PPR-10).

## References

Alliance on the Fight for 15-year Free Education. (2015). *A response to the report of the Committee on Free Kindergarten Education*. Hong Kong: Alliance on the Fight for 15-year Free Education.

Apple, M. W. (2004). Schooling, markets, and an audit culture. *Educational Policy, 18*(4), 614–621.

Audit Commission. (2013). *Pre-primary education voucher scheme*. Hong Kong: Audit Commission. Retrieved from http://www.aud.gov.hk/pdf_e/e60ch03.pdf
Ball, S. J. (1994). *Education reform: A critical post-structural approach*. Buckingham; Philadelphia: Open University Press.
Barnett, W. S. (2004). *Better teachers, better preschools: Student achievement linked to teacher qualifications*. Retrieved from http://nieer.org/resources/policybriefs/2.pdf
Braun, A., Vincent, C., & Ball, S. J. (2008). 'I'm so much more myself now, coming back to work' – Working class mothers, paid work and childcare. *Journal of Education Policy, 23*(5), 533–548.
Burchinal, M. R., Cryer, D., Clifford, R. M., & Howes, C. (2002). Caregiver training and classroom quality in child care centres. *Applied Developmental Science, 6*(1), 2–11.
Census and Statistics Department. (2012). *Statistics on households with children under the age of six*. Hong Kong: Census and Statistics Department.
Census and Statistics Department. (2014). *Women and men in Hong Kong key statistics*. Hong Kong: Census and Statistics Department. Retrieved from http://www.statistics.gov.hk/pub/B11303032014AN14B0100.pdf
Center for Quality of Life. (2014). *Hong Kong quality of life index*. Hong Kong: Center for Quality of Life, Chinese University of Hong Kong. Retrieved from http://www.cuhk.edu.hk/hkiaps/qol/eventdoc/QoL%20report/QoL%202013%20report_eng.pdf
Chan, L. K. S., & Chan, L. (2003). Early childhood education in Hong Kong and its challenges. *Early Childhood Development and Care, 173*(1), 7–17.
Chen, K. C. (2008). The discourse in the equity of preschool education voucher policy in our country. *Education Research, 16*, 133–145.
Cleveland, G., Forer, B., Hyatt, D., Japel, C., & Krashinsky, M. (2007). *Final project report: An economic perspective on the current and future role of nonprofit provision of early learning and childcare services in Canada*. Retrieved from http://www.childcarepolicy.net/wp-content/uploads/2013/04/final-report.pdf
Committee on Free Kindergarten Education. (2015). *Children first: Right start for all: Report of the Committee on Free Kindergarten Education*. Hong Kong: Education Bureau. Retrieved from http://www.edb.gov.hk/attachment/en/edu-system/preprimary-kindergarten/kg-report/Free-kg-report-201505-Eng.pdf
Council of Non-profit-making Organisations for Pre-primary Education. (2015). *Comments on the report of the Committee on Free Kindergarten Education*. Hong Kong: Council of Non-profit-making Organisations for Pre-primary Education.
Cryer, D., Tietze, W., & Wessels, H. (2002). Parents' perceptions of their children's child care: A cross-national comparison. *Early Childhood Research Quarterly, 17*, 259–277.
Curriculum Development Council. (2006). *Guide to the pre-primary curriculum*. Hong Kong: Government Printer.
Dahlberg, G., & Moss, P. (2005). *Ethics and politics in early childhood education*. London: RoutledgeFalmer.
Dahlberg, G., Moss, P., & Pence, A. (2007). *Beyond quality in early childhood education and care: Postmodern perspectives (Second edition)*. Oxon: Routledge.
Davis, E. E., & Connelly, R. (2005). The influence of local price and availability on parents' choice of childcare. *Population Research and Policy Review, 24*, 301–334.
Economic Analysis Division. (2012). *Half-yearly economic report 2012*. Hong Kong: Economic Analysis Division. Retrieved from http://www.hkeconomy.gov.hk/en/pdf/er_12q2.pdf

Education and Manpower Bureau. (2006). *Item for Finance Committee*. Hong Kong: Education and Manpower Bureau. Retrieved from http://www.legco.gov.hk/yr06–07/english/fc/fc/papers/f06–29e.pdf

Education Bureau. (2008). *Replies to initial written questions raised by Finance Committee members in examining the estimates of expenditure 2008–09*. Hong Kong: Education Bureau. Retrieved from http://www.legco.gov.hk/yr07–08/chinese/fc/fc/w_q/edb-c.pdf

Education Bureau. (2010). *Pre-primary education voucher scheme*. Hong Kong: Education Bureau. Retrieved from http://www.legco.gov.hk/yr09–10/english/panels/ed/papers/ed0111cb2–665–6-e.pdf

Education Bureau. (2015). *Replies to initial written questions raised by Finance Committee members in examining the estimates of expenditure 2015–16*. Hong Kong: Education Bureau. Retrieved from http://www.edb.gov.hk/attachment/sc/about-edb/publications-stat/figures/edb-c.pdf

Education Commission. (2000). *Learning for life: Learning through life: Reform proposals for the education system in Hong Kong*. Hong Kong: Education Commission.

Equal Opportunities Commission. (2012a). *Study on equal learning opportunities for students with disabilities under the integrated education system*. Hong Kong: Equal Opportunities Commission. Retrieved from http://www.eoc.org.hk/EOC/Upload/ResearchReport/IE_eReport.pdf

Equal Opportunities Commission. (2012b). *Study on racial encounters and discrimination experienced by South Asians report*. Hong Kong: Equal Opportunities Commission. Retrieved from http://www.eoc.org.hk/EOC/Upload/UserFiles/File/ResearchReport/201203/Race_eFull%20Report.pdf

Ertas, N., & Shields, S. (2012). Child care subsidies and care arrangements of low-income parents. *Children and Youth Services Review, 34*, 179–185.

Forestier, K. (2006, November 25). Still much to debate on voucher scheme. *South China Morning Post*. Retrieved from http://www.scmp.com/node/572907

Granell, R. (2002). Education vouchers in Spain: The Valencian experience. *Education Economics, 10*(2), 119–132.

Ho, M. S. (2006). The politics of preschool education vouchers in Taiwan. *Comparative Education Review, 50*(1), 66–89.

Hong Kong Christian Service. (2002). *A study on the quality of preschool education*. Hong Kong: Hong Kong Christian Service.

Hong Kong Government. (1965). *Education policy*. Hong Kong: Government Printer.

Hung, F. S. (2006). Privatization of Hong Kong school education. In W. K. Tsang (Ed.), *Education blueprint for the 21st century? Discourse on the education reform in the Hong Kong special administrative region* (pp. 319–348). Hong Kong: Hong Kong Institute of Educational Research and the Chinese University Press.

Johansen, A. S., Leibowitz, A., & Waite, L. J. (1996). The importance of childcare characteristics to choice of care. *Journal of Marriage and the Family, 58*(3), 759–772.

Kim, J., & Fram, M. S. (2009). Profiles of choice: Parents' patterns of priority in childcare decision-making. *Early Childhood Research Quarterly, 24*, 77–91.

Lau, Y. K. (2015, June 1). *From the perspective of family impact assessment*. Hong Kong: The Hong Kong Council of Social Service. Retrieved from http://c4e.hkcss.org.hk/chi/reference-detail.php?n=1&c=811

Lee, I. F. (2006). Rethinking the Taiwanese preschool vouchers. *Hong Kong Journal of Early Childhood, 5*(2), 33–40.

Lee, V., & Wong, E. (2002). *Education voucher system*. Hong Kong: Research and Library Services Division, Legislative Council. Retrieved from http://www.legco.gov.hk/yr01-02/english/sec/library/0102rp06e.pdf

Leung, S. L., Leung, C., & Chan, R. (2007). Perceived child behaviour problems, parenting stress, and marital satisfaction: Comparison of new arrival and local parents to preschool children in Hong Kong. *Hong Kong Medicine Journal, 13*, 464–471.

Li, H., Wong, J. M. S., & Wang, X. C. (2010). Affordability, accessibility and accountability: Perceived impacts of the pre-primary education vouchers in Hong Kong. *Early Childhood Research Quarterly, 25*, 125–138.

Llewellyn, J. (1982). *A perspective on education in Hong Kong: Report by a visiting panel*. Hong Kong: Government Printer.

Long, P., Wilson, P., Kutnick, P., & Telford, L. (1996). Choice and childcare: A survey of parental perceptions and views. *Early Child Development and Care, 119*, 51–63.

Lui, T. L. (2011). *Zhong chan xin shi: Wei ji zhi hou* [Middle class worries: After the crisis]. Hong Kong: Up Publication.

Luke, A. (1997). New narratives of human capital: Recent redirections in Australian educational policy. *Australian Educational Researcher, 24*(2), 1–21.

Moss, P. (2009). *There are alternatives! Markets and democratic experimentalism in early childhood education and care*. Working Paper no. 53. The Hague, The Netherlands: Bernard van Leer Foundation and Bertelsmann Stiftung.

Moss, P. (Ed.) (2013). *Reconceptualising early childhood and compulsory education*. Oxon: Routledge.

Moss, P. (2014). *Transformative change and real utopias in early childhood education: A story of democracy, experimentation and potentiality*. London: Routledge.

Nelson, J. L., Palonsky, S. B., & McCarthy, M. R. (2010). *Critical issues in education: Dialogues and dialectics*. New York: McGraw Hill.

Noble, K. (2007). Parent choice of early childhood education and care services. *Australian Journal of Early Childhood, 32*(2), 51–57.

OECD. (2006). *Starting strong II: Early childhood education and care*. Paris: OECD Publishing. Retrieved from http://www.oecd.org/ dataoecd/14/32/37425999.pdf

Panel on Education, Legislative Council. (2014). *Report of Subcommittee on Integrated Education*. Retrieved from http://www.legco.gov.hk/yr13-14/english/panels/ed/ed_ie/reports/ed_iecb4-1087-1-e.pdf

Paquette, J. (2007). Equity in educational policy. In S. J. Ball, I. F. Goodson & M. Maguire (Eds.), *Education, globalization and new times* (pp. 335–359). London; New York: Routledge.

Patten, C. (1996). *1996/97 Policy address*. Hong Kong: Government Printer.

Paull, G. (2012). Childcare markets and government intervention. In E. Llody & P. Helen (Eds.), *Childcare markets: Can they deliver an equitable service?* (pp. 227–246). Bristol: Policy Press.

Penn, H. (2012). Childcare markets: Do they work? In E. Llody & P. Helen (Eds.), *Childcare markets: Can they deliver an equitable service?* (pp. 19–42). Bristol: Policy Press.

Peyton, V., Jacobs, A., O'Brien, M., & Roy, C. (2001). Reasons for choosing childcare: Associations with family factors, quality and satisfaction. *Early Childhood Research Quarterly, 16*, 191–208.

Rigby, E., Tarrant, K., & Newman, M. J. (2007). Alternative policy designs and the socio-political construction of childcare. *Contemporary Issues in Early Childhood, 8*(2), 98–108.

Rizvi, F., & Lingard, B. (2010). *Globalizing education policy*. London; New York: Routledge.

Sammons, P. (2010). Does pre-school make a difference? Identifying the impact of pre-school on children's cognitive and social behavioural development at different ages. In K. Sylva, E. Melhuish, P. Sammons, I. Siraj-Blatchford & B. Taggart (Eds.), *Early childhood matters: Evidence from the effective pre-school and primary education project* (pp. 92–113). London and New York: Routledge.

School Education Statistics Section. (2015). *Student enrolment statistics 2014/2015*. Hong Kong: School Education Statistics Section.

Siraj-Blatchford, I. (2010). A focus on pedagogy: Case studies of effective practice. In K. Sylva, E. Melhuish, P. Sammons, I. Siraj-Blatchford & B. Taggart (Eds.), *Early childhood matters: Evidence from the effective pre-school and primary education project* (pp. 149–165). London and New York: Routledge.

Sparkes, J., & West. A. (1998). An evaluation of the English Nursery Voucher Scheme 1996–1997. *Education Economics, 6*(2), 171–184.

Stein, J. G. (2001). *The cult of efficiency*. Toronto: House of Anansi Press.

Tronto, J. C. (2013). *Caring democracy: Markets, equality, and justice*. New York; London: New York University Press.

Tsang, Y. K. (2006). *Policy address 2006–2007*. Hong Kong: Government Printer. Retrieved from http://www.policyaddress.gov.hk/06-07/eng/p43.html

United Nations Committee on the Rights of the Child. (2013, October 29). *Concluding observations on the combined third and fourth periodic reports of China, adopted by the Committee at its 64th session (September 16 – October 4, 2013)*. Retrieved from http://www.cmab.gov.hk/doc/en/documents/policy_responsibilities/Concluding%28eng%29.pdf

Vincent, C., Braun, A., & Ball, S. (2010). Local links, local knowledge: Choosing care settings and schools. *British Educational Research Journal, 36*(2), 279–298.

Weikart, D. P. (Ed.) (1999). *What should young children learn? Teacher and parent views in 15 countries: The IEA Preprimary Project, Phase 2*. Ypsilanti: High/Scope Educational Research Foundation.

Yuen, G. (2010). The displaced early childhood education in the postcolonial era of Hong Kong. In N. Yelland (Ed.), *Contemporary perspectives on early childhood education* (pp. 83–99). London: Open University Press.

Yuen, G. (2015). Markets, choice of kindergarten, mothers' care responsibilities and the voucher scheme in Hong Kong. *Children and Youth Services Review, 48*, 167–176.

Yuen, G., & Grieshaber, S. (2009). Parents' choice of early childhood education services in Hong Kong: A pilot study about vouchers. *Contemporary Issues in Early Childhood, 10*(3), 263–279.

Yuen, G., Lai, K. C., & Law, K. Y. (2010). *The work of early childhood teachers after the implementation of the pre-primary education voucher scheme*. Hong Kong: Strategic Planning Office, Hong Kong Institute of Education.

Yuen, G., & Lam, M. S. (2016). *A critical examination of a voucher scheme as played out within the context of Hong Kong's early education market*. Manuscript submitted for publication.

Yuen, G., & Yu, W. B. (2010). *Parents' choice in the use of full-day early childhood education service*. Hong Kong: Education Policy Forum, Hong Kong Institute of Education.

Yuen, G., & Yu, W. B. (2014). *Cross-sectoral professional dialogue 2013–2014*. Hong Kong: Faculty of Education and Human Development and Department of Education Policy and Leadership, Hong Kong Institute of Education.

# 3 Parental choice in the new education market

Aided-turn-direct subsidy scheme schools in focus

*Jacqueline Chak-Kei Woo*

## Introduction

The adoption of market rules in the education sector has fundamentally changed Hong Kong's school choice policy as well as other education policies in many ways. Most significantly, there is a new emphasis on competition, choice, accountability, performativity of schools. The introduction of the Direct Subsidy Scheme (DSS) exemplifies the adoption of market rules in the education sector. DSS has also generated many controversies, one of which mainly focuses on top traditional aided-schools joining DSS and charging high tuition fees. Various members in the community are concerned that families with low social-economic status would be deterred from applying these schools. More importantly, while DSS was originally introduced to enhance parental choice, with these aided-schools leaving the public sector and joining the DSS and charging tuition fees, many poor families perceive that their choices of school have actually decreased. This chapter analyses the DSS in Hong Kong as a choice policy. It first gives an account of the DSS as a school choice policy in the education market; second, a case study is presented to illustrate the reactions of different stakeholders involved in DSS, and finally, it further discusses the implications of DSS as a school choice policy in Hong Kong in the twenty-first century.

## Background

Since the late 1970s, educational reform has swept across industrialised countries: policy-makers in various regions have adopted neo-liberal, free-market ideology in reforming their education policies (Ball, 1993, 2003; Gewirtz, Ball, & Bowe, 1995; Lauder & Hughes, 1999; Levin, 1998; Tsang, 2002, 2006; Whitty & Power, 2003). Traditional public schooling that supposedly would provide free and equal opportunities in accessing education seem to be in need to be reformed everywhere. Under such neo-liberal, free-market reform, rhetoric that was once associated with the corporate managerial world or the market, such as "accountability", "competitiveness", "performativity", "effectiveness" and "choice", to name a few, are now dominating the education system. The adoption of market policies in the public education system has also introduced what Ball (1990) describes as an "education market" (59) that is characterised by five principles: choice, diversity, funding, competition and organisational style (Ball, 1990, 60–61).

These changes in the public education system are mainly a response to globalisation and the changing socio-economic environment. As the global market continues to expand, there is an intensification of economic competition among different nation-states and a reorganisation of the worldwide labour market. Consequently, parents and employers have changed their expectations and demands for the education system, which has a key role in preparing efficient and productive workforce (Burbules & Torres, 2000; Ho, Morris, & Chung, 2005; Mok, 2006; Plank & Sykes, 2003).

In Hong Kong, the market-oriented education reform of the public education sector began in the 1990s. Similar to the reforms conducted in many industrialised countries around the world, "neo-liberal" ideology is adopted by the reform, marked by introducing market strategies based on the private business sector model and implementing discipline and standards to the public education system (Ho, Morris, & Chung, 2005; Lee, 2006). DSS is essentially a policy that has adopted the principle of "choice" in the new education market: believers in the market actually emphasise that an increase of choice would benefit the education system, bringing efficiency and improvement to schools and even more equity to all families.

## School choice in Hong Kong: The Direct Subsidy Scheme

In terms of choice in Hong Kong, prior to the reform of the public education sector in the 1990s, most students attended government or aided-schools (from here on referred to as government-supported schools) that followed governmental regulations. There was also a weak private school sector, in which there were only few private schools for students to choose from. The limited choices of private schools included expensive private "international schools" that offered overseas curriculum and private independent schools, that most working-class, even many middle-class families in Hong Kong found them unaffordable. There were CAPUT schools that received subsidies from the government on a per capita grant basis. In addition, there were some private schools under the "Bought Place Scheme" (BPS), which were of rather poor academic and physical quality; as well as "patriotic" schools which upheld political ideology that was not popular in the mainstream society (Cheung, 2002; Sweeting, 1993, as cited in Tse, 2008; Wong, 2006).

Prior to DSS, among the government-supported schools in the public education sector, the choice of school is mostly bounded by the school net (also known as school district in other countries), and the allocation of school often depends on the central allocation determined by the government, with the exception of students who got accepted by schools via "Discretionary Place".[1] In addition, these government-supported schools are very similar in terms of their curriculum, admission procedure and teachers' hiring and firing practices. There is little diversity among the public government-supported schools. In other words, there is very little room for school choice, except for parents with financial resources, who could enrol their children in the schools there, or they could send their children to the expensive and limited private schools of their choice, such as one of the "international schools" that offer curriculum and facilities that are vastly different from the local government-supported schools.

Serious discussions on expanding school choice in Hong Kong emerged in the late 1980s, when the Education Commission's Report No.3 introduced a new policy called the Direct Subsidy Scheme (DSS) (Education Commission, 1988). The timing of the report coincided with the tenth anniversary of the implementation of compulsory education in Hong Kong. It was also a time when discussions on whether the quality of public education has declined and the talk on introducing market rules to improve the education system has become popular (Tsang, 2002). Existing private schools as well as government-aided schools in the public sector were invited to participate in DSS. One of the goals of this policy was to develop an independent and strong private education sector (Education Commission, 1988, Paragraph 4.12) in order to benefit the existing education system as a whole. Under this scheme, participating DSS schools would operate, to a certain extent, according to the market principles. They are not bounded by any school net and could charge a restricted amount of school fees and receive the government funding, which is subject to the number of students a particular school has admitted. In other words, DSS schools would have to compete for students in order to stay in business and to receive government funding. Such policy design uses "school choice" as a "driving force for continuous improvement" (Legislative Council Panel on Education, 2000) for all schools. This policy is essentially introducing "privatisation of education in terms of school operation", a type of privatisation where a private service (i.e., education in this case) is financed by the government "through contracting out . . . instead of direct government services" (Tse, 2008, 8). In the eyes of the Hong Kong government, not only school choice is a "driving force" for quality education, policymakers also believe that DSS would bring diversity in school programmes, and its flexibility in various aspects such as curriculum design, admission of students and resources management could help prepare students to face the needs of the workplace and the community in the twenty-first century. In addition, the government believes that DSS could meet the demand of the affluent Hong Kong community members for better quality education, as DSS schools could charge fees in order "to provide above-standard facilities" to the community (Legislative Council Panel on Education, 2000). The scheme was finally introduced in 1991 to promote "a vibrant private school sector" and to increase "diversity and choice" in the education system of Hong Kong (Education Bureau, 2015), suggesting an adoption of education market.

The discussions on expanding choice for parents further intensified in the late 1990s, at a time when Hong Kong launched a series of policies to restructure its public education system. First of all, beginning in 1998, schools were required to follow the Medium of Instruction (MOI) policy (Education Department, 1997), and as a result, most secondary schools had to use Chinese as the medium of instruction (CMI) in classrooms, except only about a quarter of over 400 secondary schools were allowed to remain using English as the medium of instruction

(EMI). Such an arrangement was strongly opposed by many schools and parents, as English has traditionally been the preferred MOI. Since the implementation of the MOI policy, there were simply not enough EMI schools to meet the demands of parents. Second, a comprehensive education reform was also introduced to the public education system in 2000 (Education Commission, 2000).[2] However, this ambitious comprehensive education reform was not very popular among the general public. In fact, it has even intensified the demand for school choice among parents (Tse, 2008).

Furthermore, the revised version of DSS in 2001 now permits all participating schools to charge over twice as much as the funding that government would provide to each student (Tsang, 2002). In addition to receiving recurrent subsidy from the government (as long as the school kept the tuition fee below two and one-third of the average unit cost of an aided-school spot), any participating school would have to set up a scholarship scheme and to offer to parents fee remission (Education Bureau, 2015). In addition, the government began to allow aided primary schools to participate in DSS starting from school year 2000–2001 (Chan & Tan, 2008, 470). This has attracted more schools to participate in DSS. In fact, this revised version of DSS has further exemplified the characteristics of market rules. In 2015, the school fee of DSS schools, including some aided-turn DSS schools, varies from basically nothing to close to HK$100,000 per year.

The years following the implementation of the MOI policy and a comprehensive education reform, as well as the revision of DSS, saw a significant increase of DSS schools: from top traditional aided-schools to newly built schools, many schools have decided to join DSS. As at February 2015, there are a total of 82 DSS schools (61 offering classes at the secondary level, 21 at the primary level). Among them, nine are aided-turned-DSS schools. Many of these DSS schools are EMI ones and some of them also break away from the traditional curriculum and introduced innovative themes. For instance, one DSS school introduced cutting-edge science subject such as biotechnology as a compulsory subject for all secondary one students; another one has designed thematic studies that are tailor-made for boys; and another one has even offered the International Baccalaureate Diploma Programme in addition to the mainstream curriculum.

DSS has proven to be a multi-functional scheme. Since its implementation in the early 1990s, it has successfully resolved the issues concerning the future of BPS private schools, and it enabled the once-marginalised patriotic schools to receive government subsidies (Adamson & Li, 1999, 49; Wong, 2006, 54). Even quite a number of reputable and top-notch elite aided-schools have been attracted to join the DSS since the scheme was revised in 2001, setting a high academic standard for the scheme (Wong, 2006, 54).

One of the biggest concerns about accessing these elite aided-turn-DSS schools has been their high tuition fees. In most of the newspapers and public discussions in recent years, the "elite" aided-turn-DSS schools are no longer the choice of families from working-class background, and they perceive that they would never be able to afford to send their children there. For these families, the objective of introducing DSS to increase parental choice, as proposed by the government, was not achieved. Choices of school, for these families, have been further limited by DSS.

## A case study on aided-turn-DSS schools

Among the most notable controversies over DSS is concerned about top traditional aided-schools joining DSS (hereafter as aided-turn-DSS schools). A case study of three aided-turn-DSS schools was conducted in 2010–2011 so as to illustrate the reactions of different stakeholders of these schools. These three aided-turn-DSS schools are with long history and highly reputable in Hong Kong. These three schools all have both primary and secondary schools. Their secondary sections use English as the medium of instruction. These schools have traditionally been considered as popular elite schools that are highly sought-after by parents. They are very competitive and are always oversubscribed. All of them participated in DSS after a major revision in the policy of DSS in 2001, which allows them to charge tuition fee up to two and one-third of the average unit cost of an aided-school. The stakeholders that were involved in this study include the principals from the three aided-turn-DSS schools as well as eighteen parents, six from each of these three schools.

### *The principals*

From the interviews conducted with the three principals, all three schools wanted more autonomy in student admission. All three schools were dissatisfied with the quality of the students who were placed in their schools via the government-run school allocation system when they were still government-supported schools. As traditional elite schools with legacy and prestige, they were concerned about their reputation, and wanted to remain elitist. By becoming DSS schools, they had full autonomy in deciding which students, or which families rather (as all the schools would interview the parents during the admission process), were suitable in their school communities. These schools have also made changes in their curriculum and certain management style, changes that they believed were most suitable for their students. If they had continued to stay in the public school sector, they would not be able to act on their preferences freely with such great degree of autonomy.

The principals – the gatekeepers of the schools – have strongly influenced which candidates could successfully get into an aided-turn-DSS school. This was especially true in one of the three schools in the case study, where the principal was the sole interviewer and decision maker on the admission results. In general, in all the schools participating in this study, the principals' thoughts and expectations are embodied in the schools' admission interviews, dominating the culture of the admission process.

### *Parents choosing aided-turn-DSS schools*

A total of 18 parents, 6 from each of the 3 aided-turn-DSS schools, were interviewed for this case study.

When asked about how they helped their children to apply for DSS schools, most of the parent interviewees implied that they have used their social capital to help their children. For instance, some of the interviewees invited their friends of high social status to write a recommendation letter for their children. Some of them had very close relationships with their children's teachers that they could discuss extensively with them and getting professional advice on how to choose the most suitable school for their children. Interviewees would also do extensive research on various schools. They mostly had sophisticated Internet skills – checking school websites, reading reviews of different schools from online community forums. Some of these interviewees quit their full-time jobs in order to commit themselves to raising their children. They could afford to spend a lot of time preparing their children for the school choice process. For instance, some of these full-time mothers took their children to several DSS schools for site-visits during school hours, so that they could have a better idea of different schools and their students.

From the interviews with the parents, minimising sense of risk and perceived "benefits" from enrolling in aided-turn-DSS schools are two issues worthy of special attention.

The introduction of DSS has changed what school choice means in Hong Kong altogether, helping choosers to minimise the sense of risk and uncertainty. Parent interviewees, all from the middle-class, implied that DSS as a choice policy has helped them to minimise their sense of risk and uncertainties instead.

Parent interviewees identified the factors that brought them the sense of risk and uncertainty in the field of school choice before the introduction of DSS. First, parents were deeply dissatisfied with government policies, such as policy of school places allocation at the primary school as well as secondary school levels, and the MOI policy. Second, the social context also made these parents uncomfortable sending their children to government-supported schools. One main reason, as expressed by some of the interviewees, was that they were reluctant to let their children interact with new immigrants from the Chinese mainland, and they did not want to network with families that were different from them. Some individuals were prejudiced against new immigrant families, and they did not want their children to interact with these "others". Some did not want to form any sort of parental network with these parents who had "other" kinds of values, or "other" types of dispositions. They found the selective aided-turn-DSS schools as "a sanctuary", where they could "escape" from the "unfortunate" fate of sending their children to government-supported schools in which the student population is diverse with family backgrounds likely to differ from theirs.

DSS has also provided parents with a special and alternative route to prestigious schools in view of an increasing number of traditional elite government-supported schools with long history of joining DSS. These parents included those who tried their luck via the government-run school placement systems, namely Primary One Admission (POA) or Secondary School Places Allocation (SSPA) systems, but their children did not get into the dream school of their choice, and those who had no confidence in these school placement outcomes that they decided to look for alternative school choices. They saw these aided-turn-DSS schools as their "safety-net" to quality education (Tse, 2008). In the case of their children could not get into a desirable school via the government-run school place allocation system, these parents were able to deploy their cultural, social and economic capitals and helped their children to get into one of these elite schools without much difficulty.

The interviewees were asked what quality education means in order to reveal the dominating habitus among the parent interviewees in the field of DSS schools. In general, they wanted the schools to have a well-rounded approach education beyond textbooks. They did not emphasise earning top scores, but rather, they were more concerned about whether the schools could prepare their children with skills applicable to the real world, such as presentation skills, leadership skills, positive learning habits and motivations, work ethics as well as strong English proficiency. To many interviewees, schools that could provide good English learning environment, specifically, using English as the MOI, is synonymous with quality education.

A strong sense of distinction was also found among the parent interviewees. They were convinced that their children were different. Common government-supported schools were unable to provide their children with the curriculum or activities that would suit their children's unique personalities or unique achievements. DSS schools – as they enjoyed high autonomy – would be able to provide a suitable school environment for their children to excel.

DSS schools, particularly those elite schools involved in the case study, provide students with valuable capitals, such as being a part of the strong networks with other middle-class families, and long-lasting alumni networks for students. As what Bourdieu described as "social capital", it is generally present to define "group membership, fix boundaries and create a sense of belonging" (Ball, 2003, 80). Many parent interviewees described their strong commitment they had for their children's school. Some were heavily involved in the Parent-Teacher Association, while others proactively stayed in touch with teachers and other parents, establishing a strong network so they could exchange information and stay supportive for each other.

Quite a few interviewees also expressed their excitement and satisfaction in the unique "bond" and sense of community that they have developed with other parents, and to some, with the teachers. They enjoyed being in a community of like-minded individuals, who share similar values, enjoy similar activities and have similar parental skills and views of education. Such communal association is one of the appeals that school choice has for many parents (Feinberg & Lubienski, 2008).

These interviewees also valued strong parental involvement and close relationships with other parents and the teachers. Regarding forming close relationship with other parents, most of these interviewees actually were quite honest about their preference of a selected and exclusive community, in which only parents with similar backgrounds were welcome. The "backgrounds" refer to their educational background, their values as well as their attitudes towards how to nurture their children. Some interviewees were quite blunt about who "the others" they wanted to exclude, including the new immigrants from China who had low educational background. Some of the interviewees perceived these immigrants as rude and unreasonable parents who did not care much about their children, and the children from these families would be unruly. Moreover, a few interviewees mentioned that they could not mingle with the arrogant, snobbish, extravagant wealthy families.

In other words, most of the interviewees only associated themselves with the educated, assertive "middle-class" who were proactive in choosing schools for their children and invested a lot in nurturing their children.

## Social implications

As an OECD report stated, ". . . choice in itself has often been a stimulus for change in schools and school systems" (Hirsch, 2002, 7), it shows how important school choice is in the discussion of today's education. Education has traditionally played an important role in social mobility to individuals in Hong Kong. Parents in Hong Kong have always put extreme emphasis on education of their children. Choosing a school for children has always been one of the most major events in the academic life of the children. The importance of education is even more amplified in today's society, which is characterised by more intense global competition but growing uncertainty in job security, parents would only intensify their search for quality education for their children in order to secure a promising future for their children.

And the cases of aided-turn-DSS schools in Hong Kong carry significant social implications in terms of class differentiation, social closure and reshaping the relative strengths of the private vs. public school sector.

### *Class differentiation and the importance of economic, social and cultural capital in the aided-turn-DSS schools*

"Capital" essentially represents "resources" and "power" (Ho, 2006, 296). According to Bourdieu (1986), "capital" refers to the resources and assets that are circulating in our social world. It requires time to collect and accumulate, and it has an exchange value in different settings in our social world. It has the "potential capacity to produce profits and to reproduce capital itself either in the same form or in other forms" (47).

Prior to the introduction of the DSS, school choice for most Hong Kong people mainly refers to choosing among government-supported schools, and students had to rely on the results of the government-run school places allocation system. In this system, the economic capital, and to a certain extent, cultural capital, were useless in helping students to get into the preferred school. The centrally controlled school allocation system, to them, is like a "lottery" system beyond their control. Even if they had the financial resources to move to their desired school district, it still does not guarantee a school place of their desire.

For these top traditional aided-schools, they have always been highly sought after by all parents. One reason is that these schools have long history and developed their own unique culture. Such culture is well-established. Many factors have contributed to the achievements of these elite schools, such as the practice and preservers of the leaders and the alumni's heritage. This heritage is being passed from one generation to the next. This so-called "heritage" could also be referred to as the social capital or "the aggregate of the actual or potential resources which are linked to possession of a durable network" (Bourdieu, 1986, 50).

However, in this study, it has shown that the introduction of the DSS in the field of school choice has opened up new possibilities for parents to re-evaluate the volume and types of capital they possess, and to possibly strategize school choice in more detailed ways.

Any expansion of school choice, hence, would be welcomed by many parents, as most believed that choice policy would give them more power to decide on what is best for their children. However, many individuals may not be aware that the new choice policies may not necessarily benefit all parents. Nor they would notice that the design of the school choice policy like DSS could directly or indirectly contribute to class inequality. Some scholars believe that under this new education market, the actions of the middle-class, such as exercising their school choice, could "produce or contribute to the perpetuation, inscription and reinvention of social inequalities both old and new" (Ball, 2003, 5). For instance, parents applied for the schools of their choice strategically, and they made full use of relevant capitals they had. They started planning well ahead of the application process. The background of the parent interviewees were very much similar to the "privileged/skilled choosers" described in the study conducted by Gewirtz, Ball, and Bowe (1995). They were knowledgeable on how to exercise their right to choose and valued their right to choose very much. They also used their resources to "decode school system and organisations" (Gewirtz, Ball, & Bowe, 1995, 182) and strategically bring advantages to their children. Moreover, they were inclined to choose selective and oversubscribed schools.

In addition, the aided-turn-DSS schools, including the three schools in the case study, mostly charged relatively high school fees, between HK$15,000 and HK$45,000 per year. The affordability of these schools certainly affected a family's decision in school choice. All the parent interviewees came from middle-class families, and they observed that most, if not all, of the students of these three schools came from middle-class background. This clearly showed that one very important factor regarding the access to DSS schools hinged on the financial resources of the families.

However, among the three DSS schools in the case study, the financial resources of the family is no longer the only thing that plays a key role in school choice. Instead, cultural capital plays an even more important role in determining the admission success of the students, as parents who choose DSS schools could strategize and prepare their children for the admission interviews and related materials, such as the portfolios, required by many schools. Furthermore, the way that these interviewees form their social network are quite class-specific. These interviewees used emails and intranets extensively to communicate with the teachers. Some quit their jobs to become full-time parents to nurture their children, and as a result, they could spend more time staying closely in touch with the school. They also proactively organise gatherings and family activities so as to create opportunities to bond with other families. All these efforts require resources, including time, cultural and educational resources and personal initiation and sophistication.

## Social closure

The actions taken by the interviewees in order to help their children to get into aided-turn DSS schools have given them advantages in the contesting field of school choice. This has indirectly resulted in excluding others. This phenomenon echoed what Parkin defined as "closure", that is, "the attempt by one group to secure for itself a privileged position at the expense of some other group through a process of subordination . . . intentionally or otherwise, give rise to a social category of ineligibles or outsiders" (Parkin, 1979, 45).

From this study, it is argued that middle-class parents, with their privileged capitals, are strategizing in school choice, resulting in social closure. This phenomenon is uniquely found in the field of the aided-turn-DSS schools, a social space that has already accumulated decades of social and cultural capitals, and a type of school that is much more competitive among parents as compared with other DSS schools.

## Strengthening the private school sector in Hong Kong and erosion of the public sector

In other industrialised countries, where the private school sector has long been strong and vibrant, families have long engaged in school choice by cashing in the useful capitals to strengthen their chance of success in choice. However, in the unique circumstances in Hong Kong, historically the public school sector has always been much stronger than the private school sector. It was not until recently that there has been a uniquely local phenomenon: with a growing number of prestigious aided-schools leaving the public school sector, there were more and more valuable capitals that had accumulated in these elite schools being transferred to the private educational sector. The location of these capitals has been changed and redistributed, especially since the revision of DSS policy in the early 2000s. Under this new field of school choice, by meticulous strategizing, the privileged choosers could exclude others from accessing these valuable capitals that once belonged to the public. This echoed what Bourdieu (1986) described in his much quoted essay, "Forms of Capital": "And the structure of the distribution of the different types and subtypes of capital . . . represents the immanent structure of the social world . . . which govern its functioning in a durable way, determining the chances of success for practices" (46–47).

## Conclusion and policy implications and recommendations for policy-makers

The introduction of DSS originally aims to enhance parental choice and to diversify the educational system. However, in reality, DSS is highly controversial especially among those aided-turn-DSS schools with rich history and prestigious status in Hong Kong. In 2013, St. Stephen's Girls' College (SSGC), a prestigious aided-school located in the Central and Western District on Hong Kong Island with 109 years of history faced immense opposition from its alumni, parents and students when it expressed desire to join DSS. If SSGC were successfully admitted into DSS, each student would have to pay HK$30,000 (primary school) or HK$35,000 (secondary school) per year. One could imagine the main opposing argument was that if SSGC had left the public school system and joined DSS, most poor families would not consider applying for SSGC, even though it could provide quality education. Many lamented that the social mobility of poor children would be eventually affected. It is estimated that in Central and Western District alone, tuition fee-charging DSS primary and secondary school placements made up approximately 41 per cent and 39 per cent of the total school placements available in the district (*China Daily*, July 19, 2013). It is clear that DSS has limited school choice for many working-class parents in this district. In view of the pressure, SSGC had to suspend its plan of joining DSS.

With more and more top traditional aided-schools leaving the public school system, it is important that policy-makers revise the existing DSS, while school administrators continue to review their current admission procedures and scholarship arrangement so that all families, regardless of their backgrounds, could enjoy fair opportunities for school choice and enjoy quality education.

The Education Bureau of the Hong Kong government has clearly stated that the objectives of the DSS are to "provide high-quality schools other than government and aided-schools, to provide parents with more school choice and to diversify our school system" (Education Bureau, 2015). However, there is growing evidence that many of the "traditional elite" aided-turn-DSS schools, including the three schools in the case study, have become rather exclusive for the middle-class and other well-to-do families. The case study presented in this chapter has illustrated the controversy of DSS by showing how middle-class parents at the chosen aided-turn-DSS schools are sophisticated "active choosers" who know how to make good use of their resources – they have access to valuable capitals ("wealth") and have the "will" to help their children to maximise their chance of getting into competitive schools. Consequently it made parental choice of aided-turn-DSS schools an exclusive privilege for them.

The admission procedures and high tuition fees of DSS schools have clearly deterred many poor families from choosing DSS schools. All the three principals interviewed in the case study used the provision of scholarships as the answer to any doubt on whether aided-turn-DSS schools are open to everyone regardless of their economic background, given the fact that most aided-turn-DSS schools now charge a significant amount of tuition fee. However, according to the report released by the Audit Commission (2010), fourteen DSS schools failed to give away more than 50 per cent of their scholarships or fee remission. In addition, only 65 per cent of all DSS schools had posted information about fee remission or scholarships on their websites. Among them, only 23 posted details of the fee remission or scholarships (Audit Commission, 2010).

Certain legislators have criticised DSS has become a policy that is catered for the wealthy and middle-class families (*Oriental Daily*, March 6, 2011). In other words, the presence of DSS does not provide more school choices to many working-class parents. These parents are still using the government-run school allocation system to wait for school placements for their children, while watching a growing number of free traditional elite aided-schools leaving the public schooling system and participating in DSS charging high tuition fees and setting tedious admission interviews. Tsang (2002) commented that DSS could weaken the public schooling system. It has been over twenty years since the implementation of DSS, and it is already more than ten years since the first former government-aided school joined DSS. It is time for policy-makers to seriously reflect upon the social inequality that DSS has indirectly created, and to begin the process of considering whether it is time to revise the policy of DSS. In November 2010, the Audit Commission of Hong Kong government made a series of recommendations to make DSS scholarships more accessible to everyone. It is necessary to check if these recommendations would have any positive effects. Policy-makers should continue to monitor the situation and introduce further measures to assist the poor to access these elite aided-turn-DSS schools.

As EMI schools are still being treated as the "holy grail" nowadays, and as many DSS schools offer EMI, the fierce competition for DSS schools is hence exacerbated by the idea of accessing to an EMI school. Policy-makers should face the reality: there are not enough EMI schools to satisfy the needs of the parents. It has been over ten years since the forceful implementation of EMI and CMI policy. And the "fine-tuning" to medium of instruction policy implemented in 2010 did not seem to ease the dissatisfaction of the general public. In particular, the middle-class parents want their children to access EMI schools. Policy-makers would need to revise, if not terminate, the medium of instruction policy and let schools have the autonomy to make the professional decision on the suitable language policy.

## Notes

1 There is a limited choice of schools available: all government and government-aided schools that participate in the Secondary School Placement Allocation could reserve up to 30 per cent of their secondary places for students who apply via the Discretionary Places stage, regardless of which school net the applicant belongs to. Students are allowed to apply to two schools of their choice. While on the primary school level, schools could reserve up to 30 per cent of their primary one places to admit students who applied via the Discretionary Place route (www.edb.gov.hk).
2 In 1999, the Education Commission released a document on education reform introducing the first round of consultation paper on education reform. The public response was overwhelming. There were several rounds of consultation, which included conducting over three hundred consultation sessions and collecting over thirty thousand written comments and suggestions (Education Commission, 2000, Paragraph 1.7, 1.8). In 2000, multiple and extensive reform policies were introduced.

## References

Adamson, B., & Li, S. P. T. (1999). Primary and secondary schooling. In M. Bray & R. Koo (Eds.), *Education and society in Hong Kong and Macau* (pp. 35–60). Hong Kong: Comparative Education Research Centre, the University of Hong Kong.

Audit Commission. (2010). *Governance and administration of direct subsidy scheme schools*. (Report No. 55 of the Director of Audit). Retrieved from http://www.aud.gov.hk/pdf_e/e55ch02sum.pdf

Ball, S. J. (1990). *Politics and policy making in education*. London: Routledge.

Ball, S. J. (1993). Education markets, choice and social class: The market as a class strategy in the UK and the USA. *British Journal of Sociology of Education, 14*(1), 3–19.

Ball, S. J. (2003). *Class strategies and the education market: The middle classes and social advantage*. London: Routledge Falmer.

Bourdieu, P. (1986). The forms of capital. In A. H. Halsey, H. Lauder, P. Brown & A. S. Wells (Eds.), *Education: Culture, economy and society* (pp. 46–58). Oxford: Oxford University Press.

Burbules, N. C., & Torres, C. A. (2000). Globalization and education: An introduction. In N. C. Burbules & C. A. Torres (Eds.), *Globalization and education: Critical perspectives* (pp. 1–26). New York: Routledge.

Chan, D., & Tan, J. (2008). Privatization and the rise of direct subsidy scheme schools and independent schools in Hong Kong and Singapore. *International Journal of Educational Development, 22*(6), 464–487.

Cheung, A. (2002). *Private schools and government policy in Hong Kong, 1988–2001: Perceptions of private secondary school principals (China)*. Unpublished doctoral thesis. Brigham Young University, USA.

*China Daily*. (2013, July 19). Does DSS foster discrimination? Retrieved from http://www.chinadailyasia.com/news/2013-07/19/content_15079082.html

Education Bureau. (2015). *Direct subsidy scheme*. Retrieved from http://www.edb.gov.hk/en/edu-system/primary-secondary/applicable-to-primary-secondary/direct-subsidy-scheme/index.html

Education Commission. (1988). *Education Commission report No.3*. Hong Kong: Government Printer.

Education Commission. (2000). *Learning for life, learning through life: Reform proposals for the education system in Hong Kong*. Hong Kong: Government Printer.

Education Department. (1997). *Medium of instruction: Guidance for secondary school*. Retrieved from http://www.edb.gov.hk/index.aspx?nodeID=1904&langno=1

Feinberg, W., & Lubienski, C. (2008). Introduction. In W. Feinberg & C. Lubienski (Eds.), *School choice policies and outcomes: Empirical and philosophical perspectives* (pp. 1–20). New York: SUNY Press.

Gewirtz, S., Ball, S. J., & Bowe, R. (1995). *Markets, choice, and equity in education*. Buckingham; Philadelphia: Open University Press.

Hirsch, D. (2002). *What works in innovation in education: School: A choice of direction*. CERI Working Paper. Organisation for Economic Co-operation and Development.

Ho, L. S., Morris, P., & Chung, Y. P. (2005). Driving for excellence: An introduction to the volume. In L. S. Ho, P. Morris & Y. P. Chung (Eds.), *Education reform and the quest for excellence: The Hong Kong story* (pp. 1–6). Hong Kong: Hong Kong University Press.

Ho, S. C. (2006). Xue xiao pai ju jia zhang can yu de ji zhi: Budiao de shi jiang luo ji de ying yong [Application of Bourdieu's The Logic of Practice in the mechanism of parental involvement in schools]. In W. K. Tsang (Ed.), *Nian yi shi ji jiao yu lan tu? : Xianggang te qu jiao yu gai ge yi lun* [Education Blueprint for the 21st Century? Discourse on the Education Reform in the Hong Kong Special Administrative Region] (pp. 295–317). Hong Kong: The Chinese University of Hong Kong Press and Hong Kong Institute of Educational Research (in Chinese).

Lauder, H., & Hughes, D. (1999). *Trading in futures: Why markets in education don't work*. Buckingham, England; Philadelphia: Open University Press.

Lee, C. K. (2006). Xue xiao gai ge yu nian yi shi ji Xianggang jiao yu [School reform and the 21st Century Hong Kong Education]. In W. K. Tsang (Ed.), *Nian yi shi ji jiao yu lan tu? : Xianggang te qu jiao yu gai ge yi lun* [Education Blueprint for the 21st Century? Discourse on the Education Reform in the Hong Kong Special Administrative Region] (pp. 27–51). Hong Kong: The Chinese University of Hong Kong Press and Hong Kong Institute of Educational Research (in Chinese).

Legislative Council Panel on Education. (2000). *Modification to direct subsidy scheme*. Hong Kong Special Administrative Region.

Levin, H. M. (1998). Educational vouchers: Effectiveness, choice, and costs. *Journal of Policy Analysis and Management, 17*(3), 373–393.

Mok, K. H. (2006). *Education reform and education policy in East Asia*. London; New York: Routledge.

*Oriental Daily*. (2011, March 6). Zhi zi xiao gui zhu huo, jian guan da shu lou [DSS schools becoming elitists, more monitor is needed]. Retrieved from http://orientaldaily.on.cc/cnt/news/20110306/00176_011.html

Parkin, F. (1979). *Marxism and class theory: A bourgeois critique*. London: Tavistock.

Plank, D., & Sykes, G. (2003). Preface: Why school choice. In D. Plank & G. Sykes (Eds.), *Choosing choice: School choice in international perspective* (pp. vii – xxi). New York: Teachers College Press.

Sweeting, A. (1993). *A phoenix transformed: The reconstruction of education in postwar Hong Kong*. Hong Kong: Oxford University Press.

Tsang, W. K. (2002). *Xin jing ying zhu yi yu xin zhi jie zi zhu ji hua: dui qin shi Xianggang te qu jiao yu zi ben de pi pan* [New elitism and new Direct Subsidy Scheme: Critique on the erosion of education capital in HKSAR]. Hong Kong: The Chinese University of Hong Kong Press and Hong Kong Institute of Educational Research (in Chinese).

Tsang, W. K. (2006). Xianggang te qu jiao yu gai ge yi lun: dao lun [The Education Reform in the Hong Kong Special Administrative Region: Introduction]. In W. K. Tsang (Ed.), *Nian yi shi ji jiao yu lan tu? : Xianggang te qu jiao yu gai ge yi lun* [Education Blueprint for the 21st Century? Discourse on the Education Reform in the Hong Kong Special Administrative Region] (pp. 3–24). Hong Kong: The Chinese University of Hong Kong Press and Hong Kong Institute of Educational Research (in Chinese).

Tse, T. K. C. (2008). Choices for whom? The rhetoric and reality of the direct subsidy scheme in Hong Kong (1988–2006). *Education and Urban Society, 40*(5), 628–652.

Whitty, G., & Power, S. (2003). Making sense of education reform: Global and national influences. In C. A. Torres & A. Antikainen (Eds.), *The international handbook on the sociology of education: An international assessment of new research and theory* (pp. 305–324). Lanham, MD: Rowman & Littlefield Publishers.

Wong, C. L. (2006). Bian ge zhong de xue xiao ling dao: Xianggang "ai guo xue xiao" de ge an yian jiu [*School Leadership in the Context of Change: A case study of "Patriotic Schools" in Hong Kong*]. Doctoral dissertation, The Chinese University of Hong Kong, Hong Kong (in Chinese).

# 4 Unlocking the dilemma of language policy in the post-1997 era

*Anita Yuk-Kang Poon*

## Introduction

Hong Kong has experienced dramatic changes on all fronts since its reversion to China on 1 July 1997. The language policy scene is one of the arenas that witnessed such changes. Medium of instruction (MOI) and language enhancement continue to be the foci of concern of the Hong Kong SAR government. Two language policies – the compulsory Chinese-medium-instruction (CMI) policy and the biliterate/trilingual policy (BTP) – were put forward in the wake of the handover of sovereignty. The former is meant to rectify the previous English-dominant MOI policies with a view to enhancing the quality of learning of content-based subjects through using L1 (first language), which is presumably the best learning medium for all students. The latter aims at raising the standards of two written languages (i.e., Chinese and English) and three spoken languages (i.e., Cantonese, English and Putonghua) in order to enhance the competitiveness of Hong Kong in the era of globalisation. These two language policies seem to belong to the same category of acquisition planning and could go side by side. This chapter would, however, contend that the two language policies are driven by two different forces with overt and covert aims that underpin the education reform, thus ironically producing unintended contrasting outcomes.

The language policy scene of Hong Kong is first described and analysed, highlighting the important changes in language policy and issues raised over the past five decades. The compulsory CMI policy and the BTP introduced after the handover are examined in the context of education reform in order to identify the two driving forces at play. Then there is an analysis of the unintended consequences of the post-1997 language policies. Some recommendations are finally put forward with a view to resolving some of the problems raised.

## Language policy scene over the past five decades

The changeover of sovereignty on 1 July 1997 was a watershed in the language policy scene of Hong Kong. It not only saw the launching of new language policies, but also marked a fundamental change in the nature of language policy in the territory. All the language policies implemented prior to 1997 are language-in-education policies. They belong to the second type of language policy – viz.

the government-led language policy that deals with acquisition planning (i.e., related to learning) in the absence of language planning (Poon, 2000, 2010). The language policies put forward after the handover were originally meant to be language-in-education policies only. However, the scope of post-handover language-in-education policies is gradually broadening to the wider societal level. While maintaining the focus of acquisition planning, language policies in the post-1997 era begin to look into the area of corpus planning, which is concerned with "the nature of the language itself" (Kloss, 1969, 81) (i.e., the structure and form of a language itself). The changes in the language policy scene of Hong Kong are highlighted subsequently.

## Pre-1997 period

"Supremacy of English" best describes the language situation of Hong Kong during this period, albeit 95 per cent of its population are ethnic Chinese speaking Cantonese as their first language. "Diglossia" (Ferguson, 1972; Fishman, 1971), which refers to different statuses and functions allocated to the languages used in a society, was evident prior to the 1980s because of colonialism. English being the colonists' language functioned as a "high" language in the domains of education, government administration, legislature and the judiciary while Chinese was used as a 'low' language at home and in social communication by the majority of the population (Luke & Richards, 1982; Poon, 2010). The diglossic situation gradually subsided after Chinese was enacted as a co-official language in 1974. However, it does not mean that Chinese was able to compete with English systemically as well as in the perceptions of Hong Kong people. English continued to be the dominant language supported by Chinese in the above-mentioned domains prior to 1997, not because of colonialism but because of the changing status of English in Hong Kong. The economy of Hong Kong took a further great leap forward after the boom in the 1970s and turned Hong Kong from being one of the "four little dragons in Asia" to an international centre of trade and commerce in the 1980s. English was no longer perceived as a colonial language but rather, as an international language permitting universal communication (Johnson, 1994; Poon, 2010). Thus the demand for English started to escalate. Meanwhile, Hong Kong saw a need to expand its education in order to provide sufficient skilled labour for its changing economy. Nine-year free and compulsory education was introduced in 1978, subsequently raising the literacy rate as well as increasing the number of English speakers in Hong Kong. Two kinds of language policies – MOI policies and language enhancement policies – implemented during this period are dealt with in the sections that follow.

## MOI policies

While helping to upgrade the quality of human capital, mass education, on the other hand, brought along undesirable consequences, among which was a drop in English standards. The impact was first felt in the early years of the 1980s among secondary schools. Since schools then were free to select their MOI, there were far more English as medium of instruction (EMI) schools than Chinese as medium of instruction (CMI) schools. In the elite education era (prior to 1971 when six-year free and compulsory education was introduced) students were able to make a transition from CMI primary schools to EMI secondary schools rather smoothly. However, studies reveal that students in the mass education era had difficulty coping with English-medium learning because of their declining English standards (e.g., Johnson, Chan, Lee, & Ho, 1984; Pennington, 1995). Why did students still choose to remain in EMI schools? It was for the obvious reason that English as an international language was accorded great value in Hong Kong starting from the 1980s as mentioned previously. Why did the then Hong Kong government adopt a laissez-faire MOI policy? The international visiting panel accurately summarised the tricky situation of policy dilemma during the 1980s as follows:

> *whether to jeopardise the educational progress of the majority [. . .] in order to guarantee a sufficient number of competent English speakers; or to value the whole group [. . .] but accept the loss in capacity to deal with the international environment and hence a possible decline in the economic prosperity.*
> (Llewellyn, Hancock, Kirst, & Roeloffs, 1982, 30)

In fact the Hong Kong government had made several attempts to tackle the issue of MOI prior to 1990 but to no avail.

The issue of declining English standards mentioned above was deepening while mass education was entering its second decade of implementation. The adverse impact on schools was students' inability to learn through English *only*. Since switching to CMI was the last thing schools would do, using an alternative strategy in the classroom – mixed code (i.e., mixing Chinese with English) – was a common phenomenon in EMI schools during the 1980s till the mid-1990s (Education Commission, 1984; Pennington, 1995). Such a strategy was helpful in terms of student learning and maintenance of school reputation as an EMI school, and yet ironically contributing to further decline of English standards. Meanwhile, the Hong Kong government made another effort to push Chinese-medium education. It endorsed the Education Commission's proposal of "positive discrimination" in favour of schools which adopt Chinese as the medium of teaching by giving them additional resources to strengthen the teaching of English (Education Commission, 1984, 43). However, the policy of 'positive discrimination' was not well received. The number of CMI schools continued to drop during the 1980s, and there remained only 52 out of 392 secondary schools. The issue of MOI remained unresolved while the problems of declining English standards and use of mixed code were deepening.

Approaching the 1990s, Hong Kong underwent another transformation in its economy and successfully established itself as an international financial centre. There was a direct need to further upgrade its workforce if Hong Kong wanted to sustain this role. To expand its higher education was the first and foremost task after 1989. The drastic expansion in higher education brought the issues of declining English standards and mixed code teaching to the limelight again because the unresolved problems had a severe bearing on universities, which adopted EMI in the majority of their programmes. The Hong Kong government thus made a more thorough attempt to tackle the MOI in junior secondary schools. A more clear-cut MOI policy called the Streaming Policy was proposed in 1990 to replace the laissez-faire policy (Education Commission, 1990). The aim of the Streaming Policy was to rectify the problem of mixed code – which was viewed as a contributing factor of declining English standards – through putting students of different language abilities in three different types of schools, namely, EMI schools, CMI schools and two-medium schools. In the initial stage of implementation (1994–1997) schools were free to claim which type of school they were. Meanwhile, the Education Department would conduct assessments on students' language abilities. In the second stage of implementation schools would need to abide by the Education Department's "guidance" (Education Commission, 1990) to select an appropriate type of school that suited the language profiles of their students based on hard data.

*Language enhancement policies*

While tackling the thorny issue of MOI, the Hong Kong government has been dealing with the problem of language standards since the early 1980s. Despite its reluctance to admit that students' language standards, especially English, have dipped, the Hong Kong government did make strenuous efforts to combat the falling trend. Several full reports exclusively on the language issue were published prior to 1997 (Education Department, 1989; Education Commission, 1994, 1996) in addition to the Education Commission Reports (ECR) No. 1, 2 and 4 that contributed some sections on how to improve language standards (Education Commission, 1984, 1986, 1990).

Some measures were proposed to enhance languages in general, and English particularly at schools and higher education. The following are some language enhancement measures implemented in schools prior to 1997: revising the Chinese and English syllabi in primary and secondary schools, adding the listening component in the English paper in the public examinations, introducing task-oriented curriculum to the English curriculum, providing additional resources for remedial English classes adopting split-class teaching, increasing library funds for language learning in schools, providing additional Chinese and English-language teachers in secondary schools, trying out the Expatriate English Teachers scheme in secondary schools and the like. Compared with the school sector, higher education did not receive extra money to do language enhancement prior to 1990, except for Colleges of Education, which were recommended to recruit expatriate lecturers of English to train local English teachers during the 1980s. With an expansion in higher education during the 1990s, additional funding was assigned to universities to run extensive Chinese and English-language enhancement programmes, set up self-access language learning centres and offer bridging courses for Secondary 6 and 7 students to make the transition from CMI secondary education to EMI tertiary education. In addition, the minimum entrance requirements regarding English-language proficiency were strictly enforced.

## Post-1997 period

The end of colonial rule on 1 July 1997 did raise the status of Chinese in Hong Kong as evident in the wider use of Chinese in the domain of legislature and the judiciary.[1] Contrary to people's expectation, English continues to enjoy supreme status, especially in the hearts of Hong Kong's people. Being an open economy in the era of globalisation, Hong Kong is bound to be affected by economic downturns elsewhere. Fortunately, even after suffering from severe economic downturns (e.g., the Asian financial crisis in 1998, 9/11 attack in 2001, SARS in 2003, global financial tsunami in 2008), Hong Kong is able not only to maintain the status of international financial centre, but also to form part of a financial network on par with New York and London (Elliott, 2008, January 28), and has already surpassed London as the world's second largest international financial centre in recent years. The demand for competent English speakers is insurmountable in post-1997 Hong Kong, so English is even more valued by the populace in general and parents specifically (Li, 2002). English is perceived as a necessary skill for survival as well as "a gate-keeper for upward and outward social mobility" (Lai, 2009, 81) in the competitive age of globalisation.

However, the decline in English standards has persisted until the present time despite billions of dollars expended on schools and universities in the pre-1997 language enhancement policies as mentioned previously. This trend is evidenced by both quantitative and qualitative data. According to the results of 2014 Territory-wide System Assessment – a public assessment of Primary 3, Primary 6 and Secondary 3 students on English, Chinese and mathematics – the scores on the English subject were the lowest among the three subjects, and only 69.3 per cent of Secondary 3 students achieved basic competency in English (77.0 per cent in Chinese and 79.9 per cent in mathematics) (Hong Kong Examination and Assessment Authority, 2014). In fact, there was a drop because 71.7 per cent of the same cohort of students achieved basic competency in English when they were in Primary 6 in 2011 (Hong Kong Examination and Assessment Authority, 2011). Perceptions of educators echoed prominent public figures' strong criticism of Hong Kong students' English proficiency (Poon, 2009; Wong, 2008, March 14).

The political and economic developments since 1997 have gradually changed the landscape of language in Hong Kong. Hong Kong used to be a bilingual city in which Cantonese and English were spoken, and Putonghua (Mandarin), the national language of China, did not have any place in the colony. After almost two decades' rapid economic growth, mainland tourists started to flood to Hong Kong, first in organised groups in the mid-1990s, and later as individual travellers when Beijing implemented the scheme called "Visit Hong Kong as an Individual Traveller" after the SARS epidemic in 2003. The number of visitors to Hong Kong, the majority of whom are from mainland China, has dramatically surged from 15 million in 2003 to 47 million in 2014 (Hong Kong Tourism Board, 2014). Working people in Hong Kong, especially those in the tourism and related industries, need to speak Putonghua as an additional language. Hong Kong has thus evolved into a trilingual city. Apart from the economic factor, the political change – the handover of sovereignty to China – does play a vital role in the spread of Putonghua in Hong Kong. Although Putonghua has not yet gained an official status in Hong Kong after the handover, it is bound to become a dominant language in the territory as Hong Kong is in the process of being amalgamated into China both economically and politically. The impact of amalgamation on language policies is explored in subsequent sections.

*Compulsory Chinese medium-of-instruction policy*

As mentioned previously, the streaming policy, which started in September 1994, was presumably a well-planned long-term language policy aiming at resolving the age-old problem of MOI. Taking everyone by surprise, the Education Department suddenly issued a "Firm Guidance" (Education Department, 1997a) three months prior to the handover, requesting *all* secondary schools to change to CMI when the streaming policy was about to complete its first full cycle. Opposition from schools, students and parents had never been so strong in history against the government's education policies (*Ming Pao Daily*, May 3, 1997). Some schools and Parent-Teacher Associations even advertised in the newspapers reiterating their firm support for EMI education (*Sing Tao Daily*, May 3, 1997). The "Firm Guidance" was subsequently revised as "Guidance" (Education Department, 1997b), allowing 114 schools to be exempted from the compulsory CMI policy. Because of the change of MOI policies, the number of CMI schools escalated from 12 per cent during the laissez-faire period to 38 per cent during the streaming policy period, and further to 70 per cent when the compulsory CMI policy was in force in September 1998.

The compulsory CMI policy triggered a third round of debate in the community on whether to adopt CMI or EMI. The debate became politicised again mainly because the decision-making of the policy itself was political (Poon, 1999). The debates before the handover were basically confined to the education sector whereas those after 1997 involved other stakeholders. For the pro-Beijing groups, nationalism should come first and the return of Hong Kong's sovereignty to the PRC is a golden opportunity for enforcing mother-tongue rather than the colonial language as MOI in *all* secondary schools. The new policy-maker under the administration of the Hong Kong SAR was inclined towards the patriotic view, especially when the education scene was taken into consideration (i.e., the problems of dipping English standards and subsequent use of mixed code getting more serious). The education groups which had been fighting for CMI for decades for the educational development of students also joined hands with the government. On the other hand, parents and the majority of schools continued their pledge for EMI, which they believed was beneficial to the educational and career advancement of their children. Meanwhile, for the first time in history the business sector exerted immense pressure on the government to raise English standards in order to sustain Hong Kong's position in the world economy as a result of globalisation. English-medium education was a legitimate option.

The compulsory CMI policy was implemented between September 1998 and August 2010. The effectiveness of the policy was in doubt according to some studies (Poon, 2009; Tsang, 2002, 2004, 2008). Their findings contended two proclaimed benefits of CMI (i.e., students would be better motivated in learning content-based subjects and their academic results would improve when learning through their mother-tongue). The teachers were not satisfied with the students' motivation, and did not agree that the students learning through CMI were more motivated and performed better than their past students learning through EMI (Poon, 2009). According to Tsang (2002, 2004, 2008), junior secondary students at CMI schools outperformed their counterparts at EMI schools in science and social studies subjects by 30 per cent, but the situation was gradually reversed when the same cohorts of students went up to senior forms; even worse, their chances of entering university were only half that of EMI students mainly because their results in English subject had dropped persistently and were not able to meet the entrance requirement of universities. This is corroborated by an increase by almost fourfold in the number of candidates opted for Syllabus A, an easier paper, of the English subject in Hong Kong Certificate of Education Examination (HKCEE), from 7,567 in 1997 to 29,322 in 2008 (Hong Kong Examination and Assessment Authority, 2009).

An additional drawback of the compulsory Chinese MOI policy is that it intensified the competition among students and between schools pertaining to English-medium education. The number of EMI schools had been dramatically reduced under this policy; yet the demand for English-medium education, which is believed to be a key factor for English enhancement, has never been as high in the history of Hong Kong because of the latest economic development as mentioned previously. CMI schools became even more unpopular than before 1997, and they were ironically classified as second-rate schools.

The change in policy-makers in 2007 instituted a policy change in MOI. The most alarming effect of the compulsory CMI policy mentioned above – further decline in English standards – drew the attention of the then secretary for education. Upon assuming his new role in 2007, Michael Suen explored the possibility of changing the compulsory CMI policy, which had gone through a formal review after one cycle of implementation (Education Commission, 2005) and was scheduled to continue. The framework of a policy called "fine-tuning medium-of-instruction policy", which the EDB openly claimed to be a "fine-tuning" of the compulsory CMI policy but was in effect a new policy, was put forward for consultation in June 2008. After taking into consideration the stakeholders' concerns, Suen announced in May 2009 that the fine-tuning MOI policy would be in place in September 2010 (Education Bureau, 2009). The sole reason for this policy change is "to enrich the English-language environment within schools and to enhance opportunities for students to use and be exposed to English . . . so as to better prepare them for further studies and work in future" (Education Bureau, 2010, 7). The new policy softens the boundary between schools in terms of MOI. Secondary schools are no longer bifurcated into EMI schools and CMI schools. Instead, schools are given the flexibility to determine their MOI "by class", "by subject", "by session" or "by group" as long as they follow closely the three prescribed criteria for using EMI (i.e., students' English-language ability as assessed by the Education Bureau, content-based subject teachers' English capability and English-language support measure provided by the school) (Education Commission, 2005). For offering an EMI class, 85 per cent of students in that class should be English-capable.

The fine-tuning MOI policy is well received by schools. According to the schedule, a review of this policy will be held in 2015–16. However, because of the shrinking student population, some EMI schools were not able to admit sufficient English-capable students in the past two years, so they should be required to offer some CMI classes and could no longer keep the label of EMI schools. The secretary for education, Eddy Ng, announced in July 2015 that the review would be put off for six years in order to maintain the stability of MOI arrangements at schools (*Ming Pao Daily*, 2015, July 4).

*Biliterate/trilingual policy*

The BTP was first proposed in the ECR No. 6, a year before the handover, and formally announced by the first chief executive of Hong Kong SAR, Tung Chee-Hwa, in his first policy address in October 1997. "Biliterate/trilingual" refers to two written languages (i.e., Modern Standard Chinese and English) and three spoken languages (i.e., Cantonese, English and Putonghua) in the context of Hong Kong. Initially it was meant to be a language-in-education policy enabling students to enhance their language ability and become biliterate and trilingual in order to remain competitive in the age of globalisation. Billions of dollars have been invested on four areas of work in the education sector. First, a massive curriculum reform, which formed part of the holistic education reform, was launched in 2001 (Curriculum Development Council, 2001) to promote new pedagogy and curriculum in English and Chinese language teaching plus all other subjects. A Language Teaching Support Unit was set up within the Education and Manpower Bureau (now renamed as Education Bureau) in 2003 to provide support for language teachers in their implementation of the new curriculum. Second, schools were given additional funding to support language enhancement, for instance, to set up Multi-media Language Centres. Third, various measures were launched to enhance the quality of language teaching at school, such as setting a language benchmark for English and Putonghua teachers, providing a Professional Development Incentive Grant for language teachers, introducing a mandatory overseas immersion programme as a graduation requirement for full-time teacher education programmes in English Language teaching, and offering scholarships to full-time students attending teacher education programmes in English-language teaching. Fourth, at the level of university, language requirement became more stringent by introducing a mandatory pass in both Chinese and English subjects in public examinations as a basic entry requirement, and adopting International English-Language Testing System (IELTS) as the English Exit Test for all universities on a voluntary basis.

Special emphasis has been given to promote Putonghua under the BTP. First and foremost, the school curriculum was revised in 1998 to make Putonghua a compulsory subject in primary and junior secondary curricula, so millions of dollars were allocated to schools to train Putonghua teachers. Then, in 2000

Putonghua was introduced as an elective subject of HKCEE.[2] A more drastic move was taken in 2003 to "fully endorse the Curriculum Development Council's *long-term* vision to use Putonghua to teach Chinese language" (PMIC) instead of Cantonese (SCOLAR, 2003, 36). However, the Standing Committee on Language Education and Research (SCOLAR) did not recommend any firm policy or timetable for PMIC as their studies indicated that there were no conclusive findings about positive effects of PMIC on enhancing students' competency in Chinese language. Nevertheless, in 2008 SCOLAR allocated HK$200 million to launch a 4-year intensive support scheme to assist selected schools in using Putonghua to teach Chinese language through on-site support by mainland experts and local consultants, seminars/workshops as well as local or mainland exchange activities (SCOLAR, 2008, January 3). The Support Scheme was carried out in four phases, providing support to 40 primary and secondary schools in each phase, and each school received support for three consecutive years (Education Bureau, 2015). Meanwhile, SCOLAR has continued to promote the use of Putonghua through a variety of inter-school competitions throughout the years since 2002.

In response to the Hong Kong government's education reform proposed in 1999, a "Coalition on Education in the Business Sector" was set up in 1999 by the Federation of Hong Kong Industry and 10 Chambers of Commerce to examine Hong Kong's education system and propose ways to improve it from the perspective of the business sector (*Ming Pao Daily*, 1999, September 3). The major concern of the business sector was the persistent declining English standards, so the coalition took the initiative to look into several areas of concern: co-operation between the business sector and schools, the English standards of those school graduates joining the business sector, vocational training and continuing education. The Hong Kong government fully supported the initiative of the coalition and officially launched a one-year "Workplace English Campaign" on 28 February 2000, with a view to enhancing the English proficiency of employees to meet the increasing demands of Hong Kong as international financial centre (*South China Morning Post*, 2000, February 29). It was not only a historic collaboration between the Hong Kong government and the business sector to promote English systematically, but it was also a breakthrough in the Hong Kong government's language policy, viz. an extension of language policy from the education sector to the wider community. A sum of HK$62 million was injected into the campaign to support a number of initiatives (e.g., subsidising four types of lower-level working people who account for approximately one-third of Hong Kong's workforce and who need English at work – i.e., secretaries, clerks, frontline service personnel and telephone operators) to take English courses and to sit for relevant English tests, setting language benchmarks in writing and speaking for employees of different industries in Hong Kong (Workplace English Campaign, 2009, October 30).

In addition to the education and workplace sectors, the BTP gradually gained momentum after 2000 and reached the wider society in different domains as a result of the Hong Kong government's efforts. For example, in the media domain, a Putonghua radio channel was set up on the government service – Radio

Hong Kong; SCOLAR and some commercial TV and radio stations have jointly produced some programmes on use of English-language and Putonghua in different industries. In the public transport service domain, Putonghua was added as the third language in the announcements on the trains and mass transit railway stations. In addition, SCOLAR has sponsored different organisations to provide various activities to promote English and Putonghua (e.g., an English Drama Fest and a Vocational Putonghua Public Speaking Contest).

Although significant resources have been used on promoting biliteracy and trilingualism since 1997, the English standards of students have further declined as evident in the results of TSA – a public assessment for Primary 3, Primary 6 and Secondary 3 students mentioned previously. The employers in the business sector continue to be dissatisfied with the English standards of their employees as revealed in some surveys conducted by the Hong Kong General Chamber of Commerce and the American Chamber of Commerce. On the other hand, Putonghua has continued to spread in Hong Kong. The proportion of population aged 5 and over able to speak Putonghua as another language has significantly increased from 16.9 per cent in 1991 to 24.2 per cent in 1996, and then to 46.5 per cent in 2011 (Census and Statistics Department, 2011).

## Discussion

The following sections discuss the dilemma of the two post-handover language policies presented above, the reasons behind the dilemma as well as the unintended consequences created by them.

### *Dilemma of language policy after 1997*

The compulsory CMI policy and the BTP are presumably a continuation of the MOI policy and the language enhancement policy implemented prior to the changeover of sovereignty in 1997. A detailed examination of policy-making and nature of these two post-handover language policies reveals that they have deviated from the former policies. Regarding policy-making in education, the pre-1997 Hong Kong government tried to adopt a rational approach, which included the processes of problem identification, analysis of problem, consideration of possible alternatives and predicted outcomes (Poon, 2000). A well-established and extensively used mechanism – the advisory system – used to play a pivotal role in the process of policy-making in different bureaus (formerly called branches) of the government. Advisory committees, which consisted of specialists from different sectors of the society, were set up for policy input. The formulation of education policy in the school sector had to go through several steps: (1) An advisory body like the Board of Education or the Education Commission compiled a report based on the data collected through using the rational approach; (2) a territory-wide consultation on the report was conducted, and the Education Commission modified the report before submitting it to the Education and Manpower Branch; (3) the Education and Manpower Branch made recommendations to the Executive Council (decision-making body of the government)

(Poon, 2000, 170–176). Nonetheless, the advisory system has broken down under the leadership of the Hong Kong SAR government after the handover as governance in education has taken a reversing path and become recentralized (Poon & Wong, 2004). First, the advisory role of the Education Commission was undermined in the aftermath of the handover, so the compulsory CMI policy and the BTP had not gone through rigorous policy-making procedures and public consultations as those in the pre-1997 period. Even worse, the Hong Kong SAR government twisted the meaning of documents in order to give legitimacy to the policies. As mentioned previously, while the implementation of the streaming policy was in full swing, in April 1997 the Education Department (1997a) suddenly issued a so-called consultation paper entitled "Arrangements for Firm Guidance on Secondary Schools' Medium of Instruction" to secondary schools, requiring *all* secondary schools to change their MOI to Chinese according to the 'firm guidance' stipulated in the ECR No.4 and confirmed by the ECR No. 6 (Education Commission, 1990, 1996). Again, a detailed look at the context of the ECR No. 4 shows that the issuing of the 'firm guidance' was related to the implementation of the streaming policy, which started in September 1994. According to the time frame, the streaming policy would have completed one full cycle by August 1997, so a "firm guidance" would inform schools what appropriate MOI (i.e., EMI, CMI or two-medium) to adopt in the school year 1997–1998 based on hard data of their students' language ability. The Education Department's claim that all secondary schools should follow the "firm guidance" of the ECR No. 4 to adopt CMI was a sheer lie. Likewise, the BTP, which was proposed in the ECR No. 6, was meant to enhance the two spoken languages and three written languages of students. There was no mention about using PMIC, except a recommendation to train Chinese language teachers to teach Putonghua as a subject "as a long-term goal" (Education Commission, 1996, 22). This "long-term goal" was twisted as "the Curriculum Development Council's long-term vision to use Putonghua to teach Chinese language" (SCOLAR, 2003, 36). SCOLAR even endorsed it but did not recommend any firm policy or timetable to implement PMIC, as mentioned previously (SCOLAR, 2003). Nonetheless, four and a half years later, SCOLAR suddenly launched an intensive support scheme worth HK$200 million to implement PMIC in both primary and secondary schools as described in the previous section. Though never announced or even formulated, the PMIC policy is *de facto* in place. According to an unofficial survey conducted by two concern groups in 2014, "about 70 per cent of the city's 569 local primary schools and 40 per cent of its 514 secondary schools use Putonghua for Chinese-language lessons" (Yau & Yung, 2014, September 2).

Apart from policy-making, the nature of the two post-handover language policies deviates from that of the pre-1997 ones. The streaming policy takes into account the demands of various stakeholders, attempting to strike a balance between the CMI-camp and the EMI-camp, so it is a compromise policy. By contrast, the compulsory CMI policy is an outcome of "a political move – a gesture to appease China" (Poon, 1999, 139), so it tilts in favour of the CMI-camp. As for the pre-1997 language enhancement policy, it is a genuine language-in-education policy aiming at raising language standards of students, and it involves acquisition planning only. The BTP, however, goes beyond the education sector and becomes a society-wide language policy encompassing language use in the workplace, the media and the wider community. It involves not only acquisition planning, but also corpus planning. Some form of standardisation pertaining to the use of written Chinese is conforming to the mainland norm (e.g., the use of some terminology, the use of abbreviated form of a term, the translation of foreign names and countries) (for examples of such standardisation, see Poon, 2010, 54–55).

As discussed in the previous sections, the English standards have been declining since the early 1980s, and the trend cannot be reversed even after decades' efforts devoted to language enhancement. Logically, the Hong Kong SAR government should not have launched the compulsory CMI policy, which is obviously not conducive to building an English-rich environment in schools. The negative effects of the policy, especially that pertaining to English standards as mentioned previously, are evident after twelve years' implementation. Why was the decision of the compulsory CMI policy, which would definitely counteract the effects of the BTP, made at the point of the handover? How are the compulsory CMI policy and the BTP related to the education reform launched in the aftermath of the handover? These are crucial questions to ponder.

## Reasons behind the dilemma

The compulsory CMI policy, the BTP and the education reform were launched simultaneously right after the handover. The pace of implementation of these policies was unprecedentedly rapid. The first two were positioned as a continuation of the language-in-education policies implemented prior to 1997 with some new elements in place in 1998, including the "guidance" in the compulsory CMI policy and "Putonghua" in the BTP, thus having no proper consultation. The third one, on the other hand, was a new initiative, so it took time to formulate the framework and the "Blueprint for the 21st century" (Education Commission, 2000) was out in September 2000 after three rounds of public consultations. To unlock the dilemma of the two post-1997 language policies, the following three points need to be considered.

First, the compulsory CMI policy and the BTP, which apparently contradict each other in terms of the outcomes as discussed previously, are underpinned by the education reform. Why was a massive all-embracing reform covering all areas (i.e., academic structure, curriculum, examination and assessment, admissions system, teacher training and qualifications and life-long learning at senior secondary level and beyond) initiated at the turn of the millennium? The education system of Hong Kong was criticised as "examination-driven" and "fraught with hurdles and dead-ends" (Education Commission, 1999, 29 & 15), unable to cope with the challenges posed by a knowledge economy as a result of globalisation. Hence, it was imminent to reform the education system with an explicit aim to "enable every person to attain all-round development . . . capable of life-long learning, critical and exploratory thinking, innovating and adapting to change" (Education Commission, 2000, 30) with a view to maintaining Hong Kong's competitiveness in the global economy. In fact, a closer examination of the reform document reveals that economic development is one of the two forces governing the education reform. Politics is another hidden driving force involved during the process of the reform, as evident in different aspects of the reform (e.g., education governance, academic system, curriculum and assessment). Although the "nation" (i.e., China) as a beneficiary of the education reform is mentioned by passing pertaining to the aims of education for the 21st century – "contribute to the future well-being of the nation and the world at large" (Education Commission, 2000, 30), national re-integration can be seen as a covert aim of the reform. It is, therefore, argued that the counteracting effect of the compulsory CMI policy and the BTP is due to the overt and covert aims of the education reform. If the overt aim is in conflict with the covert aim, it is always the former that gives way. For example, one aim of the BTP is to enhance English, but EMI is perceived by the patriots as a product of colonialism (Poon, 2009), so the first mission of the Hong Kong SAR government pertaining to language policy is to promote CMI, which is a symbol of nationalism and a means of achieving national re-integration, albeit its adverse effect on English enhancement. In addition, the overt aim of the BTP is for economic reason – to enhance the competitiveness of Hong Kong students in the age of globalisation, and Putonghua is a necessary skill as the economy of China is getting stronger. Stealthily the Hong Kong SAR government is more proactively promoting the teaching and learning of Putonghua. It has even started implementing PMIC without formally setting a related language policy. All these measures are for serving the covert aim of the education reform because Putonghua is a symbol of nationalism and PMIC is a means to achieving national re-integration.

Second, education reform together with reforms or changes in other domains such as the civil service, the media, the electoral reform, the public transport system, town planning, the financial structure and the like after 1997 serves a higher goal – amalgamation with the mainland not only politically, but also economically and culturally. Hong Kong has been included in the PRC's long-term blueprint for the development of Pan-Pearl River Delta, announced on 9 January 2009 (Huang, 2009, January 9). This further affirms that the covert aim of the education reform overrides the overt aim when conflicts between the two arise.

Third, the dilemma is also caused by changing governance in education. Governance involves "who controls what and how" and it takes the forms of centralization and decentralisation. Bray (1999, 207) defines centralization and decentralisation as "deliberate processes initiated at the apex of hierarchies." Governance in education undergoes changes as a result of the interplay between political, economic and social forces. During the period of decolonization (1970s–1997), Hong Kong saw decentralisation in different sectors, including education, in the aspects of decision-making and school administration, and yet some areas in education remained centralised such as teacher registration and certification, and assessment. Poon and Wong (2004, 148) argue that "educational governance is now taking a different paradigmatic course, from decentralisation back to centralization" in the post-1997 era. Recentralization is increasingly evident in structural changes (e.g., the restructuring of the government's educational institutions, and the breaking down of the advisory system in education), major educational policy changes (e.g., the MOI policy and education reform) and practices of top government officials in charge of education. For instance, in 2003, the secretary for education made an impromptu announcement of merging some universities without seeking the consent of the universities concerned. Adopting a centralising path in its governance in general and in education specifically is inevitable for a polity like Hong Kong because Hong Kong obtains its legitimate power from its sovereign state, the PRC, which is governed by one-party dictatorship, although Hong Kong is bestowed with the Basic Law that presumably upholds the "one country, two systems" principle (Poon & Wong, 2004). This is the root problem that accounts for the dilemma of language policy in the post-1997 era.

## Unintended consequences of post-handover language policies

Some unintended consequences have emerged after the BTP and the compulsory CMI policy have been implemented for almost two decades. First of all, ample support in monetary terms has been provided to both the school and university sectors, including students and teachers, to raise English standards. This is one of the primary goals of the BTP. Under the compulsory CMI policy, CMI schools were given HK$3 million each over six years to support English enhancement. Even every EMI school was also provided with HK$ 0.5 million to enhance English. Ironically, though, the English standards keep dipping after the handover.

A second unintended consequence concerns the status of CMI schools. The intention of the compulsory CMI policy is to boost the image of CMI schools through additional provisions. Ironically, due to the limited supply but immense demand, EMI schools are sought after by students and parents even more intensely than prior to 1997. The lower status of CMI schools affects students' self-concept and thus their academic performance (Yip & Tsang, 2007). On the contrary, the fine-tuning MOI policy has boosted the confidence and motivation of the students in some former Band 2 CMI schools, if not all, which are paving the way for being upgraded to EMI schools (Poon, Lau, & Chu, 2013).

Furthermore, equity in education is at stake. With the launch of the compulsory CMI policy in 1998, the Hong Kong government purported that learning through one's L1 was a legitimate and the most effective medium of learning, and no students would be disadvantaged regardless of their English standards (the reason why each CMI school was provided with HK$3 million to enhance English). However, research indicates that CMI students had only half of the chance to enter university as opposed to EMI students, as mentioned previously (Tsang, 2008). In addition, high–socio-economic status (SES) families can afford to send their children to Direct Subsidy Scheme (DSS) schools, international schools or overseas if they are not admitted to local EMI schools, but do low-SES students have such options? Official statistics shows that only 0.8 per cent of those households with monthly income less than HK$10,000 had members studying outside Hong Kong, but this percentage reached 9.5 per cent for those households with monthly income of HK$60,000 and over (Census and Statistics

Department, 2011). Hence, social mobility of CMI students, low-SES students and new immigrants from mainland China in particular, is thus restricted.

Last, it is not obligatory that language policy or other public policies will achieve what it intends to achieve because there are other social, political or economic forces at play. The covert aim of the two post-handover language policies is to boost national identity in order to hasten national re-integration. However, the public opinion poll on local people's identity conducted by the University of Hong Kong (2014) since August 1997 has revealed a far more complicated picture in terms of accepting a Chinese identity. The year 2009 is a critical year for social movements and the development of civil society in Hong Kong. The protest against constructing a high-speed rail that is linked to China's network by a group of young activists between mid-2009 and early 2010 aroused the civic consciousness of Hong Kong people, triggering a series of social movements subsequently, for example, anti-national education curriculum in 2012, protest against North East New Territories Development Plan, which will effectively dissolve Hong Kong-China border, in 2013 and Occupy Central and Umbrella Movement, which is civil disobedience against the PRC's control over Hong Kong's electoral reform, in 2014. These social movements provide an insight to understand why the upward trend of national identity was reversed in 2009 despite the Hong Kong government's strenuous efforts to promote the two language policies.

## Conclusion and recommendations

The present chapter has traced the development of post-handover language policies through reviewing and analysing the two types of language policy instigated prior to 1997 – MOI policy and language enhancement policy, which provide a backdrop for understanding the compulsory CMI policy and the BTP implemented immediately after the handover. The dilemma of these two policies – their counteracting effects – has been unlocked when they are examined in the light of education reform, the changing governance generally and particularly in education as well as the political, economic and social changes in Hong Kong during the past 18 years.

Let us conclude this chapter by answering the following two questions: (1) How far have challenges facing the education system been dealt with by the reform initiatives pertaining to language enhancement and MOI? (2) How efficient has the government been responsive to the problems arising from MOI?

Concerning the first question, it appears that the effort expended by the Hong Kong government to raise English standards and to improve teaching and learning through changing the MOI from L2 to L1 is not proportionate to the outcomes. The first three unintended consequences discussed in the previous section (i.e., failure to enhance English standards, CMI schools being turned into second-rate schools, low-SES students being disadvantaged under the compulsory CMI policy) provide an unfavourable, if not negative, answer to the question. Based on the statistics reported previously, even the covert aim of promoting national identity has been achieved to the least extent. As for the second question, the Hong Kong government always focuses only on two language problems (i.e., declining English standards and use of code-mixing in EMI schools) and responds to them, though not very efficiently. There are, in fact, some untreated problems arising from MOI that "might become detrimental when merged with other language problems," including rote learning, motivation, self-concept and social mobility (Poon, 2013, 44).

Finally, Hong Kong is facing severe language-related challenges ahead. Externally, globalisation is gaining momentum and English skill is an important factor contributing to global economy. However, the English standards in Hong Kong continue to dip. Internally, governance and policy-making in education have been politicised since the handover. The new MOI arrangement announced by the EDB in July 2015 mentioned previously is a further typical example of political decision. Those EMI schools unable to meet the requirements are allowed to remain EMI in the next six-year cycle because the government wants to avoid protests from schools and parents in this time of social instability after its electoral reform package was voted down in the Legislative Council on 24 June 2015. An implication of this move is that more and more students in the EMI schools will encounter problems when using EMI as a medium of learning, and this will undermine the effect of the fine-tuning MOI policy, which is presumably a good compromise policy. It is recommended that the government should stick to the original objective and schedule of the fine-tuning MOI policy. While taking all factors into consideration, decision-making in education should not be politicised. In addition, a long-term goal to resolve the problem of language standards is to have overall planning and adopt models of bilingual education such as the one proposed by Poon (2000, 2013) in formulating the fine-tuning MOI policy. The teaching of L1 and L2 should be planned holistically together with the planning of teaching medium in the entire school curriculum.

## Notes

1 English was used exclusively in all levels of courts prior to the handover, and Chinese is now permitted in the regional courts.
2 This examination was equivalent to the O-Level of Britain's GCE examination. It was attended by Secondary 5 students until 2010 after the new 6-year secondary school curriculum was introduced in 2009.

## References

Bray, M. (1999). Control of education: Issues and tensions in centralization and decentralization. In R. F. Arnovoe & C. A. Torres (Eds.), *Comparative education: The dialectic of the global and the local* (pp. 207–232). Lanham, MD: Rowman & Littlefield Publishers.
Census and Statistics Department. (2011). *Hong Kong 2011 population census summary results*. Hong Kong: Government Printer.
Curriculum Development Council (2001). *Learning to learn – The way forward in Curriculum*. Hong Kong: Government Printer.
Education Bureau. (2009). *Speech of Secretary for Education delivered to the Parent-Teacher Associations on 'Fine-tuning policy' on 5 January 2009*. Retrieved on

August 21, 2015, from http://www.edb.gov.hk/en/about-edb/press/speeches/sed/2012/20090223151271.html

Education Bureau. (2010). *Enriching our language environment, realizing our vision: Fine-tuning of medium of instruction for secondary schools.* Hong Kong: Government Printer.

Education Bureau. (2015). *Discussion paper for Legislative Council Panel on Education: Using Putonghua as the medium of instruction for teaching the Chinese language subject in primary and secondary schools in Hong Kong.* (LC Paper No. CB(4)748/14–15(01). Retrieved on June 2, 2015, from http://www.legco.gov.hk/yr14–15/english/ . . . /ed20150413cb4–748-1-e.pdf

Education Commission. (1984). *Education Commission report no.1.* Hong Kong: Government Printer.

Education Commission. (1986). *Education Commission report no.2.* Hong Kong: Government Printer.

Education Commission. (1990). *Education Commission report no.4.* Hong Kong: Government Printer.

Education Commission. (1994). *Report of the working group on language proficiency.* Hong Kong: Government Printer.

Education Commission. (1996). *Education Commission report no.6.* Hong Kong: Government Printer.

Education Commission. (1999). *Review of education system: Framework for education reform.* Hong Kong: Government Printer.

Education Commission. (2000). *Reform proposals for the education system in Hong Kong.* Hong Kong: Government Printer.

Education Department (1989). *Report of the Working Group Set Up to Review Language Improvement Measures.* Hong Kong. Government Printer.

Education Commission. (2005). *Report on review of medium of instruction for secondary schools and secondary school places allocation.* Hong Kong: Government Printer.

Education Department. (1997a). *Arrangements for firm guidance on secondary schools' medium of instruction.* Consultation paper.

Education Department. (1997b). *Medium-of-instruction guidance for secondary schools.* Hong Kong: Government Printer.

Elliot, M. (2008, January 28). A tale of three cities. *Time*, 30–33.

Ferguson, C. A. (1972). Diglossia. In P. P. Giglioli (Ed.), *Language and social context* (pp. 232–251). Middlesex, UK: Penguin.

Fishman, J. A. (1971). *Advances in sociology of language.* The Hague: Mouton.

Hong Kong Examination and Assessment Authority. (2009). *HKCEE statistics of entries and results over the years.* Retrieved on November 13, 2009, from http://www.hkeaa.edu.hk/tc/HKCEE/Exam_Report/Examination_Statistics/

Hong Kong Examination and Assessment Authority. (2011). *Reports of TSA.* Retrieved on May 30, 2015, from http://www.bca.hkeaa.edu.hk/web/TSA/en/2011tsaReport

Hong Kong Examination and Assessment Authority. (2014). *Reports of TSA.* Retrieved on May 30, 2015, from http://www.bca.hkeaa.edu.hk/web/TSA/en/2014tsaReport

Hong Kong Tourism Board. (2014). *A statistical review of Hong Kong tourism 2014: Number of visitors to Hong Kong.* Retrieved on May 24, 2014, from http://partnernet.hktb.com/b5/index.html.

Huang, C. (2009, January 9). Beijing reveals blueprint for delta's economic growth. *South China Morning Post*, EDUT4.

Johnson, R. K. (1994). Language policy and planning in Hong Kong. *Annual Review of Applied Linguistics, 14*, 177–199.

Johnson, R. K., Chan, R. M. K., Lee, L. M., & Ho, J. C. (1984). *An investigation of the effectiveness of various language modes of presentation, spoken and written, in Form III in Hong Kong Anglo-Chinese Secondary Schools*. A joint-project of Education Department and University of Hong Kong.

Kloss, H. (1969). *Research possibilities on group bilingualism: A report*. Quebec: Les Presse de l'Universite Laval.

Lai, M. L. (2009). 'I love Cantonese but I want English' – A qualitative account of Hong Kong students' language attitudes. *The Asia-Pacific Education Researcher, 18*(1), 79–92.

Li, D. (2002). Hong Kong parents' preference for English-medium education: Passive victims of imperialism or active agents of pragmatism? In A. Kirkpatrick (Ed.), *English in Asia: Communication, identity and education* (pp. 29–62). Melbourne: Language Australia.

Llewellyn, Sir J., Hancock, G., Kirst, M., & Roeloffs, K. (1982). *A perspective on education in Hong Kong: Report by a visiting panel*. Hong Kong: Government Printer.

Luke, K. K., & Richards, J. C. (1982). English in Hong Kong: Functions and status. *English World Wide, 3*(1), 47–64.

*Ming Pao Daily*. (1997, May 3). Publicity of mother tongue teaching can hardly change parents' minds.

*Ming Pao Daily*. (1999, September 3). Company directors visit schools.

*Ming Pao Daily*. (2015, July 4). Fine-tuning of MOI will defer for six years.

Pennington, M. C. (1995). Pattern and variation in use of two languages in the Hong Kong secondary English class. *RELC Journal, 26*(2), 80–105.

Poon, A. Y. K. (1999). Chinese medium instruction policy and its impact on English learning in post-1997 Hong Kong. *International Journal of Bilingual Education and Bilingualism, 2*(2), 131–146.

Poon, A. Y. K. (2000). *Medium of instruction in Hong Kong: Policy and practice*. Lanham, MD: University Press of America.

Poon, A. Y. K. (2009). Reforming medium of instruction in Hong Kong: Its impact on learning. In C. H. Ng & P. D. Renshaw (Eds.), *Reforming learning: Issues, concepts and practice in the Asian-Pacific region* (pp. 199–232). Dordrecht: Springer.

Poon, A. Y. K. (2010). Language use, language policy and planning in Hong Kong. *Current Issues in Language Planning, 11*(1), 1–66.

Poon, A. Y. K. (2013). Will the new fine-tuning medium-of-instruction policy alleviate the threats of dominance of English-medium instruction in Hong Kong? *Current Issues in Language Planning, 14*(1), 34–51.

Poon, A. Y. K., Lau, C. M. Y., & Chu, D. H. W. (2013). Impact of the fine-tuning medium of instruction policy on teaching and learning: Some preliminary findings. *Literacy Information and Computer Education Journal, 4*(1), 946–954.

Poon, A. Y. K., & Wong, Y. C. (2004). Governance in education in Hong Kong: A decentralizing or a centralizing path? In Y. C. Wong (Ed.), *One country two systems in crisis: Hong Kong's transformation since the handover* (pp. 137–166). Lanham, MD: Lexington Books.

SCOLAR. (2003). *Action plan to raise language standards in Hong Kong*. Hong Kong: SCOLAR, Education and Manpower Bureau.

SCOLAR. (2008, January 3). *SCOLAR intensifies support for schools to teach Chinese in Putonghua*. Retrieved on May 30, 2015, from http://www.language-education.com/eng/news_08_0103.asp

*Sing Tao Daily.* (1997, May 3). Many secondary schools were perplexed.
*South China Morning Post.* (2000, February 29). 120 firms sign for English scheme.
Tsang, W. K. (2002). *Evaluation on the implementation of the medium-of-instruction guidance for secondary schools report.* Hong Kong: Hong Kong Institute of Educational Research, the Chinese University of Hong Kong.
Tsang, W. K. (2004). *Further evaluation on the implementation of the medium-of-instruction guidance for secondary schools final report.* Hong Kong: Hong Kong Institute of Educational Research, the Chinese University of Hong Kong.
Tsang, W. K. (2008). *The effect of medium-of-instruction policy on education advancement.* Hong Kong: The Chinese University of Hong Kong.
The University of Hong Kong. (2014, December). *Public opinion programme on national identity.* Retrieved on May 26, 2015, from http://hkupop.hku.hk/english/popexpress/ethnic/eidentity/poll/datatables.html
Wong, A. (2008, March 14). Hong Kong is falling short of greatness. *South China Morning Post*, EDT4.
Workplace English Campaign. (2009, October 30). Retrieved on October 30, 2009, from http://www.english.gov.hk/eng/html/wec_hkweb_hkweb.htm
Yau, E., & Yung, V. (2014, September 2). *Cantonese or Putonghua in schools? Hongkongers fear culture and identity 'waning'.* Retrieved on June 10, 2015, from http://www.scmp.com/lifestyle/family-education/article/1583037
Yip, D. Y., Coyle, D., & Tsang, W. K. (2007). Evaluation of the effects of the medium of instruction on science learning of Hong Kong secondary students: Instructional activities in science lessons. *Education Journal, 35*(2), 78–107.

# 5 In search of equal and excellent basic education in Hong Kong
## Insights from programme for international student assessment

*Esther Sui-Chu Ho*

## Introduction

In Hong Kong and many other countries, a fundamental question which has been posed for basic education is: "Can schools simultaneously achieve high-quality of achievement and foster more equal educational opportunity?" It is obvious that these are two major goals for basic education. Are these goals compatible? Can basic education be both excellent and equal?

The concept of "equality" has several references in education. There was a time when people believed schools were "equalisers," if their definition of equality was simply that everyone was provided with a free public school education. Coleman (1968) traced the evolution of the concept of equality in education and noted that it has gone through at least five stages of development: (1) equal access of inputs such as school finances and expenditures; (2) common curriculum which schools provide for all children, regardless of their backgrounds; (3) differential curriculum (college, general, and vocational) which schools offer for students, regardless of their background, so that they can choose a curriculum best suited to their occupational goals or academic interests; (4) desegregated schooling with the understanding that equality of educational outcomes cannot be achieved via separating schools for different races; and finally (5) equality of results concerning the extent to which schools are able to provide equality of educational results given different students inputs (16–17). According to Coleman (1968), the first stage of defining equality is concerned with "input"; the second and third stages are associated with "processes" from different points of view; the fourth and fifth stages of the equality are related mainly with "outputs." In this chapter, equality of education is defined mainly as the academic outputs for students with different individual characteristics and family and social backgrounds.

A large body of research has examined the role of schooling in influencing social equality. Status attainment research examines the relationship between background characteristics and social stratification through the schooling process. Earlier studies in this tradition demonstrate that schools can indeed mitigate the negative effects of social origins on status attainment by increasing educational and occupational aspirations, academic achievement, which leads to a higher income (e.g., Campbell, 1983). Critics of status attainment research question the ability of schools to facilitate the attainment of social equality. They argue that the continuation of the social stratification found in society is ensured through specific educational processes, practices and policies that characterise contemporary schools (e.g., Bowles & Gintis, 1976). In particular, researchers point out the disadvantages faced by the working-class, female, and ethnic minority groups in schooling outcomes and life chances.

This chapter examines the overall quality and equality of opportunity in the basic education in Hong Kong and demonstrates to what extent this education system achieves high-quality as well as equality of opportunity for 15-year-old students. First, it reviews the quality of secondary education in Hong Kong by assessing its overall performance on the reading, mathematical and scientific literacy scales from an international perspective. Then it assesses the equality of educational outcomes by examining the achievement gaps of students from different social backgrounds in terms of gender, immigration status, family structure, parent occupation, parent education and family's economic, social and cultural status. In particular, the following research questions will be addressed in this article:

- How does student performance change over time?
- How do the variations in student performance between schools change over time?
- To what extent do gender, an immigrant background and individual economic, social and cultural background affect a student's performance respectively?
- To what extent does social and academic segregation within and between schools affect a student's performance?

## The context of Hong Kong education in search of quality and equality

Hong Kong is one of the most densely populated areas in the world. In 2015, its population is about 7.26 million, with approximately 93.6 per cent of ethnic Chinese, most of whom are migrants from China. The remaining 6.4 per cent are immigrants from India, Pakistan and Nepal and foreign domestic helpers from the Philippines, Indonesia and Thailand. Moreover, some immigrants are British, Americans, Australians and Japanese, largely employed in the commercial, financial and educational sectors (Census and Statistics Department, 2015).

Hong Kong's education system has always been a hybridization of the West and the East (Morris & Adamson, 2010). Its schooling system is influenced by the legacies of the Chinese tradition and the British colonialism. It is outstanding performance on mathematics and science since the 1990s (Martin et al., 2000; Mullis et al., 2000) and reading since the 2000s (Ho et al., 2003) in Trends in International Mathematics and Science Study (TIMSS), Progress in International Reading Literacy Study (PIRLS) and Programme for International Student Assessment (PISA) supported that Hong Kong's basic education system had good performance in terms of cognitive measures since the 1990s (Mourshed, Chijioke, & Barber, 2010). However, the concern of equality of education remains at the opportunity of "access" and "participation". It is not until the first cycle of PISA that the equality of "outcomes" has become a common vision and desirable goal of the basic education. PISA is the first international study which defines effective basic education with both the "quality" and "equality" of learning "outcomes" for all students regardless of the social, cultural and economic background. Raising the quality and closing the gap between different sub-groups are the major concerns in each cycle of PISA since 2000.

## Database and methodology

The primary database used in this article is from Organisation for Economic Co-operation and Development (OECD)'s PISA. Starting from 2000, PISA has taken place every three years. The assessment covers the domains of reading, mathematical and scientific literacy. In each cycle, about 50 per cent of the testing time (2 hours in total) will be devoted to a major domain among the three for detailed investigation, whereas a summary profile will be provided for the remaining domains. Major literacy domains are respectively reading in 2000 and 2009; mathematics in 2003 and 2012; and science in 2006 and 2015. This chapter uses mainly the most recent assessment, PISA 2012, in which around 510,000 students from 65 countries/regions participated. PISA 2012 Main Survey was conducted in Hong Kong in April and May 2012 by the Chinese University of Hong Kong. A two-stage stratified sampling design was used. In the first stage, schools were stratified based on their school type (government, aided and independent – international schools and schools under the Direct Subsidy Scheme) and student intake (high, medium and low) according to the information provided by the Education Bureau. This stratified sampling method ensures that schools of different background are appropriately represented in the sample. In the second stage, thirty-five 15-year-old students were randomly selected from each sample school. A total of 4,670 students from 148 schools were accepted for final analysis according to OECD sampling standards.

To understand the equality of outcome between different sub-groups, I considered first one variable at a time for each analysis. Then T-test or ANOVA was performed to assess the achievement gap between high-performing and low-performing students; between girls and boys; between immigrant and local students; between students with parents from high and low SES (as measured by parents' occupational status, level of education and economic, social and cultural resources). Finally, multi-level analysis has been used to address a crucial policy issue in Hong Kong, that is, the extent and impact of school segregation on student performance.

## Results and discussions

In this session, the quality of Hong Kong's secondary school system is reviewed by assessing the overall performance on reading, mathematical and scientific literacy scales in PISA2000+ to PISA2012. Then the equality of educational outcomes is assessed by examining the achievement gap between students from different social backgrounds in terms of gender, immigration status and family's economic, social and cultural status. Finally, multi-level analysis is used to examine the impact of social and academic segregation among schools on the student performance.

## Quality of Hong Kong's basic education

Table 5.1 shows the mean performances in each of the three domains of the top participating countries/regions. The OECD average in PISA 2012 is 494 in mathematics, 501 in science and 496 in reading. The overall performance of Hong Kong students is above the OECD average in each of the three domains.

In mathematics, Hong Kong achieved a mean score of 561, ranking third among the 65 participating countries/regions. In science, Hong Kong ranks second with a mean score of 555. In reading, Hong Kong's mean score of 545 ranks it second.

Table 5.2 shows the comparison of the performance of Hong Kong students from 2002 to 2012.

*Table 5.1* Performance of 15-Year-Old Students in Mathematical, Scientific and Reading Literacy in PISA 2012 (Top 10)

| Mathematics | | | Science | | | Reading | | |
|---|---|---|---|---|---|---|---|---|
| Countries/ Regions | Mean | S.E. | Countries/ Regions | Mean | S.E. | Countries/ Regions | Mean | S.E. |
| Shanghai-China | 613 | (3.3) | Shanghai-China | 580 | (3.0) | Shanghai-China | 570 | (2.9) |
| Singapore | 573 | (1.3) | Hong Kong-China | 555 | (2.6) | Hong Kong-China | 545 | (2.8) |
| Hong Kong-China | 561 | (3.2) | Singapore | 551 | (1.5) | Singapore | 542 | (1.4) |
| Chinese Taipei | 560 | (3.3) | Japan | 547 | (3.6) | Japan | 538 | (3.7) |
| Korea | 554 | (4.6) | Finland | 545 | (2.2) | Korea | 536 | (3.9) |
| Macao-China | 538 | (1.0) | Estonia | 541 | (1.9) | Finland | 524 | (2.4) |
| Japan | 536 | (3.6) | Korea | 538 | (3.7) | Ireland | 523 | (2.6) |
| Liechtenstein | 535 | (4.0) | Vietnam | 528 | (4.3) | Chinese Taipei | 523 | (3.0) |
| Switzerland | 531 | (3.0) | Poland | 526 | (3.1) | Canada | 523 | (1.9) |
| Netherlands | 523 | (3.5) | Canada | 525 | (1.9) | Poland | 518 | (3.1) |
| OECD average | 494 | (0.5) | OECD average | 501 | (0.5) | OECD average | 496 | (0.5) |

Source: PISA 2012 Results: What Students Know and Can Do (Volume I) – OECD (2014), Table I.2.3a, Table I.4.3a, Table I.5.3a, Figure I.2.14, Figure I.4.1 and Figure I.5.1

Note: Shaded area indicates scores significantly different from those of Hong Kong.

*Search of equal and excellent education* 77

Table 5.2 Comparison of Hong Kong Students' Performance in Mathematics, Science and Reading in PISA from 2000+ to 2012 Inclusive

| Cycle | Mathematics | | Science | | Reading | |
|---|---|---|---|---|---|---|
| | Mean | S.E. | Mean | S.E. | Mean | S.E. |
| 2000+ | 560 | 3.3 | 541 | 3.0 | 525 | 2.9 |
| 2003 | 550 | 4.5 | 539 | 4.3 | 510 | 3.7 |
| 2006 | 547 | 2.7 | 542 | 2.5 | 536 | 2.4 |
| 2009 | 555 | 2.7 | 549 | 2.8 | 533 | 2.1 |
| 2012 | 561* | 3.2 | 555** | 2.6 | 545*** | 2.8 |

Source: PISA 2012

\* indicates significant difference in mathematics performance between 2012 and 2006.
\*\* indicates significant differences in science performance between 2012 and 2006, 2012 and 2003, 2012 and 2000+.
\*\*\* indicates significant differences in reading performance between 2012 and 2009, 2012 and 2006, 2012 and 2003, 2012 and 2000+.

The results indicate that the mean score of mathematics for Hong Kong is 561 in PISA 2012, which is significantly higher than that in PISA 2006 (547), but similar to those in all other cycles of PISA. In scientific literacy, there are significant differences among students' performances in the different PISA cycles. The mean score achieved by Hong Kong in PISA 2012 is 555, which is significantly higher than those in PISA 2006 (542), PISA 2003 (539) and PISA 2000+ (541), but similar to that in PISA 2009 (549). In reading literacy, the mean score for Hong Kong is 545 in PISA 2012, which is significantly higher than those in PISA 2009 (533), PISA 2006 (536), PISA 2003 (510) and PISA 2000+ (525).

## Variation of student performance in Hong Kong

All countries face formidable challenges to educate a diverse student body and to narrow the performance gaps among students. Of the 39 countries which have the data of 2003 and 2012, the total variance increased in 17 countries (the difference is statistically significant in only 5 countries) and decreased in 22 countries (with significant differences for 12 countries) (Ho et al, 2005; Ho et al, 2015).

Table 5.3 shows the change of the variance in mathematics performance that lies between and within schools from 2003 to 2012 in selected countries/economies.

In Hong Kong, the total variance reduced from 10,029 to 9,275, and the difference of 754 is not statistically significant. When we partition the total variance into between-school and within-school variances, we find that the between-school variance decreased from 4,806 to 3,924, yet the difference is insignificant. This finding is similar to that of reading (from 3,357 to 3,143) in PISA 2009. However, the within-school variance increased from 5,184 to 5,330, with the increase also being insignificant. This pattern is again similar to that of reading

Table 5.3 Change of Between- and Within-School Variance from 2003 to 2012 in Mathematical Literacy

| Country / Region | PISA 2003 | | | PISA 2012 | | | Change between 2003 and 2012 (PISA 2012 – PISA 2003) | | | | |
|---|---|---|---|---|---|---|---|---|---|---|---|
| | Total variance | Between-school variance | Within-school variance | Total variance | Between-school variance | Within-school variance | Total variance Diff. | S.E. | Between-school variance Diff. | Within-school variance Diff. |
| Macao-China | 7566 | 1163 | 6410 | 8931 | 4442 | 6181 | **1365** | (455) | 3279 | –230 |
| Korea | 8536 | 3523 | 4972 | 9818 | 3840 | 5864 | **1282** | (581) | 317 | **892** |
| Finland | 7004 | 318 | 6664 | 7276 | 530 | 6533 | 272 | (268) | 212 | –131 |
| Canada | 7588 | 1301 | 6290 | 7896 | 1563 | 6342 | 308 | (222) | 262 | 52 |
| Japan | 10110 | 5350 | 4738 | 8748 | 4620 | 4094 | **–1362** | (688) | –730 | **–644** |
| Sweden | 8979 | 831 | 8133 | 8420 | 1042 | 7266 | –559 | (413) | 211 | **–866** |
| Hong Kong-China | 10040 | 4806 | 5184 | 9277 | 3924 | 5330 | –762 | (707) | –882 | 146 |
| United States | 9074 | 2198 | 6807 | 8077 | 1916 | 6164 | **–997** | (338) | –282 | **–642** |
| Chinese Taipei | m | m | m | 13368 | 5613 | 7710 | m | | m | m |
| Singapore | m | m | m | 11102 | 4070 | 7033 | m | | m | m |
| Shanghai-China | m | m | m | 10199 | 4767 | 5401 | m | | m | m |
| United Kingdom | m | m | m | 8935 | 2517 | 6421 | m | | m | m |
| *OECD Average* | *8801* | *3027* | *5800* | *8481* | *3117* | *5372* | *–263* | *(88)* | *84* | *–359* |

Source: "PISA 2012 Results: What Students Know and Can Do (Volume II)" – OECD (2014), Table II.2.8a and Table II.2.8b.

Note: m represents missing data. Values that are statistically significant are indicated in bold in PISA 2009 (from 3,646 to 4,360). The contention is that with the reform of the Secondary School Places Allocation mechanism which from the year 2000 reduced student streaming from 5 to 3 allocation bands, the heterogeneity of students within schools increased considerably. It is likely that teachers would face greater difficulty in handling learning differences and learning needs of individual students. The increased within-school variance found in the present study supports this conjecture. The finding has implications for the management of learning differences in the classroom. We may want to study the class size and other instructional policies of countries/regions with similar level of within-school variance for policy reference.

Unlike Hong Kong, the total variance of Finland was 6,976 in PISA 2003, which increased to 7,275 in 2012. Finland's between-school variance was the second lowest (318) in PISA 2003 and the lowest (530) in PISA 2012. On the other hand, its within-school heterogeneity has remained relatively high, suggesting that Finland is successfully making efforts to cater for the needs of students with varied ability by adopting special instructional treatments such as small class size and other measures.

For other East Asian societies, the total variance of Korea, Japan and Macao started with 8,530, 10,085 and 7,560 respectively in PISA 2003. The total variance of Korea and Macao increased to 9,816 and 8,929 respectively in PISA 2012 whereas that of Japan reduced to 8,747. All these changes in between-school variance are significant. For Korea, the significant increase in variance locates mainly within-school (892). For Macao, the significant increase in variance locates mainly between schools (1,909). Conversely, Japan's variance reduced substantially both between and within-school, yet only the reduction in within-school variance is significant statistically. All the four East Asian societies (Korea, Japan, Macao and Hong Kong) have a higher between-school heterogeneity than the OECD average, suggesting that they need to address the problem of academic segregation among schools. For the problem of high within-school learning diversity, there should be lessons that East Asian societies can learn from the Nordic countries such as Finland and some other countries, including Canada and Australia.

## *Gender disparity in academic achievement*

In many previous international studies, there were consistent gaps between males and females, with males tending to be ahead in mathematics and science (Martin et al., 2000; Mullis et al., 2000) and females universally so in reading (Johnson & Cheung, 1995). Consistent with previous studies and previous cycles of PISA, Figure 5.1 shows that males perform better than females on mathematical literacy scale by 15 points; female students perform significantly better than males on reading literacy scale by 25 points in the current PISA 2012 study. The pattern of gender difference in science is less consistent and not significant in all the five cycles of PISA.

In mathematics, boys perform significantly better than girls in 36 out of 65 countries/regions and more poorly than girls in 5 countries in PISA 2012. Boys

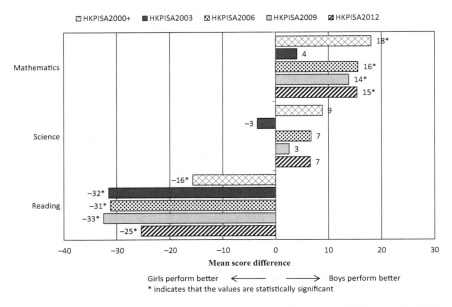

*Figure 5.1* Gender differences in reading, mathematical and scientific literacy in PISA 2000+, PISA 2003, PISA2006, PISA 2009 and PISA 2012

across OECD countries score on average 11 points higher than girls do (OECD, 2013, and see also Table 5.4).

In Hong Kong, boys score 15 points higher than girls, and the difference is statistically significant and is slightly higher than the OECD average gender gap of 11 points. Figure 5.1 also shows the change of gender gap from PISA 2000+ to PISA 2012 in Hong Kong. In PISA 2000+, in mathematics, boys outperformed girls by 18 points, which is statistically significant. However, in PISA 2003, this gender gap narrowed to a statistically insignificant margin of just 4 points. In PISA 2006, 2009 and 2012, boys again outperformed girls by statistically significant differences of 16, 14 and 15 points respectively.

As for science, 27 out of 65 countries/regions have significant gender differences in PISA 2012 (OECD, 2013). It is particularly interesting to find that a great number of countries have girls performing better than boys. Specifically, girls outperformed boys in 17 countries (OECD, 2013). In Hong Kong, boys outperform girls by 7 points in PISA 2012, but this difference is not significant statistically.

In reading, girls perform significantly better than boys in all countries/regions including Hong Kong in PISA 2012. The achievement gap in reading ranges from a low of 15 to a high of 75 point scores (OECD, 2013). The gender gap in Hong Kong is 25 points in PISA 2012, which is smaller than the 33-point gap in PISA 2009, the 31-point gap in PISA 2006 and 32-point gap in PISA 2003 and much larger than the 16-point gap in PISA 2000+. However, it is smaller than the OECD average in this cycle, which is 38 points.

Table 5.4 Gender Differences in Student Performance in PISA 2012

| Country/Region | Mathematics Boys (B) Mean score | S.E. | Girls (G) Mean score | S.E. | Difference* (B – G) Score dif. | S.E. | Country/Region | Science Boys (B) Mean score | S.E. | Girls (G) Mean score | S.E. | Difference* (B – G) Score dif. | S.E. | Country/Region | Reading Boys (B) Mean score | S.E. | Girls (G) Mean score | S.E. | Difference* (B – G) Score dif. | S.E. |
|---|---|---|---|---|---|---|---|---|---|---|---|---|---|---|---|---|---|---|---|---|
| Singapore | 572 | (1.9) | 575 | (1.8) | –3 | (2.5) | Finland | 537 | (3.0) | 554 | (2.3) | –16 | (3.0) | Finland | 494 | (3.1) | 556 | (2.4) | –62 | (3.1) |
| Finland | 517 | (2.6) | 520 | (2.2) | –3 | (2.9) | Sweden | 481 | (3.9) | 489 | (2.8) | –7 | (3.3) | Sweden | 458 | (4.0) | 509 | (2.8) | –51 | (3.6) |
| Sweden | 477 | (3.0) | 480 | (2.4) | –3 | (3.0) | United States | 497 | (4.1) | 498 | (4.0) | –2 | (2.7) | Macao-China | 492 | (1.4) | 527 | (1.1) | –36 | (1.7) |
| Macao-China | 540 | (1.4) | 537 | (1.3) | 3 | (1.9) | Macao-China | 520 | (1.3) | 521 | (1.2) | –1 | (1.7) | Canada | 506 | (2.3) | 541 | (2.1) | –35 | (2.1) |
| United States | 484 | (3.8) | 479 | (3.9) | 5 | (2.8) | Singapore | 551 | (2.1) | 552 | (1.9) | –1 | (2.6) | Chinese Taipei | 507 | (4.3) | 539 | (4.3) | –32 | (6.4) |
| Chinese Taipei | 563 | (5.4) | 557 | (5.7) | 5 | (8.9) | Chinese Taipei | 524 | (3.9) | 523 | (4.0) | 1 | (6.4) | Singapore | 527 | (1.9) | 559 | (1.9) | –32 | (2.6) |
| Canada | 616 | (4.0) | 610 | (3.4) | 6 | (3.3) | Canada | 527 | (2.4) | 524 | (2.0) | 3 | (2.1) | United States | 482 | (4.1) | 513 | (3.8) | –31 | (2.6) |
| Korea | 523 | (2.1) | 513 | (2.1) | 10 | (2.0) | Korea | 539 | (4.7) | 536 | (4.2) | 3 | (5.1) | Hong Kong-China | 533 | (3.8) | 558 | (3.3) | –25 | (4.7) |
| Shanghai-China | 500 | (4.2) | 488 | (3.8) | 12 | (4.7) | Shanghai-China | 583 | (3.5) | 578 | (3.1) | 5 | (2.7) | United Kingdom | 487 | (4.5) | 512 | (3.8) | –25 | (4.6) |
| Hong Kong-China | 568 | (4.6) | 553 | (3.9) | 15 | (5.7) | Hong Kong-China | 558 | (3.6) | 551 | (3.1) | 7 | (4.2) | Japan | 527 | (4.7) | 551 | (3.6) | –24 | (4.1) |
| Japan | 545 | (4.6) | 527 | (3.6) | 18 | (4.3) | Japan | 552 | (4.7) | 541 | (3.5) | 11 | (4.3) | Shanghai-China | 557 | (3.3) | 581 | (2.8) | –24 | (2.5) |
| United Kingdom | 562 | (5.8) | 544 | (5.1) | 18 | (6.2) | United Kingdom | 521 | (4.5) | 508 | (3.7) | 13 | (4.7) | Korea | 525 | (5.0) | 548 | (4.5) | –23 | (5.4) |
| OECD Average | 499 | (0.6) | 489 | (0.5) | 11 | (0.6) | OECD Average | 502 | (0.6) | 500 | (0.5) | 1 | (0.6) | OECD Average | 478 | (0.6) | 515 | (0.5) | –38 | (0.6) |

Source: "PISA 2012 Results: What Students Know and Can Do (Volume I)" – OECD (2014), Table I.2.3a, Table I.4.3a and Table I.5.3a

Note: Values that are statistically significant are indicated in bold.
* The minor discrepancy in the difference is due to rounding of numbers.

Overall, the results shows that the advantage of girls in reading literacy and that of boys in mathematical literacy in Hong Kong are significant since PISA 2000+ but the lead of boys in scientific literacy is no longer significant. These patterns may have resulted from the broader societal and cultural context of educational policies and practices in favour of girls in language subjects and in favour of boys in mathematics curriculum.

Previous findings of the Third International Mathematics and Science Study, where gender differences in science performance among eighth-grade students were much larger, almost always favoured boys (Martin et al., 2000). One of the possible reasons for these differences in the results between PISA and TIMSS may be due to the fact that PISA had a higher proportion of open-ended and contextualised items in which girls tend to do better, rather than multiple-choice items in which boys tend to do better. This may have contributed to the higher performance by females in science in PISA (Yip, Chiu, & Ho, 2004).

## *Equality of immigrant and local students*

There are two theories regarding the relationship between immigrant status and achievement. One theory argues that some immigrants are able to achieve more in spite of discrimination, because their culture places a premium on academic success, effort and persistence, deferred gratification and social mobility (Hirschman & Falcon, 1985, 84). For instance, the cultural value of Chinese immigrants is believed to be the major factor for the academic success of Asian students in the United States (Coleman, 1987). Another interpretation is that the differential attainments of certain immigrants are due to prior educational and occupational differences. For instance, Jewish immigrants in the United States had a substantial social class advantage in terms of their education and occupation relative to other immigrants from Eastern and Southern Europe (Steinberg, 1981).

In PISA, the immigration status of a student is classified into three categories: (i) native; (ii) second-generation; and (iii) first-generation. "Natives" refers to students who are born in the country of assessment with at least one of their parents born in the same country. "Second generation" refers to students who are born in the country of assessment but both of their parents are foreign-born. "First generation" refers to foreign-born students whose parents are also foreign-born.

In PISA 2012, the percentages of second-generation students and first-generation students are 20.2 per cent and 13.9 per cent (23.8 per cent and 15.7 per cent in 2009) respectively, totalling 34.1 per cent (39.4 per cent in 2009) of the sample. Comparing with the respective OECD average of 5.4 per cent and 5.1 per cent (6.3 per cent and 3.9 per cent in 2009) of second-generation and first-generation students, Hong Kong has many more immigrant students in the secondary school system than the OECD countries.

Figure 5.2 reveals the comparatively large score differences in favour of native and second-generation students. First-generation students' performance is consistently lower in all three domains over the five cycles of PISA.

Search of equal and excellent education  83

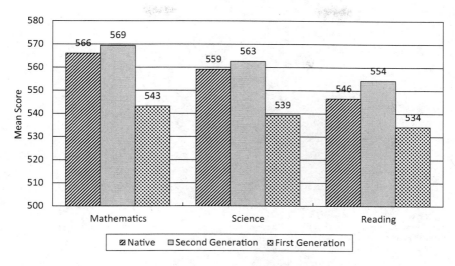

*Figure 5.2* PISA 2012 Literacy Performance of Hong Kong Students by Immigration Status

In mathematical literacy, the native students (566) and the second-generation students (569) perform equally well. The first-generation students (543) score about 25 points lower than the native and second-generation students. The size of the difference, though statistically significant, has reduced substantially from the 40-point difference in PISA 2009. The patterns in scientific and reading literacy are similar to that seen in mathematical literacy. In particular, for scientific literacy, the native students (559) and second-generation students (563) perform equally well, whereas the first-generation students (539) are 20 and 24 points lower than the native students and second-generation students respectively. The sizes of the differences for the first-generation students are again of statistical significance. For reading literacy, the second-generation students score an average of 554, which is slightly better than the 546 average for the native students. The first-generation students' average score of 534 is significantly lower than the average scores of both native and second-generation students. The above findings reveal that, in PISA 2012, first-generation students still score significantly lower than other students in all three domains.

It is interesting to find that Hong Kong is the only society with superior performance among second-generation students in mathematics, science and reading, when compared with the OECD average, while the general pattern in OECD countries shows higher scores among native students (See Table 5.5).

In Hong Kong, the majority of the immigrant students are from other parts of the Chinese mainland. When these immigrants arrive in Hong Kong, they realise that good academic qualifications are necessary for improving their standard of living. Therefore, immigrant parents may make greater efforts to motivate their children in the aspect of academic performance. Therefore, the second-generation

*Table 5.5* Literacy Scores of Hong Kong and OECD Average by Immigration Status in PISA 2012

|  | Native Score | S.E. | Second Generation Score | S.E. | First Generation Score | S.E. |
|---|---|---|---|---|---|---|
| **Hong Kong** | | | | | | |
| Mathematics | 566 | (3.8) | 569 | (4.1) | 543 | (5.2) |
| Science | 559 | (3.0) | 563 | (3.6) | 539 | (4.4) |
| Reading | 546 | (3.2) | 554 | (4.1) | 534 | (5.1) |
| **OECD Average** | | | | | | |
| Mathematics | 500 | (0.5) | 467 | (3.0) | 461 | (2.6) |
| Science | 508 | (0.5) | 470 | (2.8) | 456 | (2.6) |
| Reading | 502 | (0.5) | 473 | (2.9) | 461 | (3.0) |

Source: PISA 2012

students are more likely to perform better. Another aspect peculiar to Hong Kong is that it is easier for immigrants from China to adapt to the language and culture in Hong Kong as both societies are Chinese in origin. Further research is needed to identify the major driving force for the second-generation students to learn and to perform well.

The disadvantage of the first-generation students remains to be addressed both in practise and in future studies. Recent research indicates that when grade level is controlled for in the analysis, the difference in scores of the first-generations will disappear. Pong (2009) argued that the first generation students might have school adjustment problems, but the major barrier is the retention of students in lower grade levels (i.e., the system where students have to repeat a study year if their scores are low). More first-generation students have to repeat lower grade levels in Hong Kong. A significant reason for this might be their limited English proficiency. Further studies should be conducted to examine to what extent and in what way the age of arrival in Hong Kong is related to the adjustment of immigrant students. The ethnicity of the immigrant students needs to be scrutinised – Chinese and non-Chinese immigrant students might have different degrees of difficulty in adjusting to new schooling and a new instructional language.

## *Equality of students from different socio-economic status*

Socio-economic status is a major factor affecting a student's learning outcomes. The "family resource hypothesis" (Harker, Nash, Durie, & Charters, 1993) explains the consistent association. The hypothesis suggests that SES is likely to affect parental involvement by providing different amounts of cultural, social and economic capitals for children's education. For instance, occupation provides income, which is actually economic capital that can be directly invested to provide learning material and an appropriate environment for children's education. Parents' education can be seen as cultural capital that provides the competence and confidence for parents to interact with school teachers. Social networks can also be regarded as a type of social capital (Coleman, 1990), which provides parents with the appropriate obligations and expectations, information channels and norms, hence facilitating negotiations with school teachers.

An index of family economic, social, and cultural status (ESCS) is derived by the OECD, on the basis of the indices of parental education and occupation, and the number and type of home possessions related to education (See OECD, 2013, Chapter 2). Table 5.6 shows the ESCS indices and the scores in mathematical, scientific and reading literacy for each participating country/region in PISA 2012. The ESCS index is standardised in all the OECD countries to have a mean of zero and a standard deviation of one. Greater values represent more advantaged family backgrounds, and smaller values represent less-advantaged family backgrounds. A negative value implies that the socio-economic and cultural status is below the OECD average, and a positive value indicates that it is above the OECD average.

The second column of Table 5.6 shows the average ESCS index for each of the participating countries/regions. The ESCS index of Hong Kong is -0.79 (-0.47 in PISA 2009 and -0.67 in PISA 2006), which is far below the OECD average. The major reason for this negative value is that the educational levels of parents in Hong Kong are comparatively lower than those of many OECD countries. The average mathematical, scientific and reading literacy performance of each of the countries/regions are shown in the third columns of Table 5.6. The figures indicate that Hong Kong students perform well (561 in mathematics, 555 in science, and 545 in reading) despite the low ESCS of their families.

The fourth column of Table 5.6 shows the relationship between ESCS and students' performance in each domain for each participating country/region. This relationship can be understood as the "socio-economic gradient", which is a useful index for analysing the equality or distribution of educational outcomes of students of different socio-economic status. The results show that socio-economic gradient varies substantially across the participating countries/regions in 2012. The PISA 2012 average slope of OECD countries is 39, 38 and 37 for mathematics, science and reading respectively. These are similar to 45 for mathematics in PISA 2003, 40 for science in PISA 2006, 41 and 36 for reading in PISA 2000 and 2009. These slopes indicate that a 1 unit change in the ESCS is associated with a change of 39 points on mathematics, 38 points on science and 37 points on the reading scale.

The average socio-economic gradients for Hong Kong in PISA 2012 are 27, 21 and 20 in mathematics, science and reading respectively, which are all statistically significant but much lower than the OECD average gradients. Figures for previous cycles of PISA which are similar to 2012 are 31 for mathematics in PISA 2003, 26 for science in PISA 2006 and 28 and 16 for reading in PISA 2000 and 2009. The above results suggest that Hong Kong has continued to thrive on achieving high overall performance while on a lower socio-economic gradient than OECD countries. In other words, students from a variety of socio-economic backgrounds perform equally well in Hong Kong. Also, the relationship between ESCS and literacy performance, which was already relatively weak in 2000, is weakened further in 2012.

Let us take mathematics for further illustration. Figure 5.3 shows the relationship between ESCS and mathematical literacy scores of 9 countries/regions

Table 5.6 Relationship between Literacy Performance and the Index of Economic, Social and Cultural Status

| Country / Region | PISA index of economic, social and cultural status | | Mean score | | Slope of the socio-economic gradient[Note] | | Percentage of explained variance in performance | |
|---|---|---|---|---|---|---|---|---|
| | Mean index | S.E. | Score | S.E. | Score point difference in the domain associated with one unit of ESCS | S.E. | R sq | S.E. |
| **Mathematics** | | | | | | | | |
| Macao-China | −0.89 | (0.01) | 538 | (1.0) | 17 | (1.5) | 2.6 | (0.4) |
| Canada | 0.41 | (0.02) | 518 | (1.8) | 31 | (1.2) | 9.4 | (0.7) |
| **Hong Kong-China** | **−0.79** | **(0.05)** | **561** | **(3.2)** | **27** | **(2.6)** | **7.5** | **(1.5)** |
| Finland | 0.36 | (0.02) | 519 | (1.9) | 33 | (1.8) | 9.4 | (0.9) |
| United States | 0.17 | (0.04) | 481 | (3.6) | 35 | (1.7) | 14.8 | (1.3) |
| Sweden | 0.28 | (0.02) | 478 | (2.3) | 36 | (1.9) | 10.6 | (1.1) |
| Shanghai-China | −0.36 | (0.04) | 613 | (3.3) | 41 | (2.7) | 15.1 | (1.9) |
| Japan | −0.07 | (0.02) | 536 | (3.6) | 41 | (3.9) | 9.8 | (1.6) |
| United Kingdom | 0.27 | (0.02) | 494 | (3.3) | 41 | (2.4) | 12.5 | (1.2) |
| Korea | 0.01 | (0.03) | 554 | (4.6) | 42 | (3.3) | 10.1 | (1.4) |
| Singapore | −0.26 | (0.01) | 573 | (1.3) | 44 | (1.4) | 14.4 | (0.9) |
| Chinese Taipei | −0.40 | (0.02) | 560 | (3.3) | 58 | (2.5) | 17.9 | (1.4) |
| OECD Average | 0.00 | (0.00) | 494 | (0.5) | 39 | (0.4) | 14.8 | (0.2) |
| **Reading** | | | | | | | | |
| Macao-China | −0.89 | (0.01) | 509 | 0.9 | 11 | (1.4) | 1.5 | (0.4) |
| **Hong Kong-China** | **−0.79** | **(0.05)** | **545** | **2.8** | **20** | **(2.5)** | **5.2** | **(1.2)** |
| Canada | 0.41 | (0.02) | 523 | 1.9 | 30 | (1.3) | 8.1 | (0.7) |
| Shanghai-China | −0.36 | (0.04) | 570 | 2.9 | 33 | (2.0) | 15.6 | (1.8) |
| Korea | 0.01 | (0.03) | 536 | 3.9 | 33 | (2.8) | 7.9 | (1.2) |

| | | | | | | | | |
|---|---|---|---|---|---|---|---|---|
| Finland | 0.36 | (0.02) | 524 | 2.4 | 33 | | 7.5 | (0.9) |
| United States | 0.17 | (0.04) | 498 | 3.7 | 33 | | 12.6 | (1.3) |
| Japan | -0.07 | (0.02) | 538 | 3.7 | 38 | | 7.9 | (1.5) |
| Sweden | 0.28 | (0.02) | 483 | 3 | 38 | | 9.1 | (1.1) |
| United Kingdom | 0.27 | (0.02) | 499 | 3.5 | 40 | | 11.8 | (1.1) |
| Chinese Taipei | -0.40 | (0.02) | 523 | 3 | 42 | | 15.1 | (1.4) |
| Singapore | -0.26 | (0.01) | 542 | 1.4 | 43 | | 15.2 | (0.9) |
| *OECD Average* | *0.00* | *(0.00)* | *496* | *0.5* | *38* | | *13.1* | *(0.2)* |
| Science | | | | | | | | |
| Macao-China | -0.89 | (0.01) | 521 | 0.8 | 13 | | 2.1 | (0.6) |
| **Hong Kong-China** | **-0.79** | **(0.05)** | **555** | **2.6** | **21** | | **6.0** | **(1.3)** |
| Canada | 0.41 | (0.02) | 525 | 1.9 | 29 | | 7.8 | (0.7) |
| Shanghai-China | -0.36 | (0.04) | 580 | 3.0 | 33 | | 15.3 | (2.0) |
| Korea | 0.01 | (0.03) | 538 | 3.7 | 29 | | 6.7 | (1.1) |
| Finland | 0.36 | (0.02) | 545 | 2.2 | 33 | | 7.9 | (0.9) |
| United States | 0.17 | (0.04) | 497 | 3.8 | 36 | | 14.2 | (1.4) |
| Japan | -0.07 | (0.02) | 547 | 3.6 | 36 | | 7.3 | (1.4) |
| Sweden | 0.28 | (0.02) | 485 | 3.0 | 38 | | 10.4 | (1.2) |
| United Kingdom | 0.27 | (0.02) | 514 | 3.4 | 45 | | 13.5 | (1.2) |
| Chinese Taipei | -0.40 | (0.02) | 523 | 2.3 | 40 | | 16.7 | (1.4) |
| Singapore | -0.26 | (0.01) | 551 | 1.5 | 46 | | 16.5 | (1.0) |
| *OECD Average* | *0.00* | *(0.00)* | *501* | *0.5* | *38* | | *14.0* | *(0.2)* |

Source: "PISA 2012 Results: What Students Know and Can Do (Volume I & II)" – OECD (2014), Table I.2.3a, Table I.4.3a, Table I.5.3a, Table II.2.1 and Table II.2.3

Note: Single-level bi-variate regression of performance in the specific domain on the ESCS, the slope is the regression coefficient for the ESCS.

(Hong Kong, Shanghai, Chinese Taipei, Macao, Japan, Korea, Singapore, Finland, and Canada) whose mean scores are statistically and significantly above the OECD average. The relationship is shown in the form of socio-economic gradient lines. The slope of the gradient lines indicates the extent to which inequality in mathematics performance could be attributed to family socio-economic and cultural background. A steeper gradient indicates a greater impact of family background on mathematical literacy performance, which equates to greater inequality. In contrast, a slighter gradient indicates a smaller impact of family background on performance and hence suggests less inequality. As can be seen, the slopes of the socio-economic gradient lines vary widely across the participating countries/regions.

In Figure 5.3, the gradient line of Hong Kong has the second most gradual slope (Macao the first and Canada the third among the selected countries/regions) on the graph, indicating that Hong Kong's 15-year-olds perform well in mathematics and the impact of ESCS is modest. It can be argued that Hong Kong is providing education opportunity with relatively high quality and high equity for students regardless of their socio-economic and cultural background.

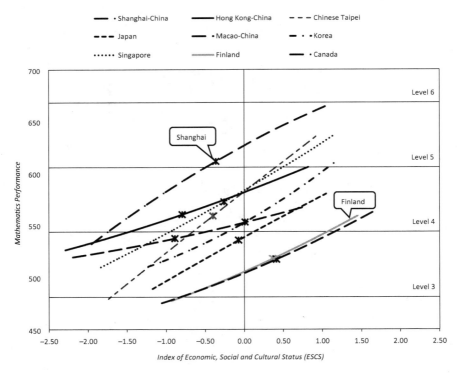

*Figure 5.3 Relationship between Student Performance in Mathematics and ESCS in Nine Countries/Regions*

## Impact of Academic and Social Segregation on Inequality of School Performance in Hong Kong

After the academic structure reform starting in 2009, Hong Kong has a "6–3–3" school system of which the first twelve years have been free since the academic year 2008/09. After six years of elementary schooling, each student attends secondary school. At the time of this study, the results of the school examination and government examination of primary school students at the end of grade 5 and the whole year of grade 6 were used to allocate students to secondary schools. Hong Kong grouped students into five ability levels before 2000. After that year, the tracking system was reduced to three ability levels (or bands), with about 33 per cent of students in each band. This academic segregation in school intake is expected to be a major factor for inequality of school performance in Hong Kong. Besides the academic segregation, social segregation between schools should also be considered. Accordingly, Table 5.7 shows the results of the multi-level analysis, which examines the effect of the students' individual SES, prior academic ability and school's academic intake and social composition on students' reading performance. "School mean SES" and "school banding" are used as the two major indicators of academic segregation and social segregation among schools.

Results of Model 1 indicate that social intake of the school is a significant predictor of the reading performance at the school-level. Although the students' SES does not have significant impact on students' reading performance, school mean SES shows a strong and significant impact. With one unit increase in the school mean SES, the performance increases by about 55 points. The between-school

*Table 5.7* Impact of School Segregation on Students' Reading Performance

|  | Model 1 | | Model 2 | |
| --- | --- | --- | --- | --- |
|  | *Coefficient* | *SE* | *Coefficient* | *SE* |
| **Intercept** | 546.16*** | 3.88 | 545.68*** | 2.13 |
| *School-level factors* | | | | |
| School mean SES | 54.64*** | 6.86 | 3.99 | 4.89 |
| School Banding |  |  | 25.48*** | 3.52 |
| **Student level factors** | | | | |
| SES | 0.03 | 1.41 | −1.03 | 1.31 |
| AAI |  |  | 2.53*** | 0.12 |
| **Variance components** | | | | |
| Between-School |  | 2060.22 |  | 506.98 |
| Within-School |  | 4124.44 |  | 3600.98 |
| **Variance explained** | | | | |
| Between-School |  | 34.73% |  | 83.94% |
| Within-School |  | 3.20% |  | 15.49% |

Source: PISA 2012

variation explained is about 35 per cent. These findings are consistent with that of PISA 2000+ (Ho et al., 2003), in which the regression coefficient of school mean SES was 96 points and the between-school variation explained was 42 per cent. In other words, the impact of school mean SES decreases from the first cycle in 2002 to the current cycle of 2012.

Model 2 extends Model 1 by adding academic intake at the individual and school levels. School banding varies from 1 (high ability) to 3 (low ability). The results indicate that academic intake has significant effect on reading performance. When school academic intake (banding) changes from low to medium or from medium to high, reading performance increases by about 25 points. In PISA 2000+, the respective increase is 53 points. The effect of school mean SES is reduced in Model 2 from 66.17 to 10.62, which is still significant. The percentage of between-school variation explained by the two intake variables is about 84 per cent, which is slightly higher than the 81 per cent in PISA 2000+. In other words, a large extent of inequality in school performance can be explained by the academic and social segregation. Only about 16 per cent of the between-school variation remained unexplained in 2012.

Similar analysis models are used to test for mathematics, and Table 5.8 shows a very similar pattern.

The results of the final model suggest that both student prior academic intake and school average banding have significant effects on mathematics performance. When the school academic intake is one band higher, students' mathematics performance increases by about 31 points. For every unit increase in individual AAI, the students' mathematics performance increases by about 3 points. The effect

*Table 5.8* Impact of School Segregation on Students' Mathematics Performance

|  | Model 1 Coefficient | SE | Model 2 Coefficient | SE |
|---|---|---|---|---|
| **Intercept** | 562.64*** | 4.18 | 561.88*** | 1.96 |
| *School-level factors* |  |  |  |  |
| School mean SES | 66.17*** | 7.10 | 10.62** | 3.94 |
| School Banding |  |  | 30.83*** | 3.36 |
| **Student level factors** |  |  |  |  |
| SES | 2.67 | 1.47 | 1.27 | 1.33 |
| AAI |  |  | 2.65*** | 0.15 |
| **Variance components** |  |  |  |  |
| Between-School |  | 2370.64 |  | 361.96 |
| Within-School |  | 5177.58 |  | 4581.46 |
| **Variance explained** |  |  |  |  |
| Between-School |  | 42.27% |  | 91.19% |
| Within-School |  | 3.12% |  | 14.27% |

Source: PISA 2012

of school mean SES is reduced from about 66 points in Model 1 to about 11 points in Model 2, which is still significant. The percentage of between-school variation explained by the individual SES and school mean SES is about 42 per cent in Model 1, which is slightly higher than the Model 1 for explaining reading performance (35 per cent). As for Model 2, the percentage of between-school variation explained by the two intake variables is 91 per cent, which is higher than the Model 2 for reading (81 per cent). In other words, a larger extent of inequality in school performance on mathematics can be explained by the academic and social segregation between schools. Only about 9 per cent of the between-school variation in mathematics remains unexplained in 2012.

Results of the HLM analysis on scientific literacy are very similar to that of reading and mathematics. The contextual effect of mean SES is the strongest and students' AAI is also significant in predicting students' scientific literacy. A more accurate analysis could be done in PISA2015 as science will be the major domain and full student data could be used for the analysis of segregation effect on students' scientific literacy.

## Conclusions and implications

This chapter has examined the overall literacy performance of Hong Kong 15-year-old students and identified the disparity of literacy performance across students of different backgrounds and across different schools. The chapter has given a detailed picture of Hong Kong students' performance in mathematic, scientific and reading literacy from an international perspective and the influence of various background factors, such as gender, immigration status, economic, social and cultural status and academic and social segregation among schools.

Findings from PISA 2012 show that first, Hong Kong continues to rank high among participating countries/regions in mathematics, science and reading. Second, there are small disparities between different sub-groups, including gender, immigration status and family socio-economic cultural status. These results suggest that Hong Kong's education system is doing quite well in providing equal access to education and is beneficial to most of the students regardless of an individual's social, cultural or economic background. This pattern is consistent over the past 10 years from 2002 to 2012. It appears that Hong Kong's education system has achieved both excellence and equality in academic results when compared with other participating countries.

However, there is substantial inequality of performance among schools in Hong Kong in terms of the academic and social segregation. In other words, PISA shows us that the schools that students attend are strongly predictive of their performances. Evidence from multilevel analysis indicates that the between-school variation in student performance in reading and mathematical literacy is largely explained by the school's social composition and academic intake. Only 16 per cent of the between-school variation in reading and 9 per cent in mathematics remains unexplained after controlling for the social and academic intake factors.

To conclude, there is evidence of input inequality, in the sense that schools with a larger proportion of students from lower SES and lower academic backgrounds are schools in which educational conditions are relatively less favourable. From the perspective of policy-makers, changing the five-banding system to three-banding system appears to be a promising policy to create a more homogenous schooling system. However, changing the existing banding system into a more comprehensive one could be too drastic. Compensatory policies and special programmes for disadvantaged learners might potentially counter the inequities that presently exist between schools.

Policy-makers should also be aware that Hong Kong has a very high percentage of immigrant students among the 65 participating countries/regions. Of the total of 34.1 per cent of immigrant students, 13.9 per cent (17.4 per cent in 2002) are the first generation (both students and their parents are foreign-born) and 20.2 per cent (26.4 per cent in 2002) are the second generation (students were born in Hong Kong but their parents were born in foreign countries) (Ho et al., 2003). The disadvantage seen in the first-generation students' performances is substantial and consistent over the past 10 years. Although the second-generation students perform as well as local students consistently in all cycles of PISA studies in Hong Kong, special adjustment programmes should still be designed to address the needs of these newly immigrant students. For parents who are non-natives, specific parent education and involvement programmes are needed to help with their language acquisition. With a growing number of immigrants in Hong Kong, the government should have specific educational and social policies to support the adaptation of this particular group of students to their new schooling and living environments in Hong Kong.

In sum, this chapter has probed into the quality and equality of Hong Kong's basic education. The goal of excellence and equality of education appears to be incompatible in previous discourses, yet this conflict is not universal or inherent in the education system as reflected in the findings of Hong Kong. Readers may be curious to know the criteria whereby Hong Kong can claim to excel and to provide educational equality in school performances, and under what conditions Hong Kong can bring about relatively high levels of achievement among the top and average performing students without leaving the disadvantaged students too far behind. Possible reasons could be the core curriculum with less differentiation that is equally demanding for all students (Chiu & Khoo, 2005); better disciplinary climate, and academic press (Ho, 2009); greater demands for students' time in school work and homework (Bray, 2010); regular assessment with feedback to students (Koh, Lim, & Habib, 2010); high parental aspiration, expectation and involvement (Chiu & Ho, 2006; Ho, 2010; Ho & Willms, 1996); school decentralisation and school climate (Ho, 2005, 2006) and so on. All these are interesting topics for future studies with the rich data of PISA from 2002 to 2012. Yet, the inequality of student performance among schools is consistently problematic. A longitudinal study is needed to examine to what extent and how the comprehensive school reforms for reducing academic segregation among schools can change this pattern over time.

# References

Bowles, S., & Gintis, H. (1976). *Schooling in capitalist America: Educational reform and the contradictions of economic life.* New York: Basic Books.

Bray, M. (2010). Researching shadow education: Methodological challenges and directions. *Asia Pacific Education Review, 11*(1), 3–13.

Campbell, R. T. (1983). Status attainment research: End of the beginning or beginning of the end? *Sociology of Education, 56*(1), 47–62.

Census and Statistics Department. (2015). *Population-overview.* Retrieved form http://www.censtatd.gov.hk/hkstat/sub/so20.jsp

Chiu, M. M., & Ho, S. C. (2006). Family effects on student achievement in Hong Kong. *Asia Pacific Journal of Education, 26*(1), 21–35.

Chiu, M. M., & Khoo, L. (2005). Effects of resources, inequality, and privilege bias on achievement: Country, school, and student level analyses. *American Educational Research Journal, 42*(4), 575–603.

Coleman, J. S. (1968). The concept of equality of educational opportunity. *Harvard Educational Review, 38*(1), 7–22.

Coleman, J. S. (1987). Families and schools. *Educational Researcher, 16*(6), 32–38.

Coleman, J. S. (1990). *Equality and achievement in education.* Boulder, CO: Westview Press.

Harker, R., Nash, R., Durie, A., & Charters, H. (1993). *Succeeding generations: Family resources and access education in New Zealand.* New York: Oxford University Press.

Hirschman, C., & Falcon, L. M. (1985). The educational attainment of religio-ethnic groups in the United States. In A. C. Kerckhoff (Ed.), *Research in sociology of education and socialization* (Vol. 5, pp. 83–120). Greenwich, CT: JAI Press.

Ho, S. C. (2005). Effect of school decentralization and school climate on student mathematics performance: The case of Hong Kong. *Educational Research for Policy and Practice, 4*(1), 47–64.

Ho, S. C. (2006). Educational decentralization in three Asian societies: Japan, Korea and Hong Kong. *Journal of Educational Administration, 44*(6), 590–603.

Ho, S. C. (2009). Characteristics of East Asian learners: What we learned from PISA. *Educational Research Journal, 24*(2), 327–348.

Ho, S. C. (2010). Family influences on science learning among Hong Kong adolescents: What we learned from PISA. *International Journal of Science and Mathematics Education, 8*(3), 409–428.

Ho, S. C., Chun, K. W, Yip, D. Y., Wong, K. M, Chiu, M. M., Sze, M. M., Lo, N. K., Chung, Y. P., Tsang, W. K., Man, Y. F., & Ho, W. K. (2003). *The first HKPISA report: Monitoring the quality of education in Hong Kong from an international perspective.* Hong Kong: HKPISA Centre, the Chinese University of Hong Kong.

Ho, S. C., & Willms, J. D. (1996). The effect of parental involvement on the achievement of eighth grade students. *Sociology of Education, 69*(2), 126–141.

Ho, S. C., Wong, K. L., Lau, K. C., & Lau, K. L. Eds. (2015). *The fifth HKPISA report: PISA2012- volume 1.* Hong Kong: Hong Kong PISA Centre, Chinese University of Hong Kong.

Ho, S. C., Wong, K. M, Yip, D. Y., Chun, K. W, Law, H. Y., Sze, M. M., Lam, C. C., Chiu, M. M., Lo, N. K., Chung, Y. P., & Tsang, W. K. (2005). *The second HKPISA report: Monitoring the quality and equality of education in Hong Kong* from an international perspective – From PISA 2000 to PISA 2003. Hong Kong: HKPISA Centre, the Chinese University of Hong Kong.

Johnson, R. K., & Cheung, Y. S. (1995). *Reading literacy in Hong Kong: An IEA world literacy project on the reading proficiency of Hong Kong students in Chinese and English*. Hong Kong: Department of Chinese and Bilingual Studies, Hong Kong Polytechnic University.

Koh, K., Lim, L., & Habib, M. (2010). *Building teachers' capacity in classroom-based formative assessment*. Paper presented at the 36th International Association for Educational Assessment. Annual Conference. Thailand: Bangkok.

Martin, M. O., Mullis, I. V. S., Gonzalez, E. J., Gregory, K. D., Smith, T. A., Chrostowski, S. J., Garden, R. A., & O'Connor, K. M. (2000). *TIMSS 1999 international science report: Findings from IEA's repeat of the Third International Mathematics and Science Study at the eighth grade*. Chestnut Hill, MA: Boston College.

Morris, P., & Adamson, B. (2010). *Curriculum, schooling and society in Hong Kong (Vol. 1)*. Hong Kong, China: Hong Kong University Press.

Mourshed, M., Chijioke, C., & Barber, M. (2010). *How the world's most improved school systems keep getting better*. London: McKinsey & Company.

Mullis, I. V. S., Martin, M. O., Gonzalez, E. J., Gregory, K. D., Garden, R. A., O'Connor, K. M., Chrostowski, S. J., & Smith, T. A. (2000). *TIMSS 1999 international mathematics report: Findings from IEA's repeat of the Third International Mathematics and Science Study at the eighth grade*. Chestnut Hill, MA: Boston College.

OECD. (2013). *PISA 2012 Results, volume II: Excellence through equity: Giving every student the chance to succeed*. Paris: OECD.

OECD. (2014). PISA 2012 results: What students know and can do – student performance in mathematics, reading and science (volume I, Revised edition, February 2014), PISA. Paris: OECD.

Pong, S. L. (2009). Grade level and achievement of immigrants' children: Academic redshirting in Hong Kong. *Educational Research and Evaluation, 15*(4), 405–425.

Steinberg, S. (1981). *The ethnic myth: Race, ethnicity and class in America*. Boston: Beacon Press.

Yip, D. Y., Chiu, M. M., & Ho, S. C. (2004). Hong Kong student achievement in OECD/ PISA study: Gender differences in science content, literacy skills and test item formats. *International Journal of Science and Mathematics Education, 2*, 91–106.

# 6 Shadow education
## Features, expansion and implications

*Kevin Wai-Ho Yung and Mark Bray*

## Introduction

Recent years have brought significant global growth in the scale and intensity of private supplementary tutoring across the globe (Aurini et al., 2013; Bray, 2009). This tutoring is widely called shadow education because it operates alongside regular schooling and to some extent mimics it in curriculum. The growth of tutoring has far-reaching implications. Major issues include social inequalities (Dang & Rogers, 2008), impact on the lives of students and their parents (Cayubit et al., 2014; Park et al., 2011) and backwash on teaching and learning in mainstream schooling (Kwo & Bray, 2014; Yung, 2015). In the scale of private tutoring, Hong Kong ranks high alongside other East Asian jurisdictions, such as Japan, South Korea, Taiwan and Singapore (Bray & Lykins, 2012; Dawson, 2010; Kim & Lee, 2010; Roesgaard, 2006). Private supplementary tutoring can help slow learners to catch up with their peers in class, but it can also create tension with mainstream education and may conflict with the initiatives of education reforms. Despite its contribution to human capital, it can exacerbate social inequalities and cause financial burdens for individuals and families.

This chapter presents the features of shadow education in Hong Kong and identifies major reasons for its expansion since 1997, when Hong Kong became a Special Administrative Region of the People's Republic of China. It commences with the definition of private supplementary tutoring, and then describes the scale, subjects, intensity and different modes of tutoring in Hong Kong. Next the chapter turns to the driving forces for students to seek private supplementary tutoring. Subsequent sections consider a number of implications and likely future trends.

## Definition of shadow education

In the academic literature, the shadow education metaphor has been used since the 1990s (Bray, 1999; Marimuthu et al., 1991; Stevenson & Baker, 1992). Like all metaphors, the vocabulary should be treated with caution. In particular, some parts of the tutoring industry elaborate on rather than exactly mimicking regular schooling. Nevertheless, the core of the metaphor seems valid. The mimicry has been clearly evident in Hong Kong with new courses in tutorial centres emerging as soon as the mainstream curriculum was reformed, for instance, to include a senior secondary subject called liberal studies after 2009 (Chan & Bray, 2014).

For present purposes, in line with a dominant strand in the literature (e.g., Bray, 1999; Kwok, 2001; Lee et al., 2009) shadow education is taken to have three central characteristics:

- *Privateness.* This dimension limits tutoring to that provided by individuals or organisations in exchange for a fee. It does not include unpaid tutoring offered by families, friends or volunteers, or extra lessons provided by teachers free of charge.
- *Supplementation.* Shadow education supplements the provision of schools and is provided outside school hours.
- *Academic subjects.* The principal academic subjects in Hong Kong are Chinese, English, mathematics and other subjects that feature in the public examinations. Domains that are learned mainly for leisure and/or personal development such as music, art and sports are excluded from the focus.

Hong Kong's shadow education is widely known in Cantonese as $bou^2\ zaap^6$ (補習). "補" literally means to supplement (either for remedial purpose or enhancement) and "習" means to learn, study or practise. Shadow education also exists at pre-primary and post-secondary levels, but different issues arise in these levels and should be addressed separately.

## Features of shadow education

Students in Hong Kong seek shadow education to support their mainstream schooling, and in particular to perform well in examinations set by their schools and externally. The forms range from one-to-one individual tutoring to large lectures. This section presents the scale, subjects, intensity and modes of tutoring in Hong Kong's shadow sector.

### *Scale*

Obtaining precise data on the size and shape of private supplementary tutoring is difficult. Tutors, students and parents are not always willing to expose their activities, in part because shadow education may not be viewed as a legitimate form of education. In addition, the variations in forms and intensity of private supplementary tutoring may make measurement difficult.

Nevertheless, a picture may be formed with data from various studies (Table 6.1). The research shows a range of figures, in part reflecting the representativeness or otherwise of the studies and the methods used for data collection. As such, the studies cannot necessarily be compared with each other in a precise way. However, they all show that shadow education was significant in scale at both primary and secondary levels. The largest and perhaps most systematic of the studies was the 2004/05 expenditure survey of 13,600 households reported by the Census and Statistics Department (2005, 23). Among the households with primary school children, 36.0 per cent had made expenditures on shadow education; and respective figures for lower secondary, middle secondary and upper secondary were 28.0 per cent, 33.6 per cent and 48.1 per cent. A more detailed study, albeit with a smaller sample, was conducted by Bray and colleagues in 2011/12 (Bray et al., 2014; Zhan et al., 2013). They surveyed 1,646 Secondary 3 and Secondary 6 students in 16 secondary schools. Among the Secondary 3 students, 53.8 per cent reported that they had received private supplementary tutoring within the previous 12 months, and 71.8 per cent of Secondary 6 students did so.

Another indicator of expansion is the number of tutorial centres. In November 1998, Hong Kong had approximately 390 registered tutorial centres plus an estimated 70 unregistered ones (Ombudsman, 1999, 14). Fifteen years later (i.e., November 2013) the website of the government's Education Bureau listed 1,185 registered tutorial centres. These were only institutions serving primary and secondary students (i.e., excluding ones for pre-primary and post-secondary students). The statistics also excluded institutions to teach adults foreign languages, business, computing, etc. For comparison, Hong Kong had 1,083 primary and secondary schools in 2013/14 (Education Bureau, 2014, 7).

*Table 6.1* Data on participation rates in shadow education in Hong Kong

| Year | Data |
| --- | --- |
| 1998 | A survey in four primary schools found that 41 per cent of Grade 3 and 39 per cent of Grade 6 pupils received tutoring (Liu, 1998). Another study of 392 students in six secondary schools suggested that 46.2 per cent of Form 4, 28.8 per cent of Forms 5 and 6, and 64.0 per cent of Form 7 received tutoring (Tseng, 1998). |
| 1998/99 | Among 630 respondents in six secondary schools of different bands, 35.1 per cent of Secondary 1–3, 46.6 per cent of Secondary 4–5 and 70.3 per cent of Secondary 6–7 received tutoring (Kwok, 2001). |
| 2004/05 | A government expenditure survey of 13,600 households reported that 36.0 per cent of families with primary school children spent money on tutoring. For lower secondary the figure was 28.0 per cent, for middle secondary it was 33.6 per cent and for upper secondary it was 48.1 per cent (Census and Statistics Department, 2005). |
| 2009 | A telephone survey of 521 students reported that 72.5 per cent of upper primary students received tutoring (Ngai & Cheung, 2010). |
| 2010 | A study of 898 secondary students indicated respective rates of tutoring as 72.5 per cent, 81.9 per cent and 85.5 per cent at Secondary 1–3, Secondary 4–5 and Secondary 6–7 (Caritas Community and Higher Education Service, 2010). |
| 2011/12 | A survey of 1,646 students in 16 secondary schools found that 53.8 per cent of Secondary 3 students and 71.8 per cent of Secondary 6 students received tutoring (Bray, 2013). |

## Subjects and intensity

The greatest demand in private supplementary tutoring is for the core examination subjects. At the secondary level, these subjects are Chinese, English, mathematics and liberal studies. The survey conducted by Bray et al. (2014, 31) found that greatest demand was for English, with 65.2 per cent of sampled students having received private tutoring in this subject during the previous 12 months. English typically has the greatest demand because it is not only an important subject in schools and public examinations but also the medium of instruction in many secondary schools, especially the elite ones (Yung, 2015). Moreover, since the 1997 resumption of Chinese sovereignty, the government has adopted a language policy of biliteracy (Chinese and English) and trilingualism (Cantonese, Putonghua and English). The status of English remains high. Mathematics and Chinese are also very popular, with 52.7 per cent and 31.8 per cent of sampled students receiving tutoring in 2011/12 (Bray et al., 2014, 31). These findings were consistent with those of other studies (Bray & Kwok, 2003; Ngai et al., 2013).

A related question concerns the intensity of tutoring. The research by Bray and colleagues indicated that during the ordinary season of schooling, as opposed to the examination season or vacations, sampled students spent an average of 2.19 hours per week on English, 2.19 hours on mathematics and 1.88 hours on Chinese (Bray, 2013, 22). During the examination season the number of hours increased to 2.50 for English, 2.85 for mathematics and 2.33 for Chinese; and during the vacation season the figures were 2.00, 2.09 and 1.70. Secondary 6 students reported that during the examination season they spent an average of 8.32 hours a week in tutoring for all subjects (Bray, 2013, 22).

## Modes

Shadow education can take various forms, including one-to-one, small-group, live lectures, video-recorded lectures and on-line (Yung, 2015; Zhan et al., 2013). The most prominent kind of tutoring in Hong Kong is in tutorial centres run by entrepreneurs with multiple outlets. Some tutorial companies advertise their tutors as "kings and queens" (Kwo & Bray, 2011). They employ flashy tutors who are like celebrities or "stage actors" (Ng, 2009), dressed trendily and using teenage vocabulary to appeal to youngsters. The companies highlight tutors' credentials in promotional leaflets and billboards and advertise the outstanding examination results of tutees, selling "the educational dream of success in Hong Kong's exam-oriented culture" (Koh, 2014, 15). Students sit in classrooms of 45 students maximum as regulated by the Education Ordinance (Hong Kong Special Administrative Region, 2003), but the classrooms may have glass walls so that over 100 students can have lessons at the same time (Lee, 2010; Yung, 2011). Some tutors' lessons are recorded and played in video classes with teaching assistants helping to deliver notes. Because of the growing demand for shadow education, it has increasingly been provided in the form of institutional arrangements rather than just as an informal activity. One Hong Kong tutorial company has become publicly listed on the Hong Kong stock exchange (Modern Education Group Limited, 2011).

In contrast to the tutoring in formal settings is informal tutoring by university students or others on a one-to-one basis or in small groups. This kind of tutoring is less visible but not uncommon. The 2011/12 research mentioned above found that 53.5 per cent of Secondary 3 students who reported having received private tutoring within the previous 12 months had done so in small groups, and 44.3 per cent had done so on a one-to-one basis (Zhan et al., 2013, 500). Small-group tutoring usually involves two to seven students, because work with eight or more students needs registration as a "school."[1] This type of tutoring commonly helps students to check homework and revise the content taught in school. Some parents hire private tutors to take care of the students' individual needs which cannot so easily be done by school teachers or group tutors.

Another mode of tutoring which has been gaining popularity worldwide is on-line tutoring. It ranges from personalised individual instructions by means of audio/video conferencing to automated tutorials adapting to students with different abilities. In Hong Kong, on-line tutoring was the least common form identified in the 2011/12 survey (Bray et al., 2014; Zhan et al., 2013), though may have grown in popularity since that time.

## Causes of expansion

Many of the forces contributing to expansion of shadow education have roots which are not allied to the 1997 change of sovereignty. They include the impact of globalisation and the advance of technologies. Nevertheless, some factors have at least some relationship with the political changes in 1997 and thereafter. This section remarks on how 1) education reform, 2) massification of post-secondary education, 3) increase in academic and social competition, 4) changes of language policy, and 5) adjusted regulations on shadow education have contributed to expansion.

### *Education reform*

Hong Kong's secondary and tertiary education has undergone a structural reform from 3+2+2+3 (three years of junior secondary schooling, two years of middle secondary, two years of senior secondary, and three years for a standard university degree) to 3+3+4 (three years for junior secondary, three years for senior secondary, and four years for university). The old structure was based on the system in England, while the new structure matches the dominant arrangement in the People's Republic of China. The New Senior Secondary (NSS) curriculum was a major initiative of the post-1997 government. It emphasised inquiry-oriented and student-centred approaches in classroom teaching and learning, though some mismatch was evident between the planned curriculum and the realities in classrooms (Morris & Adamson, 2010; Morris & Scott, 2003). Carless and Harfitt (2013) pointed out that policies imported from elsewhere are not always congruent with local situations. Hong Kong is rooted in Confucian-heritage cultures, where teachers play authoritative roles and are regarded as a source of knowledge transmission (Berry, 2011; Carless, 2011). The mismatch between traditional teaching approaches and the new curriculum objectives may lead to superficial implementation of innovations and hence frustration with classroom teaching and learning. Moreover, while teachers may attempt to encourage interactions in class, students may avoid speaking out because of the fear of losing face. Therefore, students may seek additional support from shadow education that adopts one-way knowledge transmission approaches and in this respect align with traditional teaching and learning styles. Some students may deliberately choose to attend video-recorded classes so that they do not need to speak in front of peers (Yung, 2011, 48).

Another factor has been the introduction of the Hong Kong Diploma of Secondary Education (HKDSE) examination. Students sit for the examination at the end of secondary schooling, and the results are the major criterion for admission to higher education. Despite the reduction of the number of public examinations to one from two (the Hong Kong Certificate of Education Examination previously taken at the end of Secondary 5, and the Hong Kong Advanced Level Examination previously taken at the end of Secondary 7), the demand for private supplementary tutoring did not decrease. Ngai et al. (2013) showed an overall increase in the enrolment rate and intensity in private tutoring between 2009 and 2012, a transition period between the previous and the current education system. The increase may be due to students' mind set of "one examination seals the fate", knowing that the HKDSE results determine whether they can study a degree programme at a university, or an associate degree or higher diploma at a self-funded post-secondary institute. This idea has been promoted in advertisements by many tutorial companies, which highlight the university admission rate and the importance of high HKDSE scores.

In addition, some reform initiatives may have created challenges for school teachers, leading to lower teaching quality at school and students' need to seek private supplementary tutoring. An example was the implementation of School-Based Assessment (SBA) across most subjects in the New Senior Secondary curriculum (CDC & HKEAA, 2007; Yan, 2014). SBA aimed to promote assessment for learning and a positive backwash effect on teachers and students, but many teachers felt ill-equipped (Lam, 2015), and students lacked guidance and motivation (Kwo & Bray, 2014). Moreover, as noted by Davison (2013), the implementation of SBA in societies with strong examination cultures is extremely challenging. For some teachers and students, it became another high-stakes summative assessment (Cheng et al., 2010), and many students sought help from their tutors to get the tasks done.

## *Massification of post-secondary education*

Higher education in Hong Kong has expanded rapidly since the 1990s, but the expansion has not necessarily reduced competition or eased the pressure of participation in shadow education. Bray and Lykins (2012, 24) pointed out that expansion simply changes the question from "post-secondary place or no post-secondary place?" to "*which* post-secondary place?" Indeed the expansion of post-secondary education may have increased the demand for private supplementary tutoring since families which previously would have considered post-secondary education to be out of reach now consider it within reach.

In the 1980s, only around 10 per cent of the cohort aged 17–20 were able to secure places in local tertiary education (Jung & Postiglione, 2015, 119). Provision expanded during the 1990s, and expanded further in the 2000s. In 1999, the government published a consultation document titled *Education blueprint for the 21st century – review of academic system: Aims of education* (Education Commission, 1999). One proposed target was to provide 60 per cent of senior secondary students with opportunities to pursue higher education. In response, most local tertiary education institutions have launched self-financed programmes and associate degree programmes with government support in subsequent years. However, the number of places for publicly-funded degrees has been maintained at around 14,500 each year (Wan, 2011). These degree places tended to be allocated to the elite secondary students who scored the highest in public examinations. Self-financed degrees and sub-degrees were less positively regarded by employers and the public because they were generally perceived as a route for students who performed less well academically. Many students regarded sub-degree programmes as a stepping stone to universities, but Kember (2010, 177) observed that they could be "an expensive route to nowhere" because few students were in fact able to enter the traditional universities through that route. To save the potential time and cost needed for the sub-degree programmes, many families invested in private supplementary tutoring so that they could "pay now to save later" (Bray & Lykins, 2012, 25).

## *Increasing competition*

The Census and Statistics Department (2012) showed that the 0–14 age group had decreased from 18.2 per cent of the total population in 1997 to 11.6 per cent in 2011, and that the 15–24 age group had decreased from 14.4 per cent in 1997 to 12.4 per cent in 2011. Yet while the number of local youth was decreasing, the proportion of non-local undergraduates was rising, intensifying the competition for Hong Kong students seeking to enter higher education.

Rapid increase in the inflow of non-local undergraduates from Mainland China and other parts of the world after 1997 reflected the government policies of internationalisation in higher education and promotion of links with Mainland China. In 2013/14, 15 per cent of students in government-funded undergraduate programmes were non-local compared to 9 per cent in 2006/07 and 1 per cent in 2000/01 (University Grants Committee, 2014, 33). Although universities have quotas for non-local students and have allocated at least 80 per cent of places for locals, the perception of increased competition for higher education may lead to insecurity among local students and their parents. Shadow education is then seen as a way to increase competitiveness over the international and mainland applicants.

## Language policy

Language policy has a significant impact on the medium of instruction (MOI) in schools and can influence the demand for private supplementary tutoring. Chinese (spoken Cantonese) is the mother-tongue of most Hong Kong students and has long been the MOI in most primary schools. Most tertiary institutions, by contrast, have been using English as the principal MOI. Whether Chinese or English should be the MOI for secondary education has aroused much controversy since 1997 (Lo & Lo, 2014; Tsui, 2007). During most of the colonial period, secondary schools were allowed to choose their preferred MOI, and during the 1980s and 1990s over 90 per cent of them labelled themselves as schools using English as the medium of instruction (EMI) even if in practise they used much Cantonese (Falvey, 1998). Shortly after the handover, the Hong Kong government adopted the language policy of biliteracy and trilingualism, aiming to improve connexions with Mainland China and keep the official status of English as a language for global communication. This has led to an emphasis on both Chinese and English in schools and university admission, and hence a high enrolment rate of private tutoring in these two subjects. At the same time, the government announced that all secondary schools were required to use Chinese as the MOI unless the schools could demonstrate that their teachers and students could cope with EMI. In the end, 114 schools (approximately 25 per cent) were permitted to use EMI in 1998. These schools were perceived as prestigious and superior to those using Chinese as the medium of instruction (CMI). In order to get into EMI schools, primary students needed to perform well academically. Therefore, many parents sent them for shadow education so that they could compete for a school place. At the same time, secondary students preparing for university studies using English, particularly those in CMI schools, sought shadow education to improve their English.

In 2009, due to much public discontent and pressure from the education sector, the policy was "fine-tuned" to allow schools flexibility to choose their MOI for different subjects. More schools chose to use EMI, particularly for "high-status subjects" that were considered important for university admission (Morris & Adamson, 2010, 154). The adjustment of the policy to some extent meant a return to the pre-1997 practice. Learning through a second language may be challenging for some students, so they seek shadow education in order to catch up by hearing the content again in Chinese. In the tutorial sector, in fact most English lessons are taught through Cantonese. This practice would not be permitted in the school sector.

## The regulatory framework

Regulations for tutorial centres that insist on registration and on various managerial procedures but which in other respects are very flexible have permitted and perhaps encouraged expansion of the sector. In Hong Kong, centres with eight or more tutees in a class are officially classified as Private Schools Offering Non-Formal Curriculum (Education Bureau, 2012) and are treated as regular schools with certain regulatory exemptions. The requirements for operation include availability of information to clients, tutors' academic qualifications and class size, but do not cover curriculum, textbooks or the modes of teaching (Bray & Kwo, 2014, 37). The flexibility encourages entrepreneurs to start tutoring businesses and teachers to switch to tutoring so they can avoid the bureaucratic policies and curricula demanded by schools.

The Hong Kong government also avoids intervention on fees in the shadow education industry. Unlike Bangladesh, Mainland China, South Korea and Thailand, where the authorities either set a ceiling on fees or approve the prices set by individual companies (Bray & Kwo, 2014, 40–41), the Hong Kong authorities avoid what they consider to be over-regulation. Until 2003, tutorial centres were required to seek approval for fee levels, but this requirement was removed to avoid administrative work and encourage flexibility. Therefore, tutors can charge a lot for courses, or offer large numbers of classes, either live or by video recording, making tutoring a huge business that generates extremely high incomes. For example, a large tutorial company reported a profit of over HK$40 million in the 2010 financial year (Modern Education Group Limited, 2011), and top tutors could make a million dollars a year (Kedmey, 2013; Ng, 2009). This may appeal to entrepreneurs and teachers who decide to become tutors, hence increasing the supply of private tutoring.

Accompanying the supply is advertising to create demand. The lack of regulation on tutoring advertisements may have also expanded the scale of shadow education. In the mid-2000s Hong Kong saw a boom of advertisements for tutorial centres on tall buildings, on public transport and in the mass media. Modern Education Group Limited (2011) indicated that their marketing expenses increased from approximately HK$15 million in 2008 to over HK$20 million in 2010 (215). The advertisements described tutors as celebrities and emphasised stylish hairstyles and fashionable clothes (Kwo & Bray, 2011; Ng, 2009). Some advertisements boasted about tutors' qualifications and/or their students' achievements in public examinations, and some sought to promote feelings of insecurity which they hinted could be quenched by enrolling in tutorial courses. Koh (2014, 806) argued that the repetitive exposure to tutorial centre advertisements had "spellbinding subliminal effects".

## Implications of the expansion of shadow education

The expansion in the scale and intensity of private supplementary tutoring has diverse implications. On the positive side, tutoring can increase the learning and therefore human capital of students. It also provides jobs for tutors, and it provides domestic support, role models and advice for young people outside school time. However, shadow education may also contribute to stratification; and it can have a backwash on mainstream education. These dimensions are considered in the following sections.

## Employment

Since shadow education has become such a significant industry, it provides much employment not only for the tutors but also for ancillary staff, accountants, maintenance workers and others. As indicated above, in November 2013, the Education Bureau website listed 1,185 registered tutorial centres providing academic training for students in primary and secondary schooling. Some of these enterprises had many outlets. At the extreme, 574 branches were registered for Kumon. The Modern Bachelor Education Centre had 75 registered outlets, while King's Glory had 47, Beacon College had 33 and Modern Education had 31. The company that operates Modern Education reported having 312 employees in June 2014 (Hong Kong Education [Intl] Investments Limited, 2014, 20). Statistics are not publicly available for other companies, but the large ones may be assumed to have had substantial workforces, and the large numbers of small companies would have had correspondingly large numbers of employees.

Alongside these companies were many individuals working informally. Some were university students earning extra pocket money while others were people who had completed their own education and chose to work in the tutoring sector on an informal basis.

## Domestic support, role modelling and advice

In addition to its educational function, tutoring has a child-minding function for some families. Especially in families in which both parents are in formal employment, tutoring provides a structure for children to be supervised after the end of the school day until a parent or other adult is available to collect them. Secondary students are less in need of adult supervision of this sort, but tutoring nevertheless provides a structured occupation which relieves the anxieties of parents who feel that the youths might not otherwise be so gainfully occupied.

Focusing particularly on private tutors who work in students' homes, Ho (2010) analysed from a sociological angle 12 roles performed by tutors. They were:

- knowledge disseminator,
- motivator,
- role model/idol/gender role facilitator,
- preacher/inspector,
- adviser,
- elder sister/brother/mother,
- cousin,
- peers/friends/playmates,
- mediator/messenger,
- listener/social worker,
- mother, and
- babysitter.

Striking about this list is that only the first was about knowledge dissemination. Ho observed (67) that it was the "primary role of a private tutor", but that in her interviews "every informant just talks about it briefly and then switches the topic". The social roles received much more emphasis in Ho's analysis. For example, some parents expect the private tutors to be a role model of their children. As reported from a tutor in her study, the parents from a family wanted their children to learn from her independence and the ability to make money when she was still studying. The private tutors are generally expected to have "a standard code of ethics, such as no smoking, no drinking, no swearing, knowing how to dress properly, presenting good behaviour, and also adopting a polite attitude" (68). One tutor indicated that role modelling even went to the stage of idolisation (69). For instance, in his case, the student mimicked his style of clothing, tone of speaking and even personality. He was told that the student who used to speak foul language and behave violently became more gentle and polite after following him as a model.

Tutors may also provide advice to both parents and students (70). Ho (2010) found that parents tend to listen to private tutors' advice because they consider tutors having narrower generation gap with their children and more experienced with teenage issues such as dating and self-esteem. On the other hand, students tend to share their personal issues with private tutors rather than their parents or siblings. They may seek the tutors' advice in different areas such as relationships, academic difficulties, time management and personal growth.

These roles, it must be underlined, were for tutors who worked individually with students in domestic settings. Tutoring in company premises has a set of parameters, and the mass tutorial lectures are very different in style and function. Nevertheless, even the mass tutorial lectures have a socialisation function which can have positive dimensions in constructive use of students' out-of-school time. Chan and Bray (2014) pointed out that students can fulfil their social needs through tutoring by interacting with tutors before lectures and attending lessons with their peers.

## *Social stratification*

Less positively, shadow education maintains and exacerbates social stratification. The expansion of shadow education, some of it (especially in the mass tutorial schools) at a relatively modest price, has made private supplementary tutoring accessible not only to rich families but also to middle-class and low-income families. Nevertheless, rich families can obviously afford more and better tutoring than low-income ones.

Shadow education also calls into question the notion of fee-free education espoused by the United Nations and the Hong Kong government. The 1948 Universal Declaration of Human Rights stated that education should be free, at least in the elementary and fundamental stages (United Nations, 1948, Article 26). This principle was also enshrined in the declarations of the World Education Forums led by UNESCO in 2000 and 2015 (UNESCO, 2015; World Education Forum, 2000, 43). Hong Kong has followed international norms, in 1978 introducing nine years of free and compulsory education and in 2008 extending it to 12 years. Yet while fee-free schooling has become a global norm, shadow education has been a form of hidden privatisation of education. In many settings, rich, middle-income and poor households have all come to view shadow education as a necessity (Chugh, 2011; Dang & Rogers, 2008; Dawson, 2010; Kim & Lee, 2010; Pallegedara, 2012). When the majority of students are receiving tutoring, those who cannot afford it are disadvantaged, at least psychologically. Perceptions of the need to receive shadow education may lead to financial burden for families. The 2011/12 Hong Kong survey led by Bray and colleagues found that half of the respondents receiving tutoring either agreed (34.1 per cent) or strongly agreed (17.3 per cent) that the costs were a burden to their families (Bray, 2013, 22).

## *Backwash on regular schooling*

Shadow education has also impacted on the dynamics of teaching and learning in mainstream schools. Tutoring can help slow learners to keep up with their peers, which decreases disparities within the classroom; but it can increase disparities when the high achievers receive more tutoring than others. Other backwash effects relate to teachers' attitudes. In some countries, much tutoring is provided by teachers on a part-time basis. These teachers may put more effort into their private than their public classes, and perhaps even cut the content of regular class time in order to promote demand for supplementary lessons from their own students (Dawson, 2010; Kobakhidze, 2014). In Hong Kong, few teachers also work as tutors because they are relatively well paid and are guided by the Code for the Education Profession which states that a teacher "shall not take advantage of his/her professional relationships with students for private gain" (Hong Kong Council on Professional Conduct in Education, 1995, Section 2.22). However, when shadow education is very widespread, teachers may assume that their students have external support and then provide less internal support.

Students' attitudes towards schooling are another concern. Since students or their families are paying money to their tutors, they may pay more attention to their tutors than to mainstream schooling which is free of charge (Fung, 2003, 188). This dimension is also related to students' choice. As students can choose their tutors but not their school teachers, they tend to appreciate their tutors more. This phenomenon may be especially prevalent in star tutoring, where tutors are advertised as celebrities. In contrast, it is not normal for schools to promote their teachers as "stars", so students may find school teachers less fashionable or appealing. Moreover, students perceive that their school teachers play the roles of counselling and instilling values and knowledge, while seeing tutors as more knowledgeable in examinations and skilful in teaching (Zhan et al., 2013). Shadow education has been criticised as eroding students' creativity and encouraging them to depend on passive learning; but students may find tutors more helpful than teachers in meeting pragmatic needs for examination techniques.

The extra time and effort needed for tutorial classes may also have a negative backwash. Tutorial centres in Hong Kong typically operate after school hours until 10:00 p.m., and from 9:00 a.m. to 10:00 p.m. during weekends. This means that students can attend lessons till late at night on top of their regular schooling. Such routines may lead to inefficiencies in school lessons if students are fatigued during the daytime. The intensive academic schedule may also deprive students of time for sports, socialisation and hobbies, which are important for all-round education.

## Conclusion

Private supplementary tutoring has been a shadow but an important part of education in Hong Kong and has expanded since the 1997 resumption of Chinese sovereignty. Much of the impetus may be unrelated to the political transition, but some factors are related. The expansion has had a significant impact on the lives of young people and on their families, and also has wider implications. While private supplementary tutoring may to some extent compensate for shortcomings in mainstream schooling, it can undermine educational reforms and exacerbate social inequalities.

Despite its existing scale, it seems likely that the shadow will expand further and will intensify because of the increasingly fierce academic competition among students due to the growing emphasis on achievements in standardised assessments. As such, stakeholders in the education system need to address the issues it raises and to seek to ameliorate the challenges. Nevertheless, one lesson from countries such as Mauritius and South Korea is that once shadow education has entered the culture, it is very difficult to remove (Bray, 2009). Policy-makers would be wise to recognise the existence and implications of shadow education more fully. Even if they insist on a relatively loose regulatory framework, they may do more to help families to become better informed consumers and may encourage the industry to engage in more extensive self-regulation (Bray & Kwo, 2014). In addition, policy-makers and school managers may encourage teachers to discuss the phenomenon more extensively in order to identify appropriate ways for regular schooling to respond to its shadow.

## Note

1 The Education Ordinance (Chapter 279) defines a school as "an institution, organisation or establishment which provides for 20 or more persons during any one day or 8 or more persons at any one time, any nursery, kindergarten, primary, secondary or post-secondary education or any other educational course by any means, including correspondence delivered by hand or through the postal services."

## References

Aurini, J., Davies, S., & Dierkes, J. Eds. (2013). *Out of the shadows: The global intensification of supplementary education*. Bingley: Emerald.

Berry, R. (2011). Assessment trends in Hong Kong: Seeking to establish formative assessment in an examination culture. *Assessment in Education: Principles, Policy & Practice, 18*(2), 199–211.

Bray, M. (1999). *The shadow education system: Private tutoring and its implications for planners.* Paris: UNESCO International Institute for Educational Planning (IIEP).

Bray, M. (2009). *Confronting the shadow education system: What government policies for what private tutoring?* Paris: UNESCO International Institute for Educational Planning (IIEP).

Bray, M. (2013). Benefits and tensions of shadow education: Comparative perspectives on the roles and impact of private supplementary tutoring in the lives of Hong Kong students. *Journal of International and Comparative Education, 2*(1), 18–30.

Bray, M., & Kwo, O. (2014). *Regulating private tutoring for public good: Policy options for supplementary education in Asia.* Hong Kong: Comparative Education Research Centre and Bangkok: UNESCO.

Bray, M., & Kwok, P. (2003). Demand for private supplementary tutoring: Conceptual considerations, and socio-economic patterns in Hong Kong. *Economics of Education Review, 22*(6), 611–620.

Bray, M., & Lykins, C. (2012). *Shadow education: Private supplementary tutoring and its implications for policy makers in Asia.* Hong Kong: Comparative Education Research Centre, the University of Hong Kong, and Mandalyong City: Asian Development Bank.

Bray, M., Zhan, S., Lykins, C., Wang, D., & Kwo, O. (2014). Differentiated demand for private supplementary tutoring: Patterns and implications in Hong Kong secondary education. *Economics of Education Review, 38*(1), 24–37.

Caritas Community and Higher Education Service. (2010). *Private supplementary tutoring of secondary students: Investigation report.* Hong Kong: Caritas. Retrieved from http://klncc.caritas.org.hk/private/document/644.pdf

Carless, D. (2011). *From testing to productive student learning: Implementing formative assessment in Confucian-heritage settings.* New York: Routledge.

Carless, D., & Harfitt, G. (2013). Innovation in secondary education: A case of curriculum reform in Hong Kong. In K. Hyland & L. L. C. Wong (Eds.), *Innovation and change in English language education* (pp. 172–185). Abingdon: Routledge.

Cayubit, R., Castor, J., Divina, E., Francia, R., Nolasco, R., Villamiel, A., Villoria, A. I. S., Troy, M., & Zarraga, M. (2014). A Q analysis on the impact of shadow education on the academic life of high school students. *Psychological Studies, 59*(3), 252–259.

CDC [Curriculum Development Council], & HKEAA [Hong Kong Examinations and Assessment Authority]. (2007). *English language education key learning area: English language (curriculum and assessment guide) Secondary 4–6.* Hong Kong: CDC and HKEAA.

Census and Statistics Department. (2005). *Latest 2004–05-based consumer price indices.* Hong Kong: Hong Kong Special Administrative Region. Retrieved from http://www.censtatd.gov.hk/FileManager/EN/Content_908/cpi_slide.pdf

Census and Statistics Department. (2012). *Demographic trends in Hong Kong 1981–2011.* Hong Kong: Hong Kong Special Administrative Region. Retrieved from http://www.statistics.gov.hk/pub/B1120017032012XXXXB0100.pdf

Chan, C., & Bray, M. (2014). Marketized private tutoring as a supplement to regular schooling: Liberal Studies and the shadow sector in Hong Kong secondary education. *Journal of Curriculum Studies, 46*(3), 361–388.

Cheng, L., Andrews, S., & Yu, Y. (2010). Impact and consequences of school-based assessment (SBA): Students' and parents' views of SBA in Hong Kong. *Language Testing*, 28(2), 221–249.

Chugh, S. (2011). *Dropout in secondary education: A study of children living in slums of Delhi*. New Delhi: National University of Educational Planning and Administration.

Dang, H. A., & Rogers, F. H. (2008). The growing phenomenon of private tutoring: Does it deepen human capital, widen inequalities, or waste resources? *World Bank Research Observer*, 23(2), 161–200.

Davison, C. (2013). Innovation in assessment: Common misconceptions and problems. In K. Hyland & L. L. C. Wong (Eds.), *Innovation and change in English language education* (pp. 263–275). Abingdon: Routledge.

Dawson, W. (2010). Private tutoring and mass schooling in East Asia: Reflections of inequality in Japan, South Korea, and Cambodia. *Asia Pacific Education Review*, 11(1), 14–24.

Education Bureau. (2012). *Education (exemption) (Private Schools offering non-formal curriculum) Order*. Cap 279, Section 9(3). Hong Kong. Retrieved from http://www.legislation.gov.hk/blis_pdf.nsf/6799165D2FEE3FA94825755E0033E532/8346DC44CC7651F4482575EE00565682?OpenDocument&bt=0

Education Bureau. (2014). *Student enrolment statistics 2013/14*. Hong Kong: Education Statistics Section, Education Bureau.

Education Commission. (1999). *Education blueprint for the 21st century – review of academic system: Aims of education*. Hong Kong: Education Commission.

Falvey, P. (1998). ESL, EFL & language acquisition in the context of Hong Kong. In B. Asker (Ed.), *Teaching language and culture: Building Hong Kong on education* (pp. 73–85). Hong Kong: Addison Wesley.

Fung, A. (2003). Cram schooling in Hong Kong: The privatization of public education. *Asian Anthropology*, 2, 179–195.

Ho, N. H. (2010). Hong Kong's shadow education: Private tutoring in Hong Kong. *The Hong Kong Anthropologist*, 4, 62–85.

Hong Kong Council on Professional Conduct in Education. (1995). *Code for the education profession of Hong Kong*. Retrieved February 25, 2015, from http://cpc.edb.org.hk/english/code02.htm

Hong Kong Education (Intl) Investments Limited. (2014). *Annual report 2014*. Hong Kong: Hong Kong Education (Intl) Investments Limited.

Hong Kong Special Administrative Region, Government of (2003). *Education ordinance*. Cap.279. Hong Kong: Government of the Hong Kong Special Administrative Region.

Jung, J., & Postiglione, G. A. (2015). From massification towards the post-massification of higher education in Hong Kong. In J. C. Shin, G. A. Postiglione & F. Huang (Eds.), *Mass higher education development in East Asia* (Vol. 2, pp. 119–136). Dordrecht: Springer.

Kedmey, D. (2013). Rich and famous: Why Hong Kong's private tutors are millionaire idols. *Time*, 30 December. Retrieved from http://world.time.com/2013/12/30/rich-and-famous-why-hong-kongs-private-tutors-are-millionaire-idols/#ixzz2oz0uMufN

Kember, D. (2010). Opening up the road to nowhere: Problems with the path to mass higher education in Hong Kong. *Higher Education*, 59(2), 167–179.

Kim, S., & Lee, J. H. (2010). Private tutoring and demand for education in South Korea. *Economic Development and Cultural Change*, 58(2), 259–296.

Kobakhidze, M. N. (2014). Corruption risks of private tutoring: Case of Georgia. *Asia Pacific Journal of Education, 34*(4), 455–475.

Koh, A. (2014). The "magic" of tutorial centres in Hong Kong: An analysis of media marketing and pedagogy in a tutorial centre. *International Review of Education, 60*(6), 803–819.

Kwo, O., & Bray, M. (2011). Facing the shadow education system in Hong Kong. *International Institute for Asian Studies (IIAS), The Newsletter, 56*(Spring), 20.

Kwo, O., & Bray, M. (2014). Understanding the nexus between mainstream schooling and private supplementary tutoring: Patterns and voices of Hong Kong secondary students. *Asia Pacific Journal of Education, 34*(4), 403–416.

Kwok, P. (2001). *A multi-level social analysis of demand for private supplementary tutoring at secondary level in Hong Kong*. Ph.D. thesis, The University of Hong Kong.

Lam, R. (2015). Language assessment training in Hong Kong: Implications for language assessment literacy. *Language Testing, 32*(2), 169–197.

Lee, C. J., Park, H. J., & Lee, H. (2009). Shadow education systems. In G. Sykes, B. L. Schneider, D. N. Plank & T. G. Ford (Eds.), *Handbook of education policy research* (pp. 901–919). New York: Routledge; American Educational Research Association.

Lee, C. W. (2010). *Shadow education: A comparative study of two tutorial schools in Hong Kong*. M.Ed. dissertation, The University of Hong Kong.

Liu, P. K. (1998). *Private tuition for primary students in Hong Kong*. B.Ed. (Primary) project report. Hong Kong: University of Hong Kong.

Lo, Y. Y., & Lo, E. S. C. (2014). A meta-analysis of the effectiveness of English-medium education in Hong Kong. *Review of Educational Research, 84*(1), 47–73.

Marimuthu, T., Singh, J. S., Ahmad, K., Lim, H. K., Mukherjee, H., Osman, S., Chelliah, T., Sharma, J. R., Salleh, N. M., Yong, L., Lim, T. L., Sukumaran, S., Thong, L. K., & Jamaluddin, W. (1991). *Extra-school instruction, social equity and educational quality* [in Malaysia]. Singapore: International Development Research Centre.

Modern Education Group Limited. (2011). *Global offering*. Hong Kong: Modern Education Group Limited.

Morris, P., & Adamson, B. (2010). *Curriculum, schooling and society in Hong Kong*. Hong Kong: Hong Kong University Press.

Morris, P., & Scott, I. (2003). Educational reform and policy implementation in Hong Kong. *Journal of Education Policy, 18*(1), 71–84.

Ng, Y. H. (2009). Tutors are like actors. *Deccan Herald*. Retrieved from http://www.deccanherald.com/content/8619/tutors-like-actors.html

Ngai, A., Chan, S. C., & Cheung, S. (2013). *Private tutoring of primary and secondary school students in Hong Kong*. Hong Kong: Hong Kong Federation of Youth Groups.

Ngai, A., & Cheung, S. (2010). *Students' participation in private tuition*. Youth Poll Series No. 188. Hong Kong: Hong Kong Federation of Youth Groups.

Ombudsman. (1999). *Report of the investigation report on registration of tutorial schools*. Hong Kong: Office of the Ombudsman.

Pallegedara, A. (2012). Demand for private tutoring in a free education country: The case of Sri Lanka. *International Journal of Education Economics and Development, 3*(4), 375–393.

Park, H., Byun, S., & Kim, K. (2011). Parental involvement and students' cognitive outcomes in Korea: Focusing on private tutoring. *Sociology of Education, 84*(1), 3–22.

Roesgaard, M. H. (2006). *Japanese education and the cram school business: Functions, challenges and perspectives of the juku*. Copenhagen: NIAS Press.

Stevenson, D. L., & Baker, D. P. (1992). Shadow education and allocation in formal schooling: Transition to university in Japan. *American Journal of Sociology, 97*(6), 1639–1657.

Tseng, L. C. J. (1998). *Private supplementary tutoring at the senior secondary level in Taiwan and Hong Kong*. M.Ed. dissertation, The University of Hong Kong.

Tsui, A. B. M. (2007). Language policy and the social construction of identity: The case of Hong Kong. In J. W. Tollefson & A. B. M. Tsui (Eds.), *Language policy, culture, and identity in Asian contexts* (pp. 121–142). London: Lawrence Erlbaum Associates.

UNESCO. (2015). *The education for all agenda: 2015–2030*. Paris: UNESCO.

United Nations. (1948). *Universal declaration of human rights*. New York: United Nations. Retrieved from http://www.un.org/events/humanrights/2007/hrphotos/declaration%20_eng.pdf

University Grants Committee. (2014). *Annual report 2013–2014*. Hong Kong: University Grants Committee. Retrieved from http://www.ugc.edu.hk/eng/doc/ugc/publication/report/AnnualRpt1314/full.pdf.

Wan, C. (2011). Reforming higher education in Hong Kong towards post-massification: The first decade and challenges ahead. *Journal of Higher Education Policy and Management, 33*(2), 115–129.

World Education Forum. (2000). *The Dakar framework for action – Education for all: Meeting our collective commitments*. Paris: UNESCO.

Yan, Z. (2014). School-based assessment in secondary schools. In C. Marsh & J. C. K. Lee (Eds.), *Asia's high performing education system: The case of Hong Kong* (pp. 274–287). New York, NY: Routledge.

Yung, K. W. H. (2011). *Shadow education in Hong Kong: The experience of learners of English*. MA in Applied Linguistics dissertation, The University of Hong Kong.

Yung, K. W. H. (2015). Learning English in the shadows: Understanding Chinese learners' experiences of private tutoring. *TESOL Quarterly, 49*(4), 707–732.

Zhan, S., Bray, M., Wang, D., Lykins, C., & Kwo, O. (2013). The effectiveness of private tutoring: Students' perceptions in comparison with mainstream schooling in Hong Kong. *Asia Pacific Education Review, 14*(4), 495–509.

# 7 Curriculum reform
## Why, how, what and where it is headed for

*Chi-Chung Lam and Ngai-Ying Wong*

## Introduction

The handover of the sovereignty of Hong Kong to China in 1997 not only brought about the change of government administration and political structure, but has also marked major curriculum reform in schools in Hong Kong since then. The curriculum reform, launched formally in 2001, was a reaction of the new government as part of a major strategy to face the new political arena, strengthen economic competitiveness, fix social problems, and enhance educational quality.

The new millennium marked a new chapter of education in Hong Kong. In 2000, the HKSAR government proposed a large-scale education reform (Education Commission, 2000). One year later, the reform proposal was formally launched (Curriculum Development Council, or CDC, 2001). The education reform was comprehensive and the curriculum reform is a central part of it. The former comprises redefinition of educational goal (1999, which was initiated earlier in 1992), assessment reform (ROPES report in 1998), incorporation of IT in education (1998), life-long and life-wide learning (2000) and teacher education reform, in the form of benchmarking (2000).

The curriculum reform was large in scale, involving a paradigm shift of teaching and learning. Integrated curriculum was preferred over the conventional subject-based curriculum. The constructivist teaching approach was promoted. Four reform initiatives, including reading to learn, IT in education, project learning, and moral and civic education, were chosen as the foci of curriculum changes.

This large-scale and radical education reform was further expanded in 2009 when the government introduced a new academic structure, changing the long-established English system of "5-year secondary, 2-year sixth form and 3-year university" to a "6-year secondary (3-year junior secondary and 3-year senior secondary) and 4-year university" system that is adopted in the United States and the Chinese mainland (Education and Manpower Bureau, 2005). The curriculum and assessment system of the senior secondary sector was also changed in light of the new 3–3–4 academic structure. Unlike many of the large-scale educational reforms in the 1980s and 1990s, the level of implementation of the 21st-century reform has been much higher and it has been claimed by the government as having led to improvements in at least some areas of education. Despite this, not all the goals of the reform have been achieved. Furthermore, parents, students, teachers and schools have paid a heavy price in implementing the reform initiatives. The intensification of work among teachers and the high examination pressure on students cause grave concern about the curriculum reform initiatives. Hence, in this paper, the key discussion questions are: What has contributed to the high level of implementation and some degree of success? How should the school curriculum be further developed in the future?

## Scale and nature of the reform

The current wave of curriculum reform was formally launched in 2001, but it was contemplated in the mid-1990s when the handover of sovereignty was being planned. One of the masterminds, K. M. Cheng, a member of the Education Commission at the time of the conception of education reform, explained that the curriculum reform was a response to the implementation failure of previous reform initiatives in the 1980s and 1990s suggested by the Education Commission, the highest level of consultative committee on educational matters in Hong Kong:

> *By the end of the colonial era, the seven Education Commission reports made more than 279 recommendations, but few of them could comfortably claim effective implementation. Hence the system was there, rather comprehensive compared with other systems, but the system did not quite deliver. The system and government machinery were more apt for times when developments in quantity and structure were the chief goals. They did not quite evolve into mechanisms that would cope with issues of quality and require co-ordination and value decisions. The system was therefore stagnant.*
>
> (K. M. Cheng, 2002, 158)

However, if one delves into the curriculum reform documents published in 2000 and 2001, it would not be difficult to see that the goals of reform were more than what was suggested in the previous Education Commission reports in the 1980s and 1990s. In the late 1990s, the newly established HKSAR government proposed that the aim of education for the 21st century should be to enable everyone "to attain all-round development in the domains of ethics, intellect, physique, social skills and aesthetics according to his/her own attributes" (Education Commission, 2000, 4). They rationalised that by developing these qualities, he/she will be "capable of life-long learning, critical and exploratory thinking, innovating and adapting to change; filled with self-confidence and a team spirit; willing to put forward continuing effort for the prosperity, progress, freedom and democracy of their society, and contribute to the future well-being of the nation and the world at large" (ibid.).

In essence, the reform aims to promote whole-person development of the younger generation. It is argued that young people should be taught how to learn and develop a positive attitude towards life-long learning. To equip students with life-long learning skills, nine generic skills – including collaboration skills, communication skills, creativity, critical thinking skills, information technology skills, numeracy skills, problem-solving skills, self-management skills, and study skills – should be emphasised in school education. To achieve these, the school curriculum needs to be broad and balanced; curriculum integration and school-based curriculum development should be encouraged. The structure of school curriculum was changed from subject-based to key learning area (KLA)-based. The eight KLAs are: English-Language Education; Chinese Language Education; Mathematics Education; Technology Education; Arts Education; Physical Education; Personal, Social and Humanities Education; and Science Education. The means of learning should be broadened to include life-wide learning. The Education Commission realised that the scale of the reform was large and radical in nature, hence identifying four main foci of reform – namely moral and civic education, reading to learn, project learning and information technology for interactive learning – for the first phase of development (i.e., 2001 to 2006). These changes mean that the conception of learning has been broadened from transmission of knowledge in the classroom to the active learning of students in a wide range of arenas and through many different means.

In 2004, the HKSAR government announced its intention to change the secondary and tertiary academic structure from the English tradition to the Chinese mainland system. In other words, the 6-year secondary and 4-year tertiary education system would be adopted. The government decided in 2005 that the new system would be implemented starting from Secondary 4 in 2009. The new structure is expected to have the following benefits for students (Education and Manpower Bureau, 2005, 10–11; see also CDC, 2009, 2):

- Enhanced language and mathematical abilities
- A broadened knowledge base
- Increased competence in generic skills
- Increased exposure to other learning experiences
- Having multiple progression pathways for further studies and career development

The 2-year Secondary 4 to Secondary 5 HKCEE (similar to the GCSE level) and the 2-year A-level curriculum were combined into a new senior secondary curriculum leading to the Hong Kong Diploma of Secondary Education Examination (HKDSE) at the end of Secondary 6. Students are required to take 4 core subjects (namely Chinese Language, English Language, Mathematics, and Liberal Studies) and one to three elective subjects. These elective subjects include traditional subjects like Geography, Economics, Physics, Biology as well as newly developed integrated subjects like Combined Science, and Business, Accounting, and Financial Studies (BAFS). For the less academic-oriented students, they can choose Applied Learning courses such as Jewellery Arts and Design, Introduction to Cantonese Opera, New Media Communication Strategies, Marketing and On-Line Promotion. These courses are from six areas of studies: Creative Studies; Media and Communication; Business, Management and Law; Services; Applied Science; Engineering and Production (Education Bureau, 2015). A total of 40 Applied Learning courses are offered in the 2015–2017 cohort.

The philosophy, approach, teaching strategies and assessment methods of the 2009 senior secondary curriculum reform are in line with the spirit of the curriculum reform in 2001 (Education and Manpower Bureau, 2005). For example, constructivist teaching is preferred over the transmission strategy. In brief, the development of generic skills is stressed and the slogan "learning to learn" is advocated. Furthermore, the initial intention was that all senior secondary subjects would include a component of school-based assessment

In another vein, the 2001 curriculum reform was a continuation of the Target Oriented Curriculum (TOC) launched in the mid-1990s. In simplistic terms, the TOC was a curriculum initiative that involves the standardisation of curriculum, popular in the U.K. and U.S.A. at the start of the 1990s (Wong, Han, & Lee, 2004). Schools and teachers were requested to design curriculum and instruction according to the levels of the attainment standards and the progress of the learner. The attainment standards were also used as a reference in standardised assessments. This line of thinking was materialised in 2004 when the government formally introduced the Territory-Wide System Assessment [TSA], which is used to monitor the standards of all Primary 3, Primary 6 and Secondary 3 students' English Language, Chinese Language and Mathematics standards. The TSA data form part of the quality assurance system at the school and the territory-wide level.

The curriculum reform in 2001 and 2009 was similar to the epistemological shift in the curriculum described by Barnett, Parry, and Coate (2001) (see Table 7.1). The curriculum changed from the traditional practices of promoting knowing what to knowing how. It is not surprised that these changes are widely described as fundamental, radical, paradigmatic and large-scale (Y. C. Cheng, 2009).

*Table 7.1* Epistemological Shifts in the Curriculum

| Traditional curricula | Emerging curricula |
| --- | --- |
| • Knowing what | • Knowing how |
| • Written communication | • Oral communication |
| • Internal | • External |
| • Personal | • Interpersonal |
| • Disciplinary skills | • Transferable skills |
| • Intellectual orientation | • Action orientation |
| • Concept-based | • Issue-based |
| • Knowledge-based | • Task-based |
| • Pure | • Applied |
| • Proposition-based learning | • Experiential learning |

Source: Barnett, Parry, and Coate (2001).

## Forces leading to the curriculum reform

Why did the HKSAR government launch such comprehensive and fundamental changes? As has been pointed out by K. M. Cheng (2002), the reform attempts in the 1980s and early 1990s did not materialise. Classroom practices did not differ from before (Education Commission, 2000). As the new leadership of the HKSAR planned to exercise the sovereignty, it was just natural that they adopted a proactive stance in educational matters. This drive to reform was further propelled by the handover of sovereignty in 1997.

In light of the globalisation trend, neighbouring cities such as Singapore and Shanghai were considered as a strong economic threat to Hong Kong. It was clear that Hong Kong could not rely on low labour cost nor land cost. If Hong Kong were to maintain its economic competitiveness in the information age, the economic force needed to be well-educated and were ready to face the economic challenges. The traditional curriculum was too conservative to nurture a labour force good for innovative economic tasks. Moreover, in the information age, technology advances in a phenomenal rate. If the labour force could not continue to learn and develop, many middle-aged people would lose their competitiveness. Hence, life-long learning skills and attitudes were considered as essential attributes of the school leavers.

However, the reform initiatives launched in the early 1990s, notably the Target Oriented Curriculum (TOC), failed to be implemented, not to mention changing the conventional transmission model of teaching. There is therefore the need to reinvigorate the reform drive (Wong & Tang, 2012).

The political change in 1997 also had a significant impact on the curriculum reform (Wong & Tang, 2012). The importance of moral and civic education was enhanced as the government wanted to promote national identity among the students. Even though civic education was promoted since the mid-1980s, its implementation had not been successful. Moreover, the core aims of civic education at that time were rule of law and nurturing of valuing skills. After the handover of sovereignty in 1997, promoting national identity and nationalistic feeling became much more important.

The insurmountable examination pressure on school students had been a major concern of the public (Education Commission, 2000; Morris, 1996). As the norm-referenced assessment dominated examinations in both school and territory level, examinations unavoidably created many failures. To prepare students for examination and ensure high achievement standards, students were given huge amount of homework. Students spent much of their after-school hours on completing homework (Lam & Tang, 2014). The voice of releasing students from this unhealthy pressure was loud and clear (Education Commission, 2000).

Educational reform had swept through many countries. In the West, curriculum reform was introduced in the United States, England and Wales (Hargreaves & Shirley, 2009). In Asia, Taiwan launched a large-scale curriculum reform in the mid-1990s. Singapore introduced information technology in education in 1996. These moves were widely reported in Hong Kong, which created a feeling that curriculum reform was a worldwide trend (Wong, Han, & Lee, 2004). If Hong Kong did not follow suit, it would lag behind. The above factors combined generated a strong momentum for curriculum reform in the late 1990s and early 2000s.

## Level of implementation and outcomes of the reform

Curriculum reform is not something new in Hong Kong. Since the 1970s, a series of reform initiatives had been launched by the government. Similar to many other curriculum reforms in other parts of the world, most of these curriculum reforms in Hong Kong failed to be fully implemented, not to mention achieving concrete impressive results. Tang and Morris (1989), for example, found that schools had not developed civic education as suggested by the government. The implementation of most of the large-scale curriculum and assessment reforms proposed in the 1990s failed to achieve the goals set. The TOC introduced in the early 1990s was fiercely criticised by schools and teachers. Despite the huge investment of resources supporting its implementation in schools, it has not been widely adopted by schools (Lam, 1997, 2003).

Unlike the previous reforms in the 1980s and 1990s, the 2001 curriculum reform and 2009 new senior secondary curriculum and assessment reform have established their roots in schools in Hong Kong. A series of implementation surveys and inspection reports shows that schools have incorporated the four curriculum initiatives (namely project learning, reading to learning, civic and moral education, IT in education) in the school curriculum, and student-centred teaching became more common (Education Commission, 2003, 2004, 2006). Moreover, the use of interactive learning activities in classroom teaching is more common (Chan, 2008). More schools and teachers ventured into school-based curriculum to cater for their students' characteristics (Education Commission, 2006).

The 2009 new senior secondary curriculum was implemented as planned. Schools offered quite a large number of elective subjects for students to choose. In 2012, 58 per cent of the Secondary 6 students chose elective subjects from more than one key learning area. In terms of teaching, more enquiry teaching and collaborative learning were adopted by teachers (Education Bureau, 2013).

The reform initiatives are not only adopted and widely implemented, but are also described as having achieved impressive performances of Hong Kong school students in international comparative studies (see for example, Chan, 2008). Judging from the ranking of Hong Kong in the PISA studies from 2000 to 2012, Hong Kong students' performance has been impressive (see Table 7.2). In 2012, eleven years after the curriculum reform, the competency of Hong Kong's 15-year-old students in reading, mathematics and science ranked 2nd, 3rd and

*Table 7.2* The ranking of Hong Kong in the PISA studies

| Subject | Year | | | | |
| --- | --- | --- | --- | --- | --- |
| | 2000 | 2003 | 2006 | 2009 | 2012 |
| Reading | 6 | 10 | 3 | 4 | 2 |
| Mathematics | 1 | 1 | 3 | 3 | 3 |
| Science | 3 | 3 | 2 | 3 | 2 |

Source: Programme for International Student Assessment, Hong Kong Centre [http://www.fed.cuhk.edu.hk/~hkpisa/output/output.htm]

2nd respectively in this international study. Only Shanghai and Singapore could outrank Hong Kong. This achievement is even more remarkable if one takes into account that Shanghai and Singapore only joined the PISA study in 2009. One may say that Hong Kong has improved and outperformed all its counterparts in the 2000 study.

If we go beyond the simple indicator of ranking, it could also be found that Hong Kong students have improved significantly in reading, and such improvement could be attributed to the introduction of "reading to learn" reform initiative in the 2001 curriculum reform (HKPISA Centre, 2008). Hong Kong students' improvement in reading is also revealed in the Progress in International Reading Literacy Study (PIRLS) which assesses Grade Four students' reading comprehension ability. The ranking of Hong Kong jumped from 14th in 2001 to 2nd in 2006. In the PIRLS 2011 study, Hong Kong was quoted as one of the four top-performing countries/regions. The score of Hong Kong students have also further improved from 2006 to 2011 (Mullis, Martin, Foy, & Drucker, 2012).

Moreover, the social gradient of Hong Kong students in the PISA study is comparatively less than that of many other places and countries (He & Lu, 2010). This suggests that differences between students of different socioeconomic background are relatively small. One can refer to Esther Sui-Chu Ho's chapter of this book for further details.

As the first cohort of the 2009 senior secondary curriculum students only completed their secondary education in 2012, and many are still in their tertiary studies, there is yet solid evaluation data to show its impact on students' learning outcomes. Nevertheless, from the various international comparative evaluation studies of school students' performance, it could be concluded that the curriculum reform in Hong Kong in 2001 has not adversely affected the primary and junior secondary students' academic learning outcomes (Lam, Li, & Yu, in press).

## Causes of the high level of implementation

Lin and Zhang (2006) have attempted to explain the reasons contributing to the higher level of implementation of the 2001 curriculum reform. They suggested that a range of factors interacted to achieve such a high level of change at the school and classroom levels.

The HKSAR government was so serious about the education reform that it pumped huge sums into public funding to support its implementation. In the financial year of 2003–2004, the public expenditure on school education was 50 per cent more than that in 1996–1997 (Education Commission, 2003), despite the serious Asian financial crisis in 1998 and the SARS outbreak in 2003. This increase in funding for school education continued in the mid-2000s and 2010s. For example, from 2005–2006 to 2007–2008, the government invested an extra HK$1.65 billion to ease the workload of teachers. The average unit cost of primary school place and secondary school place was also increased from HK$30,381 and HK$39,485 in 2008–2009 to HK$47,320 and HK$54,170 respectively in 2013–2014 (Lam, Li, & Yu, in press).

Investing public funding alone usually was not effective in bringing about curriculum changes at the school level. This was the case in the TOC. The Hong Kong government had pumped in large amount of money in implementing the TOC in the early 1990s, but it had not established its root in schools at all (Lam, 1997). A major force pushing schools and teachers to adopt the reform at the classroom level in this new round was the neo-liberal implementation strategies adopted by the HKSAR government. Since the early 1990s, the Hong Kong government had followed the neo-liberal strategies adopted by the Thatcher government in the United Kingdom. The School Management Initiative was launched in 1991, promulgating the importance of relaxing centralised bureaucratic control in schools. Behind this move was the rationale of holding the schools accountable for the educational service provided. Lam (2014) sums up the development:

> *Under this initiative, schools were required to compile school report and profile which should include information such as school aims, operating plans and students' performance (Education and Manpower Bureau [Branch] & Education Department, 1991). The report and profile, after being submitted to the Education Department, "are published in public domains such as the internet" (Ng & Chan, 2008). The release of school profile is to provide information for parents to choose schools (Ng & Chan, 2008). This request is reasonable as parents and students need the information for making informed decisions about school choice. Hence, school teachers and principals did find it difficult to argue against it.*
>
> (313–314)

The government strategy of using the mass media to discredit the standard of educational service (K. M. Cheng, 2002) further highlighted the need of an accountability culture and system. In 1997, a new quality assurance system, similar to what was introduced in many Asia-Pacific places (Mok et al., 2003), was launched. Schools were required to perform school self-evaluation, followed by periodic external school review. The external school review report was released to the school management committee, which included teachers, alumni and parent representatives. The school management needed to draft response statements and plans to improve the service in light of the report. Hence, the external school review was part of a high-stakes monitoring system. The school review was conducted with reference to a set of performance indicators developed by the government. Implementing the reform initiatives formed part of the performance indicators. For example, in the classroom observation evaluation form used in the external school review, one of the criteria was whether teachers had integrated the four curriculum initiatives in their teaching. With this new managerialism system and the performativity culture (Ball, 1998), schools and teachers found it difficult not to follow the education policy.

The danger of school closure with the shrinking of student intake amplified the power of these neo-liberal strategies (Mok, 2007). Since the turn of the new millennium, the primary student intake started to drop because of record-low birth rate. "The primary school enrolment dropped from 445,607 in 2000 to 366,531 in 2006, and the drop was 79,076 students, nearly 21.6 per cent primary school population" (Cheng, 2009, 78). The shrinking of student population, notably first in the primary schools, meant that schools which were less popular among parents faced real threat of school closure. The government, instead of taking this opportunity to introduce small-class teaching, decided to close down the schools failing to attract enough students. The threat of school closure shifted the balance of the power of schools and parents. Schools had to find ways to "sell" themselves to parents.

## Costs of the reform

Although there are hard data showing the achievements in academic learning outcomes, other aspects of learning and student development are lagging behind. One of the major goals of curriculum reform is to enhance whole-person development, promoting not only the development of academic competencies, but also moral, aesthetic and physical development (CDC, 2001). A government-commissioned survey on the implementation of the new senior secondary curriculum found that the learning activities for aesthetic development and physical education were less well developed (Education Bureau, 2013). A number of survey and studies also found that obesity problems among school students have worsened, and the physical fitness of school students has declined (CDC, Hong Kong Examinations and Assessment Authority, and Education Bureau, 2013).

The inadequacies in the development of non-academic aspects of education are closely related to the failure in tuning down examination pressure among school students. One of the major arguments for the curriculum reform in 2001 was the exceedingly high examination pressure upon students. Similar to other Confucian-Heritage Culture areas, such as South Korea, the Chinese Mainland, Japan, examination has long been taken as of prime importance in schooling (Lee, 1996; Wong, 2004). When the curriculum reform was first put forward, relieving the examination pressure was expected to be a key benefit to students. Similarly, this was a major argument for introducing the new senior secondary curriculum as students only need to take one public examination, that is, HKDSE, instead of two, namely the Hong Kong Certificate of Education Examination and Hong Kong Advanced Level Examination. However, this expected outcome has not materialised. Senior secondary students reported that they felt badly pressed by the workload and examination pressure (Education Bureau, 2013). The primary school students have not been exempted from examination too. In order to prepare students for the Territory-wide System Assessment in Primary 3 and 6, most if not all schools push their students to buy exercises and mock test papers. This often starts at Primary 2, while Primary 3 and 6 students are most affected (Wong, Lam, & Chan, 2009).

The reform launched in 2001 has led to the intensification of teachers' work. A study on teacher workload conducted by the Education and Manpower Bureau in 2006 found that "On average, teachers worked about 10 hours a day on a school day. . . . Work often extended to the weekends and holidays though the intensity decreased significantly during the holidays. For non-school days other than long holidays like Christmas and the summer vacation, teachers usually worked 4.6 hours a day. The overall data showed that teachers on average worked a total of 2,607 hours a year, or about 50 hours a week" (The Committee on Teachers' Work, 2006).

Another study conducted in 2011 showed that the workload problem was even worse. On average, teachers had to work 58 to 59 hours a week (Strategic Planning Office, Hong Kong Institute of Education, 2011). Yeung (2010) highlighted that the work pressure on teachers to fulfil the tasks involved in implementing the reform initiatives and the managerial measures worsened as the reform was implemented. Teachers complained about having to spend time on activities like the marketing activities of the school, preparing documents for external school review, running teacher-parent association and participating in teacher-parent activities, because these activities were seen as not related to the enhancement of teaching and learning of students at all. "Many [teachers] even put aside other essential duties (such as talking with students) and work to the expectation of the officials as well as the demand of parents" (Yeung, 2010, 199). This problem was acknowledged by the government after two teachers committed suicide in 2006. A special commission on teacher workload and pressure suggested to provide more funding to provide extra manpower to ease the problem (Education and Manpower Bureau, 2006). The dissatisfaction of teachers did not simply result from heavy workload. The managerial measures adversely affected teachers' professional status. They had to meet the demands of the parents even when their demands were not in line with the professional practices. The undesirable effects of managerial measures are not unique to Hong Kong. Brauckmann and Pashiardis (2010), for example, have elaborated on the adverse effects of quality assurance system.

The emphasis on developing integrated programmes and generic skills, particularly limiting the choice of elective subjects to one to three, has significantly hindered the development of academic subjects other than the four core subjects (i.e., Chinese Language, English Language, Mathematics, and Liberal Studies). The number of elective subjects taken by HKDSE students is much lower than the old HKCE and HKAL. In a Legislative Council paper, it is reported, "It is worth noting that the average number of elective subjects taken per day school candidate was 4 for the 2010 HKCEE, 2.8 for the 2012 HKALE, and 2 for the HKDSE" (Legislative Council Panel on Education, December 8, 2014, 2). If this trend continues, the breadth and depth of general knowledge of secondary school graduates would be seriously affected. Wong, Lam, and Chan (2009) warned that students' subject knowledge of mathematics might fall.

## The way forward

The high level of implementation of reform initiatives is not cost-free. The neoliberal strategies have led to some side effects on the system. Moreover, the pressure exerted through the managerial and performativity measures has its limitations in further enhancing students' whole-person development outcomes.

Hong Kong is still facing the challenge of how to cater for individual differences among school students and achieving whole-person development. The extension of inclusive education and the constant increase in number of students with special education needs means that the practices adopted since the 2001 curriculum reform need to be reviewed if schools are to achieve their ultimate goals of lifelong whole-person development for the younger generation.

The reform launched since 2001 has crafted a school culture that is more open to changes and accepts school self-evaluation practices (Lam, 2014). Instead of exerting even higher pressure on school teachers to achieve excellence in educational services, a sustainable development of school education should be in place. The key for sustainable development is teacher development (Fullan, 2010; Hargreaves & Shirley, 2009). Barber, Donnelly, and Rizvi (2012) point out that teachers play a pivotal part in education quality. An education system could not achieve beyond what teachers could do. The importance of promoting teacher development is made even more pronounced in light of the urgency in catering for individual differences in schools. In the present round of education reform, the HKSAR government still believes in finding a way of teaching that would cure all the ills in schools. For example, it was postulated that constructivist paradigm, student-centred teaching strategies and integrated programmes should be adopted (Curriculum Development Council, 2001). However, there is no solid evidence supporting the superiority of integrated curriculum over subject-based curriculum (Lam, 2002), nor are student-centred teaching strategies necessarily more effective than direct instruction (Hattie, 2009). The power of curriculum design and development should be vested in the professional hands of teachers rather than someone at the drawing board on policy.

In light of the scale and severity of the challenge to cater for individual differences, the strategy should be investing more on promoting teacher development in schools. If this is successfully done, more teachers would have solid subject knowledge, pedagogical content knowledge and pedagogical skills so that they could develop authentic school-based curriculum and tailor the curriculum for their students effectively. Moreover, even the most talented and well-trained teachers need time and professional space to design and deliver their work. Even though the rapid technological advances have led to higher automation in economic activities, teaching remains a labour-intensive professional activity. The government has to provide adequate resources to create the necessary working environment conducive to quality teaching.

Another important move would be reconstructing mutual trust between the stakeholders, including the Education Bureau, school sponsoring bodies, the principals, teachers, parents and the public as a whole. As has been pointed out above, the government has successfully discredited the work of the schools and the teachers at the early stage of the present round of reform. In recent years, the government has also attempted to downplay the consultation mechanism when planning educational policies. Some education policies were launched without reaching a consensus among the stakeholders. These actions have damaged the trust between the stakeholders. In education, mutual trust between the government, schools, teachers, parents and students is important. According to Bryk and Schneider (2003), the importance of trust in schools in the United States suggests that re-building trust is important if we are to enhance the quality of service in schools.

"Drastic reform – conflicts – compromises and amendments – distortions and grievances – outburst – another drastic change" seems to be a repeating formula. Curriculum reform is often seen more as a starting point of what we want to engineer in the decades to come rather than a summarization of day-to-day experience we accumulate in the past. As such, curriculum reforms were often initiated out of the vacuum, either through shopping around other countries or vague ideologies. Many ideas were not well-thought-out and were difficult to implement. Facing disputes and resistance, curriculum decision makers try to compromise. The School-Based Assessment (SBA) is an example. Besides testing performances that cannot be reflected in traditional paper-and-pencil tests, it aimed at releasing the intensive pressure of public examinations (so-called determining the whole life with one exam). However, the whole concept does not work in a place with heavy examination culture. SBA not only fails to release the examination pressure, it intensifies the workload of the students and teachers. Because of the importance of the public examination, the students take SBA very seriously. Hence, they spend extra hours and effort after Secondary 4 to ensure that their SBA work is of the best quality that they can achieve. The examination pressure cascades down from Secondary 6 to Secondary 5, and even to Secondary 4.

The distortion of the educational arena becomes more serious with the lowering of birth rate. Facing the threat of having to close down, schools are forced to comply with the curriculum reform and the marketization initiatives. The bargaining power of teachers was weakened. Over-load, over-time, under-paid, short-term contracts become common practices. Much of teachers' time is devoted to non-teaching tasks, such as fund-raising, promoting the school and pleasing various stakeholders, leaving teaching and nurturing as something of a lower priority.

Looking ahead, to reverse the above, we probably need courage to rebuild our professionalism more than introducing another round of reform. We need to re-awaken the soul more than adopting new hardware like curriculum design. "Less is more" has often used to inspire on student learning, and the same may be true for curriculum and teaching. Teachers need nurturing and free space to implement the curriculum according to their professionalism.

## References

Ball, S. J. (1998). Perfomativity and fragmentation in 'postmodern schooling'. In J. Carter (Ed.), *Postmodernity and the fragmentation of welfare* (pp. 187–203). London, UK: Routledge.
Barber, M., Donnelly, K., & Rizvi, S. (2012). *Oceans of innovation: The Atlantic, the Pacific, global leadership and the future of education.* London, UK: The Institute for Public Policy Research.
Barnett, R., Parry, G., & Coate, K. (2001). Conceptualising curriculum change. *Teaching in Higher Education, 6*(4), 435–449.

Brauckmann, S., & Pashiardis, P. (2010). The clash of evaluations: In search of the missing link between school accountability and school improvement – Experiences from Cyprus. *International Journal of Educational Management, 24*(4), 330–350.

Bryk, A. S., & Schneider, B. (2003). Trust in schools: A core resource for school reform. *Educational Leadership, 60*(6), 40–45.

Chan, K. K. (2008). *Curriculum reform: Building on strengths for continuous intensification*. Hong Kong, China: Education Bureau.

Cheng, K. M. (2002). Reinventing the wheel: Educational reform. In S. K. Lau (Ed.), *The first Tung Chee-hwa administration: The first five years of the Hong Kong special administrative region* (pp. 157–174). Hong Kong, China: The Chinese University Press.

Cheng, Y. C. (2009). Hong Kong educational reforms in the last decade: Reform syndrome and new developments. *International Journal of Educational Management, 23*(1), 65–86.

The Committee on Teachers' Work. (2006). *Final report*. Hong Kong: Education and Manpower Bureau.

Curriculum Development Council. (2001). *Learning to learn: The way forward in curriculum*. Hong Kong, China: Author.

Curriculum Development Council. (2009). *Senior secondary curriculum guide – The future is now: From vision to realisation (Secondary 4–6)*. Hong Kong, China: Government Logistics Department.

Curriculum Development Council, Hong Kong Examinations and Assessment Authority, and Education Bureau. (2013). *The new senior secondary learning journey – Moving forward to excel*. Hong Kong, China: Education Bureau.

Education Bureau. (2013). *Progress report on the new academic structure review the new senior secondary learning journey – moving forward to excel*. Hong Kong, China: Author. Retrieved from http://334.edb.hkedcity.net/doc/eng/Full Report.pdf

Education Bureau. (2015). *Applied learning*. Retrieved from http://www.edb.gov.hk/en/curriculum-development/cross-kla-studies/applied-learning/index-1.html

Education Commission. (2000). *Learning for life, learning through life: Reform proposals for the education system in Hong Kong*. Hong Kong, China: Author.

Education Commission. (2003). *Progress report on the education reform (2)*. Hong Kong, China: Author.

Education Commission. (2004). *Progress report on the education reform (3)*. Hong Kong, China: Author.

Education Commission. (2006). *Progress report on the education reform (4)*. Hong Kong, China: Author.

Education and Manpower Bureau. (2005). *The new academic structure for senior secondary education and higher education – Action plan for investing in the future of Hong Kong*. Hong Kong, China: Author.

Education and Manpower Bureau. (2006). *The Committee on teachers' work final report*. Hong Kong, China: Author. Retrieved from http://www.legco.gov.hk/yr06-07/english/panels/ed/papers/ed0212cb2-1041-6-e.pdf

Education and Manpower Branch & Education Department. (1991). *The school management initiative: Setting the framework for quality in Hong Kong schools*. Hong Kong: Government Printer.

Fullan, M. (2010). *All systems go: The change imperative for whole system reform*. Thousand Oaks, CA: Corwin.

Hargreaves, A., & Shirley, D. (2009). *The fourth way: The inspiring future for educational change*. Thousand Oaks, CA: Corwin Press.
Hattie, J. A. C. (2009). *Visible learning: A synthesis of over 800 meta-analyses relating to achievement*. London, UK: Routledge.
He, R., & Lu, N. (2010). An analysis of the issues of educational quality and equality of Hong Kong and East Asian societies from a perspective of international evaluation plan [in Chinese]. *Educational Research, 1*, 75–82. [note: The first author same as Ho, S. C., just different in transliterations].
HKPISA Centre. (2008). *The third HKPISA report: PISA 2006*. Hong Kong, China: Author.
Lam, C. C. (1997). *The design and implementation of Target Oriented Curriculum* [in Chinese]. Hong Kong, China: Cosmos.
Lam, C. C. (2002). Is integrated curriculum really better than discipline-based curriculum? [in Chinese]. *Curriculum and Instruction Quarterly, 5*(4), 141–154.
Lam, C. C. (2003). The romance and reality of policy-making and implementation: A case study of the Target-Oriented Curriculum in Hong Kong. *Journal of Education Policy, 18*(6), 641–655.
Lam, C. C. (2014). The role of quality assurance system in the implementation of curriculum reform. In C. Marsh & J. C. K. Lee (Eds.), *Asia's high performing education systems: The case of Hong Kong* (pp. 307–319). New York, NY: Routledge.
Lam, C. C., Li, L., & Yu, Y. C. (in press). How should educational reform in Hong Kong develop in the future? [in Chinese]. *Education Research*.
Lam, C. C., & Tang, W. Z. (2014). The quality and quantity of homework in Hong Kong primary schools: An indicator of curriculum reform implementation [in Chinese]. *Journal of Curriculum Studies, 9*(1), 33–64.
Lee, W. O. (1996). The cultural context for Chinese learners: Conceptions of learning in the Confucian tradition. In D. Watkins & J. Biggs (Eds.), *The Chinese learner: Cultural, psychological and contextual influences* (pp. 25–41). Hong Kong: Comparative Education Research Centre; Melbourne: Australia Council for Educational Research.
Legislative Council Panel on Education. (2014, December 8). *The registration of HKDSE examination of various subjects*. Legislative Council Paper No. CB(4)210/14–15(04).
Lin, Z., & Zhang, S. (2006). An analysis of the curriculum reform implementation strategies in Hong Kong [in Chinese]. *Exploring Education Development, 12A*, 8–13.
Mok, M. M. C. (2007). Quality assurance and school monitoring in Hong Kong. *Educational Research for Policy and Practice, 6*(3), 187–204.
Mok, M. M. C., Gurr, D., Izawa, E., Knipprath, H., Lee, I. H., Mel, M. A., & Zhang, Y. M. (2003). Quality assurance and school monitoring. In J. P. Keeves & R. Watanabe (Eds.), *International handbook of educational research in the Asia-Pacific region* (pp. 945–958). Dordrecht, the Netherlands: Kluwer Academic.
Morris, P. (1996). *The Hong Kong school curriculum: Development, issues and policies (Second edition)*. Hong Kong: Hong Kong University Press.
Mullis, I. V. S., Martin, M. O., Foy, P., & Drucker, K. T. (2012). *PIRLS 2011 international results in reading*. Chestnut Hill, MA: TIMSS & PIRLS International Study Center, Boston College.
Ng, P. T., & Chan, D. (2008). A comparative study of Singapore's school excellence model with Hong Kong's school-based management. *International Journal of Educational Management, 22*(6), 488–505.

Strategic Planning Office, Hong Kong Institute of Education. (2011). *Report on the workload of teachers in Hong Kong primary and secondary schools.* Hong Kong, China: Author.

Tang, C. K., & Morris, P. (1989). The abuse of educational evaluation: A study of the evaluation of the implementation of the civic education "guidelines". *Educational Research Journal, 4,* 41–49.

Wong, N. Y. (2004). The CHC learner's phenomenon: Its implications on mathematics education. In L. Fan, N. Y. Wong, J. Cai & S. Li (Eds.), *How Chinese learn mathematics: Perspectives from insiders* (pp. 503–534). Singapore: World Scientific.

Wong, N. Y., Han, J. W., & Lee, P. Y. (2004). The mathematics curriculum: Toward globalization or Westernization? In L. Fan, N. Y. Wong, J. Cai & S. Li (Eds.), *How Chinese learn mathematics: Perspectives from insiders* (pp. 27–70). Singapore: World Scientific.

Wong, N. Y., Lam, C. C., & Chan, A. M. Y. (2009). Is basic competence still basic? [in Chinese]. *EduMath, 28,* 2–9.

Wong, N. Y., & Tang, K. C. (2012). Mathematics education in Hong Kong under colonial rule. *BSHM Bulletin: Journal of the British Society for the History of Mathematics, 27*(2), 119–125.

Yeung, S. S. Y. (2010). Using school evaluation policy to effect curriculum change? A reflection on the SSE and ESR exercise in Hong Kong. *Educational Research Journal, 25*(2), 187–209.

# 8 Civic education in Hong Kong

From the colonial era to the post-occupy movement era

*Yan-Wing Leung, Eric King-Man Chong, and Timothy Wai-Wa Yuen*

## Introduction

As pointed out in the previous chapters, after the return of sovereignty to China, Hong Kong became a SAR of the People's Republic of China in 1997, and a string of education reforms were introduced to improve the quality of education, by the first chief executive, Tung Chee-Hwa. The preparative work for the education reform started before 1997, and the reform blueprint was released in September 2000 by the Education Commission. It embraces a wide range of critical issues, including the focus of this chapter, civic education (used interchangeably with moral, national and civic education later). The education reform was triggered by two major challenges – first, the challenges from the emergence of a competitive, knowledge-based economy arising from globalisation, and second, the changing local political, social and economic contexts caused by the change of sovereignty. In addressing the first group of challenges, the HKSAR government introduced reform measures to nurture students to become competitive in the knowledge-based economy. In addressing the second sets of challenges, the HKSAR government was enthusiastic to demonstrate its strong determination and ability to bring about sustainable social developments to show that under the policy of "One Country, Two Systems", Hong Kong would be governed more effectively and efficiently than under the colonial administration.

In the education reform, two conflicting concerns about the changing role of government in education were identified. In response to the globalisation issue, the HKSAR government intends to allow individual schools and education institutions greater autonomy in exchange for accountability, efficiency, responsiveness and responsibility (Whitty, 2002). In addressing the changing local contextual issue, there is a growing intention for the government to be more interventions in some areas of education, especially in civic and national education (Scott, 2005).

Even though there has been a consensus that education should be a priority of public policy and reform, there have been inevitable controversies over what and how reforms should be proposed and implemented. It is difficult to have the interests of diverse stakeholders being well taken care of or even compromised. This is particularly valid and sensitive in the case of civic education, which is never neutral or ideologically free, with character dependent on the world-view in which it is embedded (Howard & Patten, 2006). The type of civic education demanded by the central government in Beijing, with very strong focus on patriotism, is so much different from that expected from the civil society of Hong Kong, with focus on education for democracy, human rights and social justice (Chong, Yuen, & Leung, 2015). This great and uncompromising difference in the expectation of the central and HKSAR governments and the local civil society are part of the reasons paving the road to the two massive social movements to be detailed later.

In this chapter, we start with sketching the relationship between civic and national education with the education reform. Then we review the general context of Hong Kong related to the development of civic education, followed by four stages with reference to the major policy documents, before the Anti-National Education Movement. Particular attention has been drawn to the re-depoliticizing effect on civic education and the request for strengthening of national education. The third section focuses on the Anti-National Education Movement, the causes, processes, impacts and results. It also discusses briefly the type of civic education proposed by the *Civic Education Guidelines from Civil Society* published in 2012, as a response from the local civil society. The fourth session focuses on exploring some of the issues and factors triggered by the Occupy Movement, and the underpinning rationales, that may influence the future development of civic education within the context of increasing tension between the government and civil society. The last section ends the chapter by first concluding that Hong Kong needs a version of civic education of its own, which helps to sustain its uniqueness and contribute to the nation as a special administrative region under the policy of "One Country, Two Systems", and second recommending some concrete suggestions that help in addressing the identified issues and sustaining its uniqueness.

## Civic education in the Hong Kong context

Before the handover, Hong Kong had already developed into an international city in both the economic and civic sense. The Western notions of democracy, human rights, role of civil society and understanding of the state have long taken root and blossomed from a more humanistic and right-respecting attitude in the later part of the colonial rule, together with the upholding of the rule of law, the eradication of corruption, the open nature of the society with free access to information and a Western-style education. The relative progress and the achievement of stability and prosperity in the later part of its colonial history further strengthened Hong Kongers' beliefs about such social institution and civic values. Since Hong Kong's uniqueness contrasted starkly with the socialist system upheld in Mainland China, the reunification was achieved under the principle of "One Country, Two Systems", which allowed Hong Kong to retain her capitalist economic structure and the existing way of living. Apart from defence and foreign affairs, Hong Kong is to practise self-rule, with a high degree of autonomy, detailed in the *Basic Law*, the mini-constitution of Hong Kong.

Nevertheless, both before and after 1997, the government of Hong Kong has treated Hong Kong as an apolitical city. Regardless of the granting of substantial civil and social rights, political rights and an empowering, active mode of citizenship was denied to Hong Kong citizens. Though the scenario of political participation has improved, since the signing of the Sino-British Joint Declaration in 1984 on the transfer of sovereignty in 1997 (Fairbrother, 2005), Ghai (2001) claimed that the *Hong Kong Basic Law* has laid down a political structure with a restricted franchise, hindering the development of an active and participatory citizenship. Unfortunately, the "restricted franchise" has become the core issue resulting in the outbreak of the massive Occupy Movement in 2014. However, this minimal participatory citizenship fits the expectation of both the HKSAR and the PRC governments of keeping Hong Kong as an apolitical, commercial Chinese city (Vickers & Kan, 2003). Nonetheless, regardless of the government's intention to depoliticize Hong Kong, Hong Kong has a vibrant civil society, where dissenting voices are heard and participation is encouraged (Leung, Yuen, & Leung, 2011).

Civic education can broadly be understood as the education required to nurture "good citizens". Citizens are defined as "members of political communities, with legally conferred rights and responsibilities, associated identities and participation" (Delanty, 2000; Oldfield, 1990), with the political communities referring to multiple levels, comprising local, national, regional and global communities (Heater, 1990). The core of civic education is political education, as it defines the relationship between a citizen and the political communities. But the attributes of 'good citizens' are often controversial. Westheimer and Kahne (2004) argued that civic education programmes are about "what good citizenship is" and "what good citizens do", and the anticipated characteristics of "good citizens" and "good society" determine the orientations of the associated civic education programmes. However, in reality, civic education, with conservative ideologies, has always been used as means by the government to minimise the intention of people in political participation, so as to preserve the status quo (Leung, Yuen, & Ngai, 2014). This is particularly relevant to the civic education in Hong Kong as the central government always preferred Hong Kong to remain an apolitical commercial city.

Civic education in Hong Kong has been shaped by its own colonial history and socio-economic and political development on the one hand; and the political development and foreign policies in China on the other. Generally speaking, because of the pragmatic nature of Hong Kong education, with great emphasis on academic knowledge and examinations, civic education is only reactive and remedial in addressing short-term civic issues and seldom used for enhancing participation (Fairbrother & Kennedy, 2011; Leung & Yuen, 2012). Its development can be divided into several stages (Leung, Yuen, & Ngai, 2014; Morris, Kan, & Morris, 2000). Since this chapter focuses on the development in post-1997 era, the pre-1997 stages are only briefly discussed.

## Stage one (from World War II to mid-1980s): Depoliticization by the state and schools

From the end of World War II to the mid-1960s, the government depoliticized education in order to counteract threats to its legitimacy and to preserve the stability by empowering the director of education to control school subjects, textbooks, teaching materials and political activities in schools (Morris & Chan, 1997). Hence, civic education in Hong Kong, particularly the political part of it, sank into a dormant stage till the 1980s, resulting in apolitical and docile people who were conservative, and would avoid any form of political participation but worked hard to earn a decent living.

## Stage two (mid-1980s–1997): The politicisation of the intended curriculum

Against the impending transfer of sovereignty of Hong Kong to the PRC, representative government began to develop. From an interventionist perspective, the Hong Kong government published the *Guidelines on Civic Education in Schools* in 1985 (CDC, 1985) (hereafter *1985 Guidelines*) and 1996 (CDC, 1996) (hereafter *1996 Guidelines*) to help students to face the forthcoming legal and political changes. The intervention could be considered as mild because schools were delegated with the power to decide how to implement it based on their school context. The *1985 Guidelines* was described as conservative, advocating a type of citizens who accept and conform to a traditionally established way of life, while the *1996 Guidelines* was described as more liberal, aiming at nurturing "good citizens" with the knowledge, values and dispositions to participate actively in communities at different levels with a critical mind (Leung, Chai-Yip, and Ng, 2000). This was considered as an important breakthrough as the study of previously sensitive and forbidden materials, including social and political aspects of the PRC, was then allowed (Morris & Chan, 1997).

## Stage three (1997–2008): Re-depoliticization of civic education and official affirmation of national education

Dissatisfied with the insufficient attention given to national identity in the previous civic education guidelines in the colonial era, under the new round of education reform led by Tung, the SAR government issued a few education documents containing guiding principles for moral and civic education, with particular emphasis on the cultivation of national identity. The document *Learning to Learn: The Way Forward in Curriculum Development* (CDC, 2001) tried to re-depoliticize civic education again by integrating civic education with sex education, religious education, ethics and health living, and minimising the political content (Leung & Ng, 2004). Five paramount values including national identity (with emphasis on cultural identity), a positive spirit, perseverance, respect for others and commitment to society and nation are proposed in the main text, while values like human rights and democracy are marginalised to the appendix. At the same time, national education, with emphasis on the achievements of the PRC and avoidance of her politics, is being promoted with the aim of cultivating national identity and patriotism in an apolitical sense. This document gives an impression that the government aims to nurture "uncritical and depoliticized patriots", who are in line with the expectation of the government to keep Hong Kong as an apolitical, commercial and financial city (Tse, 2007; Vickers & Kan, 2003). Though the current intervention instrument remained school-based, unlike the previous interventions in 1985 and 1996, schools were strongly supported with resources from the government and NGOs to implement school-based national education activities.

### Stage four (2009 onward): Civic education through liberal studies

As part of the educational reform, aiming mainly at equipping youth to face the competitive knowledge-based global economy, a new compulsory subject for senior secondary students (S4-S6), Liberal Studies (LS), was introduced in September 2009. The subject aims at enabling students to understand the contemporary world and its pluralistic nature by helping them to make connexions among different disciplines, examining issues from a variety of perspectives and constructing personal knowledge of immediate relevance to themselves in today's world (CDC, 2007).

Although the overall education reform aims mainly at addressing global economic competitions, LS was also assigned a task of nurturing citizenship and was described as a potential vehicle for civic education (Leung & Yuen, 2009). It allows for the first time all senior secondary students to study explicitly topics of political knowledge and recommended pedagogies emphasising students' construction of knowledge, with learning and teaching structured around enquiry into contemporary and perennial issues, supported by experiential learning and involving non-governmental organisations (CDC, 2007). These characteristics are useful for the cultivation of informed, rational and active citizens (Boehnke & Boehnke, 2005; Finkel, 2003). This might be considered as a stronger intervention as the subject is mandatory. However, parallel with the development of LS, there is always a strong force pressing for the strengthening of national identity through national education. Although much policy and resources input have been channelled to national education from the government, it is still considered by the PRC government as unsatisfactory. Hence, came a much stronger intervention (Leung & Ngai, 2011; Tse 2007).

## The anti-national education movement

In fact, the emphasis on national identity has increasingly influenced school education since 1997 (Yuen & Byram, 2007). Following the visit of then President of PRC, Hu Jintao, to the tenth anniversary of HKSAR in 2007, proclaiming that there was a need to enhance national education in Hong Kong schools, then Chief Executive Donald Tsang had officially endorsed the need to strengthen national education in Hong Kong primary and secondary schools in his *Policy Address 2008 and 2009* respectively (Chong, 2013). Because of this strong intervention from the central government, resources and support in the forms of teaching plans, subsidised study tours to China, and various celebrative programmes in regard to Chinese history, culture, economic, sports and aerospace technology achievements are provided by the Education Bureau to the schools.

The policy of strengthening national identity through national education culminated in a government's proposal of a mandatory curriculum of Moral and National Education (MNE) for all schools (CDC, 2012). This official national intention, however, was met with massive protests and demonstrations in 2012 with the alleged claims that this MNE curriculum may lead to "indoctrination". The discontent and public outcry was intensified by the discovery of biased and misleading government subsidised teaching resource and organised visits to the Chinese Mainland, aiming only at presenting a positive picture of China to the students (Ngai, Leung, & Yuen, 2014). In addition, it was also criticised as too much inclined towards arousing students' emotion without paying sufficient attention to the possible abuse of affective education (Leung, 2003; Leung & Lo, 2012). Also, critics argued that national citizenship is just one aspect of multiple citizenship and cannot be used to replace civic education (Leung, 2012). As the pressure of Anti-National Education Movement built up in the summer 2012 and continued at the beginning of school year of 2012/13, Chief Executive C.Y. Leung was forced reluctantly to shelve the proposal, and most schools reverted to the original practice of school-based civic education, a shift from strong and mandatory intervention to weak and school-based intervention.

The impacts of the movement are many. First of all, it had the effect of further strengthening Hong Kong youth's political awareness and their eagerness to participate politically (Leung, Yuen, & Ngai, 2014). They felt that they should participate in the civic affairs that affect their lives with responsibility (Haste & Hogan, 2006), as evidenced in their subsequent participation in other social movements.

Second, the movement has alerted the civil society on the guard against indoctrination, which will suppress willfully the development of students' critical disposition (Spiecker & Straughan, 1991). This awareness has enhanced the call for developing critical thinking as an important aim of civic education. Along similar line of argument, the idea of "critical patriots" was proposed as a counter proposal to the official version of blind love (Fairbrother, 2003; Leung, 2007). Third, the movement has demonstrated that with concerted efforts, the vibrant civil society was able to exert significant impacts on the government's policy decisions even against a tough stance taken by the government.

Last, the movement has given birth to the *Civic Education Guidelines from Civil Society* (Leung et al., 2012) published by the Alliance for Civic Education (an NGO on civic education) in 2012 in response to the reversion to school-based civic education (hereafter *Guidelines 2012*). It was distributed to all Hong Kong secondary schools for reference in designing their school-based civic education. The *Guidelines 2012* proposes that civic education in Hong Kong has to be reconstructed both in conceptual, curricular, and pedagogical terms (Chong, Yuen, & Leung 2015). It reclaimed the "civic mission of schools" (Battistoni et al., 2003; Gould et al., 2011), calling for the cultivation of politically-literate, critically-thinking and actively-participating citizens, who are willing and competent to uphold universal core values such as democracy, human rights, rule of law, social justice, respect for diversity, etc., in different levels of political communities. It suggests that political education should be the core of civic education so as to rectify the depoliticized scenario in Hong Kong. It also recommends that time slots for civic education should be built in the timetable and teaching and learning strategies that minimise indoctrination and enhance critical thinking should be adopted, for example, teaching of controversial issues in an open classroom ethos (Hahn, 1998; Hess, 2001).

After the anti-national education movement in 2012, there came another massive civil society's movement – the Occupy Movement that significantly challenged the authority of the HKSAR government, and it has caused a huge media impact across the world. Under the political climate of central government's campaign to tighten control over China's most freewheeling city of Hong Kong (Torode, Pomfret, & Lim, 2014), and in the high tide of controversies over electoral reforms for the 2017 chief executive election, the Occupy Movement broke out in the autumn of 2014.

## The occupy movement and the development of civic education

The Occupy Movement is a sit-in protest in Hong Kong involving mass civil disobedience that began in September 2014. Also widely known as the Umbrella Movement, the protest began after the National People's Congress Standing Committee (NPCSC) came to a decision regarding proposed reforms to the Hong Kong electoral system, which was widely seen to be highly restrictive against the democratic development of Hong Kong. University and secondary school students led a strike against the decision beginning on 22 September 2014. Demonstrations began outside the HKSAR government headquarters, and occupied a few major city intersections, including Admiralty, Causeway Bay and Mong Kok. They remained closed to traffic for 79 days until December 2014 (Wikipedia, 2014). The comments on the Occupy Movement are controversial. If it is evaluated against the objective of overturning the decision of the NPCSC on universal suffrage, the movement might be considered as a failure, as the decision remained the same. However, the movement precipitated a rift in Hong Kong society, and galvanised youth – a previously apolitical section of society – into political activism or heightened awareness of their civil rights and responsibilities. However, why did so many youths get involved in the movement?

Drawing upon the data collected before the outbreak of the movement, a government-sponsored study (CPU, 2015) commented that many of the young people who are critical of the government (named as "dissidents" in the study), were prompted by "positive" beliefs and values about themselves, the society and the polity, including the idea of democracy. This echoed with what the financial secretary, John Tsang, commented in *2015–16 Budget*: ". . . behind and beyond material fulfilment, the people of this city, our younger generations in particular, are hungering for spiritual contentment" (Tsang, 2015, 48, Paragraph 178). This pursuit after post-materialist values is termed a "spiritual contentment" in Tsang's speech, which seems to be a shared phenomenon among youths in democratic societies across the globe (Saha, 2000). Nevertheless, what exactly has triggered the "dissidents" to participate in the massive civil disobedient movement?

Ironically, before and during the onset of the Occupy Movement, LS, the innovative subject strongly supported by the government in the education reform, was seriously accused by the pro-establishment supporters of arousing students' interest to participate in the Occupy Movement. Different requests have been suggested to curtail the subject contents linked to local politics, and these requests aroused many debates on the nature and functions of the subject. Though we agree with the argument that the protests had galvanised young people into political activism or heightened awareness of their civil rights and responsibilities, we have reservation that LS has a direct activating effect on the youths (Leung & Guo, 2014). Similarly, Cummingham and Lavalette (2004) had pointed out that there was little connexion between strikes and civic education as taught in schools. However, we are well aware of the warning raised by Porter (1993) that on one hand we are excited to learn that apolitical youth had developed into political activism, and on the other hand, we are worried that without an appropriate political education for cultivating civic virtues or democratic culture, this may develop into populist movement, unhealthy to the democratic development in Hong Kong. Uncritical advocacy for participation without civic knowledge may be dangerous (Ainley & Schulz, 2011; Cohen & Chaffee, 2013).

Looking ahead, probably how will and should civic education be developed after the Occupy Movement? On one hand, because of the enhanced political awareness, sense of local identity and sense of pursuing for autonomy in public affairs, the youths may have developed various views on democratic development of Hong Kong and hence affecting the development of civic education ahead. Meanwhile, with the outbreak of the two massive social movements, the pressure of intervention into civic education from the central government has been strengthened. Before and during the Occupy Movement, the central government had repeatedly requested Hong Kong people to be re-educated with a better understanding of "One Country, two Systems" policy and the Basic Law, as they attributed the movement was partially caused by the misunderstanding of the Basic Law by Hong Kong people, with too much emphasis on the "Two Systems" perspective than that of "One Country" (Ong, 2015). This intervention gave rise to rigorous debates and controversies, which led to increasing tension between the government and civil society. In the following discussion, we shall explore seven issues triggered by the social movements that may influence the future development of civic education within the context of increasing tension between the government and civil society.

### *Issue 1: The importance of political literacy*

Although we argue that LS has not triggered the students to demonstrations, we contest that LS has provided students with background information about the social and political systems of Hong Kong. The LS subject can arouse students' awareness of the important social and political issues and different views and perspectives on the issues. LS can also provide students with basic concepts, knowledge and values as analytical tools for examining the issues making their own judgement (Yuen, Leung, & Lu, in press).

As pointed out by Haste and Hogan (2006), social movement activity is always a response to issues that are perceived as personally relevant and entailing personal responsibility. After the NPCSC's resolution on a restrictive nomination scheme of the chief executive election in 2017 was announced on 31 August 2014, this significant issue was immediately taken up for teaching and learning in some LS lessons in secondary schools. Some students compared the proposal with Article 25 of the *International Covenant on Civil and Political Rights* and came up with an academic judgement that the decision did not meet the three criteria of a "genuine universal suffrage": "equal rights to vote, equal right to stand for election, equal right to nominate". It is clear that without enriched political literacy, students could not have the competence in analysing the issues comprehensively and came up with their own judgements. As Hong Kong is developing its own democratic system, politically-literate citizens are becoming more and more important.

## *Issue 2: Morality and political action*

Accompanying the academic judgement, some students might have also made a moral judgement on the political issue that the decision was political unjust because in their views, not only a "false universal suffrage" has been imposed on Hong Kong people, they felt that the NPCSC had completely denied the wish of Hong Kong citizens to have a genuine universal suffrage in the past many years. Moved by the moral claim or moral conviction on a political arena (Nussbaum, 1999; Skitka & Mullen, 2002), some students might feel moral passion of upset and even anger, which further motivated them to take political action and participate in the Occupy Movement. Some even argued that it is their moral obligation and personal responsibility to be engaged (Haste & Hogan, 2006; Ngo, 2015; Skitka & Bauman, 2008), as reflected from the slogan, "living in an era of confusion, we should have a sense of obligation", which has become popular among the dissident youth in the movement. As the political system develops, students are anticipated to be facing similar decision-making more frequently.

## *Issue 3: Civil disobedience*

The Occupy Movement, by intention, is an act of non-violent civil disobedience with love and peace (Tai, 2013). Though acts of civil disobedience are bound to be illegal and against the law, they are becoming more and more common in youth political participation across the globe (Saha, 2000). However, in reality, violence of various degrees broke out in the Occupy Movement. During the movement, most members of the two oppositional camps held strong moral convictions for their own beliefs and ideologies. Unfortunately, some members of both camps showed intolerant behaviours to members of the opposition camp, and this occasionally led to conflicts and violence of various degrees. Though the small number of non-peaceful protectors defended their acts by arguing that their mild physical violence was triggered by structural violence of the system (Galtung, 1990), their behaviours were considered by many as unacceptable (*Hong Kong Economic Journal*, July 31, 2015; Wong, 2010).

Moreover, in the movement some protestors were not willing to compromise even on non-principled issues, such as strategies and forms of actions. Unfortunately these uncompromising attitudes and actions were reinforced by the unwillingness of the central government to allow space of negotiation (Fong, 2015). Though we understand that the unwillingness of the central government might have reinforced the youth's uncompromising attitudes and actions, we are worried that the uncompromising attitudes and actions, particularly those involving physical violence, may become the seed of populist movement.

### *Issue 4: Competing civic identities*

The dual civic identities, national (Chinese) identity and local (Hong Kongers) identity of the Hong Kong people, have always been competing with each other, especially when the national identity is perceived as suppressing the local identity (Leung & Ngai, 2011). The NPCSC's resolution was perceived by many Hong Kong people as a serious threat to their political rights and local identity. The threatened local identity bounded back and became exclusive, counteracting the perceived threatening national identity. This exclusive local identity is further reinforced and consolidated by other recent events, such as the issue of "parallel goods traders" and some local narratives, resulting in a strong sense of detachment and separation from China (Chan, 2012). For example, Kwong and Ho (2015) argued that Hong Kong should be considered as a self-governing political community and should set boundary controls to protect Hong Kong from the mainland. We contest that this exclusive nature of local identity, particularly those with violence, may buttress the development of the populist movement.

### *Issue 5: Social media*

In the Occupy Movement and many previous protests and demonstrations, social media has helped to mobilise youths to participate. But whether they walked out after thoughtful consideration of the political conversation in the social media or were simply emotionally influenced by like-minded people, as an echo chamber in the social media, is both an issue and a worry that should be attended to (Andersson, 2012; Dahlgren, 2007; Lo, 2015).

### *Issue 6: A sense of empowerment or disempowerment*

During the Occupy Movement, some participants, especially students, felt empowered, as they thought they had a strong sense of autonomy in influencing political decisions affecting Hong Kong and they may wish to be more engaged in daily life politics. However, on the other hand, many more young people felt frustrated, powerless, hopeless and lost, especially after the movement was over and the occupied sites were cleared because apparently it seemed that nothing had changed.

*Issue 7: Intervention from the government*

As discussed, the central government has accused that misunderstanding in the *Basic Law* is the cause of the Occupy Movement. In 2013, *The Practice of the "One Country, Two Systems" Policy in the Hong Kong Special Administrative Region* was published by the State Council of the PRC to re-interpret the *Basic Law* from the "One Country" perspective so as to rectify the perceived misunderstandings among the Hong Kong people (Information Office of the State Council, PRC, 2014). In June 2015, teaching materials based on the State Council's document were published for schools. This caused hot debates and controversies in civil society because the documents were considered as suppressing the "the two system" and violating the policy of "One Country, Two Systems". The education community is particularly sensitive to the teaching materials as it may lead to indoctrination similar to what had happened in the Anti-National Education Movement (Cheung, 2015).

In the following discussion, we shall recommend some ideas for the planning of civic education ahead, which may be useful for addressing the above issues and sustaining the uniqueness of Hong Kong. However, since the Occupy Movement was a recent, significant and powerful social event, with on-going impacts, the following recommendations should be considered as preliminary scratch of pilot, exploratory ideas that have to be evaluated by future research.

## Policy recommendations and conclusion

The development of civic education in Hong Kong is intertwined with and framed by her political history – colonial rule, reunification with China, and the experimental implementation of "One Country, Two Systems". As explained in the previous sections, the concern of the British colonial regime for maintaining governability in view of its own lack of legitimacy led to depoliticisation of civic education and playing down of any form of national identity discussion. When sovereignty over Hong Kong reverted to the People's Republic of China, the new ruling elite in Hong Kong, whether under pressure from the central government or by its own initiative, would like to press forward national education for fostering a sense of national identity which is important in buttressing unity now that Hong Kong has become a part of China and to maintain a high degree of autonomy with her own unique socio-economic system. However, because of the uniqueness of Hong Kong that it has long been a cosmopolitan city, embracing universal core values and practices, including freedom, human rights, democracy, justice, rule of law, etc., the attempt to implement national education was much resisted. People perceived that the proposed national education was based on a model akin to indoctrination, which is contradictory to an education that respects the individual right of independent thinking and plurality of ideas.

The aspiration for a democratic form of government is understandable not just because of the social beliefs Hong Kongers shared but also because of the stipulations in the *Basic Law* that there will be universal suffrage for both the Chief Executive and the Legislative Council. This helped to explain the frustration and disappointment a lot of people shared when a more restrictive form of election was imposed. Youths and students became the backbone of the Occupy Movement. For the majority of protestors who could insist on peaceful demonstration, the movement in principle could be a way that they communicated their political demand to the ruling elite and the central government. But in reality, violence and other uncivilised behaviours broke out. The inability to draw a hard and fast line with those protestors who chose not to be peaceful and not to demonstrate the civility that civil disobedience normally requires unfortunately tarnished the course of the movement somehow.

Last, we contend that the most severe challenge ahead of civic education teachers in Hong Kong is, in face of more interventions from the central government, what and how we are going to prepare Hong Kong youths to face 2047, the year when the policy of "One Country, Two Systems" ends, and safeguard the core values of Hong Kong, including freedom, human rights, democracy and justice. We believe that whilst the ruling elite and the Chinese government should be more responsive to the political aspiration of the Hong Kong people, civic education should be strengthened to help implement and sustain the "One Country, Two Systems" policy in Hong Kong beyond 2047. Hong Kong needs a version of civic education of its own that fits its uniqueness, as a cosmopolitan city embracing universal core values and practices, which are invaluable asset to both Hong Kong and China. We argue that the issues of concern identified above are highly relevant to the building and consolidation of Hong Kong's uniqueness and would like to make some tentative, concrete suggestions, addressing the issues as discussed in the previous section for further deliberation.

*Addressing issues 1 and 2.* In order to equip students to become competent in making informed, independent moral judgement and decision on political issues, and on whether they should take action, civic education should on one hand strengthen political education as its core, so that students could be better equipped with the necessary political knowledge, concepts, values and competence. On the other hand, they should also be equipped with relevant knowledge and competence in making moral decisions, including the relationship between morality and politics, approaches of making moral decisions, and so on (Chow, 2014; Sandel, 2009). More liberal and critical forms of civic education, for example, civic education with critical pedagogy, human rights education and social justice education, should be explored in addition to the common conservative practices (Leung, 2008).

*Addressing issue 3.* Political education should be strengthened to nurture citizens with civic qualities or democratic personalities so as to prevent the enhanced youth political activism from developing into a populist movement. Students should be educated that though they have the right to hold fast to their moral/political convictions, they should uphold civic virtues/democratic personality such as open mindedness, respecting reasoning and respecting views from different ideologies at the same time. In addressing the issue of "unwillingness to compromise", the democratic personality, "willingness to compromise", compromise in forms and strategies without giving up core principles and values by Cohen (1971) is highly relevant. In addressing the issue of violence, they have to learn about the nature and forms of violence, such as physical violence, structural violence, cultural violence and peaceful resolution of conflicts.

*Addressing issue 4.* Though we understand that identity is a personal choice and it is legitimate for Hong Kong's people to focus on local identity and issues (Fong, 2015), we contest that in an age of globalisation, it is more appropriate for Hong Kong's citizens to hold fast to their Hong Kong identity and related core values and on the other hand, to develop inclusive, multiple citizenship identities, because single, simplistic loyalty may easily lead to exclusion and suppression of other identities (Heater, 1990). Second, it is impractical for Hong Kong to be separated from China, simply because Hong Kong does not have sufficient resources to survive alone. Therefore, we suggest that civic education should discuss ideas such as identity politics, inclusive and exclusive nature of identities, multiple citizenships and critical patriotism with students so that they are better prepared to make informed decisions on the issues related to identities, in an open, tolerant and inclusive manner.

*Addressing issue 5.* Civic education teachers have to be equipped with competence to engage students in in-depth democratic deliberation in the social media, so as to enhance the positive impacts and minimise negative impacts of the social media.

*Addressing issue 6.* Civic education teachers should help in the re-building of hopes and empowerment in students through encouraging active participation of students in school governance. Students should be treated as here and now citizenship and allowed to take part in the decision-making processes of significant school matters. Through the active participatory experiences and associated critical reflection, students could regain hopes, a sense of autonomy and be empowered (Leung et al., 2014; McQuillan, 2005).

*Addressing issue 7.* In addressing to this potential indoctrinatory issue by the government, civic education teachers have to be more sensitive to the content of the teaching materials and textbooks, no matter where they come from. They should be critically aware of whether different perspectives and interpretations of the controversial issues related to "One Country, Two Systems", and *Basic Laws* are fairly presented, to prevent biased presentations of political information, so as to minimise the danger of indoctrination.

In conclusion, teachers' ideologies and values will affect how they interpret and take their stands in the issues. However, as professional teachers, the paramount principle is that civic education teachers should hold fast to their professional obligation to ensure that students are taught impartially, though it is their right to hold fast to and share their own ideologies and values (Huddleston, 2003). In the learning of controversial issues, students should be exposed to different perspectives, together with rationales. They should be encouraged to make informed decisions based on comprehensive and in-depth understandings of the issues and context, and to be responsible for the decision they made. Civic education teachers, as professionals, should protect our students from being indoctrinated by different parties, and nurture them to become informed and active citizens who are equipped with critical thinking skills. In a nutshell, civic education teachers should be competent in managing their ideological selves by their professional selves in performing their professional duties. With the concerted efforts of civic education teachers, perhaps we may be able to equip our youths with necessary knowledge, values and competence to face the challenges of 2047.

## References

Ainley, J., & Schulz, W. (2011, April 8–12). Expected participation in protest activities among lower secondary students in 38 countries. In *Annual Meetings of the American Educational Research Association in New Orleans*.

Andersson, E. (2012). The political voice of young citizens: Educational conditions for political conversation- school and social media. *Utbildning & Demokrati, 21*(1), 97–119.

Carnegie Corporation of New York and CIRCLE (2003). *The civic mission of schools*. New York: CIRCLE and Carnegie Corporation of New York. Retrieved from http://civicyouth.org/PopUps/CivicMissionofSchools.pdf

Boehnke, K., & Boehnke, M. (2005). Once a peacenik- always a peacenik? Results from a German six-wave, twenty year longitudinal study. *Peace and Conflict: Journal of Pease Psychology, 11*(3), 337–354.

Central Policy Unit. (2015). *The final report on social attitudes of the youth population in Hong Kong: A follow-up study*. Hong Kong: Hong Kong Special Administrative Region. Retrieved from http://www.cpu.gov.hk/doc/en/research_ reports/social_ attitudes_of_the_youth_population_in_hong_kong.pdf

Chan, W. (2012). *On Hong Kong city state: One country, two systems, self- rule of city state, a matter of life and death for Hong Kong*. Hong Kong: Enrich Publishing (in Chinese).

Cheung, Y. F. (2015, May 5). The teaching materials that transplant the White Paper on the 'One Country, Two Systems'. *Mingpao*, A28.

Chong, E. K. M. (2013). *The controversies from civic education to national education*. HKIAPS Occasional Paper Series, No. 227. Hong Kong: Hong Kong Institute of Asia-Pacific Studies, the Chinese University of Hong Kong (in Chinese).

Chong, E. K. M., Yuen, T. W. W., & Leung, Y. W. (2015). Reconstruction of civic education: Conceptual, curricular and pedagogical responses to civic education in post-national education controversies of Hong Kong. *Citizenship Teaching & Learning, 10*(3), 251–269.

Chow, P. C. (2014). *Political morality: From a liberal point of view*. Hong Kong: Chinese University Press (in Chinese).

Cohen, A. K., & Chaffee, B. W. (2013). The relationship between adolescents' civic knowledge, civic attitude, and civic behavior and their self-reported future likelihood of voting. *Education, Citizenship and Social Justice, 8*(1), 43–57.

Cohen, C. (1971). *Democracy*. Athens: University of Georgia Press.

Cummingham, S., & Lavalette, M. (2004). "Active citizens" or "irresponsible truants"? School students strike against the war. *Critical Social Policy, 24*(2), 255–269.

Curriculum Development Committee. (1985). *Guidelines on civic education in schools.* Hong Kong: Hong Kong Education Department.
Curriculum Development Committee. (1996). *Guidelines on civic education in schools.* Hong Kong: Hong Kong Education Department.
Curriculum Development Committee. (2001). *Learning to learn: The way forward in curriculum development.* Hong Kong: Hong Kong Education Bureau.
Curriculum Development Council. (2007). *Liberal studies: Curriculum and assessment guide, Secondary 4–6 (final version).* Hong Kong: Hong Kong Education Bureau.
Curriculum Development Council. (2012). *Moral and national education curriculum guide (Primary 1 to Secondary 6).* Hong Kong: Curriculum Development Council.
Dahlgren, P. Ed. (2007). *Young citizens and new media: Learning for democratic participation.* New York: Routledge.
Delanty, G. (2000). *Citizenship in a global age: Society, culture, politics.* Buckingham: Open University Press.
Fairbrother, G. P. (2003). The effects of political education and critical thinking on Hong Kong and Mainland Chinese university students' national attitudes. *British Journal of Sociology of Education, 24*(5), 605–620.
Fairbrother, G. P. (2005). Power and right in Hong Kong's citizenship education. *Citizenship Studies, 9*(3), 293–308.
Fairbrother, G. P., & Kennedy, K. J. (2011). Civic education curriculum reform in Hong Kong: What should be the direction under Chinese sovereignty? *Cambridge Journal of Education, 41*(4), 425–444.
Finkel, S. E. (2003). Can democracy be taught? *Journal of Democracy, 14*(4), 137–151.
Fong, C. H. Ed. (2015). *Theories on the reform of Hong Kong.* Taiwan: Azoth Books (in Chinese).
Galtung, J. (1990). Cultural Violence. *Journal of Peace Research, 27*(3), 291–305.
Ghai, Y. (2001). Citizenship and politics in the HKSAR: The constitutional framework. *Citizenship Studies, 5*(2), 143–164.
Gould, J., Jamieson, K. H., Levine, P., McConnell, T., Smith, D. B., McKinney-Browning, M., & Campbell, K. Eds. (2011). *Guardian of democracy: The civic mission of schools.* Pennsylvania: University of Pennsylvania and the Campaign for the Civic Missions of Schools.
Hahn, C. (1998). *Becoming political: Comparative perspectives on citizenship education.* Albany: State University of New York.
Haste, H., & Hogan, A. (2006). Beyond conventional civic participation, beyond the moral-political divide: young people and contemporary debates about citizenship. *Journal of Moral Education, 35*(4), 473–493.
Heater, D. (1990). *Citizenship: The civic ideal in world history, politics and education.* London: Longman.
Hess, D. (2001). Teaching to public controversy in a democracy. In J. J. Patrick & R. S. Leming (Eds.), *Principles and practices of democracy in the education of social studies teachers: Civic learning in teacher education* (Vol. 1, pp. 111–131). Indiana: ERIC.
*Hong Kong Economic Journal.* (2015, July 31). Students' confrontation leads to both happiness and worries, using violence to control violence leads to worries. Retrieved from https://forum.hkej.com/node/124685
Howard, C., & Patten, S. (2006). Valuing civics: Political commitment and the new citizenship education in Australia. *Canadian Journal of Education, 29*(2), 454–475.

Huddleston, T. (2003). *Teaching about controversial issues: Guidance for schools.* London: The Citizenship Foundation.

Information Office of the State Council, PRC. (2014). *The practice of the 'One Country, two systems' policy in the Hong Kong special administrative region.* Beijing: Foreign Language Press.

Kwong, K. M., & Ho, C. T. (2015). Hong Kong's community autonomy- Some responses to the left wings. In C. H. Fong (Ed.), *Theories on the reform of Hong Kong* (pp. 33–51). Taiwan: Azoth Books (in Chinese).

Leung, Y. W. (2003). Use and misuse of affective education in nationalistic education in Hong Kong. *Pacific-Asian Education, 15*(1), 6–24.

Leung, Y. W. (2007). Understandings and teaching approaches in nationalistic education: The case of Hong Kong. *Pacific-Asian Education, 19*(1), 72–89.

Leung, Y. W. (2008). An 'action-poor' human rights education: A critical review of the development of human rights education in the context of civic education in Hong Kong. *Intercultural Education, 19*(3), 231–242.

Leung, Y. W. (2012). A review and preview of the national education debate. In Y. C. Ip (Ed.), *Awaken for next generation* (pp. 74–82). Hong Kong: Enrich Culture (in Chinese).

Leung, Y. W., Chai-yip, W. L. T., & Ng, S. W. (2000). The evolution of civic education in Hong Kong: From guidelines 1985 to guidelines 1996. In Y. C. Cheng, K. W. Chow, & K. T. Tsui (Eds.), *School curriculum change and development in Hong Kong* (pp. 351–368). Hong Kong: Hong Kong Institute of Education.

Leung, Y. W., Cheung, Y. F., Li, C. W., Chong, K. M., Ip, K. Y., Tang, Y. N., & Lo, Y. L. (2012). *Civic education guidelines from civil society.* Hong Kong: Hong Kong Christian Institute (in Chinese).

Leung, Y. W., & Guo, C. L. (2014, November 5). Is students' participation in the Occupy Movement motivated by Liberal Studies? *Mingpao*, A35 (in Chinese).

Leung, Y. W., & Lo, Y. L. (2012, August 25). Affective education without critical reflection tends to be indoctrinatory. *Mingpao*, A26 (In Chinese)

Leung, Y. W., & Ng, S. W. (2004). Back to square one: The "re-depoliticizing of civic education in Hong Kong. *Asia Pacific Journal of Education, 24*(1), 43–60.

Leung, Y. W., & Ngai, G. S. K. (2011). Competing citizenship identities in the global age: The case of Hong Kong. *Citizenship Teaching & Learning, 6*(3), 251–267.

Leung, Y. W., & Yuen, W. W. T. (2009). A critical reflection on the evolution of civic education in Hong Kong schools. *Pacific-Asian Education, 21*(1), 35–50.

Leung, Y. W., & Yuen, W. W. T. (2012). The development of civic and moral education in Hong Kong's changing context. In J. Cogan & D. Grossman (Eds.), *Creating socially responsible citizens: Cases from Asian-Pacific region* (pp. 35–67). Charlotte: Information Age Publisher.

Leung, Y. W., Yuen, W. W. T., Cheng, C. K., & Chow, K. F. (2014). Is student participation in school governance a 'mission impossible'? *Journal of Social Science Education, 13*(4), 19–34.

Leung, Y. W., Yuen, W. W. T., & Leung, Y. K. (2011, March). *The contribution of advocacy NGOs in governance: Case studies in Hong Kong.* Paper presented in International Conference on Governance and Citizenship in Asia: Paradigms and Practices, Hong Kong Institute of Education.

Leung, Y. W., Yuen, W. W. T., & Ngai, S. K. (2014). Personal responsible, participatory or justice-oriented citizen: The case of Hong Kong. *Citizenship Teaching & Learning, 9*(3), 279–295.

Lo, A. (2015, June 11). Social media amplifies hate and despair. *South China Morning Post*. Retrieved from http://www.scmp.com/comment/insight-opinion/article/1820113/social-media-amplifies-hate-and-despair?page=all

McQuillan, P. J. (2005). Possibilities and pitfalls: A comparative analysis of students' empowerment. *American Educational Research Journal*, 42(4), 639–670.

Morris, P., & Chan, K. K. (1997). The Hong Kong school curriculum and the political transition: Politicization, contextualization and symbolic action. In M. Bray & W. O. Lee (Eds.), *Education and political transition: Implications of Hong Kong's change of sovereignty* (pp. 101–118). Hong Kong: The University of Hong Kong.

Morris, P., Kan, F., & Morris, E. (2000). Education, civic participation and identity: Continuity and change in Hong Kong. *Cambridge Journal of Education*, 30(2), 243–264.

Ngai, S. K., Leung, Y. W., & Yuen, W. W. T. (2014). The turmoil of implementing national education in Hong Kong: An overview and analysis. *Social Educator*, 32(1), 5–15.

Ngo, H. Y. (2015, May 20). I am angry: Personal feeling in the umbrella movement. *Mingpao*, A36 (in Chinese).

Nussbaum, M. (1999). *Sex and social justice*. New York: Oxford University Press.

Oldfield, A. (1990). *Citizenship and community: Civic republicanism and the modern world*. London: Routledge.

Ong, L. (2015). Former Chinese official hints Beijing should control education in Hong Kong. *Epoch Times*, January 10, 2015. Retrieved from http://www.theepochtimes.com/n3/1189555-former-chinese-official-hints-beijing-should-control-education-in-hong-kong/

Porter, A. (1993). Preface: Political education and social changes. In Y. W. Leung & K. F. Lau (Eds.), *Political education in a Hong Kong setting: Theory and practice* (pp. VIII-IX). Hong Kong: Hong Kong Christian Institute (in Chinese).

Saha, L. J. (2000). Education and active citizenship. *Prospects and Issues*, 22(1), 9–20.

Sandel, M. J. (2009). *Justice: What's the right thing to do?* New York: Farrar, Straus and Giroux.

Scott, I. (2005). Education policymaking in a disarticulated system. In L. Ho, P. Morris & Y. Chung (Eds.), *Education reform and the quest for excellence: The Hong Kong story* (pp. 23–36). Hong Kong: Hong Kong University Press.

Skitka, L., & Bauman, C. W. (2008). Moral conviction and political engagement. *Political Psychology*, 29(1), 29–54.

Skitka, L., & Mullen, E. (2002). Understanding judgments of fairness in a real-world political context: A test of the value protection model of justice reasoning. *Personality and Social Psychology Bulletin*, 28(10), 1419–1429.

Spiecker, B., & Straughan, R. Eds. (1991). *Freedom and indoctrination in education: International perspectives*. London: Cassell.

Tai, Y. T. (2013). *Occupying central: Peaceful confrontation*. Hong Kong: Enrich Publishing (in Chinese).

Torode, G., Pomfret, J., & Lim, B. K. (2014, July 1). Special report – The battle for Hong Kong's soul. *Reuters*. Retrieved from http://www.reuters.com/article/2014/07/02/us-hongkong-china-specialreport-idUSKBN0F62XU20140702

Tsang, C. W. (2015). *The 2015–16 Budget: Speech by the Financial Secretary, the Hon John C Tsang*. Retrieved from http://www.budget.gov.hk

Tse, K. C. (2007). Remaking Chinese identity: Hegemonic struggles over national education in post-colonial Hong Kong. *International Studies in Sociology of Education*, 17(3), 231–248.

Vickers, E., & Kan, F. (2003).The reeducation of Hong Kong: Identity, politics, and education in post-colonial Hong Kong. *American Asian Review, 21*(4), 179–228.

Westheimer, J., & Kahne, J. (2004). What kind of citizen? The politics of educating for democracy. *American Educational Research Journal, 41*(2), 237–69.

Whitty, G. (2002). *Making sense of education policy.* London: Paul Chapman Publishing.

Wikipedia. (2014). *2014 Hong Kong Protests.* Retrieved from https://en.wikipedia.org/wiki/2014_Hong_Kong_protests

Wong, C. K. (2010, May 19). The re–interpretation of survey opinion results supporting the identification with radical approaches, *Hong Kong Economic Journal,* 19 (in Chinese).

Yuen, W. W. T., & Byram, M. (2007). National identity, patriotism and studying politics in schools: A case study in Hong Kong. *Compare, 37*(1), 23–36.

Yuen, W. W. T., Leung, Y. W., & Lu, J. Q. (2016). Liberal Studies' role in civic education: An exploratory study. *Asian Education and Development Studies, 5*(1), 59–70.

# 9 Changing governance, accountability and leadership
## Hong Kong education meets neo-liberalism

*Nicholas Sun-Keung Pang*

## Introduction

The potential effects of globalisation on education are many and far-reaching due to education's scale and nature. This chapter will provide insights for a better understanding of the nature of globalisation and neo-liberalism that has been brought by globalisation to the education system. It will examine the rationales and the needs of restructuring school education in the era of globalisation. This chapter aims to investigate how globalisation has been affecting educational governance, accountability and leadership and how education administrators and leaders have been responding to the challenges that have arisen from neo-liberalism. It first outlines what is meant by globalisation, the impacts on education administration and principle changes that have come about. Neo-liberalism that resulted from globalisation has brought a paradigm shift in educational governance, accountability and leadership in many countries. Specifically, the author argues that when the education system in Hong Kong is open to globalisation, it has oriented into those neo-liberal values of contract, market, choice, competition, efficiency, flexibility, managerialism and accountability. At the end, the author would like to call for a reflection on the benefits and the hazards that neo-liberalism have brought to us and on the values of globalisation on educational governance, accountability and leadership.

Globalisation is not a new process. Bates (2002) comments that migration of ideas, artefacts and people has been a constant part of human history but that what appears to be new is the pace with which such migrations are now accomplished and the relative weakness of the barriers constructed by nation-states in order to maintain their social, political and cultural integrity in the face of such migration. Although current concepts of globalisation are still blurred and hard to define, they are generally accepted as relating to the global reach of processes of exchange of goods, the formation of gigantic multinational or transnational enterprises, and the virtual abolition of time because of the instantaneous nature of communication all over the world (Capella, 2000). Carnoy (1999) argues that globalisation means more competition, which means that a nation's investment, production, and innovation are not limited by national borders. Globalisation has become possible only because of the technological infrastructure provided by telecommunications, information systems, microelectronic equipment and computer-controlled transportation systems.

There is no universally accepted conceptualisation of globalisation. Globalisation has many faces, thus different theorists view globalisation differently. Held (1991, 9) defines globalisation as "the intensification of worldwide social relations which link distant localities in such a way that local happenings are shaped by events occurring many miles away and vice versa." Globalisation is a product of the emergence of a global economy. The process of globalisation is seen as blurring national boundaries, shifting solidarities within and between nation-states, and deeply affecting the constitution of national and interest group identities (Morrow & Torres, 2000). The term "globalisation" is generally used to refer to a complicated set of economic, political and cultural factors. As a result of expanding world trade, nations and individuals experience greater economic and political interdependence (Wells et al., 1998). New communication technologies that facilitate expanded world trade as well as cultural interaction are considered the determinants that lead to the emergence of globalisation. It is widely believed that globalisation is transforming the political, economic and cultural lives of people all around the world, whether in the developed countries or developing ones, and that globalisation is driving a revolution in the organisation of work, the production of goods and services, relations among nations, and even local culture.

## The impact of globalisation on education

The potential effects of globalisation on education are many and far-reaching, due to its scale and nature. Because the main bases of globalisation are knowledge-intensive information and innovation, globalisation should have a profound impact on education (Burbules & Torres, 2000; Carnoy, 2002). Almost everywhere in the world, educational systems are now under pressure to produce individuals for global competition, individuals who can themselves compete for their own positions in the global context, and who can legitimise the nation-state and strengthen its global competitiveness (Daun, 2002; Pang, 2006).

Economic and technological globalisation is challenging many nation-states in different ways. Countries differ in their response to the processes of globalisation according to their size, economic and technological level, economic position in world markets, cultural composition, relationships between the nation-state and economy (Daun, 2002; Green, 1997). Carnoy (2002) argues that analysing how nation-states respond to globalisation is crucial to the understanding of the effects of globalisation on education. He posits that the approach a nation-state takes in education reform, their educational response to globalisation, depends on three key factors: their real financial situation, their interpretation of that situation and their ideological position regarding the role of the public sector in education. These three factors are expressed through the methods that a nation-state has adopted for the structural adjustment of its economy to the new globalised environment (Mok & Welch, 2003).

Globalisation is having a profound effect on education at many different levels. That education has been a national priority in many countries is largely understood in terms of national economic survival in a fiercely competitive world. It is commonly recognised that the production economy is being rapidly overtaken by the knowledge economy. Many countries have taken action to enhance their competitive edge through the development of the knowledge-producing institutions and industries (Daun & Strömqvist, 2011). The development of the knowledge economy through the enhancement of skills and abilities, that is, improved human capital, has become an important agenda in many countries' educational policy (Bates, 2002). Globalisation will have even greater effects on education in the future. Because global financial flows are so great, governments rely increasingly on foreign capital to finance economic growth. One way to attract financial capital is to provide a steady supply of skilled labour by increasing the overall level of education in the labour force.

Globalisation has brought a paradigm shift in educational policies and administration in many countries. Under the impacts of globalisation, Mulford (2002) observes that the old-fashioned values of wisdom, trust, empathy, compassion, grace and honesty in managing education have changed into those so-called values of contracts, markets, choice and competition in educational administration. More and more nation-states and education systems probe to the philosophy of neo-liberalism, which is a set of economic policies that have become widespread during the last 30 years or so. Under the influence of neo-liberalism, school administrators are probing more into the instrumental skills of efficiency, accountability and planning than the skills of collaboration and reciprocity. School education systems nowadays put more stress on the short-term, the symbolic and expediency, having the answers and sameness, than those of the past, which focused on the long-term, the real and substantive goals and objectives, discretion and reserving judgement and character.

## A probe to neo-liberalism in educational reforms

Since the 1990s activists have used the word 'neo-liberalism' for global market-liberalism ('capitalism') and for free-trade policies (MacEwan, 1999). Sometimes, 'neo-liberalism' is often used interchangeably with 'globalisation' (Hyslop-Margison & Sears, 2006). Neo-liberalism is not only just about economics, it is also a social and moral philosophy. Treanor (2015) offers a summary definition of neo-liberalism as a philosophy as below:

> *Neo-liberalism is a philosophy in which the existence and operation of a market are valued in themselves, separately from any previous relationship with the production of goods and services, and without any attempt to justify them in terms of their effect on the production of goods and services; and where the operation of a market or market-like structure is seen as an ethic in itself, capable of acting as a guide for all human action, and substituting for all previously existing ethical beliefs.*

The main core values of neo-liberalism include: (i) the rule of the market, (ii) cutting public expenditure for social services, (iii) deregulation, (iv) privatisation and (v) eliminating the concept of "the public good" (Martinez & Garcia, 2015).

In the competitive global economy and environment, many nation-states have no choice but to adjust themselves in order to be more efficient, productive and flexible. To enhance a nation-state's productivity and competitiveness in the global situation, decentralisation and the creation of a "market" in education have been the two major strategies employed to restructure education (Lingard, 2000; Mok & Welch, 2003). Decentralisation and corporate managerialism have been used by most governments to increase labour flexibility and create more autonomous educational institutions while catering for the demand for more choice and diversity in education (Blackmore, 2000; Novelli & Ferus-Comelo, 2010). The emergence of education markets has also been central to education reform for globalisation in many nation-states. Carnoy (2002) argues that if education is restructured on market principles and based upon competitive market relations where individual choice is facilitated, education will become more efficient. While it is true that many educational developments are due to globalisation, the dynamics, complexity, and mechanism of such impacts are still not fully grasped.

In studying the responses to globalisation in educational reforms in different countries, Currie (1998) identified a few interesting trends, which include: (i) a shift from elite to mass education, (ii) the privatisation of education, (iii) the practice of corporate managerialism in education governance and (iv) the spread of transnational education. These trends necessarily confront the traditional values and culture in the practice of educational governance and management (AACSB International, 2011). Based on the neo-liberal strategies nation-states adopted in school educational reforms implemented in the context of globalisation, the International Labor Organization (1996, 6-12) and Carnoy (1999) have been able to identify three different models of educational reforms and make a distinction between: (i) competitiveness-driven reforms, (ii) finance-driven reforms, and (iii) equity-driven reforms. The competitiveness-driven reforms are implemented in order to improve a country's competitiveness in the world market and the major strategies include decentralisation, improved management of educational resources and improved teacher recruitment and training. Finance-driven reforms consist of privatisation, shifting public funding from higher to lower levels of education and the reduction of costs per student as the major strategies, while equity-driven reforms are often targeted at groups that are neglected or are more affected by the consequence of structural adjustment programmes. Different countries will adopt these models of educational reform to a greater or lesser extent according to their financial situation, culture and interpretation of globalisation. Though different nation-states may have varying perceptions of globalisation and adopt different neo-liberal strategies in school educational reforms and decentralisation, marketization and choice, are the major approaches seen.

In neo-liberalism, the main argument for decentralisation stems from the assumption that increased flexibility and control allow for a better fit between educational methods and the students served, as well as greater accountability for educational results. Decentralisation is cast in the role of a reform that increases productivity in education and thus contributes significantly to improving the quality of human resources. Many schemes have been tried to achieve decentralisation of school education, such as zero-based budgeting, school consultative committees and school-based management (Brown, 1990).

Marketization in education systems is typically the legacy of the New Right's neo-liberal ideology of school reform in Western countries in the early 1980s (Cooper, 1988). The basic beliefs were that the market is the most efficient instrument to allocate resources, that competition will motivate people to raise their standards of performance and that school improvement will not occur if they are not held accountable and given the necessary resources to do their job.

The New Right's language articulated in school reform is "choice," "competition," "market mechanism" and such like. In order to promote a market mechanism in the school system and to allow schools to compete with each other, state (government) schools should be devolved, deregulated and even "privatised" (Pang, 2002), be given the chance of self-management (Caldwell & Spinks, 1988) and be accountable for their own performance. "Market" and "decentralisation" are the two prime ideological foci of the New Right's school reforms.

When the concept of a market is applied to the school system, the notion of choice is crucial. Choice may be bidirectional in the sense that schools compete for students and students also compete for schools. The two-way competition is the driving force for both schools and students to improve and to raise their standards of performance. In the face of competition, students would strive for excellence in order to get into a "good" school, and schools would ensure they provided quality education in order to compete for the best students. When market forces are introduced into the school system and competition is created, the quality of education will be assured effectively, efficiently and automatically.

When there is a market mechanism in the education system, schools are responsive and accountable. The right choice is to devolve the system to schools (Chapman & Boyd, 1986). School-based management (site-based management, self-budgeting and self-management are other terms coined) is the most popular form of school management reform to revitalise schools in terms of responsiveness, flexibility, accountability and productivity. When the functions of market and school-based management in schools are at full strength, the quality of education will be assured.

In facing the challenges arisen from globalisation, the government in Hong Kong has no choice but probe to neo-liberalism and to restructure the governance and management structure in its school education systems. The major neo-liberal strategies in school educational reforms are decentralisation, marketization and enhancing choice and flexibility.

## Restructuring educational governance, accountability and leadership in Hong Kong

After the Asian financial turmoil in 1998, the Hong Kong Special Administration Region (HKSAR) government launched a series of educational reforms in order to enhance the overall responsiveness, efficiency and effectiveness of the education system to cope with the rapid changes arising from globalisation. According to the *Reform Proposal for the Education System in Hong Kong* (Education Commission, 1999), the scope of the reform was three-pronged – to review the goals and objectives of school education in the 21st century; to streamline the whole-school education system; and to reform the school curriculum and assessment mechanisms. The government has published a time table for implementing the reform measures. Support measures for schools and teachers are being put in place to ensure that the reform can be implemented smoothly and effectively. In terms of school governance and management, according to the recommendations made in the Education Commission Report No. 7, all schools in Hong Kong should have implemented the school-based management scheme, in which decentralisation is the major ideology adopted to enhance the flexibility and change capability of the school system. Another major reform since the year of 2000 is to restructure the admission systems for different stages of education, by creating greater degrees of choice and competitiveness in order to create a market mechanism in the school system (Pang, 2002).

In the following, this author will review the changing governance, accountability and leadership structure in the Hong Kong education system since the 1990s. These strategies include (1) the implementation of school-based management in the school system, (2) the launching of a quality assurance mechanism and (3) the establishment of a continuous professional development framework for the principals. These are the major approaches seen adopted by the Hong Kong government in response to the ever-changing external environments and challenges posed by globalisation.

## *The changing governance structure in Hong Kong schools: Implementation of school-based management in the school system*

Hong Kong has had a rapid expansion in its education system in the last three decades. As the system grows more complex, central control becomes increasingly difficult. Although the government may continue to exercise its authority to make regulations, its capacity to monitor actual compliance with those regulations declines. Constant supervision of the staff of schools becomes impossible. Achievement of objectives declines. Some degree and form of decentralisation is necessary to regain achievement of system objectives.

There has been a quest for school-based management (SBM) in Hong Kong in the 1990s (Education and Manpower Branch and Education Department, 1991; Education Commission, 1997; Pang, 1999). The SBM movement happened in three phases: the first being started with the publication of the School Management Initiative (SMI) by the government in 1991, the second with the Education Commission Report No. 7, "Quality School Education," in 1997 (Pang, 1998a) and the third phase with the Amendment Bill of Education Ordinance in 2004.

The first phase was to reform school management based on the school-based management model on the basis of decentralisation. Decentralisation simply means that schools are allocated resources and money to purchase supplies, equipment, personnel, utilities, maintenance and perhaps other services according to their own assessment of what is appropriate. It intends to bring education reform in the system and to set the framework for quality in Hong Kong schools. The underpinned philosophy of the government in managing the Hong Kong education system changes from the "external-control" to "school-based". This involves the move of the locus of control for the implementation of programmes and policies "down the line" from centre toward periphery, or from larger to smaller units (the schools). A change to school-based management implies greater flexibility of decision-making, changes in role accountability (particularity for the principal), the potential enhancement of school productivity and assuring the quality of education (Pang, 1997). The basic aims of School Management Initiatives have been (Education and Manpower Branch and Education Department, 1991):

*(i) to clarify the roles and responsibilities at both the school and system levels;*
*(ii) to increase the efficiency and effectiveness in deploying resources to meet educational needs;*
*(iii) to enhance principals' and teachers' sense of professionalism through participation in decision-making;*
*(iv) to ensure accountability through self-managing effort to improve learning and teaching; and*
*(v) to assure quality in education.*

The government anticipated that the SMI scheme with its full implementation in 1993 would set the quality framework for both primary and secondary schools. However, due to improper use of strategies, the implementation of the SMI has been quite unsuccessful (Pang, 1998b). Only about one-third of the Hong Kong schools had joined the SMI scheme by 1998. With respect to the poor responses to school-based management and the failure in setting up a quality framework by the SMI, the Education Commission, after three years of investigation into the question of SBM, published its report No.7 and recommended all schools in Hong Kong to implement school-based management in the spirit of SMI by the year 2000.

In this second phrase of implementation of SBM, schools were more rationalised in school management. Schools joining the SBM were requested each year to clarify the functions and responsibilities of those involved in the delivery of education (for example, supervisors, principals, teachers, parents and the then Education Department), to formulate school development plans, to conduct school self-evaluation, to prioritise their actions and to publicise the annual school reports to the public. Teachers were guided by a sense of duty and by a set of rational rules and regulations in their actions to the schools.

The amendment of the Education Ordinance in the year 2004 signified the third phrase of development of the school-based management in Hong Kong. Under the principle of school-based management, aided-schools are given more autonomy and greater funding flexibility to manage the operation and resources of the school for the provision of quality education. In return, schools are expected to be more transparent and accountable for their operation, and all key stakeholders should be involved in the decision-making process. The Education

Ordinance (Cap. 279) and Amendment Bill (2004) requires that all aided-schools shall set up and be managed by an incorporated management committee (IMC), comprising all the key stakeholders – the sponsoring body representatives, the principal, teachers(s), parent(s), alumnus (alumni) and independent member(s) of the community (HKSAR Government, 2004). All sponsoring bodies of aided-schools in Hong Kong were expected to submit to the Permanent Secretary for Education by mid-May 2012 a draft constitution of the proposed IMC of their schools. It was anticipated that all aided-schools would set up their IMCs in the foreseeable future.

As members of the IMCs, school managers are playing an important role in leading and steering the school for improvement and providing an all-round education to students. In view of the proposed changes to the school governance framework to include stakeholders of different categories, more people with different backgrounds will become school managers. It is hoped that through training, these serving as well as potential managers could be assisted to perform their roles more effectively under the new governance framework. Further, school managers who are closely involved in the provision of school education in Hong Kong, such as teachers and principals, are expected to be more involved in school administration at the decision-making level. It is hoped that through sharing of experience and broadening of the horizon of participants in the training sessions, they could be more confident of assuming the roles of school managers under the new governance framework.

In sum, the basic beliefs in school-based management are that market is a very efficient instrument to allocate resources, that competition will motivate people to raise their standards of performance and that school improvement will not occur if they do not hold accountable and given the necessary resources to do their job. In terms of the New Right's common language, the core values are decentralisation, efficiency, effectiveness, flexibility, accountability and so forth. In order to achieve these values, schools are given the chance of self-management and to be accountable for their own performance. Market and school-based management are the two sides of a coin in the New Right's ideology of neo-liberalism (Pang, 2010).

## *The changing school accountability framework in Hong Kong: Launching of a quality assurance mechanism*

There have been rapid changes in both internal and external environments of schools in Hong Kong in the 1990s due to the impact of globalisation (Pang & Leung, 2010). The Education Commission Report No. 7 issued in 1997 recommended a two-pronged approach to ensure the quality of education in Hong Kong: an external assurance mechanism and an internal quality assurance framework. While the external quality assurance mechanism was achieved through the establishment in 1998 of a Quality Assurance Inspectorate (QAI) to which schools were accountable, the internal quality assurance framework relied on schools' own ability to evaluate themselves as part of the process of school-based management.

There have been two phrases in the implementation of quality assurance mechanism in Hong Kong schools. The first phrase in 1998–2002 was the first quality assurance cycle in Hong Kong with the mode of whole-school inspections, while the second phrase began from 2003 with the establishment of the School Development and Accountability Framework.

At the beginning, the external quality assurance mechanism worked by adopting a whole-school approach to inspection by the QAI, which assessed schools' effectiveness, identified their strengths and weaknesses, made suggestions on ways of improvement and development in the schools and released inspection reports for public reference. In order to continuously improve the quality of school education, all schools were also expected to engage in cyclical processes of planning, implementation and evaluation (Pang, MacBeath, & McGlynn, 2004). Every school was expected to work towards meeting the educational needs of its students as effectively as it could, and self-evaluation would provide information on which to base plans for improvement. As for this self-evaluation, all schools had to produce documents which outlined the long-term goals, prioritised development areas, set out specific targets for implementation, evaluated progress made in work during the previous school year and set improvement or development targets for the coming year (Pang, 2003).

However, in the initial stage, the two strategies in this two-pronged approach to assuring educational quality in Hong Kong might not have been as effective as expected. For one thing, as for the external assurance mechanism, whole-school inspections could only take place for two- or three-week periods (each time) and the QAI would not re-visit the same school for at least five to six years, given the QAI teams' manpower. Thus while whole-school inspections were implemented in Hong Kong in the 1997/98 school year, between that year and 2001/02 the number of schools inspected was only about 11.4 per cent of the total. Second, in conducting whole-school inspections in over 200 schools from 1998 to 2002, the QAI found that most of these schools had not established a self-evaluation framework, and in fact at that time there were still no appropriate school-based indicators for school self-evaluation.

In the year of 2003, the Permanent Secretary of the Education Bureau released a circular to all schools in Hong Kong and announced the newly established School Development and Accountability Framework, which modified the original two-pronged approach in the first phrase to becoming School Self-Evaluation (SSE) and External School Review (ESR).

The ESR of the quality assurance mechanism by Education Bureau (EDB) (formerly called Education Manpower Bureau [EMB]) requests individual schools to formulate a number of specific goals in compiling their SSE report annually. The ESR team then validates the SSE reports once every six years. According to Education Bureau (2013), the ESR is improvement-oriented and is conducted in a school-specific and focused mode. Its procedures focus on how schools make use of the process of "Planning-Implementation-Evaluation" (P-I-E) for sustained development and self-improvement in the SSE cycle (Education Bureau, 2013). The on-going cyclical process of SSE and ESR assists schools in initiating and sustaining improvement at the school-level to a certain extent, since through these internal and external quality assurance mechanisms, schools are able to formulate their direction of future development and strategic planning (Education Commission, 2006).

In sum, under the ever-changing and turbulent world and in coping with the challenges posed by globalisation, schools can only improve continuously when they have institutionalised a self-evaluation framework in daily practice. Practising self-evaluation enables schools (i) to develop formal procedures for setting school goals; (ii) to have the participation of teachers, parents and alumni in school management, development, planning, evaluation and decision-making; (iii) to assess their progress towards goals as well as their own performance over time; and (iv) to take appropriate steps toward self-improvement.

Evidence-based organisational change has become a trend in the school reform and improvement movement throughout the world (Pang, 2009). It is important that schools' organisational change should be based on objective and reliable evidence of school performance. To successfully institutionalise a self-renewal framework in daily managerial practices as well as to lead and manage change effectively, the principal or leader needs to: (1) acquire appropriate knowledge and understanding of the theoretical framework of school self-evaluation; (2) develop and acquire the necessary skills and attitudes for self-evaluation and manipulation of performance indicators; (3) think through his/her leadership role as a guide to action; and (4) clarify for him/herself the strategic elements essential to an effective implementation of the school development plan. Thus the principal should examine the types of knowledge, skills and attitudes which need to be developed for successful implementation of organisational change, and it also calls for the importance of continuous professional development of school principals in the globalising world.

### *The changing leadership roles in Hong Kong schools: Establishment of a continuous professional development framework for the principals*

It is widely acknowledged that the school principal holds the key to achieving school effectiveness in the midst of a rapidly changing educational environment. As school administrators, the principals are the vanguards of stability as well as agents of change, which require them to be flexible and seek re-education and re-training in facing the new challenges (Gamage & Pang, 2006).

With the implementation of the concepts of decentralisation and devolution in most school systems around the globe, the school principal-ship has become the structure which is undergoing most significant changes and facing many new challenges. Now, almost all education systems acknowledge that the school leaders should be provided with adequate professional development opportunities to equip them with skills and competencies in coping with these new challenges (Pang, 2007). Below is a review of the development of the continuous professional development of principals in Hong Kong, since the start of the new millennium.

Since 1982, the then Education Department (ED) has been providing an induction programme for newly appointed school principals in the public sector schools. The program was a nine-day Secondary School Administration Course with six months of action plan/project work to help the school leaders to acquire management concepts and skills for effective administration of their schools (ED, 1999). Other than this programme, principals received no substantial pre-service or in-service training.

The quest for quality education in Hong Kong resulted in a number of initiatives, recognising the principals as the leaders in school education who play a vital role in achieving the government's aim in providing a quality education for the young (Education Department, 1999). These initiatives have made significant demands on principals, requiring them to take on new leadership roles. The Continuing Professional Development (CPD) framework stipulated by the Education Department in 2002 suggested that the expectations on the roles of Hong Kong principals could be best conceived as school leaders: (1) who must be more professional and personally competent than ever before; (2) who must have clearly defined values and be dedicated to continually upgrading their knowledge and skills, and those of their colleagues in school; (3) who provide a vision and direction for the schools and ensure that they are managed and organised to meet their aims and targets; and (4) who develop and maintain effective networks to secure commitment in enriching students' learning (Education Department, 2002a, 6).

In consideration of the critical skills, values and attributes in leading twenty-first century schools, Pang (1998b) suggested that school administrators should empower the teachers and emphasise on rationality, participation, collaboration, collegiality, good orientation, communication and consensus in their daily management practices towards building a quality management culture. The Quality Assurance Inspection (QAI) teams stressed "professional competence" and "working relationships" (QAI reports, 2000/2002 & 2001/2002) as the two important leadership skills of principals.

In September 2002, in response to the changing roles with a view to strengthening principal's leadership, ED published its Guidelines for Principals' Continuing Professional Development. The new leadership training programme was designed to equip the principals with the necessary knowledge, skills, and attitudes to become competent to lead schools in the new millennium. Its mission is to empower principals to become effective, dynamic and accountable leaders through CPD in creating professional learning communities in facing the challenges of an ever-advancing knowledge-based society (Education Department, 2002b, 6). The values, knowledge, skills and attributes needed by Hong Kong principals as they pursue CPD within the inter-related leadership domains are clustered into the six core areas (ED, 2002b). The Chinese University of Hong Kong was invited as the first institution to offer a designated course on "Preparation for Principal-ship" (PFP) and to design a pilot training programme for the aspiring principals in terms of the CPD framework stipulated by the then ED.

Concerning the six core areas of leadership (ED, 2002a), two pertain to external changes and the need for outreaching activities (i.e., strategic direction and policy environment, and external communication and connexion). Four domains touch upon effective internal management (i.e., teaching, learning and curriculum, teacher professional growth and development, staff and resources management and quality assurance and accountability). Closely intertwined and conceptually affiliated to these core areas register some basic administrative functions that a school principal normally carries out. Additional challenges, however, are met in the face of the current school reform, which perceptually and substantially changes these basic administrative functions. The proposed training programme for the aspiring principals, described in the following pages, is based on the twin concerns of comprehending the principals' basic responsibilities and the new demands placed upon the existing ones. And the specific objectives of the PFP programme are as below (Pang, 2014):

- *To allow participants of the programme to satisfy the government's requirement for certification for principal-ship.*
- *To provide some basic skills, knowledge and proper perspectives for aspiring principals in their career advancement towards assuming full principal-ship.*
- *To prepare aspiring principals to be ready to accept emerging challenges that alters or complicates existing role expectations of principal-ship.*
- *To enhance the operational efficiency of the schools through the formal training of aspiring principals.*
- *To provide momentum for participants of the training programme to embark upon continuous professional upgrading.*

In July 2002, the then EMB announced that from 2004/05 all newly appointed principals will be required to attain the Certification for Principal-ship (CFP), in addition to complying with the appointment conditions in force at that time, before they can be considered for appointment to principal-ship. The CFP comprises of a needs analysis, a designated PFP course and a submission of a portfolio. The EMB has accredited and contracted the Chinese University of Hong Kong to deliver the PFP Programme as a pilot project during the period 2002–04 in order to help participants to fulfil the second component of the PFP requirements. As stipulated by the EMB's policy on principals' CPD, all newly appointed principals had to obtain the Certificate in Principal-ship (CIP) by September 2004. In sum, the implementation of school-based management in Hong Kong since 1991 has given principals more autonomy and flexibility in the deployment of resources, curriculum development, staff development and on other professional managerial matters in return for greater accountability. The current education reforms call for changes in students' learning attitudes and habits to cater to new learning processes and teaching strategies while recognising that the quality of school leadership is pivotal in bringing all these changes into reality (Education Department, 2002a, 1).

## Conclusion

Globalisation as conceived by New Right might entail the imposition of the concepts of competition, market, choice, decentralisation and privatisation on education, that is, the further infiltration by business forces into education. It might also lead to increased commoditization of education and making quality education only accessible to elite elements of society who can afford it (Kellner, 2000).

Globalisation has brought a paradigm shift in educational governance, administration and leadership in Hong Kong. Under the impacts of globalisation, the Hong Kong government is confronted with sets of conflicting values and dilemmas in the choice between tradition and modern values brought by globalisation (Reid, Gill, & Sears, 2010). People are facing the challenges of choosing the proper values and ethics in determining their thinking and actions in a highly competitive world. The Hong Kong government is challenged with these impacts when the education system is open to globalisation and when its traditional cultures and values meet with neo-liberalism brought along with globalisation. The traditional ethics and values of hierarchical relationships, collectivism, trust, empathy, compassion, grace and honesty in educational governance and management have changed into the new values of contract, market, choice, competition, efficiency, flexibility, productivity and accountability (Gutek, 2009; Lee & Mcbride, 2007).

It is evident that in many places, neo-liberalism has led to greater economic and social inequality; and that educational access, whilst expanded, has also become more unequal in quality. Greater decentralisation and privatisation of education has generally not increased equality in educational services, but rather lead to more inequality (Carnoy, 2002). It is not conclusive, yet whether the new values brought by neo-liberalism are good or bad to education, because the very nature of education is quite different from that of business. When the economic and market principles of neo-liberalism are applied to education, it is not certain whether it would be more beneficial or harmful to the school system.

## References

AACSB International. (2011). *Globalization of management education: Changing international structures, adaptive strategies, and the impact on institutions*. Report of the AACSB International Globalization of Management Education Task Force. Bingley, UK: Emerald Group Publishing.

Bates, R. (2002). Administering the global trap: the roles of educational leaders. *Educational Management & Administration, 30*(2), 139–156.

Blackmore, J. (2000). Globalization, a useful concept for feminists rethinking theory and strategies in education. In N. C. Burbules & C. A. Torres (Eds.), *Globalization and education: Critical perspectives* (pp. 133–155). London: Routledge.

Brown, D. J. (1990). *Decentralization and school-based management*. London: The Falmer Press.

Burbules, N. C., & Torres, C. A. (2000). An introduction to globalization and education. In N. C. Burbules & C. A. Torres (Eds.), *Globalization and education: Critical perspectives* (pp. 1–26). London: Routledge.

Caldwell, B. J., & Spinks, J. M. (1988). *The self-managing school*. London: The Falmer Press.

Capella, J. R. (2000). Globalization, a fading citizenship. In N. C. Burbules & C. A. Torres (Eds.), *Globalization and education: Critical perspectives* (pp. 227–251). London: Routledge.

Carnoy, M. (1999). *Globalization and educational reform, what planners need to know*. UNESCO, Paris: International Institute for Educational Planning.

Carnoy, M. (2002). Foreword. In H. Daun (Ed.), *Educational restructuring in the context of globalization and national policy* (pp. xv–xviii). New York: Routledge.

Chapman, J., & Boyd, W. L. (1986). Decentralization, devolution, and the school principal, Australian lessons on statewide education reform. *Educational Administration Quarterly, 22*(4), 28–58.

Cooper, B. S. (1988). School reform in the 1980s: The New Right's legacy. *Educational Administration Quarterly, 24*(3), 282–298.

Currie, J. (1998). Globalization practices and the professoriate in Anglo-Pacific and North American universities. *Comparative Education Review, 42*(1), 15–29.

Daun, H. Ed. (2002). *Educational restructuring in the context of globalization and national policy*. New York: Routledge.

Daun, H., & Strömqvist, G. Eds. (2011). *Education and development in the context of globalization*. New York: Nova Science Publishers.

Education Bureau. (2013). *External school reviews: Information for schools*. Hong Kong: The Government Printer.

Education Commission. (1997). *Education Commission report No. 7: Quality school education*. Hong Kong: the Government Printer.

Education Commission. (1999). *Review of education system: framework for education reform*. Hong Kong Special Administrative Region: Education Commission.

Education Commission. (2006). *Progress report on education reform (4)*. Hong Kong: The Government Printer.

Education and Manpower Branch and Education Department. (1991). *The school management initiative: Setting the framework for quality in Hong Kong schools*. Hong Kong: the Government Printer.

Education and Manpower Bureau. (2003). *Quality assurance inspection reports 1998/1999, 1999/2000, 2000/2001, 2001/2002*. Retrieved from http://www.edb.gov.hk/index.aspx?langno=2&nodeID=744

Education Department. (1999). *Leadership training program for principals consultation paper*. Hong Kong: The Printing Department.

Education Department. (2002a). *Continuing professional development for school excellence – Consultation paper on continuing professional development of principals*. Hong Kong: The Printing Department.

Education Department. (2002b). *Guidelines for principals' continuing professional development (CPD)*. Hong Kong: The Printing Department.

Gamage, D. T., & Pang, N. S. K. (2006). Facing the challenges of the 21st century: Preparation of school leaders in Australia and Hong Kong. *Educational Research Journal, 21*(1), 21–46.

Green, A. (1997). *Education, globalization and the nation state*. London: Macmillan Press.

Gutek. G. L. (2009). *New perspectives on philosophy and education*. Columbus, OH: Pearson.

Held, D. Ed. (1991). *Political theory today*. California: Stanford University Press.

HKSAR Government. (2004). *Education ordinance 2004 (Amendment)*. Hong Kong: The Government Printer.

Hyslop-Margison, E. J., & Sears, A. M. (2006). *Neo-liberalism, globalization and human capital learning: Reclaiming education for democratic citizenship*. Dordrecht: Springer.

International Labor Organization. (1996). *Impact of structural adjustment on the employment and training of teachers*. Geneva: ILO.

Kellner, D. (2000). Globalization and new social movements: Lessons for critical theory and pedagogy. In N. C. Burbules & C. A. Torres (Eds.), *Globalization and education, critical perspectives* (pp. 299–321). London: Routledge.

Lee, S., & Mcbride, S. Eds. (2007). *Neo-Liberalism, state power and global governance*. Dordrecht: Springer.

Lingard, B. (2000). It is and it isn't: Vernacular globalization, educational policy, and restructuring. In N. C. Burbules & C. A. Torres (Eds.), *Globalization and education: Critical perspectives* (pp. 79–108). London: Routledge.

MacEwan, A. (1999). *Neo-liberalism or democracy? Economic strategy, markets, and alternatives for the 21st century*. New York, NY: St. Martin's Press.

Martinez, E., & Garcia, A. (2015). *What is Neoliberalism?* Retrieved on October 17, 2015 from http://www.corpwatch.org/article.php?id=376

Mok, J. K. H., & Welch, A. (2003). Globalization, structural adjustment and educational reform. In J. K. H. Mok & A. Welch (Eds.), *Globalization and educational restructuring in the Asia Pacific region* (pp. 1–31). New York: Palgrave Macmillan.

Morrow, R. A., & Torres, C. A. (2000). The state, globalization and education policy. In N. C. Burbules & C. A. Torres (Eds.), *Globalization and education: Critical perspectives* (pp. 27–56). London: Routledge.

Mulford, B. (2002). The global challenge: A matter of balance. *Educational Management and Administration, 30*(2), 123–138.

Novelli, M., & Ferus-Comelo, A. Eds. (2010). *Globalization, knowledge and labour: Education for solidarity within spaces of resistance*. London: Routledge.

Pang, N. S. K. (1997). The school management reform in Hong Kong: Restructuring the accountability system. *Education Journal, 25*(1), 25–44.

Pang, N. S. K. (1998a). Should quality school education be a Kaizen (improvement) or an innovation? *International Journal of Educational Reform, 7*(1), 2–12.

Pang, N. S. K. (1998b). Organizational values and cultures of secondary schools in Hong Kong. *Canadian and International Education, 27*(2), 59–84.

Pang, N. S. K. (1999). *Educational quality, quality culture and the accelerated schools project*. Educational reform series, Occasional Paper No. 2. The Hong Kong Institute of Educational Research, Hong Kong.

Pang, N. S. K. (2002). Towards school management reform: Organizational values of government schools in Hong Kong. In J. K. H. Mok & D. K. K. Chan (Eds.), *Globalization and education: The quest for quality education in Hong Kong* (pp. 171–193). Hong Kong: Hong Kong University Press.

Pang, N. S. K. (2003). Initiating organizational change through school self-evaluation. *International Journal of Knowledge, Culture and Change Management, 3*, 245–256.

Pang, N. S. K. Ed. (2006). *Globalization: Educational research, change and reforms*. Hong Kong: The Chinese University Press, the Hong Kong Educational Research Association and the Hong Kong Institute of Educational Research.

Pang, N. S. K. (2007). The continuing professional development of principals in Hong Kong SAR, China. *Frontiers of Education in China, 2*(4), 605–619.

Pang, N. S. K. (2009). Educational evaluation and quality assurance: The case of Hong Kong. In S. M. Peng & J. C. K. Lee (Eds.), *Educational evaluation in East Asia: Emerging issues and challenges* (pp. 75–91). New York: Nova Science Publishers.

Pang, N. S. K. (2010). Educational governance and management in Sinic societies. In Yong Zhao (Ed.), *The handbook of Asian education: A cultural approach* (pp. 7–28). New York: Routledge.
Pang, N. S. K. (2014). Hong Kong Principals' continuous professional development in the era of globalization. In N. S. K. Pang (Ed.), *Professional training and development programme for school leaders and action research* (pp. 7–23). Shenzhen, China: Shenzhen Lowu Centre for Research in Educational Science & Hong Kong Centre for the Development of Educational Leadership (in Chinese).
Pang, N. S. K., & Leung, Z. L. M. (2010). The development and reforms of educational assessment in Hong Kong. In Hiroto S. Nakamura (Ed.), *Education in Asia* (pp. 121–137). New York: Nova Science Publishers.
Pang, N. S. K., MacBeath, J., & McGlynn, A. (2004). *Self-evaluation and school development*. School Education Reform Series No.19. Hong Kong: The Faculty of Education of the Chinese University of Hong Kong and Hong Kong Institute of Educational Research.
Reid, A., Gill, J., & Sears, A. Eds. (2010). *Globalization, the nation-state and the citizen: Dilemmas and directions for civics and citizenship education*. New York: Routledge.
Treanor, P. (2015). *Neoliberalism: origins, theory, definition*. Retrieved on October 17, 2015, from http://web.inter.nl.net/users/Paul.Treanor/neoliberalism.html
Wells, A. S., Carnochan, S., Slayton, J., Allen, R. L., & Vasudeva, A. (1998). Globalization and educational change. In A. Hargreaves, A. Lieberman, M. Fullan & D. Hopkins (Eds.), *International handbook of educational change* (pp. 322–348). Dordrecht: Kluwer Academic.

# 10 Should there be public reporting of school performance?
## The lessons from the school inspection reports disputes

*Thomas Kwan-Choi Tse*

## Introduction

Since the 1980s there has been an explicit move towards a consumerist accountability model, as many governments are collecting and using evidence for evaluations and monitoring purposes. Regarding education, more and more special disciplinary measures and mechanisms associated with surveillance and performativity are placed on schools, with school inspection being a tool favoured by many governments to assess schools and teachers (Perryman, 2006; Poulson, 1996; Ranson, 2003). Increasingly, the public is demanding information for choice and effectiveness-enhancement purposes. But disclosing this information to the public is a very complex and contested affair as different stakeholders may have different views on the availability and dissemination of school data (Petegem, Vanhoof, Daems, & Mahieu, 2005). Additionally, the reporting practices may carry unintended or undesirable effects and hence trigger fierce disputes.

In the past, there was no comprehensive or systematic reporting on school performance available in Hong Kong. In recent years, many parents have complained of not having enough data to guide them in selecting schools for their children (*Standard*, May 19, 2000). Also, they increasingly wanted more transparency regarding the performance of local schools, preferably in the form of a league table (Telephone survey laboratory, The Hong Kong Institute of Asia-Pacific Studies, CUHK, 2000). This demand for information has been addressed by a vast number of managerialist and quasi-market strategies introduced to the education sector from the 1990s onwards (Tsang, 1997, 2000; Tse, 2005). Among them are intensive and comprehensive assessments coupled with information disclosure to the public so as to satisfy parents' right of access to information, in tandem with a promotion of a 'consumer-centred culture' which defines the roles of parents and students as customers who exercise choices (Education and Manpower Branch, 1993; Education Commission, 1997).

This information release also serves the purposes of management, evaluation and monitoring of every school. It is assumed that with increased transparency and accountability to the public, schools will improve their effectiveness and strive for excellence.

While this release of information to the public has been a popular trend in Hong Kong and many overseas countries, so far it has only received scant attention in academic circles (except Cullingford & Swift, 2001; Cuttance & Stokes, 2000; O'Day, 2002; Petegem, Vanhoof, Daems, & Mahieu, 2005; Reid, 2006). Also, many crucial issues concerning public reporting of school performance are still subject to clarification and deliberation.

Against the knowledge gap in literature and background of Hong Kong's recent education reform afore-mentioned, this chapter examines the disputes over the school inspection reports and the consequences brought by these policy measures. My analysis is based on two main bodies of literature. The first one includes major policy papers, documents and reports published by the Hong Kong government and relevant consultative bodies. The second is nearly 530 major Chinese and English newspaper reports and comments on the measures during the period from May 1998 to August 2014 retrieved from a comprehensive electronic news database and powerful search engine called Wiser Information Portal.

This chapter has four sections in total. Following this introduction is the origins and development of the relevant measures. The third section reports the standpoints of the different camps involved in the disputes and examines four critical issues concerning generation of information, public reporting, the role of the news media and its impact in turn. The final section draws out the implications of the Hong Kong experience for the general issue about public reporting of school performance.

## Origins and development of the measures

The release of school inspection report to the public was derived from a new quality assurance mechanism named "Quality Assurance Inspection" (hereafter referred to as QAI) installed in 1997. In the past, schools in Hong Kong were subject to monitoring by different divisions of the former Education Department mainly in the form of school-subject based inspection. And the findings of the inspection were kept confidential to the public. For better co-ordination of inspection work and to provide schools with a holistic review of their strengths and areas for improvement, the government then switched to "a whole school approach" to school inspection and reorganised all the sections into a single inspection unit. Beginning in the 1997/98 school year, school's performance would be assessed against sets of complex performance indicators in four domains – management and organisation, teaching and learning, support for students and school ethos, and standard of attainment and achievement.

The school also had to conduct self-evaluation and produce an annual report towards the end of the year for parents' information. A report card was produced in the form of a written report on the inspection findings and key issues for schools' improvement and development for each individual school. In phases, QAI covered all primary and secondary schools, special schools and kindergartens from 2001 onwards.

In addition, a variety of inspections have been introduced in later days for different purposes or different kinds of schools. Meanwhile, school inspection was further modified in tandem with the implementation of school-based management since 2000, which was characterised by an increasing emphasis on self-evaluation processes on the part of schools. Starting from 2003, a new audit mode called "External School Review" (ESR) was adopted to validate confession-like school self-evaluation. Thus the authorities could combine both internal and external assessments for the twin aims of school development and accountability and save the cost and time of inspection as well. By phases, all schools would undertake their self-assessment of performance relative to previous standards and the performance of other schools in Hong Kong, and have their internal assessment reviewed by an expert external review team once every four years.

A part of the quality assurance was to make inspection findings open so as to provide a review on the overall performance of the school. At the aggregate level, these modes of inspections also aimed to provide the government and the public with information on the current position regarding the overall quality of school education. From November 1998 onwards the government annually released the inspection reports of individual schools based on the new inspection methods. For public reference, full reports were located at a resource centre and the summaries of individual inspection reports were uploaded onto the government's website starting from April 2001. Schools undergoing ESR were also required to complete a school report card and display the results on their websites for external monitoring. Still further, to increase accessibility of the information to the public, since July 2004, information on QAI summary reports and good practices of kindergartens have been linked to the electronic version of the annual *Profile of Kindergartens* so that parents could better understand the quality and the good practices of pre-primary education. These reports become official endorsement of good schools and kindergartens. Also, the overall performance of the school sector and the quality of the inspection processes were reported too in subsequent annual reports.

Besides these official rationales like transparency and right to information as stated above, the government employed the inspection or external review and their reports to compel schools to comply with certain education policies in light of normalisation and competition introduced to the school sector (*Ta Kung Pao*, June 1, 2005). Public reporting hence became a tool for accelerating policy implementation through the public or the parents' pressure put on the schools. This official tactic of monitoring the attainment of certain policy targets could be done by incorporating some mandatory items of assessment and reporting. For example, introduced in 2003, 23 items of "key performance measures" (KPM) concerning school performance were identified as common characteristics of effective schools and schools had to report relevant data (F. Law, 2003). Amongst the items required were some concerning policy compliance like composition of the school management committee, teacher qualification and professional experience, such as attainment in language proficiency. Territory-wide norms were also produced for reference and became yardsticks for schools to evaluate their progress and performance.

Yet another example of the use of this published data can be identified. Since 2001 the government has strengthened the quality assurance mechanism for early childhood education, including increasing schools' transparency and stepping up inspection to raising the quality of kindergartens (HKSAR Information Services Department, October 21, 2006; *Standard*, October 12, October 20, 2006). Later, this quality assurance mechanism was also related to a new voucher scheme starting from 2007/08 – school fee assistance provided to parents of children in non-profit-making kindergartens. And all participating kindergartens are subject to classroom inspection and have to provide information on their facilities and achievements, including the academic qualifications of the principals and teachers and special features of their curriculum, and pass the QAI for being entitled to redeem the vouchers from 2011 onwards.

## Disputes

Both QAI and later ESR reports provided school performance information to parents and the general public. The community was divided on these measures – while there was enthusiastic support for their release by the government, the parents and the media, there was strong opposition to these initiatives from the school sector as well.

As for the advocacy side, officials have stressed the benefits and urgency of releasing inspection reports to the public with the obvious rationales stated above (*Ming Pao*, November 3, 1998). Parents' representatives also supported the release of inspection reports, particularly public examination results, on the grounds of transparency and providing a reference to make school choices (*Ta Kung Pao*, September 28, 2002; *Sing Tao Daily*, December 30, 2004; *SCMP*, March 18, 2006).

As for the news media, the newspaper *Ming Pao* editorial (September 28, 2002) supported the use of public monitoring, in the way of allowing public opinion to push school to reform, even though there might be some risk from misuse of the data by parents and students. *Sing Pao* editorial (July 31, 2004) welcomed such a "sunshine test" on the grounds that this might promote healthy competition and raise the performance of the school sector as a whole. The press also viewed parents as consumers and treated the inspection reports as akin to test reports produced by the Consumer Council, that is, protecting the parents' right to information as well as realising the principle of "value for money". *Hong Kong Economic Times* (November 15, 2006) argued that the government should provide guardians with precise market updates for consideration, such as the disclosure of review reports of various kindergartens or collection of comments from graduates' guardians on the kindergartens.

By contrast, as early as in 1999, the proposal to release inspection reports provoked criticism from Hong Kong Professional Teachers Union (HKPTU), the largest teachers' union in Hong Kong (*Ta Kung Pao*, November 16, 1998). It expressed worries towards how the report would be interpreted by the mass media and the general public, and the danger that the sole focus would be put on the pass rates of public examinations or that there would be selective reporting of the negative aspects of school performance, which might adversely affect the future development of the school in focus. The comprehensiveness and objectivity of the tools of measurement – performance indicators – was also subject to query. Similarly, the proposal to release 2000/01 QAI report to the public in 2001 was faced with opposition from the kindergarten sector on the grounds of invading the privacy of kindergartens (all of them are privately owned in Hong Kong) and that an official ranking of kindergartens would come with labelling effects and affect admissions of students in future (*Ming Pao*, April 6, 2000). The government finally made concessions and deferred the release of inspection reports for one year till 2002 (*Ming Pao*, April 6, 2000).

In brief, a number of crucial and complex value issues concerning right to information, freedom of choice, transparency, accountability, freedom of the press, and teaching professionalism have arisen from the disputes over the public reporting of school performance. The following sub-sections will unpack these issues and distil them into four key questions for detailed discussion.

## How the information is generated?

School inspection aims to collect authentic and valid information about the school inspected at stake. Ensuring the objectivity and reliability of the assessment mechanisms is thus crucial. But a major point of dispute concerning public reporting of school performance was exactly the "generation of information" process itself (Reid, 2006).

In Hong Kong, while school principals generally agreed that the inspection reports could be useful for schools to evaluate themselves and learn from each other, as well as to promote a better public understanding of the quality of local school education, some practitioners criticised the government for failing to recognise or admit to inadequacies in the assessment system (*SCMP*, April 21, 2001), including the procedures of review, workload, manpower as well as expertise of the inspection team. The demand for accountability put inspection teams and school personnel into a suspicious relation, and it is not easy to build up trust between them. School visits by the inspection team constitutes intrusions into private space of school and classroom operation. School personnel tend to see the inspection teams as critics instead of critical friends. They accused the inspection practices of being fault-finding-oriented, with undue emphasis placed on looking for evidence of suspected weaknesses in a four- to eight-day school visit (L.Y.S. Law, 2003; *Ming Pao*, May 8, 2008; *Sing Tao Daily*, May 8, 2008).

Obviously school ethos, staff training and students' performance were not easily observed in a few days. Because of time constraints, inspection teams might tend to make piece-meal and superficial judgements and therefore draw dubious conclusions based on limited interviews and observations. These inadequacies were further exacerbated by a lack of responses to appeals for amendment, making inspectors the sole and ultimate authority in the assessment exercises. Some schools also refuted the inspection reports as "not reflecting reality" and "unfair" (*Oriental Daily*, April 17, 2001). The doubts over the fairness and transparency of the inspection body directly undermined the credibility of the inspections and the report as well (*The Sun*, April 18, 2001, February 20, 2002).

In addition, schools vary in their histories and traditions, intakes of students, problems encountered and priorities of development. Some commentators challenged the appropriateness of using a uniform set of criteria to evaluate all schools across the board, which meant a failure to recognise a school's uniqueness and strengths or to give sufficient consideration to the context in which personnel and teachers worked (Choi, 2005a; Tsoi, 2005). Another criticism directed at inspections was an over-emphasis on academic achievement or public examination results are unfavourable to newly-founded schools, and those schools accommodating mainly disadvantaged pupils, or located in poor socio-economic communities.

Another source of dispute lay in disparity in internal and external ratings. For instance, in the 2003/04 exercise, over half of the primary and secondary schools undergoing ESR having SSE (school self-evaluation) ratings higher than those of ESR in areas of "teaching and learning" and "self-evaluation" (*Hansard*, March 9, 2005). It clearly demonstrated the diversity of perspectives between the government and of schools which were not easy for compromise.

Bearing in mind the possible limitations of the inspection procedures, the report of under-performing school could be a mis-accusation of school ineffectiveness or failures in educating students. Accountability requires devising common standards, but it is also a difficult task when there is disagreement about what "good school performance" or "quality" should be (Silver, 1994). Dissent and resistance are more common in a model of external accountability to monitor teachers and coerce them into accepting normalising judgements of their practices, or threatened to punish them through a sophisticated network of surveillance. People differ in their perspectives and aspirations over standards and the thorny conceptual, methodological and measurement problems involved are complicated with the complexity and the multi-faceted nature of schooling processes and student performance (Fitz-Gibbon, 1996; O'Day, 2002; Reynolds & Cuttance, 1992). A hasty implementation and compilation of indicators short of a widely acceptable understanding and professional criterion could undermine the objectivity and fairness of reporting based on it, as well as validity of the rest of the tools.

The inspection reports were also refuted for reasons which lay in the inadequacy of the post-inspection process (*Oriental Daily*, April 18, 2001). Every year under-performing schools are named, and their pitfalls and areas for improvement are identified in the inspection reports. However, rarely would the government make follow-up efforts. Whether the schools being criticised would make improvements depends solely on whether they want to do so. It was unfair to schools for there not to be follow-up assessments and updates of the report. Also, since there was a considerable time lag between the inspection itself and the release of the report, it might not reflect the current status of the school (Lee & Chiu, 2003). After an inspection, a school would probably have taken action to remedy its weaknesses as mentioned in the inspection report. Therefore, the release of individual QAI reports to the public, without also releasing follow-up reports to explain how much a school had improved since the last inspection, could cause serious and unjustified harm to the schools concerned. And in many cases, this could lead to their further decline.

Among the KPM for secondary school assessment include the sensitive items of student performance such as pre-S1 attainment test, territory-wide system assessment, academic value-added performance and public examination results. For other domains of school performance, they must also be evidence-based or data-driven to support evaluation, or commonly described as "documentation" in these assessment exercises. Accordingly, the school personnel have to collect information from staff, parents and students. From the viewpoint of the schools inspected, given that school reputation (an important asset of the school) was at stake, they were under tremendous pressure as it was a matter of nothing less than survival, particularly at a time of shrinking school population and closing down many schools in recent years (H. Chan, 2005; Choi, 2005b). The school's honour and fame, how it was known to the media, the parents and the public, was related to enrolment numbers. To live with external inspection and school comparison, many schools were forced to operate in a climate of fear and distrust. Under such circumstances, schools would naturally commit time and resources to prepare to forestall criticism or negative reporting and to manipulate the impression gained by the inspection teams (Cheung, 2004; Leung, 2008; Quality Assurance Division of ED, 2003; Quality Assurance Division of EMB, 2005a). Accordingly, many schools over-reported to the inspection teams out of fear of inadequate documentation. Some schools engaged in cosmetic activities by supplying made-up information to satisfy official expectation or to meet the request for openness. These extra preparations for ESR included re-writing or re-packaging massive school documents, reports and minutes of meetings, or compiling new ones; developing excessive questionnaires to collect data, requesting teachers to submit lesson plans for the lessons to be observed to the ESR team; cancelling or cutting short normal school activities, or organising additional ones during ESR; and rehearsing meetings, lessons or student activities. Some schools also bought services from universities or consultancies in preparation of the external inspections.

Excessive meetings and paperwork in preparation for external review actually raised the level of anxiety among school principals and teachers. It also resulted in other schools following suit (Cheung, 2005). This had greatly increased teachers' workload and pressures and diverted their effort from the core business of teaching. Some surveys of teachers or studies on the impact of ESR also confirmed that school inspections were a major source of intense anxiety for teachers (Education Convergence, etc., 2006; HKPTU, 2005, 2007a, 2007b, 2008; Quality Assurance Division of EMB, 2005, 2006: 6, 8, 2008; *Sing Tao Daily*, June 1, 2005). External school inspections and self-evaluation were among the key points of contention by teachers in recent years, which reached a peak when 7,500 teachers, led by Hong Kong Professional Teachers' Union, took to the streets on 22 January 2006 to protest about stress and heavy workloads.

## How the information is disclosed?

Once information is recorded for inspection, there still exist concerns over the way of reporting and the users it is disclosed to, and these raise further questions about fullness and accuracy of information reported to the public. Given the sensitivity and importance of the information, its presentation, including wording and format carry crucial implications and impact for and on the stakeholders involved (Field et al., 1998). It forms interpretation and determines its reception by the users.

In Hong Kong, in addition to distributing full printed copies of the inspection reports to the community, these reports were disseminated by the Internet for public reference as well. The release of the QAI and ESR reports inevitably differentiated kindergartens and schools into different grades in an explicit way. In assessing school performance, with the set of Performance Indicators for Hong Kong Schools published in 2002, the government used four grades (excellent, good, acceptable and unsatisfactory) to indicate four levels of performance respectively: major strengths, strengths outweigh weaknesses, some strengths and some weaknesses, and major weaknesses. This kind of official sorting and ranking of school was undoubtedly critical to the reputation of the schools inspected, and there are a number of issues that deserve serious attention.

First, the practice of releasing only summary reports, instead of the whole report, on the Internet was criticised for causing public misunderstanding of the schools (*Oriental Daily*, April 17, 2001). In the eyes of school representatives, if there was any criticism of particular schools, there should be a report of the fine details. Without this, any criticism of the schools concerned was dismissed as biased and misleading. Also, the replies to the criticisms from the schools concerned was not included in the reports, thus denying the schools the opportunity to defend their performance and appeal for amendment, and this caused further dissent by the schools. Some principals argued that particular remarks might not reflect the full picture of school reality, and the wordings of the statements in summaries became a subject of dispute (*Apple Daily*, April 18, 2001). For example, remarks like "occasionally hindered communications between teacher and students with the use of English in instruction" actually referred to physical education lessons; and "some teachers were not well-versed with questioning technique" referred to only one novice teacher. Another issue was about the interpretation of the statements such as "students were poor in examination performance" and "students were poor in discipline". From the summaries and the selective reporting of them in the newspapers, readers were, at best, easily inclined to make over-generalizations about the schools, and at worst, got a one-sided or poor impression.

In those cases when real problems were detected, proper attribution of cause was another area of dispute as these reports did not differentiate between symptoms and root-causes. For instance, in the schools accused of a lack of creativity in teaching and learning – a common failing of many Hong Kong schools, the reason was mainly due to the limitations of the current public examination system that emphasised lower-order thinking and memorisation. Criticisms such as not providing enough opportunities for students to participate in class and for relying too heavily on textbooks, questions asked were not stimulating, and thus failed to develop in students the ability to think critically might also lie in the constraints of a tightly-packed syllabus, large class sizes, the wide range of student abilities within classes, over-load with administrative tasks and traditional pedagogical culture (*Sing Tao Daily*, April 18, 2001). Despite the goodwill of the policy-makers, many aims of current education reform were also difficult to achieve without additional resources and adequate support.

These problems have deteriorated since adopting some measures of education reforms like the reduction of school bands (that is, student intake classified into groups according to their academic performance) from five to three, and the implementation of an inclusive education programme for children with learning disabilities. Admittedly, a school's weak performance in teaching and learning was often the result of taking in a considerable number of academically weak students and those who have emotional or behavioural problems due to unfavourable family background. For these schools, teachers' restricting themselves to ask straightforward questions because of discipline concerns was also understandable and justified as open-ended questions might lead to classroom management problems (*South China Morning Post (SCMP)*, September 18, 2004). In contrast, simple questions might serve to build up students' confidence. All these issues raised the question of what standard and whose standard was being applied. Decontexualized information is meaningless and misleading.

Moreover, the "reality" as reported, while being condemned as "anti-educational" by the authority, might be exactly the result of market forces that the authority favoured. A case in point was those kindergartens denounced for writing characters, frequent dictations and a tough curriculum in the QAI reports (Quality Assurance Division of ED, 2003; Quality Assurance Division of EMB, 2005a). While the government has reformed the primary one entry assessments to prevent kindergarteners from being given writing drills, dictations or required to sit for examinations; it remains quite common for kindergarteners to do so, which lead to very adverse effects. Many kindergartens were induced to adopt the traditional approach, like writing characters and dictations, because many reputational primary schools did so (*SCMP*, March 29, November 8, 2003). It was not easy to avoid before corresponding changes were made in the primary sector. Another factor that has brought about this tendency is parents' views on their children's education. Many parents favoured more homework and dictation for their children, but did not realise playing is an effective way of learning and were worried that their children might waste their time in kindergartens. They were worried their children might not catch up with others at primary school stage. Being pressured by parents in the marketplace, many kindergartens prematurely crammed their pupils with excessive amounts of knowledge. Facing fierce competition in attracting pupils, many kindergartens also had to meet the wishes of parents who paid the tuition fees (*Ta Kung Pao*, September 28, 2002).

## What is the role of news media?

News media is a major party in using and disseminating the information of school performance. There has been increasing attention paid to the role of the news media in mediating education policy (Blackmore & Thorpe, 2003; Wallace, 1993; Warmington & Murphy, 2004). Popular news media play an important intermediary role in transmitting and presenting the information to the public.

Reporting in the news media therefore raises further questions about extraction and interpretation. What makes news as "news" usually lies in its exceptionality, rather than ordinariness. The media usually constructs news by spotlighting on the novel, exciting, troublesome and problematic areas readers or audience are interested in. For journalists, news about schooling performance is a potentially exciting story of public concern, particularly when it is related to examination results or scandals. Bad news for schools are often good news for the news media (Berliner & Biddle, 1995; Thomas, 2003).

In a fashion of market-oriented journalism, school performance is naturally a topic of interest to the public and to the news media in Hong Kong. The public reporting of school performance has attracted the interests of and scrutiny by the press, and the presentation of a story could be made sensational when the press gives exclusive attention to partial and negative information available. It was no surprise that the summary reports of individual schools and kindergartens uploaded onto the official homepage were selectively reported by the press. Despite the appeals made by the officials opposing any official ranking of schools, shortly after the issue of the inspection reports, the news media were extremely eager to compare the performances of different schools as found in inspection reports. The press was very keen on re-analysing this information in order to appraise and rank the performance of schools. Some newspapers deliberately took the words and lines of individual schools' summary reports in their reporting. Extractions of individual QAI school reports were also made special columns of newspapers or parents' magazines which serve as guidelines for choosing schools and kindergartens.

When reporting the QAI findings, there was a tendency for the news media, especially the popular Chinese newspapers to witch-hunt and uncover the weakest, to highlight the "unexpected" performance of renowned schools, and to deride the "poor" performance of individual schools (which will be discussed fully in the next section). Reports were thus focused more on under-performing schools, with less recognition of those schools which are doing well. The news discourse of derision (Ball, 1990) was coupled with stigmatisation – with the faults amplified by the newspapers' reports, which both serve to alarm the public and boost revenue for the press. Schools' poor performance was usually made a headline using exaggerated or emotion-charged phrases like "BLASTING", "SLAMMING", "POOR COMMENTS", "TEN BIG WEAKNESSES" and "NINE DEADLY SINS".

Hong Kong's education system has long been driven by public examinations, and it was widely faulted for being too stressful, too examination-oriented, prone to drilling students and producing passive learners – criticisms still levelled at some Hong Kong schools today. No surprise that general problems like rote learning, teacher-centred teaching, drilling pupils, a lack of proper questioning techniques, failure to arouse students' interests in learning, insufficiencies with developing students' creative and critical thinking, too low expectations of students were commonly found in the inspection reports (Quality Assurance Division of EMB, various years), and these pitfalls were appropriated or focused by the local newspapers.

Another focus of concern was using English as a medium of instruction (*Apple Daily*, July 1, 2005; *Hong Kong Economic Times*, July 1, 2005, March 18, 2008; *SCMP*, February 18, 2006; *Sing Tao Daily*, March 18, 2008). It was found out that in English classes or subjects taught in English, some teachers spoke a mixture of both English and Chinese while others did not often encourage students to communicate in English. With these negative reports, the press highlighted schools' and teachers' failings and put the blame on both of them for their weak performance.

Another group of victims was the traditional reputational schools, many of which were among the premium English-language secondary school sector (less than 25 per cent of secondary schools were allowed to continue to teach in English after a mother-tongue policy strictly enforced from 1998 onwards). Being the stars in the eyes of the public, their performance naturally became the focus of the media. For instance, to pick up the weaknesses, the press like *Sing Tao Daily* (April 18, 2001) tabulated the criticisms towards some renowned schools as found in the inspection reports. Their uses of traditional teaching method and school rules were also subject to reproach and disgrace in many newspapers (*Apple Daily*, February 15, 2003, November 1, 2003; *Ming Pao*, October 3, 2002; *SCMP*, March 12, 2002; *Sing Tao Daily*, February 19, 2002, March 1, 2002).

Worse than this, there were cases of careless mistakes found in the newspapers' reports. For example, *Ming Pao* (September 29, 2004) mixed up the names of individual schools in quoting remarks of QAI reports, and had to make amendments and clarifications apologising for "imprecise" headlines and confusing reports of individual schools.

## What are the consequences of reporting?

The public reporting of school performance as discussed above not only resulted in very heated disputes, but also proved an ordeal for the school sector and many teachers and students involved. More importantly, with little recognition of the merits and efforts of schools, the news media often performed "public trial" when picking on weaknesses of the schools inspected. Many schools were under great pressure when their names appeared on the newspapers. The blame placed on the schools by the public hurt many teachers and students, and the damage to school's reputations directly affected the enrolment in following academic years. For example, the QAI 2001/02 annual report severely condemned a primary school in Tuen Mun for its mal-administration and poor school performance, which was widely reported by many newspapers. The incident was made headline as "teachers kept lazy for five years, principal said helpless" by *Ming Pao* (September 28, 2002). And *Sing Tao Daily* (September 28, 2002) even used the phrase 'nine deadly sins' to dramatise its shortcomings.

The scandal directly led to the sacking of the school principal in 2002 (*Ta Kung Pao*, September 29, 2002). The impact went even further, with many pupils feeling so upset about the negative report of their school that special counselling had to be arranged for them (*Sing Tao Daily*, October 2, 2002). The school's parent-teacher association also placed an advertisement in a newspaper to defend the school at stake (*Ming Pao*, October 18, 2002). The school spokesman explained that its relatively poor standard in English was the result of accommodating a large number of immigrant children from mainland China, an important underlying factor which was not taken into account in the inspection report (*Wen Wei Po*, October 5, 2002). The new school principal, in a newspaper interview in December 2003, also admitted that the negative report was a severe blow to teachers' self-confidence (*Sing Tao Daily*, December 29, 2003). To rescue the school from under-enrolment, the school had to create a team to promote admissions. Despite these efforts, the school finally merged with another primary school and passed its management to another sponsoring body in 2004.

The release of information has also caused some changes in the school sector in the following ways. First, the gaze of the public has brought a new culture of competition among schools, and accordingly, more time, resources and efforts have been channelled to publicity and marketing strategies and therefore away from teaching. In order to do window-dressing and compete for "good students" intake (*Ta Kung Pao*, April 26, 2001), more and more schools were willing or even enthusiastic to take the lead in disclosing more detailed information by incorporating solely the positive remarks of QAI or ESR reports into their school profiles and on school websites. The threat of school closures due to the falling birth rate had further skewed school self-disclosure into something unhealthy, as mentioned on pages 167–168.

Second, as all facets of school work were subject to formal and informal scrutiny from inside and outside, principals and school management were also faced with the spectre of vastly increased accountability (Cheung, 2000; Yu, 2005). QAI or ESR exerted increasing pressure of external surveillance on school management. As schools were pushed further to opening up to the public, principals found themselves as highly visible spokespersons for their schools and had to explain inspection results to the media. Given that schools operating in a more open and competitive climate, they needed to deal with the media and project a positive image of their schools. Fierce rivalry for better student intakes among schools has also forced principals to become public relations officers, with increased contact with the parent-teacher associations and the alumni associations. Many principals found their new roles to be uncertain and rather stressful and in some cases, distracting from the core purpose of their schools. For the teachers, there remained a widespread view that school inspections meant an extra, imposed workload in relation to time and timing, in particular the tightness of the schedule which encompassed a wide variety of tasks, and time-consuming in gathering and analysing documents, holding meetings, discussing ratings, and drafting reports (Quality Assurance Division of EMB, 2005b). Falling rolls, parental choice and external accountability contributed to a heavy pressure on the teaching staff that the school had not been properly depicted in the final report. And principals, teachers and parents expressed anxiety about uploading of reports to a publicly accessible website.

## Summary and implications

This analysis of these disputes related to the generation and disclosure of QAI reports brings us back to the key policy question – "should there be public reporting of school performance?" And the answers to the questions depend very much on the fitness of original purposes and the costs involved. While the measure of releasing school inspection reports was justified in terms of right to information, parental choice, accountability, and school improvement, the issues such as legitimacy and fairness of assessment mechanisms, fullness and accuracy of reporting and proper dissemination and uses of such information also deserved special attention when formulating and implementing the relevant policy. What happened in Hong Kong showed that there were serious unintended, and sometimes highly undesirable, consequences related to the disclosure of school reports. With hindsight, the official rhetoric on the merits of information disclosure to the public did not lead to expected results as promised. And there was evidence that QAI failed in bringing about school improvement in the eyes of teachers (Chan, 2001). What is more, the disputes caused severe strife among the government, news media, the parents and the school sector, and at worst undermined the partnership of various stakeholders. These high-stakes and punitive accountability practices in the past decade have created tremendous tension within the school sector.

In the final analysis, the legitimacy problems of inspection and assessment arise from the deficient policy-making mechanism in Hong Kong, despite the fact that some officials said the QAI reports were compiled in the spirit of transparency and accountability. An irony was that the QAI exercise was lacking in this fashion, being unilaterally imposed by the government (*Ming Pao*, April 7, 2000). The black-box-like consultation mechanisms thus suffered from not taking adequate advice from teachers and other academic groups in the education sector. And the external accountability as such focused exclusively on school-level accountability, without paying much attention to the larger system at work.

As for the content and ways of information release, public reporting also requires professional accountability on the parts of government, school management, and the press – an issue should not be overlooked under the notion of consumerist accountability. It was unfortunate that the worries and warnings of the school sector finally came true. The exclusive focus on incomplete, sketchy or negative information by some news media was definitely anti-educational, destructive and unethical. Many relentless attacks on the schools not only proved harmful to parents and students, but also undermined public trust towards the overall school system. What should be reported and how it should be released to the public points are after all ethical issues. This raises the questions of information quality and ethics of information release to the public. And this requires corresponding policy measures concerning the audit and regulation of information release and uses.

Upon receiving complaints about excessive workload and documentation in preparing for the external school review, and in response to the schools' concern about making the review reports available to the public which could be selectively reported in the media to the detriment of the schools' reputation, in June 2005, the government finally made concession to the school sector and allowed school self-evaluation reports of primary and secondary schools not to be disclosed to the public (*Ming Pao*, June 9, 2004). To dispel excessive worries and alleviate pressure on schools, the government further loosened the procedures and requirements of the review process and reporting, starting from the 2005/06 school year (*Ming Pao*, July 16, 2005; Quality Assurance Division of EMB, 2005; n.d.). While sponsoring bodies and the school community, including parents, through its school management committee, would continue to receive copies of the full report, the review reports would not be uploaded to the Internet for the first four-year cycle. This was to honour the principle of accountability to the key stakeholders whilst reducing anxieties which could distract attention from the core purposes of school improvement and student learning. The changes were also intended to enhance communication and mutual trust so that to establish a candid and open culture of self-reflective and self-evaluation in schools.

In February 2006, following a massive teacher rally in January 2006 and in response to growing concern about teachers' work and stress, the government further introduced nine measures to relieve teachers' workload. Among them the mode and procedures of ESR were simplified and revised starting from the 2006/07 school year (*Standard*, February 28, 2006). In 2008, following a review on ESR of the first cycle covering all public sector schools, the second cycle commencing in 2008/09 was extended from four to six years (EDB, 2008; QAD, 2008a, 2008b). To facilitate SSE in a more focused manner and alleviate teachers' workload, the PI framework, KPM and SHS have been further simplified and refined. "Performance Indicators" (PI) areas are also reduced from 14 to 8 and the number of PI, from 29 to 23. KPM and Stakeholder Survey (SHS) have also been revised accordingly to align with the collection of data and evidence. In order to avoid excessive detail and repetition, evidence of performance is exemplified against each PI area instead of against the components of each PI.

In 2014, the streamlined ESR procedures have been further consolidated after the second cycle review (Quality Assurance and School-based Support Division of EDB, 2014). Also, greater flexibility in ESR procedures and reporting is allowed to reflect unique school context. Schools are only required to release the ESR findings to their stakeholders for information, feedback and accountability. ESR reports are not to be uploaded onto the Education Bureau's website. And if the school chooses to release the ESR report to the public, the report has to be presented in whole, not in part, but the appendices and the information of the ESR Team should be deleted. Once the school has chosen to release the ESR report to the public, this practice has to be continued for subsequent years. And schools should not use the ESR report for publicity.

These latest developments signaled a concession and compromise of the policy made after several years of bitter experiences in the school sector. And the case of Hong Kong could serve as a reference for other places contemplating similar policies. School accountability mechanism like school inspection has its own merits. But it also has its drawbacks. More importantly, public reporting of school performance does complicate the issue and exacerbate some inherent problems of school inspection. My analysis has demonstrated the ways and effects of surveillance on the school sector and described the problems of surveillance amplified with the use of public reporting. There is a problematic relationship between external control and internal organisational improvement and the nature information plays a crucial role in mediating this relationship and process of schooling (O'Day, 2002). It is ironic that a greater degree of openness or transparency would deepen a culture of performativity (Ball, 2000) and defect the cardinal educational purposes, let alone at the cost of deprofessionalisation and stress on the part of teachers. To a certain extent, public reporting, particularly in a high-stakes manner, would decrease the incentives on the part of school personnel to report authentic and valid information of school performance to the public and the parents. Also, we should not forget the very fact that information or data is mainly generated and provided by the school personnel and teachers, which could easily result in a situation abundant with misleading, messed-up and mostly useless information when threat is perceived. And information of school performance is easily dramatised and manipulated by the news media.

The negative impact of releasing school performance information could sometimes outweigh the benefits. And a proper balance between improvement and accountability must be made. What matters most is not so much about the amount of information is reported as about the nature and quality of information is collected, reported and used. Some prerequisites such as building up consensus should be met when publishing individual school data so that to prevent certain negative outcome from occurring.

# References

*Apple Daily*. (2001, April 18). Newly-released QAI reports pinpoint weaknesses of reputational schools, principals did not agree.
*Apple Daily*. (2003, February 15). QAI reports.
*Apple Daily*. (2003, November 1). Inspection reports reveal the reality of reputational schools.
*Apple Daily*. (2005, July 1). CMI students criticized for poor English, Parents furious with failure of mother tongue teaching.
Ball, S. J. (1990). *Politics and policy-making in education*. London: Routledge.
Ball, S. J. (2000). Performativities and fabrications in the education economy: Towards the performative society. *Australian Educational Researcher, 17*(3), 1–24.
Berliner, D., & Biddle, B. (1995). *The manufactured crisis: Myths, fraud, and the attack on America's public schools*. Reading, MA: Addison-Wesley.
Blackmore, J., & Thorpe, S. (2003). Media/ting change: the role of mass popular media in school reform. *Journal of Education Policy, 18*(6), 577–595.
Chan, H. (2005, March 9). Values of ESR. *Sing Tao Daily*.
Chan, Y. M. (2001). *Teachers' perceptions of 'quality assurance inspection' in relation to school improvement: A case study*. M.Ed. thesis. Hong Kong: University of Hong Kong.
Cheung, R. M. B. (2000). The changing roles and needs of school principals in Hong Kong. In *School leadership in Hong Kong: A profile for a new century* (pp. 9–10). Hong Kong: Hong Kong Centre for the Development of Educational Leadership, The Chinese University of Hong Kong.
Cheung, R. M. B. (2004, 13 December). School fears. *SCMP*.
Cheung, R. M. B. (2005, 1 February). ESR might deepen divisions among schools. *Hong Kong Economic Times*.
Choi, K. K. (2005a, January 20). Redesigning school assessment. *Sing Tao Daily*.

Choi, K. K. (2005b, July 7). Pressure of ESR. *Sing Tao Daily*.
Cullingford, C., & Swift, H. (2001). Beleaguered by information? The school reactions of headteachers to school effectiveness initiatives. *Educational Review, 53*(3), 271–283.
Cuttance, P., & Stokes, S. A. (2000). *Reporting on student and school achievement*. A research report prepared for the Commonwealth Department of Education, Training and Youth Affairs, January 2000. Department of Education, Training and Youth Affairs, Australia.
Education Commission. (1997). *Education Commission report No.7: Quality school education*. Hong Kong, Government printer.
Education Convergence, Hong Kong Primary Educational Research Association, Eye on Education (2006). *Research project on Hong Kong teachers' stress*. (August 31) http://www.edconvergence.org.hk/
Education Bureau. (2008, July 3). *Circular No. 13/2008 The school development and accountability framework – the next phase of continuous school improvement*. (Ref.: EDB(QA/INS)/ADM/196/1 II).
Education and Manpower Branch. (1993). *School education in Hong Kong: A statement of aims*. Hong Kong: Government Printer.
Field, C., Greenstreet, D., Kusel, P., & Parsons, C. (1998). OFSTED inspection reports and the language of educational improvement. *Evaluation and Research in Education, 12*(3), 125–139.
Fitz-Gibbon, C. T. (1996). *Monitoring education*. London: Cassell.
*Hansard*. (2005, March 9). Assessment of School Standard by School Self-evaluation, 5176–5179.
*Hong Kong Economic Times*. (2005, July 1). CMI schools teaching English accused of mixed with Chinese, ESR reports of EMB point to not building up English-speaking environment.
*Hong Kong Economic Times*. (2006, November 15). (Editorial) The voucher scheme for kindergartens – like neither donkey nor horse.
*Hong Kong Economic Times*. (2008, March 18). Inspection report criticize expatriate English teachers' boring teaching methods, English teaching mixed with Chinese in kindergartens.
Hong Kong Professional Teachers' Union. (2005, November 25). Quality education impossible with teachers' high burnout rate. *PTU News, 498*.
Hong Kong Professional Teachers' Union. (2007a, August 8). Facing teachers' work stress, slowing the pacing of education reform, in response to the summary report of the 'teachers' work' committee. *PTU News, 517*.
Hong Kong Professional Teachers' Union. (2007b, September 17). A critical review of educational policies in the past decade, *PTU News, 528*.
Hong Kong Professional Teachers' Union. (2008, 13 October). Another teacher takes the plunge, *PTU News, 547*.
Hong Kong SAR Information Centre. (2006). *Quality of early childhood education hinges on pursuit for self-improvement and professionalism*. (Press Release on 21 October).
Law, F. (2003, May 9). *Enhancing school development and accountability through school self-evaluation and external school review*. Letter to school principals.
Law, L. Y. S. (2003, March 1). Basic flaws threaten credibility of inspections. Mailbag, *SCMP*.
Lee, K. K., & Chiu, C. S. (2003, February 25). How to create quality inspection? *Sing Tao Daily*.

Leung, K. S. (2008) *The effects of key performance measures of Hong Kong schools on teachers' work: A power perspective.* Unpublished dissertation, CUHK.
Ming Pao. (1998, November 3). Holistic inspection satisfactory, self-evaluation results and student academic performance of some schools still not satisfactory.
Ming Pao. (2000, April 6). Groups query the release of QAI report.
Ming Pao. (2000, April 6). ED implement inspection on kindergartens in September, the report will not be released to the public in the first year.
Ming Pao. (2000, April 7). Subsidised Secondary Schools Council accuses ED for three serious faults.
Ming Pao. (2002, September 28). Teachers staying lazy for five years, principal said helpless.
Ming Pao. (2002, September 28). Problematic schools, support prior to punishment (editorial).
Ming Pao. (2002, October 3). QAI report criticizes unidirectional teaching, a small group of teachers resist change, reform in Wah Yan College (Hong Kong) encounters barriers.
Ming Pao. (2002, October 18). Siu Leun's parents put an ad to support the school.
Ming Pao. (2004, September 29). Amendments and clarification.
Ming Pao. (2004, June 9). EMB makes concession, SSE of primary and secondary schools not disclosed.
Ming Pao. (2005, July 16). ESR reports not to be publicized.
Ming Pao. (2008, May 8). Former chief inspector of ED questions ESR as unprofessional.
O'Day, J. A. (2002). Complexity, accountability, and school improvement. *Harvard Educational Review, 72*(3), 293–329.
Oriental Daily. (2001, April 17). Tops schools criticized by ED for lacking in inspiration in terms of teaching and learning.
Oriental Daily. (2001, April 18). Reputational schools criticize QAI reports unfair, only summaries put on the Internet, responses refused.
Perryman, J. (2006). Panoptic performativity and school inspection regimes: Disciplinary mechanisms and life under special measures. *Journal of Education Policy, 21*(2), 147–161.
Petegem, P. van, Vanhoof, J., Daems, F., & Mahieu, P. (2005). Publishing information on individual schools? *Educational Research and Evaluation, 11*(1), 45–60.
Poulson, L. (1996). Accountability: A key-word in the discourse of educational reform. *Journal of Education Policy, 11*(5), 579–592.
Quality Assurance and School-Based Support Division, Education Bureau. (2014). *External school review: Information for schools.* Hong Kong: The Division.
Quality Assurance Division, Education and Manpower Bureau. (2005a). *Phase I report of the impact study on the effectiveness of external school review.* Hong Kong: The Division.
Quality Assurance Division, Education and Manpower Bureau. (2005b, July 29). *School self-evaluation and external school review modification of implementation requirements* (Letter reference No. EMB(QA/INS)/ESR/1).
Quality Assurance Division, Education and Manpower Bureau. (2006). *Phase II report of the impact study on the effectiveness of external school review*, August. Hong Kong: The Division.
Quality Assurance Division, Education Bureau. (2008a). *Final report of the impact study on the effectiveness of external school review*, July. Hong Kong: The Division.

Quality Assurance Division, Education Bureau. (2008b). *The next phase of external school review: Information for schools*, 22 September. Hong Kong: The Division.

Quality Assurance Division, Education Bureau. (n.d.). *School development and accountability framework: Memorandum on school self-evaluation (SSE) and external school review (ESR)*. Retrieved from http://www.edb.gov.hk/FileManager/EN/Content_6459/memorandum_on_sse_esr_e.pdf

Quality Assurance Division, Education Department. (various years since 1998). *Quality assurance inspection annual reports*. Hong Kong: The Department.

Quality Assurance Division, Education Department. (various years since 2004). *ESR annual report*. Hong Kong: The Department.

Ranson, S. (2003). Public accountability in the age of neo-liberal governance. *Journal of Education Policy, 18*(5), 459–480.

Reid, K. (2006). An evaluation of inspection reports on primary school attendance. *Educational Research, 48*(3), 267–286.

Reynolds, D., & Cuttance, P. Eds. (1992). *School effectiveness: Research, policy and practice*. London: Cassell.

*SCMP (South China Morning Post)*. (2001, April 21). Doubts over quality assessment.

*SCMP*. (2002, March 12). Pupils forced to take passive role in elite classes.

*SCMP*. (2003, March 29). Rote learning and dictations still prevalent in HK kindergartens.

*SCMP*. (2003, November 8). Pre-schools still putting pupils under pressure.

*SCMP*. (2004, September 18). Teachers fail to develop critical skills, say reports.

*SCMP*. (2006, February 18). Usage of English as medium tool rare.

*SCMP*. (2006, March 18). Safeguard vital school inspections, say parents.

Silver, H. (1994). *Good schools, effective schools*. London: Cassell.

*Sing Pao*. (2004, July 31). Allow social forces to monitor kindergartens (editorial).

*Sing Tao Daily*. (2001, April 18). QAI reports grade students passive in reputational schools, overemphasis on examinations, lacking in diversified teaching.

*Sing Tao Daily*. (2002, February 19). School management lacking in consensus, teachers poor in performance, ED blames Chan Sui Ki (La Salle) College.

*Sing Tao Daily*. (2002, March 1). Chan Sui Ki (La Salle) College accepts Ed's criticisms.

*Sing Tao Daily*. (2002, September 28). Siu Leun being accused of committing 'nine deadly sins', ED's report denounces as 'poor' primary school.

*Sing Tao Daily*. (2002, October 2). ED's report a damage to school's reputation.

*Sing Tao Daily*. (2003, December 29). Being blasted by EMB, Siu Leun School reforms for survival.

*Sing Tao Daily*. (2004, December 30). Confidential VA indicators revealed for the first time.

*Sing Tao Daily*. (2005, June 1). 03 QAI report examine performance of 92 primary and secondary schools, 30% of English teachers performed unsatisfactorily.

*Sing Tao Daily*. (2008, March 18). English lessons in some kindergartens not satisfactory.

*Sing Tao Daily*. (2008, May 8). Former inspector of EDB criticizes ESR quality.

*Standard*. (2000, May 19). Parents favour subsidised private schools.

*Standard*. (2006, February 28). Li attempts to ease job pressures on teachers.

*Standard*. (2006, October 12). Parents to be given help with kindergarten fees.

*Standard*. (2006, October 20). Private preschools eye slice of subsidy pie.

*Sun*. (2001, April 18). Incomplete, not objective, short of support, difficult to improve, ED's inspection 'diagnosis without prescription'.

*Sun.* (2002, February 20). Inspection reports criticize some reputational schools poor management, ED's inspection being blamed for offering no assistance.
*Ta Kung Pao.* (1998, November 16). QAI report- groups contest its public release.
*Ta Kung Pao.* (2001, April 26). Taking the lead to issue summary report in school profiles, Tuen Mun's TWGH Sun Hoi Directors' College announces its inspection report.
*Ta Kung Pao.* (2002, September 28). ED names the kindergartens to reduce classwork, principals says difficult to satisfy parental demands.
*Ta Kung Pao.* (2002, September 28). Parents' alliance urge for taking back the management of school.
*Ta Kung Pao.* (2002, September 29). Siu Leun School is going to replace its head, ED says it should turn in a plan of improvement within four months.
*Ta Kung Pao.* (2005, June 1). Nearly half of the schools not in line with education reform.
Telephone survey laboratory, The Hong Kong Institute of Asia-Pacific Studies, CUHK. (2000). *Public attitudes towards renowned secondary schools* (25–31 January, 2000). Hong Kong: The Hong Kong Institute of Asia-Pacific Studies, the Chinese University of Hong Kong (in Chinese).
Thomas, S. (2003). 'The trouble with our schools': A media construction of public discourses on Queensland schools. *Discourse: Studies in the Cultural Politics of Education, 24*(1), 19–34.
Tsang, W. K. (1997). *The Deeper Meanings of ECR 7: The Cult of Market Efficiency.* Occasional Paper No. 3. Hong Kong, Hong Kong Institute of Educational Research, the Chinese University of Hong Kong (in Chinese).
Tsang, W. K. (2000). *Misuse and misunderstanding of education performance indicators: A critique on the culture of performance-indicator and league-table cult.* Occasional Paper No. 34. Hong Kong, Hong Kong Institute of Educational Research, the Chinese University of Hong Kong (in Chinese).
Tse, T. K. C. (2005). Quality education in Hong Kong: The anomalies of managerialism and marketization. In L. S. Ho, P. Morris & Y. P. Chung (Eds.), *Education reform and the quest for excellence: The Hong Kong story* (pp. 99–123, pp. 224–227, pp. 238–240). Hong Kong: Hong Kong University Press.
Tsoi, K. L. (2005, July 16). Address the public feeling, improve policy implementation. *Hong Kong Economic Times.*
Wallace, M. (1993). Discourse of derision: the role of mass media within the education policy process. *Journal of Education Policy, 8*(4), 321–337.
Warmington, P., & Murphy, R. (2004). Could do better? Media depictions of UK educational assessment results. *Journal of Education Policy, 19*(3), 285–299.
*Wen Wei Po.* (2002, October 5). The measure of principal's accountability should be in practice.
Yu, C. C. Y. (2005). Principal and teacher perceptions of the leadership role of principals in Hong Kong protestant Christian secondary schools following the change of sovereignty to China. *Post-Script, 6*(1), 1–22.

# 11 Parent and home-school relationships

Issues and challenges

*Shun-Wing Ng*

## Introduction

For the last two decades, the education sector has been changing quickly in the world. Most importantly there are two significant factors affecting educational development in Hong Kong. First, globalisation has imposed significant impacts on educational change for future developments (Arnove & Torres, 2007; Carnoy & Rhoten, 2002; Daun, 2009). Neo-liberal values have directed reforms to fill achievement gaps among students with diverse backgrounds and abilities and to measure performance of schools and teachers given market demands for accountability (Skerrett & Hargreaves, 2008). Second, the return of Hong Kong's sovereignty to China in 1997 has led to the political movement of requesting democratisation in a representative government system. These two factors have imposed great influence on education reforms in which the quest for decentralisation of power, accountability, transparency and participatory management in school education has become prevalent in the developmental process of Hong Kong's education.

Cheng (2007) argues that the period of 1990s witnessed the wave of school-based management (SBM) reforms emphasising the significance of educational accountability to the stakeholders. This accountability orientation carries the notion that parents and teachers can play a significant role in school management and school governance (Caldwell, 2004; Cheng, 1991; Ng, 2013). Indeed, the school decentralisation framework in SBM offers opportunities for a new type of school management in which the notion that parents as school partners in state education is gradually recognised at different levels of school education in Asian countries. Nowadays, government programmes currently mandate direct parent input in school governance (Nir & Ami, 2005). Motivated by Western research showing that strong family-school relationships contribute to school effectiveness, the Hong Kong government has proposed a number of measures regarding parent involvement in children's education since 1991.

Home-school partnerships have been developed because parent representatives have eventually been allowed to participate in managing schools through legislation. The bill that parents, teachers and alumni are included as school governors commencing in 2011 was passed as an Education Ordinance by the Legislative Council in July 2004. Thus, empowering parents to play a role in the self-management of schools is one of the most important innovations in helping achieve school effectiveness (Caldwell, 2004; Ng & Lee, 2015).

Many studies show that parent involvement in school is beneficial to the children (e.g., Epstein, 2013; Graves & Wright, 2011), but there are also conflicts between parents and teaching professionals in the process of developing home-school relationships (e.g., Heystek, 2006: Nir & Ami, 2005; Pang, 2008). This chapter aims to examine (1) how parents have been included in the education sector for the last twenty years; (2) in what ways their roles are evolving in their children's education; and (3) issues and challenges arising in the process of parents' involvement in school in Hong Kong. Analyses are interwoven with review of education policy documents published by the Education Bureau (EDB), formerly the Education and Manpower Bureau (EMB), of Hong Kong and the literature concerned from the perspectives of social, political and economic development at different periods of time. As a result of examining the evolving roles of parents through analysing these policy documents, four phases of how parents have been included in times of education reforms in Hong Kong are conceptualised in chronological order, namely: (1) parents as unwelcome guests: absolute quiescence and acquiescence (before 1991); (2) parents as volunteers: collaboration orientation (1991–1998); (3) parents as clients: accountability orientation (1999–2004); and (4) parents as school governors: partnership orientation (2004 and onwards).

Prior to discussing these four phases grounded from review of policy documents and research studies, the following two sections regarding relevant literature review on parent involvement and the micro-politics arising from parents' involvement in school operation will provide readers with theoretical underpinnings of the notion of parent involvement and the background about home-school relationships around the world. And these may give hints to the understanding of the situation of parents' evolving roles in school education especially in the post-colonial era in Hong Kong and the examination of the challenges facing the promotion of parent involvement in the Hong Kong schooling system.

## Parent involvement

Parents are people who influence children's attitudes towards learning and have a crucial role in education. Constructive impacts of parent involvement on students' academic outcomes have been recognised by teaching professionals (Graves & Wright, 2011). Thus, parent involvement could be defined as parents' behaviours in home and school setting supporting their children's educational progress (El Nokali, Bachman & Votruba-Drzal, 2010). In fact, research in the West demonstrates that parent involvement in school can help enhance positive development of children's self-concepts and can make contributions to the long-term development of school effectiveness (Amatea, 2007; Berns, 2007; Epstein, 2001). However, researchers and policy-makers who choose to avoid a general definition of parent involvement have interwoven different aspects of parent involvement in children's education.

To conceptualise how parent involvement or home-school co-operation occurs in different dimensions at school, many researchers have developed different frameworks on the basis of empirical evidence (e.g., Bastiani, 1989; Epstein, 1995). For examples, Bastiani (1989) conceptualises eight levels of home-school relationships, including communicating with school personnel, taking care of students' problems, supervising children's learning at home, understanding school policies, volunteering, attending parent education programmes, giving advice on the school's decision-making process and participating in community activities. Epstein (1995) suggests the following six types of family, school and community partnerships: parenting, communicating, volunteering, learning at home, decision-making and collaborating with the community. In Hong Kong, Ng (1999) has also developed a six-level model of home-school co-operation in which parents could be involved in communicating with school, helping actual learning of individual children, taking part in parent programmes, assisting in school operation, helping and participating in decision-making. The model has been employed as a research framework in many of his studies (Ng, 1999, 2003, 2007a; Ng & Lee, 2015). Encouraged by the positive evidence of getting parents involved, the Hong Kong government has initiated measures to gradually involve parents at different levels of school education (Ng, 2007a) and eventually they are invited to be involved in the decision-making process in 2011 (Ng, 2013). Nevertheless, Ng (2013) and Pang (2008) have found that there are tensions among parents, teachers, principals at the school-level and between the EDB and school sponsoring bodies during the process of parent involvement.

## Tensions in the process of parent involvement

Blasé and Anderson (1995) indicates that micro-politics exists everywhere in school, especially when new initiatives are introduced to school from outside. The notion of home-school co-operation connotes that parents and teachers value each other in the schooling process of their children where mutual respect exists. Chrispeels (1996) highlights that "co" means "two-way" and "multi-dimensional". She argues that parents and teachers can be co-learners and co-teachers.

MacBeth (1988) discerned three possible stages of progression in the development of home-school partnership among European countries. In the "self-contained stage", professional autonomy is emphasised and the school should be a closed institution in which the expertise functions of professionals carried out are neither influencing nor influenced by parents. However, teachers are gradually recognising the values and the needs to involve parents in school in the second "stage of professional uncertainty". The final one is the "stage of growing confidence" where parents and teachers envisage that the level of parent participation in school education is increasing and partnership relations between teachers and parents are being developed.

In the West, many studies have found that while parents are invited to be school managers, there are various types of tensions, conflicts and micro-politics between and within groups of actions involved in the process of decision-making

(Brown & Duku, 2008; Heystek, 2006; Huber, 2011; Nir & Ami, 2005). For example, the study of Chikoko (2008) in Zimbabwe indicates that despite the presence of a legal decentralised school governance structure in which parents form the majority, they did not have the capacity to function effectively therein, and were still marginalised in the decision-making process.

Cowburn (1986) argues that the concept of home-school partnership is devised for the school personnel to legitimately retain professional control by means of co-opting parents' support and it seems teaching professionals have built-in control over their relationship with parents. Siu (2000) echoes that power relations penetrate parent-school interactions when she explains the meaning of home-school co-operation and parent involvement. Parents are still to be controlled with reference to the will of school principals. Teaching professionals will not easily release influence and control to parents.

In sum, the findings of the above-mentioned research studies conducted in different countries inform us that there is little evidence that schools are accountable to parents and have any intention to hand over policy-making power to parents. In Hong Kong, when parents are allowed to be involved in school management, Pang (2008) argues that there has been no decentralisation of power with the establishment of the school council; rather, the level of government control over school education has increased. Ng (2007a) finds that parent representatives are always marginalised by other members in the school board in Hong Kong. Since parents are now invited to be involved at various levels of school education in Hong Kong, it is my intention to examine how parents' roles have been evolving for the last two decades. And then I discuss and analyse the issues and challenges arising in the involvement process.

## The evolving roles of parents in times of developing home-school relationships

My effort to review relevant policy documents and research studies resulted in conceptualization of the following four phases regarding parents' evolving roles in times of developing home-school relationships. Periodization of each phase is based on occurrence of the incidents at the time which was believed to be critical for promotion of parent involvement. On the other hand, some of the policy documents cited in each phase were published earlier than the period stated because they served the purpose of providing the background of the theme of the phase within that period.

### Phase I (before 1991): Parents as unwelcome guests: Absolute quiescence and acquiescence

The statement, "No parents beyond this line", cited by Green (1968) was not fantasy but a fact in a school in 1966 in Britain. The line which was clearly marked on the ground probably told parents to leave the children with the teaching professionals. The phenomenon was also prevalent in Hong Kong in the 1980s and early 1990s. Parents' rights to take part in school education had not been recognised in Hong Kong until the 1990s. The ideology among the Hong Kong teaching professionals that parents as unwelcome intruders were pervasive among all schools at that time (Ng, 1999). It was probably due to an over-demand for school places in primary and secondary schools (Llewellyn, 1982).

Parents were quiescent about being involved in their children's education. To acquire a place for either aided or free education for their children, they had to be absolutely acquiescent with the government's educational policies (Ng, 2007a). The colonial government had never had a complete and comprehensive idea of how education should look and had put little effort in taking care of other aspects in education such as school management, quality of language teaching, curriculum development and home-school co-operation (Ng, 2001). Parents who could successfully obtain a place for schooling for their children felt very fortunate and satisfied. In this regard, home-school relationships were basically focused on one-way communication; that was to transmit information from school to home. In 1981, an international panel was commissioned by the Hong Kong government to embark on a thorough study of Hong Kong education system. The panel published a report on the findings in 1982. In Hong Kong, it was difficult to find any sense of parent participation in schools in the 1980s. Owing to political reasons, the colonial government did not find it mature to exercise democratisation in the school. The panel led by Llewellyn wrote the following in the report:

> *Any move towards greater participation in educational decision-making and policy formulation would add to existing pressures for the democratisation of the territory's government generally.*
>
> (Llewellyn, 1982, 17–18)

It also stated that teacher-parent contact was limited to problem-orientation. The sharing of responsibilities in education between parents and teachers, and between home and school, was not widely accepted. In the report, it argued:

> *Parent involvement with schooling is usually limited to formal parent-teacher associations' meetings (where they exist) and to rare school visits when a child's problems prompt the teacher to call for the parent.*
>
> (Llewellyn, 1982, 18)

Regarding the development of home-school relationships, Llewellyn (1982) noted that many subsidised schools operated by private and voluntary organisations without tight government supervision tended to be run in an authoritarian and centralised fashion, leaving little room for parent participation in school.

> *Teachers in both subsidised schools and private schools operated by and large without close government supervision of their professional activities. Despite the existence of management boards, schools tend to be run autocratically.*
>
> (Llewellyn, 1982, 50)

Not only did the parents experience difficulties participating in decision-making, the school seldom considered parents' needs when formulating home-school policy. Entering the school, parents had to follow the following procedures (Chung, 1994):

> *First, parents have to obtain the prior approval from the teacher before entering the school. Second, they have to explain to the school gate-keeper for the purpose of their coming when arriving at the school. Third, they have to wait outside the general office.*
>
> (71)

In this period, the autocratic image of school authority owing to historical reasons had rendered parents no choice but to comply with what the school required. Implementation of education policies in this period only aimed at providing schooling opportunities for children of suitable age, compensating most of them with what they had lost and what they should receive. However, due to a great demand and an inadequate supply, it was difficult for parents to ask for more. In terms of involvement, parents were excluded from school, but they were asked to be involved in supervising their children at home. No wonder the parents had to be quiescent and acquiescent in this period.

In fact, the autocratic style of management of the school principals in Hong Kong had been pervasive for almost three decades. The policy document of the 'School Management Initiatives' (SMI) published in 1991 echoed Llewelyn Report in this way:

> *. . . some Principals are insufficiently accountable for their actions and see their post as an opportunity to become* **little emperors** *with dictatorial powers in the school.*
>
> (Education and Manpower Branch & Education Department, 1991, 14)

In summary, parents were passive in this phase. Home-school relations emphasising routine and one-way communications about students' academic performance and discipline problems at school and parent involvement in students' cognitive learning at home pervaded in the ethos of the school. Contact with parents other than those in crisis was not encouraged. Parents were perceived as policy-followers and unwelcome guests if they attempted to overstep the bounds of communication, intruding themselves on school daily operation. What occurred in this phase corresponds with the findings of MacBeth's (1988) and Edward's (1995) studies, that is, a "self-contained stage" where professional autonomy is emphasised and the school is a closed institution. Parents could not intrude on teachers' professional turf. The ideology of separate responsibilities between parents and teachers was pervasive in the education sector before 1990. As reiterated by Davis (1996), by virtue of their positions in the school and the professional knowledge acquired, the teacher professionals have often demonstrated a certain control over the relationships. The built-in control is sometimes, on the one hand, out of the thought of protectionism, and on the other hand, out of the sociological perspective of ethnocentrism. Nevertheless, there seemed to be a breakthrough with regard to parent involvement when the Hong Kong government proposed to include parents in the process of managing schools in the SMI in 1991.

### Phase II (1991–1998): Parents as volunteers: Collaboration orientation

In this phase, in order to explain clearly the background regarding how collaboration between home and school was being established, some documents published earlier than this period were cited for the purpose of discussion.

Following the suggestions from the Llewellyn Report, the Education Commission (EC), was established for the organisation of educational planning and policy in 1984. Since then, recommendations in the Education Commission Reports (ECRs) on educational policies for future development have been presented to the governor every two years in the colonial period and to the chief executive after the sovereignty of Hong Kong was returned to China in 1997. However, the promotion of parent involvement has been put in low priority among recommendations on educational improvement in the reports. In the first three reports, ECR 1, ECR 2 and ECR 3 (EC, 1984, 1986, & 1988), nothing regarding home-school relationships and parents' roles in education was mentioned, and much of the emphasis was made for the expansion of aided places in secondary four and five, medium of instruction and development of tertiary education.

Nevertheless, there was a turning point in 1988 when a booklet on *Better Parenting* was distributed to parents and a note on *School-Parent Liaison* enclosed in a circular on *Strengthening Home-School Communication* was issued to teaching professionals to stress the importance of communicating with parents (Education Department, 1988). The meaningfulness of home-school links seemed to be recognised by the government, but the actions mentioned above were seemingly responses to the sudden change of the social environment that demanded a solution to an alarming increase in the rate of juvenile delinquency.

In 1984 when the Sino-British Agreement regarding returning Hong Kong's sovereignty to China was signed, a more significant political change in Hong Kong aroused parents' awareness of their roles in education. It was the introduction of the representative government system to the legislative council that a representative from the education constituency and others from functional constituencies were elected as legislative councillors in 1988. They started raising the issue of power decentralisation in the school sector in the council.

In 1991, to develop in line with the democratisation process in the political arena of the society, the Hong Kong government, after sending a team of education officials overseas to study the characteristics and components of effective schools, introduced the *School Management Initiatives* (SMI) to school principals, a key and significant state policy paper recommending a reform on devolving power from the central government to schools, and from the school organisations to both teachers and parents (Education and Manpower Branch & Education Department, 1991). Cheng (2007) conceptualised the period of 1990s emphasising interface effectiveness of educational institutions as the second wave of education reforms in response to the concerns about power decentralisation and accountability to the stakeholders, including parents, teachers and professionals in the community. In fact, parents' rights of participation had not been recognised until the proposal of implementing SBM was announced in SMI in 1991 (Ng, 2007b; Pang, 2008).

One of the purposes of the SMI was to specifically define the actual roles of the school principals so that they would no longer be autocratic as indicated in the Llewellyn Report. In addition, the paper recommended greater participation of teachers, parents and alumni in the school management process. It was the first time that parents were given a larger formal stake in the management of schools themselves:

> *School management frameworks should allow for participation in decision-making, according to formal procedures, by all concerned parties including: all teaching staff; the Principal; the SMC; and (to an appropriate degree) parents and students.*
>
> (Education and Manpower Branch & Education Department, 1991, 37)

Parents seemed to be formally included as school managers. Chan, Ho, Tsang, and Wong (1993) then conducted a study on primary school teachers' attitudes towards parent participation in school with a sample of over 350 teachers and principals in 20 primary schools. They reported that parents were most welcome by teachers when they facilitated children's learning at home and rendered support to school at special events such as fund-raising and sports days. However, teachers would become very conservative and self-defensive if parents became school governors.

In 1992, the issue of home-school co-operation was subsequently elaborated in great length in the ECR 5 (EC, 1992). Members of the EC found that the culture and atmosphere in school was not conducive to closer co-operation owing to the fact that teachers and principals, on one hand, treated parents as unwelcome guests (Ng, 1999, 2013) and parents, on the other hand, often maintained unhelpful attitudes towards sharing responsibility with schools (Education Department, 1994). In the ECR 5, it stated:

> *Teachers sometimes feel they can do their job best without parent interference. Parents sometimes expect schools to take an excessive share of responsibility for raising their children. Both parents and teachers may have unrealistic expectations of what a child can achieve at a particular stage of development.*
>
> (EC, 1992, 15)

Obviously, uncooperative attitudes of both parents and teachers were the major obstacles to effective home-school connexions. To improve the situation, the commission advised schools to take initiatives to communicate with the homes and develop innovative approaches of enhancing home-school partnerships which were not too onerous for either parents or teachers. The report also recommended the establishment of a new standing committee to conduct a survey on home-school relationships. In 1993, the Committee on Home-School Co-Operation (CHSC) was set up and the study was then carried out. The report of the survey indicated that only a few of parents (7 per cent) wished to have a say in school management but nearly half of them merely wanted to be informed. Moreover, more than 50 per cent of the teachers and principals surveyed did not welcome parents to manage the school (Education Department, 1994). Shen (1995) explained that these responses, on the one hand, might be due to the assumption that schools did not have a genuine intention to invite parents to take part in school operation and the lack of transparency of school policies discouraged parent participation. On the other hand, parents did not actually understand the meaning of involvement in school.

According to Ng's (2002, 2003) studies, parents and teachers were not psychologically prepared for co-operation. Teachers demonstrated a number of constraints when parent involvement as an innovation in school management was implemented (Ng & Yuen, 2015; Pang, 2004). Understanding that there were barriers to the promotion of parent involvement in decision-making, the Education Department found that the prerequisite of making parents and schools become partners was to improve their relations in the education process. The CHSC found that the prerequisite of making parents and schools become partners was to improve their relations in the schooling process. They then put more emphasis on encouraging schools to set up Parent-Teachers Associations (PTAs) as bridges for providing parents and teachers with more and better opportunities to communicate and collaborate at schools. Currently, there were about 1400 PTAs set up in schools as of 2013 (CHSC, 2015), whereas the number was 497 in 1997 and 287 in 1994 (Ng, 2007a). Coordinated by PTAs, many parents were invited to be volunteers in the library, story tellers in the classroom, assistants in distributing lunch meals, etc. Since then, the relationship between parents and teachers has been improved through working collaboratively in the PTA committee. Indeed, the notion of parents as volunteers helped set a foundation for further levels of parent-school co-operation and facilitate parent involvement at various levels of school education.

Parent involvement became an education innovation in times of paradigm shift in the second phase of development. When SBM was introduced, there were conflicts of receptivity arising between parents and teachers. It coincides with MacBeth's (1988) assertion of progression of parent-teacher relations in which Macbeth conceptualised the phase as "professional uncertainty". Fortunately, the establishment of PTAs in every school helped provide parents and teachers with a platform to attempt to work together and develop mutual respect through collaboration on different occasions. It is believed that collaboration and communication is a prerequisite for establishing better home-school relationships, which sets a foundation partnership orientation. In this phase, many schools went beyond the bounds of ethnocentrism by inviting parents to enter schools to be volunteers with the pragmatic belief that parents' contribution to school education could help improve the academic and social development of the children. What is more, their participatory roles in school had further been recognised when schools were required to increase their transparency and to be accountable to parents and the public as indicated in the policy paper, "Quality Assurance in School Education in Hong Kong" published in 1999 in the next phase.

However, parents came to school when they were requested. They became instruments of the schools for school activities and in return, what could they obtain from the schools? The issue will be discussed in the concluding section.

## Phase III (1999–2004): Parents as clients: Accountability orientation

To highlight parents' evolving roles from being volunteers to being recognised as clients in their children's education, some documents published earlier than the period stated in this phase were adopted to demonstrate how they were recognised in the process of promoting quality education. Ultimately, schools were required to be accountable to stakeholders.

During the period of the second phase, there were ups and downs when parents and teachers worked together in the PTAs. According to the study of Ng and Yuen (2015), parents providing voluntary services for school were recognised as invaluable resources on the one hand, but parents were treated as instruments in some schools on the other. On the whole, when more collaborative experiences were accumulated, parents were gradually perceived by teachers as playing vital roles contributing to children's effective learning and school improvement.

Since 1991, the word *parents* has nearly appeared in every education policy document. In 1993, for example, the EMB published a policy document entitled *School Education in Hong Kong: A Statement of Aims*. To further ensure that the domain of home-school co-operation is one of the main targets for educational improvement in schools, the booklet aims at helping schools and parents share a common understanding of what schools are trying to achieve, and designing and evaluating projects to encourage home-school collaboration with reference to the statement of aims. Indeed, parents' rights to get involved in the school affairs have been respected and parents as partners with schools in nurturing children's personal growth have also been recognised as the primary aims in school education. The statement continues to specify the following aims:

> Aim (5): *As far as possible, parents should be able to choose the type of education best suited to their children, and should have adequate information on which to make informed choices.*
> 
> (EMB, 1993, 13)

> Aim (13): *School in partnership with parents and others, contribute to the personal growth of their students, by helping them develop a sense of morality and prepare for the physical, emotional and mental transition to adulthood.*
> 
> (EMB, 1993, 21)

Parents' rights and responsibilities in education were also recognised gradually by the government and educators. For example, Cheng, Tam, and Cheung (1996) conceptualised the meaning and function of total home-school co-operation by way of three perspectives; namely "statutory", "management" and "education".

Tam (1994) expressed his expectation on the completion of Parents' Charter in Hong Kong, the purposes of which were to explain to parents their rights and responsibilities in the schooling process of their children and to encourage schools to develop constructive relations of partnership with parents. As parents' rights were widely raised and discussed since 1994, parents as clients and schools being accountable to parents had come to be the main concern. Schools being pressured by the elected legislative councillors necessarily had to increase their schools' transparency to satisfy the needs of the general public.

In 1996, the EC published the consultation document ECR 7 entitled "*Quality School Education*". In the arena of home-school co-operation, however, the document pointed out that many schools still demonstrated the attitudes against the recommendations in the SMI. In the document, it argued:

> *School which has not yet introduced any quality assurance measure should start doing so soon. We propose that all schools should be required to practise school-based management by the year 2000 as a means to assure school education quality.*
>
> (EC, 1996, 16)

Obviously, there were still a lot of teaching professionals who were resistant to change. In the area of parent participation in management, the document again stressed:

> *To involve teachers, parents and students in school management is conducive to the development of quality school education. This will not only help the balanced development of students and gain the support of parents, but also enable the school to collate effectively views of teachers, parents and students.*
>
> (EC, 1996, 17)

A year after the consultation, the ECR 7 (EC, 1997) was published. Parent participation in school management is formally ensured. Empowerment of parents is one of the objectives in education reforms. In the report, it reiterated:

> *Education is not the sole responsibility of the Government or schools. Co-operation between schools and parents is vital. Participation of teachers, parents and students in school management and school activities is conducive to the development of quality school education.*
>
> (EC, 1997, 18).

The conception of accountability was also emphasised in the policy document entitled "Quality Assurance in School Education in Hong Kong" which has reiterated that parents participate in evaluation of school and provide comments and feedback on school matters (Education Department, 1999). Schools being accountable to parents have then become a policy while parent involvement is imposed in the process of education reform. Nevertheless, some teaching professionals had still demonstrated conservative and ethnocentric attitudes towards parents' involvement. They perceived parents' participation as intrusion and a threat to their daily teaching lives (Ng & Yuen, 2015).

Parents' roles were first marginalised during the period when education reforms strived for quantitative targets and the role of parents was found to be quiescent and acquiescent before the 1990s (Ng, 2002). Fortunately, subsequent policy documents at the end of the 20th century had provided us with marked evidence that parents' vital roles in children's schooling process were recognised and respected. The EC then published *The Reform Proposals for the Education System in Hong Kong* (EC, 2000) in which parents were praised for their recognition of the importance of education for young people. The document (EC, 2000, 151) provides the following description:

> *Parents are the closest and the most reliable mentors to students. Parents' viewpoints and guidance have a great impact on students' learning attitudes and effectiveness.*

Since then, parents' rights have been widely mentioned and discussed. The government has also posted the school's external evaluation report on the website to let parents and the public know the school performance. To be accountable to parents, schools are required to increase their transparency through uploading their annual school plans and report on their websites. Parents have legitimately been included in this phase where the notion of accountability and transparency is the prevailing ideology in this period. Understanding the school operation by examining the school plan and report, parents have now been encouraged and involved in giving advice on school matters. Most importantly, parents' managing roles in school were legitimately recognised in 2004.

## Phase IV (2004 and onwards): Parent as school governors: Partnership orientation

To highlight the process of how parents were included in school management, some policy documents published before 2004 were used for the purpose of discussion. In this phase, the power of managing schools is legitimately dispersed to parents. The innovation of increased parent involvement has marked intention to include parents as partners in the children's education. The school authority accepts parents' rights of participating in decision-making and their voice, to a certain extent, should be listened (Ng, 2007b). Edward (1995) indicated, having had his study in ten schools, that meaningful parent involvement in education is the involvement of parents in the governance structures of the school. The study of Ng and Yuen (2015) also found that parents could be treated as partners while school professionals invited them to be members of the school management board.

The policy that parents are to be involved in managing schools has become mandatory in the ECR 7. In 2000, the Advisory Committee on School-Based Management (2000) consulted the public for the number of parent representatives to be included in the School Management Committee (SMC). Parent involvement in school management was then formally introduced to school. The government of Hong Kong proposed in the *Education Bill 2002 (Amendment)* that two parent representatives with the right of voting be included as the "school governors" in the SMC in every school. However, the proposal became very political because it was opposed by some school sponsoring bodies but agreed upon by a lot of parent organisations. After serious debates and negotiation between the school sponsoring bodies and the government within a two-year consultation period, the bill was then amended and has eventually become the *Education (Amendment) Ordinance 2002* at the Legislative Council since July 2004. The ordinance stipulates that all schools in Hong Kong should establish an Incorporated Management Committee (IMC) by 2009 in which one parent governor with the right of voting and one alternate parent governor without the right of voting should be included as members. Since 2004, parents' roles as governors have been legitimately realised.

Though the ordinance is established, there has still been a long and heated debate between school sponsoring bodies and the government, and their relationships has so far been hampered (Pang, 2004) and the government ultimately announced that the deadline of establishing IMCs in all school was extended to 2011.[1] In order to persuade schools to participate in this governance scheme, the government promises the school to be funded under a block grant. Since the passing of the Education Bill, parents are empowered to be involved at different levels of school operation as outlined in Ng's (1999) model of parent involvement. Not only are they encouraged to get involved in their children's education outside school as supervisors at home, but also they are invited to be school governors and advisers inside school. According to Ng (2006) and Edward (1995), when parents are empowered to be involved in the decision-making process, they can be treated as school partners in which mutual respect and recognition are of paramount significance. This theoretical assumption also echoes MacBeth's (1988) progression model where the "stage of growing confidence" highlights that the level of parent participation in school education is increasing and partnership relations between teachers and parents are being developed.

Parents are now invited to be governors in the movement of power decentralisation in education, but there are still many tensions and challenges in managing the school between parents and school sponsoring bodies. According to Vincent (2000), it is not surprising that most of them remain marginal to the running of the school. The study of Vincent and Tomlinson (2000) revealed that parents' voices were muted in the school board and eventually, the parent governor was promoting the general interest of the principal or the governing body. Ng and Yuen (2015) came cross the similar issue in their study of micro-politics in parent involvement in three schools in Hong Kong. They concluded that the issue of inviting parents as school governors revealed the tension of the triadic relationship among parents, teachers and the principal. There was a danger that the parent representative would play the role of marionette in the school board, being manipulated by the school sponsoring body and might be accused of being assimilated as a part of the school side by the other parents. He was always in a dilemma between two courses of unfavourable actions in the meeting: to voice parents' general views or to enact the wishes of the school principal.

## Discussion: Partnership as policy rhetoric!

Overall speaking, parents are empowered in the education reform movement in Hong Kong. The discourse of home-school relationships has now moved forward from the darkest period of quiescence and acquiescence during which parents were treated as unwelcome guests to the welcoming stage where parents are invited as school governors. The current education reforms around the world emphasising democratisation and decentralisation of power have enlightened parents as clients as well as partners in their children's education and facilitated the process of parent empowerment (Vincent, 2000). In Hong Kong, parents' roles are evolving from being quiescent and acquiescent to the roles of parents as clients, consumers and partners. They have also strived for empowering themselves by getting hold of opportunities to participate in school management. From the phase of exclusion to the phases of collaboration, accountability and partnership orientation, these perspectives coincide with Vincent's (1996) assertion of parent empowerment which endows parents with certain rights and responsibilities in their involvement in school education in Hong Kong.

Since 1997, parents' rights of participating in children's education have gradually been recognised. They have been invited to participate in Parent-Teacher Associations (PTAs), manage the school, organise school activities and assist in school functions (Pang, 2004). By 2015, all schools in Hong Kong have already had their IMCs in place. Parents are now included to be school governors and treated as school partners where mutual respect and recognition are the critical essence of their relations. It seems that there is a honeymoon between parents and teachers from now on. However, implementation of parent-teacher partnerships signifies the notion of parent empowerment highlighting that "power given to a subordinate group is consequently lost by the former power-holder" (Vincent, 1996, 7).

Gore (1993) highlights that it is the teacher and other educational professionals giving some of their power to parents. The study of Nir and Ami (2005) revealed that parent governors would have militant behaviours against school when they found that schools were reluctant to meet their demands. Parents' roles were first marginalised in the first phase of the development of parent involvement. Teachers demonstrated the notions of ethnocentrism and protectionism, keeping parents away from the school. Some teachers will find the work of working with parents as extra workload. Research studies highlight that some teachers and principals resisted changes due to the fact that they were crossed by the increased parent involvement and were constrained by lack of skills and knowledge of working with parents (Ball, 1987; Ng, 2011). The teachers' inclination is relatively similar to the protective model suggested by Swap (1993). Parents as laymen were virtually excluded from the notion of home-school cooperation as promoted by the government for years across schools. Though collaboration and accountability have been emphasised nowadays in the development of home-school relationships, parents are sometimes treated as instruments of school initiatives, and they are within the control of the teaching professionals as disclosed in Ng's (2013) study.

Parents were treated as volunteers and resources in the second phase. However, to some schools, their intention of inviting parents was strictly "utilitarian" (Ng & Yuen, 2015). To be utilitarian is based on the belief that actions are good if they are useful or benefit most of us. It means that the action of welcoming parental participation carries the message of power decentralisation. With the view of market orientation, it is beneficial to the reputation of the school by which parents are attracted to choose the school for their children. Nevertheless, what do parents get in return when being involved in school education? At this stage of parent involvement, parents cannot be interpreted as partners. From the outsider's point of view, parents and teachers are cooperating harmoniously through a process of integration and collaboration. However, at the back stage, imbalance of power is implicitly demonstrated. Lareau (2000) finds that what teachers wanted was a professional-client relationship with parents rather than equal partners:

> *What teachers wanted to control is the amount of interconnectedness between home and school. They welcomed only particular types of parental involvement in schooling – involvement they defined as supportive and fruitful.*
>
> (35)

The roles parents play are in the hands of the schools. The grasp of control is to minimise teachers' tensions since greater parent involvement embodies a threat to their professionalism (Crozier, 1997). Beyond playing the role of schools' instruments, parents were not found, actually were not allowed, to play any tangible roles of governors in this phase.

Even though parents are included, they are within the control of the teaching professionals so their participation in the school management is considered pseudo. For example, in terms of the ratio between the number of the representatives from the school sponsoring body and that of the parent representative, ten to one, the establishment of parent-as-governor in the IMC in Hong Kong is of symbolic rhetoric, not to mention that parent representative being assimilated as part of the school sponsoring body and playing the role of marionette. Thus, it is apparent that parents' managerial role is intentionally marginalised by the school side (Ng, 2003). Parent involvement is of policy rhetoric, a term to disguise the school's inclination to grasp the control of parents' behaviours. It reveals that the school sponsoring body and teaching professionals resist change for fear of losing a portion of governing power (Ng, 2006). The finding of Ho's (2003) study in Hong Kong indicated that teachers generally did not accept parents having authority to make decisions. She added that parents did not consider that they should have the rights and responsibilities in school governance. Thus, it might be possible that the parent representative is willingly or unwillingly pushed to and fro between parents and the school sponsoring body in the IMC. In Phase IV, through politically incorporating limited number of parents into the governing body, the parent governor is still an instrument of school initiatives on the one hand, and it allows the management to legitimise the parents-as-governors policy to be implemented on the other.

## Conclusion

This chapter has provided insights into how parents' roles have been evolving in times of promoting parent involvement in children's education in Hong Kong in the last two decades.

Since the passing of the Education Bill regarding school-based management in 2004, parents are empowered to be involved at different levels of school operation. Not only are they encouraged to get involved in their children's education outside school as supervisors at home but also they are invited to be school governors and become partners of the school. However, based on the analysis above, the notion of parents-as-governors could be actualised only when there is mutual respect in the decision-making process. Therefore, the existing practice of partnership is of policy rhetoric, and it is an ideal for excellence in education at the moment. It is a far more complicated process than is commonly expected. Building a partnership is a dynamic process. It involves the principle of give-and-take between parents and teaching professionals. It requires mutual trust and respect. Partnership should not be equated with little more than parents passively participating in school activities, attending school seminars or receiving information from school. As Vincent and Tomlinson (2000) remark:

> *Some parents will undoubtedly be content to adopt the schools' aims and viewpoints, but others will be untouched by the promises of 'partnership' and remain distanced and alienated.*
>
> (2046)

Undoubtedly, teaching professionals generally did not accept parents' active roles in school governance. Nevertheless, it cannot be denied that most of the parents accepted a more passive role in most school governance issues (Ho, 2003; Ng, 2003). In this regard, Ho (2003) suggests taking a broader view of parent involvement encompassing home-based and school-based activities while Hornby and Lafaele (2011) argue that education professionals need to achieve a greater understanding of the barriers to parent involvement. For example, some parents are in a worse position in getting involved in school education due to social class difference (Lareau, 2000; Ng, 2000) because the power of direct participation in school is monopolised by the middle-class parents and working-class parents are always the followers of their counterpart in participating in school-based parent activities (Ng, 2001). It is suggested that the Education Bureau of Hong Kong should provide more training opportunities for school governors and stakeholders concerned on the real purposes and functions of the IMC and the operational guideline of parent involvement in school education at various levels. The school management should also design school-based teacher professional development programmes with regard to knowledge and skills for involving parents at various levels. It is not the quantity of professional development programmes that matters. Rather, what is important is the focus and quality of such programmes designed to help teaching professionals address the innovation of working with parents and sharing power of decision-making with parents effectively. Comparative studies between Hong Kong and other Asian countries on relevant and similar topics are much needed so as to formulate an effective policy that helps facilitate parents as "real" but not "rhetorical" school governors. Whether parent involvement in children's education is smoothly implemented is still an educational discourse and the politics of parent involvement is worth further investigating in Hong Kong.

## Note

1 It was proposed to commence in 2009. However, due to many schools claiming that they were not ready, the EDB announced to extend another two years for implementation of IMCs: that was 2011.

## References

Advisory Committee on School-Based Management. (2000). *Transforming schools into dynamic and accountable professional learning communities.* Hong Kong: Hong Kong Government Printer.

Amatea, E. S. (2007). *Building culturally responsive family-school relationships.* Upper Saddle River, NJ: Pearson Education and Allyn and Bacon.

Arnove, R. F., & Torres, C. (2007). *Comparative education: The dialectic of the local and global.* Lanham, MD: Rowman & Littlefield.

Ball, S. J. (1987). *Micropolitics of the school: Towards a theory of school organization.* London: Methuen.

Bastiani, J. (1989). *Working with parents – A whole school approach.* Berkshire: Nefer-Nelson.

Berns, R. M. (2007). *Child, family, school, community: Socialization and support.* Belmont, CA: Thompson Higher Education.

Blasé, J., & Anderson, G. (1995). *The micro-politics of educational leadership: From control to empowerment.* New York, NY: Teacher College Press.

Brown, B. A., & Duku, N. (2008). Participation politics: African parents' negotiation of social identities in school governance and its policy implications. *International Journal of Lifelong Learning, 27*(4), 413–429.

Caldwell, B. J. (2004). *Re-imagining the self managing school.* London: Specialist Schools Trust.

Carnoy, M., & Rhoten, D. (2002). What does globalization mean for educational change? A comparative approach. *Comparative Educational Review, 46*(1), 1–9.

Chan, K. C., Ho, S. L., Tsang, S. H., & Wong, S. C. (1993). Primary school teachers' attitudes towards parents' participation in school education (in Chinese). *Journal of Primary Education, 3*(2), 39–48.

Cheng, Y. C. (1991). The meaning and function of parents' participation in school education (in Chinese). *ICAC Moral Education Periodical, 3*, page unknown. Retrieved from http://www.me.icac.hk/upload/doc/j31.htm

Cheng, Y. C. (2007). Future developments of educational research in the Asia-Pacific region: Paradigm shifts, reforms, and practice. *Educational Research for Policy Practice, 6*(2), 71–85.

Cheng, Y. C., Tam, W. M., & Cheung, W. M. (1996). The concept of total home school cooperation. *Asian Journal of Counseling*, 4(1&2), 29–42.

Chikoko, V. (2008). The role of parent governors in school governance in Zimbabwe: Perceptions of school heads, teachers and parent governors. *International Review of Education*, 54(2), 243–263.

Chrispeels, J. (1996). Effective schools and home-school-community partnership roles: A framework for parent involvement. *School Effectiveness and School Improvement*, 7(4), 297–323.

Chung, W. M. (1994). *The days staying with children* (in Chinese). Hong Kong: Wide Angle.

Committee on Home-School Cooperation. (2015). *Number of PTAs*. Retrieved from http://www.chsc.hk/upload/attachments/02–03_to_12–13_No_of _PTAs_ (C).pdf

Cowburn, W. (1986). *Class, ideology and community education*. London: Policy Press.

Crozier, G. (1997). Empowering the powerful: A discussion of the interrelation of government policies and consumerism with social class factors and the impact of this upon parent interventions in their children's schooling. *British Journal of Sociology of Education*, 18(2), 187–200.

Daun, H. (2009). Globalized educational governance decentralization and grassroots responses. *Comparative Education and Policy Research*, 8(1), 1, 23–51.

Davis, D. (1996). Crossing boundaries: Community-family-school partnerships. *Forum of Education*, 51(1), 83–91.

Education Commission. (1984). *Education Commission report No. 1*. Hong Kong: Hong Kong Government Printer.

Education Commission. (1986). *Education Commission report No. 2*. Hong Kong: Hong Kong Government Printer.

Education Commission. (1988). *Education Commission report No. 3*. Hong Kong: Hong Kong Government Printer.

Education Commission. (1992). *Education Commission report No. 5*. Hong Kong: Hong Kong Government Printer.

Education Commission. (1996). *Consultation paper for Education Commission report No. 7*. Hong Kong: Hong Kong Government Printer.

Education Commission. (1997). *Education Commission report No. 7*. Hong Kong: Hong Kong Government Printer.

Education Commission. (2000). *Learning for life, learning through life: Reform proposals for the education system in Hong Kong*. Hong Kong: Hong Kong Government Printer.

Education Department. (1988). *Note on school-parent liaison*. Ref: ED1/26/1075/86, September.

Education Department. (1994). *Home-school cooperation research report*. Hong Kong: Hong Kong Government Printer.

Education Department. (1999). *Quality assurance in school education in Hong Kong*. Hong Kong: Hong Kong Government Printer.

Education and Manpower Branch. (1993). *School education in Hong Kong: A statement of aims*. Hong Kong: Hong Kong Government Printer.

Education and Manpower Branch & Education Department. (1991). *The school management initiatives: Setting the framework for quality in Hong Kong school*. Hong Kong: Hong Kong Government Printer.

Edward, S. J. (1995). Parents and school reform. *Journal for a Just & Caring Education*, 1(1), 80–93.

EL Nokali, N. E., Bachman, H. J., & Votruba-Drzal, E. (2010). Parent involvement and children's academic and social development in elementary school. *Child Development, 81*(3), 988–1005.

Epstein, J. L. (1995). School/family/community partnership: Caring for the children we share. *Phi Delta Kappan, 76*(9), 710–717.

Epstein, J. L. (2001). *School, family and community partnerships – Preparing educators and improving schools*. Boulder, CO: Westview.

Epstein, J. L. (2013). Ready or not? Preparing future educators for school, family, and community partnership. *Teach Education, 24*(2), 115–118.

Gore, J. (1993). *The struggle for pedagogies*. London: Routledge.

Graves, S. Jr. & Wright, L. Parent involvement at school entry: A national examination of group differences and achievement. *School Psychology International, 32*(1), 35–48.

Green, L. (1968). *Parents and teachers: Partners or rivals*. London: George Allen and Unwin.

Heystek, J. (2006). School governing bodies in South Africa: Relationships between principals and parent governors – A question of trust? *Educational Management, Administration and Leadership, 34*(4), 473–486.

Ho, E. S. C. (2003). Teachers' views on educational decentralization towards parental involvement in an Asian Educational System: The Hong Kong case. *International Studies in Educational Administration, 31*(3), 58–75.

Hornby, G., & Lafaele, R. (2011). Barriers to parental involvement in education: An exploratory model. *Educational Review, 63*(1), 37–52.

Huber, S. T. (2011). School governance in Switzerland: Tensions between new roles and old traditions. *Educational Management, Administration & Leadership, 39*(4), 469–485.

Lareau, A. (2000). *Home advantage: Social class and parental intervention in elementary education*. Oxford: Rowman and Littlefield Publishers.

Llewellyn, J. (1982). *A perspective on education in Hong Kong*. Hong Kong: Government Printer.

MacBeth, A. (1988). The future: Proposals for a school and family concordat. In J. Bastiani (Ed.), *Parents and teachers II: From policy to practice* (pp. 254–259). Berkshire: Nfer-Nelson.

Ng, S. W. (1999). Home-school relations in Hong Kong: Separation or partnership. *School Effectiveness and School Improvement: An International Journal of Research, Policy and Practice, 10*(4), 551–560.

Ng, S. W. (2001). Parents' roles in children's school education (in Chinese). *Journal of Basic Education, 10*(2) & *11*(1), 13–32.

Ng, S. W. (2002). Parent-teacher interaction: Are parents and teachers in Hong Kong ready for cooperation? *Journal of Southeast Asian Education, 3*(1), 115–139.

Ng, S. W. (2003). Are parents and teachers psychologically prepared for cooperation? *Pacific Asian Education, 15*(1), 60–76.

Ng, S. W. (2006). The micro-politics of home-school collaboration: Power! Instruments! Partners! *Educational Research Journal, 21*(1), 131–151.

Ng, S. W. (2007a). The chronological development of parent empowerment in children's education in Hong Kong. *Asia Pacific Education Review, 8*(3), 487–499.

Ng, S. W. (2007b). Development of parent-school partnerships in times of educational reform in Hong Kong. *International Journal of Educational Reform, 16*(4), 321–345.

Ng, S. W. (2011). Managing teacher balkanization in times of implementing change. *International Journal of Educational Management, 25*(7), 654–670.

Ng, S. W. (2013). Including parents in school governance: Reality or rhetoric. *International Journal of Educational Management, 27*(6), 667–680.

Ng, S. W., & Lee, T. H. T. (2015). How parents were involved in a special school in Hong Kong. *International Journal of Educational Management, 29*(4), 420–430.

Ng, S. W., & Yuen, W. K. G. (2015). The micro-politics of parental involvement in school education in Hong Kong: Ethnocentrism, utilitarianism or policy rhetoric! *Educational Review, 67*(2), 253–271.

Nir, A. E., & Ami, T. B. (2005). School-parent relationship in the era of school based-management: Harmony or conflict? *Leadership and Policy in Schools, 4*(1), 55–72.

Pang, I. W. (2004). School-family-community partnership in Hong Kong: Perspectives and challenges. *Educational Research for Policy and Practice, 3*(2), 109–125.

Pang, I. W. (2008). School-based management in Hong Kong: Centralizing or decentualizing. *Educational Research for Policy and Practice, 7,* 17–33.

Shen, S. M. (1995). The pattern and development of home school cooperation in Hong Kong (in Chinese). *Educational Journal, 23*(1), 55–66.

Siu, W. S. (2000). Home-school collaboration: A reflection from tradition to new culture in the 21st century. *The Policy Newsletter of the Social Policy Research Centre of the Hong Kong Polytechnic University, 2,* 6–9.

Skerrett, A., & Hargreaves, A. (2008). Student diversity and secondary school change in a context of increasingly standardized reform. *American Educational Research Journal, 45*(4), 913–945.

Swap, S. (1993). *Developing home-school partnership: From concepts to practice.* New York, NY: Teachers College Press.

Tam, M. K. (1994). An analysis of education & family system: From educational, social and political perspectives. *Proceedings of Lingnan College public seminar.* Hong Kong: Lingnan College.

Vincent, C. (1996). *Parent and teachers: Power and participation.* London: Falmer.

Vincent, C. (2000). *Including parents?* Buckingham: Open University Press.

Vincent, C., & Tomlinson, S. (2000). Home-school relationship: The swarming of disciplinary mechanism. In S. Ball (Ed.), *Sociology of education* (Vol. 4, pp. 2038–2058). London: Routledge-Falmer.

# 12 Changing student diversity, changing cultures and changing education policies

Cross-boundary students, Chinese immigrant students and non-Chinese speaking students in focus

*Celeste Yuet-Mui Yuen*

## Introduction

Similar to several other Asian cities, it is Hong Kong's declared aim to be recognised globally as an outstanding international metropolitan area. Styling itself "Asia's World City" since 1997 (Tung, 1998), when 150 years of colonial history came to an end, Hong Kong promotes itself as a cosmopolitan meeting place between East and West. Its international aspirations are reflected in the curriculum reform that both underlines a global outlook and places an increased emphasis on learning languages. The Chief Executive Tung Chee-Hwa in his 1998 *Policy Address* stressed that "Hong Kong . . . has the potential to become . . . the most cosmopolitan city in Asia enjoying a status similar to that of New York in America and London in Europe" (Tung, 1998, 7). Despite this objective, however, the education system remains very much a mono-cultural affair cocooned within its own distinct identity (Yuen, 2004). Findings of related Hong Kong studies reveal that teachers are largely unaware of the issues of educating students with diverse cultural backgrounds such as immigrant and minority students, and hence unprepared to address them (Grossman & Yuen, 2006; Westrick & Yuen, 2007). Over the past decade there has been a growing awareness of the need to equalise opportunities for the socially disadvantaged student groups in order to improve their education outcomes. Whilst the government has introduced some policy initiatives to address this issue, the social mobility of immigrant and minority students remains a concern.

This chapter addresses the challenges facing Hong Kong schools in relation to the cultural dimension of student diversity. It describes the changing characteristics of student populations in Hong Kong classrooms and discusses the ways in which the issues of ethnicity, race, family structure, class and culture are challenging the education system and school practice. The responsiveness of the government and the appropriateness of its support to the challenges will be evaluated. In so doing, this chapter highlights a range of school-based initiatives to accommodate the needs of increasingly diverse student bodies in Hong Kong and concludes by summarising the key strategies and approaches required towards securing this goal.

# Change in student demography

The size of the immigrant student population in Hong Kong since 1997 has been on the rise. These student groups comprise three main categories, namely (1) cross-boundary students (CBS) born to families with at least one Chinese mainland resident; (2) Chinese immigrant students (CIS) who arrived from Mainland China within seven years and (3) non-Chinese speaking students (NCS), usually referring to children born to the Indian, Pakistani, Nepalese and Filipino families. Although many of the latter were born in Hong Kong and speak fluent Cantonese, they are defined as NCS because they come from homes where the local dialect, Cantonese, is not the primary language. Due to various social and political factors, both the CBS and NCS groups record the largest growth while the CIS group the smallest. Comparing the enrolment figures in 2010/11 and 2014/15, the numbers of CBS has increased from 9,899 to 24,990 and NCS from 25,646 to 27,895 (Education Bureau, 2015).

Among the CBS, many are local-born children of doubly non-permanent resident (DNR) parents from Mainland China, and hence are entitled to the right of abode in Hong Kong. In 2011, there were 95,418 children of DNRs. It was believed that up to half of 23,000 DNR children will eventually live in Hong Kong before their twenty-first birthday (Legislative Council, 2015). The recent Mainland-Hong Kong conflicts over public, social, housing, hospital and transportation resources and the availability of certain consumer goods have led to the launch of a zero-quota policy in 2013 for Chinese mainlanders to give birth in Hong Kong (Chu, 2012; LaFraniere, 2012). Chow (2012) criticised that the large number of children of DNRs has already created negative impact on the formulation of a population policy and social solidarity in Hong Kong. Many of these CBS of DNR students do not have household registration and benefits on the mainland. Hence, they become one major student group among the pre-primary and primary schools, especially those in the boundary areas. Since there are many of them in numbers, this thus created a critical phenomenon where there is a shortage of school places for their local counterparts.

Concerns over the co-ordination between Hong Kong and Shenzhen on matters of cross-boundary transport and school placement allocation to curb the problems have made the headlines of the media (*Hong Kong Commercial Daily*, September 5, 2015; *Ming Pao*, 2013; *Ta Kung Pao*, September 15, 2015). The policy responses to CBS schooling include providing diversified school nets such as Kwun Tong, Yuen Long and Tai Po in 2014 (Legislative Council, 2015). Logistic problems aside, CBS face a myriad of social, economic, linguistic and cultural adjustments in coping with diverse circumstances (Yuen, 2010a). In response to all these, the government only provides lip service to supporting their English-language learning and advising schools to address their personal and emotional needs during lunch and recess breaks. The policies are somewhat tokenistic and lacking in planning (Yuen, 2011a, 2011b), the outcomes of which are sometimes positive and sometimes negative, varying from individual to individual.

Immigrants from India, Pakistan, Nepal and the Philippines, as well as Mainland China, typically tend to be working-class and employed in the catering, construction and security sectors. Geographically, many of them cluster in government-subsidized public housing estates or private rented cage-like residential homes in Wan Chai, Kwun Tong, Shum Shui Po, Tin Shui Wai and the North District of the New Territories (Yuen, 2013a; Yuen & Lee, 2013). There is a remarkable gap between the expectation of parents and teachers concerning student learning due to their socio-cultural differences (Oxfam Hong Kong, 2014; Yuen, 2015b). The under-representation of South Asian (SA) ethnic minorities and mainland Chinese immigrant youth in post-secondary education (PSE) in Hong Kong has raised serious social concerns over education access and equity. In 2006 there were only 1.1 per cent of SA youth in senior secondary and 0.59 per cent in PSE (Hong Kong Equal Opportunities Commission, 2011). They are mainly from low-income families and placed in less academically demanding classes. The challenge for them to make the transition from secondary education to PSE seems to too big to be overcome. Their low rate of PSE implies that they are not prepared for PSE-level work academically. That being said the findings of our past and on-going studies show that the predominant SA and Chinese immigrant youth aspire to obtain PSE and engage in the society actively. Moreover, girls are happier than boys, and older Chinese immigrant boys tended to be the least satisfied with their schools (Yuen, 2013a, 2015a; Yuen & Lee, 2013).

It is the case that the majority of students from these groups are from humble origins with low social capital (Chou et al., 2014) and multiple needs in affective, behavioural and cognitive engagement with schooling (Yuen, 2013b). Researchers and the media have paid little attention to the pedagogical process and the policy development surrounding this issue. For those teaching in such a multicultural setting, the tensions generated between the demands of the classroom and a lack of intercultural competency consistently undermine teaching professionalism. In the 2014 Policy Address, the government attempted to respond to some of the needs (Leung, 2014). For example, additional funds were made available for school-based support for schools with 10 or more ethnic minority students in Chinese learning; moreover, a Professional Enhancement Grant Scheme was launched for equipping teachers with the required competence to teach Chinese as a second language to the NCS in 2014 (Erni & Leung, 2014).

Driven by a free-market economy, Hong Kong classrooms are governed by the golden rules of (1) "struggle for survival" and (2) "survival of the fittest." Being a pragmatic society, a social assimilation approach to immigrant and ethnic minority education prevails in Hong Kong schools that seek to socialise minorities into the local culture (Yuen, 2010a). The media often portray CIS and NCS as passive members of society who need extra help to fit into the dominant culture and values (Yeung, 2013). The social reward systems and school assessment mechanisms are thus characterised by the virtue of hard work. However, students' personal and cultural strengths are largely unrecognised. Consequently, while outstanding students are celebrated, many struggling students are being marginalised, especially those who find it hard to fit in.

In Hong Kong schools, education for immigrant students has always been a lonely battle, struggling with human and financial resources, but for lower economic returns. Most of the support measures offered by schools and the government are so far not only of a remedial and piece-meal nature, but also tend to emphasise their weaknesses rather than their strengths. For instance, there was too much concentration on brushing up the English of the CBS and CIS (Yuen, 2012) and switching the simplified Chinese characters into the traditional Chinese characters and mastering oral Cantonese. As for NCS in Chinese-language classes of mainstream schools, they are normally incapable of functioning at such a level (Loper, 2004). Hence, attention is focused upon their deficiency in Chinese language and what can be done to compensate for this (Shum et al., 2011; Yeung, 2013). Provision for extra teacher assistants or a curriculum adaptation caters purely for Chinese learning needs. Only in 2014, after a long-standing public debate and lobbying by some legislative council members, a new curriculum initiative, "Learning Chinese as a second language", was launched to provide an option for those struggling with the standard Chinese curriculum (Education Bureau, 2014a). Changing student demographic profiles has entailed new challenges to classroom teaching and teacher professionalism, which will be discussed in the following section.

## Challenges facing Hong Kong classrooms

Both SA and mainland Chinese students are the fastest growing groups in Hong Kong schools. Yet there is little parallel attention given to address their educational needs, especially with regard to their specific family needs. For example, the SA parents have little knowledge of the local education system, and quite a number of mainland Chinese students live with one parent or two working parents, receiving limited parental support for homework. The busy and competitive lifestyle of these parents undermines their role as the primary teacher to their children, while teachers have to shoulder the parents' responsibilities, especially in homework supervision.

Since the 1990s, a large number of Hong Kong males have married mainland women or have fathered children by mainland women (Yuen, 2011a). Roughly 20,000 cross-boundary marriages have been registered in Hong Kong every year since 2000, of which three-quarters brides were mainland residents (Information Service Department of HKSAR, 2015). As these new family patterns tend to be associated with low social capital and/or challenging family issues, they have created new demands for the schools to respond to their diverse needs (Yuen, 2011b).

### *Identity of migrant students*

Concerning the identity of migrant students, studies on Hong Kong minority and immigrant students have revealed that they identify themselves as neither a Hongkonger nor a mainlander (Yuen, 2011b). Their circles of friends are mainly from the co-ethnic or similar cultural backgrounds in their new schooling due to language, cultural and family factors (Pong & Kwong, 2010; Shum et al., 2011; Tsung & Gao, 2012; Yuen, 2011a, 2011b). Although many of them claim to be

Hong Kong citizens, their involvement in the civic and public spheres is disproportionately less than mainstream students (Hong Kong Unison, 2013; Ngo, 2013). Empirical findings also underscore their vulnerable circumstances (Gao, 2011; Kwan & Ip, 2007; Siu, 2009) and their struggles with their identity and sense of belonging (Weiss, 1991; Yuen, 2011a, 2011b).

Second-generation ethnic minority students aspire to be full Hong Kong citizens, yet their current involvement in the civic and public spheres is disproportionately low as mentioned. Research findings also reveal that NCS, especially those with high levels of school engagement behaviourally, exhibited a stronger desire towards civic participation in the future (Yuen & Cheung, 2014). Despite their positive aspiration and outstanding results in English and other subjects, their deficiency in the Chinese language remains the key impediment in their academic and social advancement. The survey conducted by Hong Kong Unison in 2015, for instance, reported that most of NCS failed in securing a place in public-funded higher education institutions because of their inadequate oral Chinese proficiency to satisfy admission requirements (Cheung, 2015; Zhao, 2015). These aspects have been and will continue to be concerns for mainstream schooling as there are no parallel policies and support mechanisms available to address them.

School policy and ethos is the third issue worthy of attention. Education in a globalising context advocates self-directed life-long learning. Such a process gives emphasis to the learners' capacity and adaptability in mastering the necessary knowledge and skills. Intercultural awareness and racial equality, however, remain unaddressed issues despite Education and Manpower Bureau's emphasis on the principle of equal opportunities for schools to follow. In the new senior secondary school system implemented since 2009, most schools attempt to integrate some non-academic initiatives in their examination-driven curriculum as a gesture towards government policy seeking to re-engineer the school system to become more inclusive for all students. Nonetheless, this trend is still at its beginning stage, and frontline teachers are struggling between abandoning their long-established "mission" to support the meritocracy, and embracing any new approaches of honouring diversity and mixed abilities (Yuen, 2010b). All change comes at a price, and while teachers take only small steps in moving this forward, there can be no substantial and effective results at the local level. Moreover, waves of short-lived educational reforms tend to cause more harm than good to the existing system to make constant adjustments and inevitably affect the effectiveness of implementing any deeply-rooted educational reforms at the school level.

Formal schooling is the means to provide the foundation of learning to prepare learners to be independent. In this regard, teachers should be prepared to adopt strategies that are highly interactive and reflective. The ability of the teachers to facilitate greater independent self-learning and the perception of the students to assume personal responsibility in learning are both important. Rios (1996, 34) argues that the consideration of students' race/ethnicity is an essential characteristic of effective multicultural teachers. As most teachers in Hong Kong do not have a good understanding of the mainland Chinese and/or South Asian education systems, they lack the competence and sensitivity to differentiate their curricular contents, instructional and assessment strategies as well as classroom organisation to increase student engagement and achievement (Yuen, 2004; Yuen & Grossman, 2009). Consequently, the dominant survival of the fittest ethos reinforces the assimilation of the immigrant and minority students into the Hong Kong school culture.

Migrant children generally have greater difficulty in academic studies and are considered to be at risk. They need close adult assistance and monitoring, academically and emotionally (Reynolds, 1989, 129). Researchers note that home culture and parental factors (parental aspiration for academic success) are particularly paramount in building minority students' emotional resilience and academic achievement (Sharma, 2012; Yuen & Cheung, 2014). Schools with bilingual personnel and that embrace the values of multicultural education are not common, even among schools with a high percentage of minority students. Moreover, schools generally fail to address both the cultural background of SAS and the readiness of their parents in collaborating with schools. Conversely, another reason for failure is that the ethnic minority children do not get enough financial or educational support from their parents due to them being poor and not well-educated enough to appreciate the importance of schooling for their children and future careers (Yeung, 2013). The very presence of these student groups creates a need for promoting equality of education in Hong Kong schools. Meaningful and functional integration cannot be achieved simply by physical integration; there needs to be accessible opportunities and participation in the holistic education system and social advancement process. So is a systemic change that might grant such opportunity and success for all in the local education system.

## *Curriculum issues*

With regard to curriculum issues, the selective nature of Hong Kong schooling means that the current school curriculum is designed to attract academically more "able" pupils and enhance their future life chances. This agenda seems to be the main obstacle to implementing meaningful and genuine curriculum innovations such as promoting equal education opportunities and moral, citizenship and environmental awareness. The rigid class structure and timetabling, such as relatively short periods of lessons, is not conducive to effective learning for the majority of students they serve. Also, the inflexible student groupings and one-size-for-all approach to learning are found to inhibit individual-paced learning outcomes (Yuen, 2004). For a diverse learning setting, some students may need more time to organise themselves and/or complete the tasks. Most teachers consider the core subjects (Chinese, English and mathematics) to be the main thrusts of the whole-school curriculum, whilst the elaborative curriculum such as music, visual arts and physical education is given less emphasis. Deppeler, Harvey, and Loreman (2005) remind us that the teacher's belief in core and elaborative curricular directly affects their emphasis in teaching all children, including diverse learners. As indicated previously, education and life chances are tightly linked. Whilst most Chinese families are aware of this and are therefore keen to drill their children for academic examinations, many SA families tend to take a more relaxed approach and allow their children to opt for a career-oriented move away or even to drop out prematurely from their secondary education. Unless protective and preventive measures are taken, the existing information gap between the informed majority and the uninformed minority can only be widened and polarised in this education contest.

## Educating the newly-arrived Chinese immigrant students

The population of the immigrant students studying in Hong Kong has been booming since the reunification with China in 1997, but compared with the CBS and NCS, the growth of the CIS are apparently the lowest among the three main categories. As a CIS, they must meet the basic criteria of studying and/or working in Hong Kong for a minimum of seven years until they can officially become citizens in Hong Kong. Aside from the evident schooling performance due to the unfamiliar medium of instruction conducted in Cantonese and English, the disadvantaged group also faces a lot of other complications and barriers in line with their cultural and social capital that challenges their satisfaction in life and well-being.

### Difficulties encountered by CIS

Research suggests that Hong Kong's education system adopts an assimilation approach to the educational needs of immigrant and minority students (Yuen, 2010a). Although CIS are of the same Chinese origin, they face even more challenge adjusting to the academic, social and psycho-emotional demands in this society than the NCS due to their disadvantaged family circumstances. Their deficiency in English-language and lower social capital, coupled with complicated family circumstances, raise barriers against social acceptance and friendship, compounding an already low self-esteem. Although it is a well-known fact that CIS face many transient difficulties in their new schooling, such as speaking the Cantonese dialect, understanding English or adjusting to Hong Kong society, making the curriculum accessible and encouraging academic engagement remain challenges that need to be addressed. Compared to their local Chinese and SA friends, CIS reported lower levels of life satisfaction and spiritual well-being (Yuen, 2015a, 2015b; Yuen & Lee, 2013). In addition, the expectation gap between teachers and parents regarding academic performance has been a hindering factor to their academic achievement.

### Current policies of educating CIS

From September 1997, the Hong Kong government has offered the School-Based Support Scheme (SBSS) grant for schools to help all non-local students admitted to schools for the first time. The grant has been adjusted and in 2014/15 stood at HK$3,407 per primary student and HK$5,049 per secondary student. It can be used flexibly for school-based activities for social and education enrichment such as visiting the landmarks of Hong Kong society, purchasing multi-media packages for Chinese and/or English-language learning and other teaching aids (Education Bureau, 2013a). Aside from the SBSS grant, there is also a 6-month full-time Initiation Programme available for CIS and NCS prior to their joining mainstream schools (Education Bureau, 2013b). This Initiation Programme usually involves non-government organisations to enhance the learning experience, help students adjust to local communities and foster their personal development before their mainstream placement (Education Bureau, 2013b). The programme is deemed beneficial for the newcomers, especially at a younger age. It would be worthwhile to establish an archival repository to track the growth of these students and determine the hindering factors in order to tackle their school disengagement.

## Educating the ethnic minority SAS

In Hong Kong, SA students are broadly categorised as NCS, albeit many Hong Kong-born SA can handle conversations held in the local dialect, Cantonese. Nonetheless, as indicated previously, they are a minority group and are overrepresented in the low socio-economic status (SES) sector. The crux of the problem facing SA is that schools are very subtly promoting segregated, if not exclusive, education for immigrant students (The Hong Kong Council of Social Service, 2013). This is evinced by the notorious watered-down Chinese language curriculum in the schools with a high percentage of SA students and by their under-representation in higher education (Hong Kong Equal Opportunities Commission, 2012). Prejudice against immigrants was well-documented (Erni & Leung, 2014; Hong Kong Unison, 2015; Policy 21, 2012). The declared policy of equal education opportunities for all is still an illusion at the school-level. Since the Hong Kong government made a commitment to the mother-tongue teaching policy to improve the ability of students to use Chinese and English, all primary and secondary schools in the public sector except private and international primary ones have adopted Chinese as the medium of instruction (Tung, 1998). They are required to use fluent spoken Cantonese and good written Chinese to communicate at school (Shum et al., 2011). In this regard, NCS in particular are put at a disadvantage due to the language used in class and are thus alienated from their family and social lives. It is also controversial if it is fair for all local universities to require NCS to have a passing grade of Chinese Language if it bears no direct relations to their specialisation (Cheung, 2015; Hong Kong Unison, 2015; Zhao, 2015).

Most SA families tend to congregate together geographically in such districts as Kowloon West, Yau Tsim Mong and New Territories West where the rent is also more affordable. Poverty and the lack of the mainstream Chinese language are two main reasons for their children to be placed in less academically demanding schools (Hong Kong Unison, 2012). Whilst it is no surprise that SA students reported difficulties in adjusting to mainstream schools, it is however surprising to learn that some SA are educated in classes located in separate parts of the same school building (Erni & Leung, 2014). There were complaints about unfairness in school punishment between them and local Chinese owing to teachers' stereotyped perception of their behaviours. That being said, recent studies (Yuen, 2013b; Yuen & Lee, 2013) reveal that SA youth in secondary schools reported a higher level of subjective life satisfaction and school engagement evaluation than their Chinese mainstream and immigrant peers. The reasons for these mixed findings warrant further investigation.

Concerning the current policies for educating NCS, *The 2014 Policy Address* announced some measures to facilitate schools to create an inclusive learning environment, foster an environment for accommodating ethnic diversity in school, promoting respect to cultural and religious differences and strengthening communication with SA parents (Leung, 2014). The government wishes to encourage ethnic minority (mainly referring to SA) students to study in "mainstream" schools, which would help their mastery of the Chinese language and integration into community (Education Bureau, 2014b). The Education Bureau has provided schools with the "Chinese Language Curriculum Second Language Learning Framework" (hereafter "Learning Framework"), developed from the perspective of second language learners, to further address the concern from NCS (Education Bureau, 2014c). It was with the good intention that this "Learning Framework" can to assist them: (1) to learn Chinese as a second language, and (2) to bridge over to mainstream Chinese Language classes.

To facilitate the implementation of the "Learning Framework" in schools, the government has made available professional development in teaching Chinese as a second language and has enhanced funding support as well as professional support for schools. Schools admitting 10 or more students, can receive 0.8 to 1.5 million additional funding per annum for implementing the "Learning Framework" (Education Bureau, 2014c). This new initiative signifies a milestone in government policy to respond to the public debates. The next step is to enhance public perception and recognition of the new qualification framework, especially in the education and business sectors.

Besides teaching Chinese Language, the Hong Kong government encourages early adaption for NCS through informing parents to send their children to local kindergartens and providing summer bridging programmes for newcomer students (Education Bureau, 2014a). SA parents are also encouraged to join the summer bridging programmes with their children. Whilst the government has put a concerted effort to fund NGOs and high education institutions to provide language support to educating NCS, professional teacher development and home-school collaboration remain two main challenges to be addressed.

Concerning the first challenge, the Chinese language is one of the compulsory subjects and is tightly linked with the PSE and life opportunities of NCS in Hong Kong. As the "Learning Framework" (Leung, 2015, 129) was only advocated as an alternative Chinese syllabus option for the secondary and primary NCS in late 2014, its effectiveness has yet to be confirmed. At present, curriculum and instruction tailoring is largely absent, especially in secondary schools. The recent relaxation of the rigid language policy allowing individual schools to decide which subject(s) other than English-language to be taught in English or Chinese, this new initiative may lead to another new wave of inter- and intra-school competitions.

As for the barriers of home-school collaboration, immigrant and minority children are characterised by developmental challenges at school and acculturative challenges in bridging their home and school expectations and cultures (Suárez-Orozco et al., 2009; Suárez-Orozco & Suárez-Orozco, 2002). Gonzalez (2007) claims that the interaction between family structure and school environments and cultural identity and life satisfaction is very dynamic. Affluent families with educated parents make a positive influence on their children's education whilst those with little social capital have to struggle with meeting teachers' expectation and academic standards.

Positive engagement of parents in their children's educational process results in improved school attendance and outcomes (Hoover-Dempsey et al., 2005). Poor economic conditions, broken relationships and cultural barriers can hinder the involvement of Chinese immigrant and SA families in their children's schooling. Any civil society has an obligation to mobilise resources to include all families into the school and reduce the impact of such obstacles (Gonzalez, 2007). Researchers note that home culture also correlates with students' emotional resilience and academic achievement (Chee, 2010; Sharma, 2012; Yuen & Cheung, 2014). However, Hong Kong schools with children from diverse ethnic groups often fail to provide bilingual personnel and embrace the values of multicultural education to address the needs of families from different cultures (Colombo, 2013; Varela, 2008). Sharma (2012) criticised that schools generally fail to address the cultural background and parental readiness of SAS in collaborating with schools. One of the reasons for failure is that ethnic minority children could not get enough financial or educational support from their parents due to their low income and educational level and consequently an under-appreciation of the importance of schooling for their children and future careers (Hong Kong Unison, 2015; Yeung, 2013).

## Conclusion

This chapter has highlighted the changing landscape of student demography in mainstream schools in Hong Kong. The issues, challenges and policy initiatives in addressing the changing needs of CIS, CBS and NCS were discussed. In particular, the interweaving of curricular, language, pedagogical and family issues that arise with these immigrant student groups were further elaborated.

The fact is that admitting a group of diverse ethnic students does not necessarily make the school more culturally sensitive, especially in curriculum issues. The prevailing assimilation policy approach, while unspoken, is generally practised across schools. It has been argued that even under the meritocratic education system, efforts are not always rewarded due to systemic unfairness. Education access and education equity are two sides of the coin. Although there are now policies and initiatives that offer support for language learning, there are still no systematic policies that advocate equality of education opportunities for all. Immigrant and minority students are under-represented in the higher education sectors and their access to quality education is also disabled by poverty and inadequate knowledge of the education system. For the NCS, they need to learn social Chinese and academic Chinese in order to participate in school activities successfully. They must learn to read in Chinese, comprehend academic discourse, write coherently and speak and produce Chinese at cognitively complex and academically abstract levels. Likewise, CBS and CIS are required to achieve the same level of English proficiency as their mainstream peers in order to secure a place in higher education. There is no policy and practice currently available to address this issue. Most teachers are not professionally equipped and their curriculum is not responsive enough to compensate their academic needs.

Parents of CIS and NCS have different values with regard to their children's schooling. To Chinese parents, academic success is the main hope for the personal advancement of their children. Conversely, because of the socio-economic background of the SA families coupled with their cultural and religious values, parents of NCS are relatively more focused on the religious side of their children's development than their academic performances. South Asian parents nonetheless have high aspirations for the education of their children, albeit their linguistic and cultural capitals were not valued by Hong Kong society. This area remains a concern to link home and school together to achieve effective parent-teacher-community collaboration.

At the heart of a culturally-relevant pedagogy lies the awareness and competence of teachers. Teachers need to be more conscious of their own world-view towards intercultural interactions. There needs to be a change from a monocultural deficit perspective on educating CBS, CIS and NCS to an affirming perspective in which all cultures are treated equally and are all equally valued. Likewise, the government needs to invest further in teachers' professional development in order for them to upkeep themselves with the changing education landscape and the aspiration to promote education for all. Taken together, this is a pressing issue that needs to be addressed and supported by a dedicated and enlightened government policy.

## References

Chee, W. C. (2010). When the cultural model of success fails: mainland Chinese teenage immigrants in Hong Kong. *Taiwan Journal of Anthropology, 8*(2), 85–110.

Cheung, J. (2015, August 11). Ethnic pupils go nowhere with interviews. *The Standard*. Retrieved on August 23, 2015, from http://www.thestandard.com.hk/news_detail.asp?pp_cat=11&art_id=160012&sid=44983309&con_type=1

Chou, K., Cheung, K., Lau, M. & Sin, T. (2014). Trend in child poverty in Hong Kong immigrant families. *Social Indicators Research*, 117, 811–825.

Chow, N. (2012). How a population policy can be formulated in response to Hong Kong's integration with the Mainland. *Journal of Youth Studies, 15*(2), 30–39 (in Chinese).

Chu, K. (2012, February 20). Tensions grow over 'mainlanders' giving birth in Hong Kong. *USA Today*. Retrieved from http://usatoday30.usatoday.com/news/world/story/2012-02-14/chinese-mainland-pregnant-women-hong-kong/53159886/1

Colombo, M. (2013). Working in mixed classrooms: teachers' reactions and new challenges for pluralism. *Italian Journal of Sociology of Education, 5*(2), 17–45.

Deppeler, J., Harvey, D., & Loreman, T. (2005). *Inclusive education: A practical guide to supporting diversity in the classroom*. London: Routledge Falmer.

Education Bureau of Hong Kong SAR. (2013a). *Newly-arrived children-subsidy and resources*. Retrieved on July 6, 2015, from http://www.edb.gov.hk/en/student-parents/newly-arrived-children/subsidy-resources/index.html

Education Bureau of Hong Kong SAR. (2013b). *Education and support services for newly-arrived children*. Retrieved on July 6, 2015, from http://www.edb.gov.hk/en/student-parents/newly-arrived-children/overview/index.html

Education Bureau of Hong Kong SAR. (2014a). *Education support measures for non-Chinese speaking students* (2014/15 School Year). Retrieved on July 3, 2015, from http://www.edb.gov.hk/attachment/en/student-parents/ncs-students/about-ncs-students/201415BriefonSupportMeasures/English_Dec.pdf

Education Bureau of Hong Kong SAR. (2014b). *Hong Kong Education Bureau's reply to question about educational support for non-Chinese speaking students in the Legislative Council*. Retrieved on June 30, 2015, from http://www.info.gov.hk/gia/general/201407/09/P201407090500.htm

Education Bureau of Hong Kong SAR. (2014c). *Education Bureau circular no 8/2014: Enhanced Chinese learning and teaching for non-Chinese speaking students*. Retrieved on July 3, 2015, from http://www.edb.gov.hk/attachment/en/student-parents/ncs-students/new/CM_2014%2006%2005_E.pdf

Education Bureau of Hong Kong SAR. (2015). *Support for non-Chinese speaking students and students with special needs in kindergartens* (LC Paper No. CB(4)977/14–15(01)). Retrieved on July 24, 2015, from http://www.legco.gov.hk/yr14–15/english/panels/ed/ed_fke/papers/ed_fke20150514cb4–977–1-e.pdf

Erni, J. N., & Leung, L. Y. (2014). *Understanding South Asian minorities in Hong Kong*. Hong Kong: Hong Kong University Press.

Gao, F. (2011). Linguistic capital: continuity and change in educational language polices for South Asians in Hong Kong primary schools. *Current Issues in Language Planning*, 12(1), 251–263.

Gonzalez, V. (2007). A multidimensional perspective of minority and mainstream children's development and academic achievement. In V. Gonzalez (Ed.), *Minority and mainstream children's development and academic achievement: An alternative research and educational view* (pp. 3–47). Lanham, MD: University Press of America.

Grossman, D. L., & Yuen, Y. M. C. (2006). Beyond the rhetoric: A study of the intercultural sensitivity of Hong Kong secondary school teachers. *Pacific-Asian Education Journal*, 18(1), 70–87.

*Hong Kong Commercial Daily*. (2015, September 5). The cross-boundary students' problems have yet to be resolved (in Chinese). *Hong Kong Commercial Daily*. Retrieved on August 23, 2015, from http://www.hkcd.com/content/2015-09/05/content_955944.html

The Hong Kong Council of Social Service. (2013). *Poverty situation of South and Southeast Asian ethnic minorities in Hong Kong*. Retrieved on August 7, 2015, from http://www.poverty.org.hk/sites/default/files/20131218_em_e.pdf

Hong Kong Equal Opportunities Commission. (2011). *Report on the working group on education for ethnic minorities*. Hong Kong: Equal Opportunities Commission.

Hong Kong Equal Opportunities Commission. (2012). *Study on racial encounters and discrimination experienced by South Asians*. Hong Kong: Equal Opportunities Committee.

Hong Kong Unison. (2012). *Racial acceptance survey report*. Retrieved on September 23, 2014, from http://www.unison.org.hk/DocumentDownload/Researches/R201203%20Racial%20Acceptance%20Survey%20Report.pdf

Hong Kong Unison. (2013). *Submission by Unison to the Education Panel of the Legislative Council (also submitted to the Commission on poverty)*. Retrieved on July 7, 2015, from http://www.unison.org.hk/DocumentDownload/R01-Position%20papers/2013/Submissions_Edu_Panel_20130418_attach.pdf

Hong Kong Unison. (2015). *Report on the enrollment of non-Chinese speaking students in post-secondary education in Hong Kong* (in Chinese). Retrieved on September 20, 2015, from http://www.unison.org.hk/DocumentDownload/Researches/R201508%20Post%20Secondary%20Report.pdf

Hoover-Dempsey, K. V., Walker, J. M. T., Sandler, H. M., Whetsel, D., Green, C. L., & Wilkins, A. S. (2005). Why do parents become involved? Research findings and implications. *Elementary School Journal, 106*(2), 105–130.

Information Service Department of HKSAR. (2015). *Question reply: Marriage and divorce trends in Hong Kong and their impacts on various social aspects*. Retrieved on July 8, 2015, from http://gia.info.gov.hk/general/201504/15/P201504150399_0399_144864.pdf

Kwan, Y. K., & Ip, W. C. (2007). Suicidality and migration among adolescents in Hong Kong. *Death Studies, 31*(1), 45–66.

LaFraniere, S. (2012, February 22). Mainland Chinese flock to Hong Kong to give birth. *The New York Times*.

Legislative Council. (2015). *Background brief on issues related to education for cross-boundary students* (LC Paper No. CB (4) 925/14–15(07)).

Leung, C. Y. (2014). *The 2014 policy address*. Hong Kong: Hong Kong Government of the HKSAR. Retrieved from http://www.policyaddress.gov.hk/2014/eng/notices.html.

Leung, C. Y. (2015). *The 2015 policy address*. Hong Kong: Hong Kong Government.

Loper, K. (2004). *Race and equity: A study of ethnic minorities in Hong Kong's education system*. Hong Kong: The Centre for Comparative and Public Law and Unison Hong Kong – for Ethnic Equality.

*Ming Pao*. (2013). 400 students will study in cross-boundary schools in Tai Po and the Education Bureau carries out Return System. *Ming Pao*. Retrieved on August 23, 2015, from http://happypama.mingpao.com/cfm/study3.cfm?File=20130323/prepe/gmb2.txt

Ngo, J. (2013). Ethnic minorities face uphill education fight in Hong Kong, *South China Morning Post*. Retrieved on August 23, 2015, from http://www.scmp.com/news/hong-kong/article/1311812/ethnic-minorities-face-uphill-education-fight-hong-kong

Oxfam Hong Kong. (2014). *Survey on the Chinese learning challenges South Asian ethnic minority kindergarten students from low-income families face (Executive Summary)*. Hong Kong: Oxfam Hong Kong.

Policy 21. (2012). *Research on South Asian people's attitudes toward ethnic groups interactions and experiences in discrimination* (in Chinese). Hong Kong: Equal Opportunities Commission.

Pong, S. L., & Kwong, T. W. (2010). The educational progress of Mainland Chinese immigrant students in Hong Kong. *Research in the Sociology of Education, 17*, 201–230.

Reynolds, M. C. (1989). Students with special needs. In M. C. Reynolds (Ed.), *Knowledge base for the beginning teacher* (pp. 129–142). Oxford: Pergamon.

Rios, F. A. (1996). *Teacher thinking in cultural contexts*. Albany: State University of New York Press.

Sharma, A. (2012). *Low-income South Asian parents' concept of 'making it' in Hong Kong*. Ph.D. Thesis. Hong Kong: The University of Hong Kong.

Shum, M. S. K., Gao, F., Tsung, L., & Ki, W. W. (2011). South Asian students' Chinese language learning in Hong Kong: Motivations and strategies. *Journal of Multilingual and Multicultural Development, 32*(3), 285–297.

Siu, H. F. (2009). Positioning 'Hong Kongers' and 'New Immigrants'. In H. F. Siu & A. S. Ku (Eds.), *Hong Kong mobile: Making a global population* (pp. 117–148). Hong Kong: Hong Kong University Press.

Suárez-Orozco, C., Rhodes, J., & Milburn, M. (2009). Unraveling the immigrant paradox academic engagement and disengagement among recently arrived immigrant youth. *Youth & Society, 41*(2), 151–185.

Suárez-Orozco, C., & Suárez-Orozco, M. M. (2002). *Children of immigration*. Cambridge, MA: Harvard University Press.

*Ta Kung Pao*. (2015, September 15). Shenzhen police guard the cross-boundary students to go through the check point. *Ta Kung Pao*. Retrieved on September 15, 2015, from http://news.takungpao.com.hk/paper/q/2015/0915/3165824.html

Tsung, L., & Gao, F. (2012). What accounts for the underachievement of South Asians in Hong Kong? The voices of Pakistani and Nepalese parents. *Educational Research, 54*(1), 51–63.

Tung, C. H. (1998). *The 1998 policy address*. Hong Kong: HKSAR Government.

Varela, A. (2008). Embrace multiculturalism to foster parental involvement. *The Education Digest, 74*(3), 59–60.

Weiss, A. M. (1991). South Asian Muslims in Hong Kong: Creation of a 'local boy' identity. *Modern Asian Studies, 25*(3), 417–453.

Westrick, J. M., & Yuen, Y. M. C. (2007). The intercultural sensitivity of secondary teachers in Hong Kong: A comparative study with implications for professional development. *Intercultural Education, 18*(2), 129–145.

Yeung, L. (2013, May 6). South Asian students thwarted by lack of Chinese-language skills. *South China Morning Post*.

Yuen, C., & Grossman, D. (2009). The intercultural sensitivity of student teachers in three cities. *Compare, 39*(3), 349–365.

Yuen, Y. M. C. (2004). The early experience of intercultural teacher education in Hong Kong. *Intercultural Education, 15*(2), 151–166.

Yuen, Y. M. C. (2010a). Assimilation, integration and the construction of identity: The experience of Chinese cross-boundary and newly arrived students in Hong Kong schools. *Multicultural Education Review, 2*(2), 1–32.

Yuen, Y. M. C. (2010b). Dimensions of diversity: Challenges to secondary school teachers with implications for intercultural teacher education. *Teaching and Teacher Education, 26*(3), 732–741.

Yuen, Y. M. C. (2011a). Cross-boundary students in Hong Kong schools: education provisions and school experiences. In J. Phillion, M. T. Hue & Y. Wang (Eds.), *Minority students in East Asia: Government policies, school practices and teacher responses* (pp. 174–194). New York: Routledge Press.

Yuen, Y. M. C. (2011b). Towards inclusion of cross-boundary students in education, policy and practice in Hong Kong. *Journal of Education, Citizenship and Social Justice, 6*(3), 251–264.

Yuen, Y. M. C. (2012). Caught between two cultures: The everyday civic life of cross-boundary youth. *HKFYG: Journal of Youth Studies, 15*(2), 75–87.

Yuen, Y. M. C. (2013a). Ethnicity, level of study, gender, religious affiliation and life satisfaction of adolescents from diverse cultures in Hong Kong. *Journal of Youth Studies, 16*(6), 776–791.

Yuen, Y. M. C. (2013b). School engagement and civic engagement as predictors for the future political participation of ethnic Chinese and South Asian adolescents in Hong Kong. *Migration and Ethnic Themes, 29*(3), 317–342.

Yuen, Y. M. C. (2015a). Gender difference in life satisfaction and spiritual health among the junior immigrant and local Hong Kong secondary students. *International Journal of Children's Spirituality.* doi:10.1080/1364436X.2015.1061485.

Yuen, Y. M. C. (2015b). Enhancing early childhood schooling of South Asian children in Hong Kong: beliefs and perceptions of kindergarten teachers and principals. *Early Child Development and Care.*

Yuen, Y. M. C., & Cheung, A. C. K. (2014). School engagement and parental involvement: The case of cross-border students in Singapore. *Australian Educational Researcher, 41*(1), 89–107.

Yuen, Y. M. C., & Lee, M. (2013, September 23). Mapping the life satisfaction of adolescents in Hong Kong secondary schools with high ethnic concentration. *Youth and Society,* 1–18.

Zhao, S. (2015, August 11). Majority of Hong Kong's post-secondary education programmes unsuitable for non-Chinese speakers, study finds. *South China Morning Post.* Retrieved from http://www.scmp.com/news/hong-kong/education-community/article/1848164/majority-hong-kongs-post-secondary-education

# 13 Excellence without a soul?
## Higher education in post-1997 Hong Kong

*Michael H. Lee*

## Introduction

Hong Kong is not immune to a global trend of higher education reform which aim at improving the quality of education and maintaining its relevance to socio-economic needs in the age of globalisation when market forces and competitions are the core values. While universities are expected to be more adaptive (Sporn, 1999), enterprise-oriented (Marginson & Considine, 2000) and entrepreneurial (Clark, 1998, 2004), both Lucas (1996) and Readings (1998) warn against a crisis looming in higher education for universities have been under growing political pressure for reform in face of more acute competition for public or government resources which have become more limited as a consequence of more stringent budgetary control. The traditional image of universities as ivory towers being immune from the world of commerce is no longer valid. In fact, as Kennedy (1997) stated, universities are controversial places, and they have drawn intense public scrutiny on their obligations and duties in order to regain public trust. Under such a circumstance, academics' work seems to be more demanding for they have to teach, publish, serve and even risk change.

This chapter analyses the ways higher education in Hong Kong has been transformed by identifying major issues facing higher education. These issues include the institutionalisation of quality assurance mechanisms, the reorientation of the government-university relationship, the growth of private higher education institutions and the internationalisation of higher education to cater for Hong Kong's strong intention to become a regional education hub. There are five sections following this introductory section. It commences by providing a brief review on the development of higher education in Hong Kong. It is followed by an analysis of the policy context of higher education in Hong Kong since the 1990s. The next section examines major issues facing higher education in Hong Kong. The penultimate section discusses major trends shaping the development of higher education in Hong Kong, and followed by a conclusion.

## Past and present

At present, there are eight local degree-awarding higher education institutions funded by the government through the University Grants Committee (UGC), which was founded in 1965. The UGC serves as a non-statutory advisory committee responsible for advising the government on the development and funding needs of higher education institutions. It is aimed at working with the institutions to promote excellence, efficiency, cost-effectiveness and accountability in the higher education sector in order to establish Hong Kong as a regional education hub and to nurture high-quality people to promote the economic, cultural and social development of Hong Kong (University Grants Committee, 2013). The eight UGC-funded institutions are the University of Hong Kong (HKU), Chinese University (CUHK), University of Science and Technology (HKUST), City University (CityU), Polytechnic University (PolyU), Baptist University (HKBU), Lingnan University (LU) and Education University (EdUHK, formerly Institute of Education, HKIEd). Each of these eight institutions is stipulated as an autonomous statutory body with its own ordinance and governing body. Moreover, these institutions are guaranteed freedom and autonomy to manage their own affairs within the legal framework.

Apart from these eight higher education institutions, the publicly-funded degree-awarding Hong Kong Academy for Performance Arts (HKAPA) will eventually be placed under the auspices of the UGC (University Grants Committee, 2010). It should be noted that Shue Yan University (SYU) is the first private higher education institution to be granted the status of university in 2008 whereas Open University is a self-financed institution providing mainly part-time and distance-learning degree programmes to working adults. These developments are in response to the government's intention to boost the self-financing or private higher education sector for the sake of developing education services as one of the new six core industries for Hong Kong (Tsang, 2009).

In the academic year 2013–14, around 15,160 first-year-first-degree places were offered by the eight UGC-funded institutions and the publicly-funded Hong Kong Academy of Performing Arts, and also about 7,000 places in the self-financing undergraduate programmes. This covers approximately 18 per cent of the 17–20 age cohort population (Information Services Department, 2015). In fact, both the quantity and proportion of first-year-first-degree places have largely remained intact since 1994 when the massification policy was fully implemented with the provision of 14,500 first-year first-degree places in the UGC-funded institutions (University Grants Committee, 1996). This reflects the government's prudent attitude towards an unlimited increase in university places in order to avoid excess supply and thus mass unemployment of graduates. It is estimated that together with those students who opted to study in overseas universities, there are about 30 per cent of the relevant age cohort receiving university education in Hong Kong and abroad. Meanwhile, there has been more emphasis on diversifying post-secondary education through the development of privately-funded or self-financed community colleges to provide associate degree programmes in tandem with publicly-funded vocational training sub-degree programmes under the auspices of the Vocational Training Council (Tung, 2001). These two sectors accommodate around 40 per cent of the relevant age cohort to receive post-secondary education. In other words, taking both degree and sub-degree places into account, nearly 70 per cent of young people in Hong Kong should be able to access higher education.

The origin of higher education in Hong Kong was dated back in 1911 when HKU which was founded with an aim of training professionals in engineering, law and medicine (Cunich, 2012; Lin, 2002). It was not until 1963 when CUHK was formed as a federal university, comprising three privately-run post-secondary colleges, using Chinese as a medium of instruction (Sweeting, 2001). The addition of the second university, however, did not result in a much wider access to university education. In the mid-1980s, a mere 2 to 3 per cent of the relevant age cohort was offered first-year-first-degree places in the two universities (Hong Kong Government, 1978; University Grants Committee, 1996). After the June Fourth crackdown in Beijing in 1989, the Hong Kong government decided to expand the university sector by raising the participation rate to 18 per cent and increasing the number of universities through the establishment of HKUST in 1991 and the upgrading of existing polytechnics and post-secondary colleges, including CityU, HKBU, HKIEd, LU and PolyU between 1994 and 1999, in response to the brain drain problem associated with the growing emigration of local professionals (Shive, 1992).

Since the education reform was launched in 2000, private universities and self-financed community colleges have been encouraged to offer alternative paths for secondary school leavers to receive post-secondary education (Education Commission, 2000). It has witnessed the emergence of several self-financed community colleges to offer associate degree programmes since 2002 (Yung, 2002). The further expansion of higher education would be accomplished not by publicly-funded universities to provide more places but by self-financed community colleges or private universities for the cost of higher education should not be solely shouldered by the government but shared by the community (Tung, 2001). The subsequent change from a three-year to four-year first-degree academic structure since 2012, together with the imposition of six-year secondary education in 2009, would imply a further growth of the overall student population of the eight UGC-funded institutions, but it does not mean that the expansion would be necessarily financed by the government (Education and Manpower Bureau, 2005). The message of cost-sharing for higher education is even clearer when the government has been encouraging the higher education institutions to seek for social donations for their long-term infrastructural and improvement projects with the launch of the Matching Grant Scheme in 2003 (Leung, 2003).

Since the mid-2000s, the notion of developing Hong Kong as a regional education hub has been put forward and strongly emphasised by the government in line with its notion of promoting Hong Kong as Asia's world city which is comparable with New York and London (Tung, 2004). For universities, this policy direction implies the need of strengthening their international competitiveness and also the enrolment of more non-local or international students, especially those from the Chinese mainland. In 2009, education was identified by the government as one of the six major industries; others were medical services, testing and certification services, environmental industries, innovation and technology and cultural and creative industries, with a strong emphasis on internationalisation to bring in more non-local students to study in degree programmes run by both local and overseas higher education institutions in Hong Kong (Tsang, 2009). All these elements were reflected in a higher education review being conducted by the UGC in 2009, around seven years after the previous round of higher education review was conducted (University Grants Committee, 2002, 2010).

Against the background of the development of higher education in Hong Kong, the following section will turn to the policy context and conditions, leading to changes facing the higher education sector in Hong Kong since the 1990s, when it has been increasingly subject to the influence of fiscal constraints, market forces, stakeholders' needs and expectation and public sector management and reforms.

## Recent policy context

Globalisation has affected the ways higher education has evolved and transformed. Closely associated with higher education is a cluster of aims, values and general ideas, including the pursuit of truth and objective knowledge, research, liberal education, institutional autonomy, academic freedom, a neutral and open forum for debate, rationality, the development of the students' critical abilities, autonomy and character formation, the provision of a critical centre within society and the preservation of society's intellectual culture (Barnett, 1990). The university is a place of teaching universal knowledge where persons of broad knowledge, critical intelligence, moral decency and social sensitivity are produced (Newman, 1996). It is expected to serve as the protecting power of all knowledge and science, fact and principle, inquiry and discovery, and also experimentation and speculation (Kerr, 2001). They have to strive not only for survival but also performance and resources for their sustainable development amidst fierce local and global competition. Moreover, universities need to reconsider their enlightenment role in advancing the level of general understanding in society. It is a must for universities to adapt to new demands and expectations that would require radical changes in management and leadership (Barnett, 1997, 2000a, 2000b).

The impact of globalisation on the policy context of higher education has been widely attended. Globalisation refers to a set of processes leading to a rapid integration of the world into one economic space through increased international trade and the internationalisation of production and commodity culture with the dominance of laissez-faire principle (Bottery, 2000; Stromquist & Monkman, 2000). It is closely associated with neo-liberalism which "sees the market as the most effective way of determining production and satisfying people's needs" (Stromquist, 2003, 25). According to Carnoy (2000), the relationship between globalisation and educational change can be revealed not only from the expansion of higher education to cope with economic restructuring but also from the strong emphasis placed on the quality of education which is translated into some quantifiable and measurable performance indicators to be compared at the international level. Higher education is not surprisingly subject to financial constraints as a consequence of the shift towards neo-liberalism and the rise of economic globalisation (Bottery, 2000; Schugurensky, 2003). The adoption of quality assurance and performance indicators comes with intra- and inter-institutional competition among universities for revenues and resources and the application of business principles and practises in the institutional administration (Currie & Newson, 1998; Peters, Marshall, & Fitzsimons, 2000; Stromquist, 2003; Stromquist & Monkman, 2000; Taylor, Rizvi, Lingard, & Henry, 1997).

Performance assessments and indicators have become more important when the allocation of public funding to higher education in Hong Kong is not only based on student enrollments but also the competition for performance-based research funds. The General Research Fund under the Research Grants Council, which is part of the UGC, is a competitive funding scheme for research funds to be allocated based on academics' track records and the originality, merit, contribution and significance of their research projects. Moreover, there is the Research Assessment Exercise (RAE), which was at first conducted in 1993–94, to assess the research output performance of the UGC-funded institutions. The proportion of the active researchers at each cost centre is treated as a factor in determining the allocation of research funding for the next triennium. The second round of RAE was conducted in 1996 and the third in 1999. The fourth round was carried out in 2006 when the UGC decided to have the exercise undertaken at 6-year intervals instead of 3-year after the third RAE in 1999. The RAE in 2006 served as the basis for distributing of block grants for research among the eight UGC-funded institutions in the triennium of 2008–11 (University Grants Committee, 2004). The fifth round of RAE just finished in 2015.

Apart from witnessing the development of performance-based funding mechanisms in the higher education sector, universities are facing the professionalisation of management and the adoption of the more directive and assertive management style commonly found in the private sector. More professional managers are expected to play a more important role to lead universities and also to learn and borrow from other countries or institutions for the best practices of management (Bottery, 2000). Universities, like other public sector organisations, have to become more businesslike and incorporate good practices of business management whilst professional managers should be innovative, dynamic, flexible, transparent, customer-centred and strategic (Whitty, Power, & Halpin, 1998). Moreover, the language of efficiency, empowerment, rationality and transparency dominates the on-going processes of education reforms and restructuring in most parts of the world (Apple, 2001), including Hong Kong. Outcomes and outputs are measured against the goals, roles, and objectives set by universities and higher education institutions (Taylor, Rizvi, Lingard, & Henry, 1997). The notion of "fitness for purpose" has been emphasised for higher education in Hong Kong (University Grants Committee, 2002). While universities have to comply with the principle of public accountability, the collegial forms of decision-making have been considered an obstacle to managerial rationalities (Bok, 2003).

Within this policy context, the higher education sector in Hong Kong has experienced a rapid expansion as well as much intensified intra- and inter-institutional competitions for funding, students and academics since the final decade of the 20th century. These changes also gave rise to the introduction of quality assurance systems with the use of certain key performance indicators as a means of external quality audit on teaching, research and also management (Postiglione, 1996). Performance-based funding mechanisms were made to ensure the universities are more efficient, more accountable to the public, more cost-effective and more responsive to socio-economic needs (Schugurensky, 2003). Higher education practitioners and stakeholders are facing changes like the development of Hong Kong as a regional education hub, the admission of a larger number of non-local students, and the on-going restructuring of the university academic and curriculum systems (Postiglione, 2002). Moreover, there are also widespread concerns about the protection of academic freedom and institutional autonomy as well as the maintenance of internationalism (Postiglione, 1997).

Concomitant with a strong emphasis on market competition among institutions, the notion of "quality" has been interpreted from both the educational and business perspectives. Maximising the value for money and cost-effectiveness and meeting the market needs, the higher education sector is subject to greater pressure of external scrutiny with the use of several key performance indicators which are decided by the UGC. Finally, with the rise of managerialism, collegiality is taken over by corporate rationality in the decision-making processes in universities (Schugurensky, 2003).

## Major issue facing higher education nowadays

Some issues facing the higher education sector in Hong Kong have emerged in recent years, including 1) the institutionalisation of quality assurance mechanisms, 2) the reorientation of the government-university relationship, 3) the growth of private higher education institutions and 4) the internationalisation of higher education to cater for Hong Kong's strong intention to become a regional education hub. This section examines these issues and their impacts on higher education development one by one.

### *Institutionalisation of quality assurance*

The UGC defines quality assurance as "the maintenance of the highest possible standards, both in teaching and learning and in research, which are commensurating with an institution's agreed role and mission" (University Grants Committee, 2002, 18). Universities are responsible for upholding the quality of education and research in order to maintain their competitiveness in the global market competition in higher education. Meanwhile the UGC has introduced and managed a series of quality assurance mechanisms covering three major areas of higher education institutions, namely research, teaching and learning, and management. The allocation of research funds is subject to performance-based assessments and competitions. Apart from that, several reviews on the teaching and learning quality assurance processes and the institutional management were carried out. Teaching and Learning Quality Process Reviews (TLQPR) were carried out twice in 1995–97 and 2001–03. The objectives of TLQPR were to focus attention on teaching learning, to assist institutions in their efforts to improve teaching and learning quality, and to enable the UGC and the institutions to discharge their obligation to be accountable for quality (University Grants Committee, 1999).

Furthermore, Management Review (MR) was conducted in 1998–99 by the UGC to ensure individual institutions having the capacity and effective processes to manage devolved funds and resources to achieve their aims and objectives in face of financial cutback between 1999 and 2001 (French, 1999). MR was aimed to support the institutions in enhancing the quality of management, to discharge the UGC's accountability for ensuring that devolved funds and resources are managed appropriately, and to enhance the effectiveness of institutions' internal resource allocation, planning and financial processes. This review was also aimed to promote the sharing of experiences and best practices by the institutions in the areas of internal resource of allocation, planning and financial processes relative to the institutions' academic plans and objectives.

In 2007, the Quality Assurance Council (QAC) was set up as a semi-autonomous non-statutory body under the aegis of the UGC to carry out external quality audits targeting on the quality of teaching and learning in place of TLQPRs. The first audit conducted by the QAC was carried out on a four-year cycle between 2008 and 2011. The main objective of QAC audits is to assure the quality of student learning in UGC-funded institutions, and also to assure the UGC and the public that institutions can deliver on the promises they make in their mission statements in line with the notion of "fitness for purpose" especially in teaching and learning. What the QAC concerns is about the quality of student learning rather than research and managerial activities (Quality Assurance Council, c. 2007). The second round of QAC audits, which would be carried out over a two-year period, focused on promoting the enhancement of teaching and learning, and on assessing the strengths and weaknesses of current academic practice. More attention would be given to institutional strategies and policies for global engagements on the ways students can participate in an increasingly global community, together with more specific coverage of taught postgraduate programmes and research training programmes (Quality Assurance Council, c. 2011). These developments reveal an irreversible trend of institutionalising performance-based assessments and quality assurance in the higher education sector. However, the imposition of these quality assurance mechanisms has been criticised as a means not to improve the quality of education but incur much greater pressure for academics and university managers to comply with numerous quantifiable performance indicators amidst increasing rationalisation and bureaucratization of management (Cheng, 2002; Tse, 2002; Yeung, 2000).

## Reorientation of government-university relationship

The UGC, as the government's funding body and also policy adviser on higher education, has come with much greater pressure on universities to modify the governance and management systems in order to make them more accountable to the general public since the expansion of higher education in the mid-1990s. For instance, HKU was the first UGC-funded institution that underwent the governance review in 2003. One of the most significant changes was that the faculty deans would no longer be elected, but appointed by the top management according to the vice-chancellor's recommendation (University of Hong Kong, 2003).

Apart from this, a few other controversial incidents have aroused widespread concerns over the changing government-university relationship, especially since the handover in 1997.

According to the Basic Law, all educational institutions, including universities and higher education institutions, should be allowed to preserve institutional autonomy and academic freedom (National People's Congress, 1990, Article 137). Both institutional autonomy and academic freedom remain the most sacred values upheld by the academic community in Hong Kong. However, since 1997, there have been a few incidents triggering controversies over political interference in academic work. The first of such incidents happened in 1999 when the opinion polls on the popularity of the government conducted by a HKU's research centre were not welcomed by the former Chief Executive Tung Chee-Hwa, whose aide paid a visit to HKU's vice-chancellor to seek for his promise for not proceeding to opinion polls targeting on the performance of the government. The incident ended with the resignation of the vice-chancellor and the removal of the aide of the chief executive. This government's action was suspected as an abrupt infringement of the core academic value of academic freedom in a sense that academics should bear zero tolerance over political intervention into their work in research and teaching alike (Currie, Petersen, & Mok, 2006; Postiglione, 2002).

The second incident, which took place in 2002, is concerned about the merger plan between CUHK and HKUST as put forward by then Secretary for Education Arthur Li, who was CUHK's vice-chancellor in 1997–2002. The plan was to integrate the two universities into a strong comprehensive world-class university in Hong Kong. Nevertheless, due to the strong resistance of academics in both universities, the merger plan was not pursued but replaced by other viable initiatives of institutional collaboration and integration (University Grants Committee, 2004). The government subsequently proposed an idea of merging CUHK with HKIEd so as to strengthen the latter's research capacity and also its reputation in the local and international academic communities. Rather than a merger, a deep collaboration approach was deemed more appropriate and thus adopted. As a consequence, both institutions engaged in offering some joint undergraduate programmes with an aim of improving the quality of teachers' training in Hong Kong. These two merger proposals were perceived as attempts by the government to intervene directly into how certain universities should be run and to impose important policies with a top-down approach regardless key stakeholders' responses and reactions.

The third incident happened in 2007 when the senior management of HKIEd, after the contract of its president Paul Morris was not renewed, disclosed that then Permanent Secretary for Education Fanny Law filed a complaint to the institution against a few academics whose critics and commentaries published in the local press had obstructed the smooth implementation of education reforms and policies. Moreover, Arthur Li was accused of posing a threat to the HKIEd's senior management on cutting the number of student enrollments if the merger plan with CUHK was not accepted. Meanwhile, the senior management was also asked to issue a statement condemning a group of surplus teachers and a teachers' union for protesting against the government's refusal to secure those surplus teachers' jobs in primary and secondary schools. In face of these controversies between the government and HKIEd, then Chief Executive Donald Tsang appointed an independent commission to inquire into these allegations. While the two allegations against Arthur Li and the government's improper interference with institutional autonomy of HKIEd were not established, another one against Fanny Law on her improper interference with academic freedom enjoyed by a few academics working in HKIEd was established (Yeung & Lee, 2007). These incidents mentioned above inevitably aroused widespread concerns about the preservation of academic freedom and institutional autonomy by universities and higher education institutions.

## *Growth of private higher education*

The first decade of the 21st century witnessed the emergence and growth of private higher education in Hong Kong, which has long been dominated by the publicly-funded universities and higher education institutions. It is believed that private higher education can not only diversify the sector but also provide more choices for students to choose from and also provide alternative pathways for students to receive higher education without relying overwhelmingly on the UGC-funded institutions.

A breakthrough development took place in 2008 when the formerly post-secondary college, Shue Yan College, was granted the university status as SYU. Other privately-run post-secondary colleges, such as Chu Hai College of Higher Education, Hang Seng Management College and the Caritas Francis Hsu College, which is run by the Catholic Diocese in Hong Kong, have also planned to develop as private universities in the future. In addition, the government has also looked for renowned overseas universities to set up branch campuses in Hong Kong. For instance, the Savannah College of Art and Design (SCAD) set up its first Asian branch campus in Hong Kong in 2011 and the Booth School of Business of the University of Chicago decided to move its Asian campus from Singapore to Hong Kong in 2014. The emergence of overseas universities' branch campuses in Hong Kong suggests the good potential for Hong Kong to be developed as a regional hub of higher education.

In addition, there has been much more rapid development of community colleges which provide associate degree programmes for secondary school leavers since the early 2000s, when the government decided to ensure more opportunities of higher education, although they would not be exclusively provided by the publicly-funded universities. The UGC recommended in its third major review of higher education in 2010 to set up a single oversight body such as Further Education Council to oversee the quality of the non-publicly funded higher education institutions, including self-financed community colleges. The UGC also expressed its concerns about the credibility of self-financed associate degree programmes for which a clear identity and character should be constructed together with a more stringent quality assurance mechanism to strengthen the public confidence on the sector (University Grants Committee, 2010). This recognises the rapid development of privately-funded community colleges is not problem-free. Apart from the widespread concerns over the quality and credibility of associate degrees, there are also worries about the highly limited opportunity for associate degree holders to continue their study for degree programmes at the publicly-funded universities in Hong Kong. Moreover, the employability of associate degree holders is also questioned for their credentials are not fully recognised by some professions such as nursing (Kember, 2010).

## *Internationalisation for education hub*

Internationalisation is without doubt a popular issue widely discussed in many countries (De Wit, 2002; Knight, 2004). In Hong Kong's context, the concept of internationalisation can be analysed from two dimensions. On the one hand, internationalisation suggests a significant rise in the number of non-local or international students studying in Hong Kong's universities. In 2003–04, there were 2,871 non-local students enrolled in the UGC-funded institutions, accounting for about 4 per cent of the overall student enrolment. In the academics years 2011–12 and 2012–13, the numbers of non-local students studying in the UGC-funded institutions increased to 10,770 and 13,661 respectively, or around 14 per cent of the overall enrolment in both academic years. Moreover, a majority of non-local students were originated from the Chinese mainland with a much higher percentage at over 80 per cent as compared with those from other places in Asia or the rest of the world. In 2003–04, 2,536 students or about 88 per cent of non-local students were from the Chinese mainland, with most of them enrolling in research postgraduate programmes (Trade Development Council, 2005). From 2011–12 to 2014–15, around 75–80 per cent of non-local students were from the Chinese mainland, which contrasts with around 12–18 per cent from other parts in Asia and 4–5 percent from the rest of the world (University Grants Committee, 2013, 82; University Grants Committee, 2015). Although there had been an increase in the number of non-local students from outside the Chinese mainland over the past decade, there is still room for the UGC-funded institutions to strike a better balance between the proportion of the mainland Chinese students and the ones from Asia and other parts of the world. A possible reason for more non-local students to study in Hong Kong's universities is that they are allowed to stay in Hong Kong for employment for one year after graduation (University Grants Committee, 2010).

On the other hand, internationalisation means more than the recruitment of non-local or international students. It also refers to the integration of the universities in Hong Kong into an active network of relationships with international counterparts. One way is to demonstrate their "world-class" performance through a series of international university-ranking exercises. Certain universities in Hong Kong have been ranked high in several international league tables on higher education (see, for instance, Quacquarelli Symonds, 2014; *The Times Higher Education Supplement*, 2015). Some universities made use their institutional reputation to explore their markets for higher education outside Hong Kong, including the Chinese mainland and other parts of Asia. Some of them have been exploring opportunities of having collaboration with universities in the Chinese mainland to jointly offer self-financed taught postgraduate programmes and courses in China (Trade Development Council, 2005).

Moreover, internationalisation is a process leading to the making of Hong Kong as an "education hub" (Tung, 2004). The competitiveness of Hong Kong lies in the provision of high-quality higher education by a number of high-quality or internationally recognised world-class universities to non-local students. These non-local students can possibly become valuable talents to contribute to Hong Kong's long-term socio-economic development. In this sense, the development of Hong Kong as a regional education hub is to create a larger pool of local and non-local talents to keep the city on the track of sustainable development in the long run. Meanwhile, internationalisation also implies a fundamental change of the character of higher education, which is not just a public good but also a commodity for economic exchange as the cases shown in the United Kingdom, the United States, Australia, Canada and Singapore. This denotes the movements of some UGC-funded institutions to provide higher education outside Hong Kong like CUHK set up its first branch campus in Shenzhen in September 2014.

Nevertheless, there are a few unresolved problems facing Hong Kong universities for the on-going process of internationalisation. One of them is concerned about the composition of non-local student population, which has been dominated by mainland Chinese students. It is necessary for Hong Kong universities to find ways to attract not only the Chinese mainland students but also more students from Asian countries as well as other parts of the world to ensure a greater diversity of nationalities and cultural backgrounds (University Grants Committee, 2010). In view of pulling in more non-local students to study in Hong Kong universities, another unresolved problem to be tackled is the insufficient provision of hardware facilities, most particularly student accommodation. The consistent shortage of university student accommodation in Hong Kong, where land and housing shortage has been a major policy issue over the past few years, not only discourages the coming of non-local students but also instigates competition on the limited availability of on-campus accommodation between them and local students. In fact, competition between local and non-local students is not only about student accommodation, but also opportunity to go for further studies in local universities where a majority of research graduate students have been recruited outside Hong Kong, most particularly the Chinese mainland, in recent years (University Grants Committee, 2013, 2015). While it witnessed a significant increase of non-local students studying in Hong Kong universities, the welfare and interest of local students should not be neglected, for the universities are publicly-funded.

Internationalisation comprises core elements like exchanges of academics, students and knowledge across national boundaries, the recruitment of non-local or international students, the export of higher education by local institutions outside Hong Kong, and the import of higher education from overseas universities in Hong Kong. Apart from recruiting more non-local students, especially those from the Chinese mainland, Hong Kong universities have in recent years embarked on constructing collaborative relationships with the counterparts in the Chinese mainland in the forms of joint teaching and research projects as well as academic exchange programmes. The Chinese mainland has become the most important market of higher education for the eight UGC-funded institutions.

In short, internationalisation does bring about both opportunities and dangers to the higher education sector in Hong Kong. Further expansion of higher education is expected for an ever-growing market of higher education in Hong Kong's hinterland, the Chinese mainland, where demands for world-class higher education, including publicly-funded undergraduate and research postgraduate programmes as well as self-financed taught postgraduate programmes run by UGC-funded institutions would become more prominent. Moreover, more attention should be given to whether and how overseas institutions which set up their branch campuses in Hong Kong can survive on the self-sufficient basis in the long run, for they can mainly rely on the tuition fees as their incomes. The challenge is how to increase the number of students who can afford as much as HK$250,000 or US$32,000 a year for tuition fees at SCAD as a big contrast to HK$42,000 or US$5,400 charged by the UGC-funded institutions. An even more critical issue concerns how to get in more overseas students to study in this emerging education hub. It is important to rectify the common impression that what has been achieved since the early 21st century in Hong Kong higher education is not about "mainlandization" or regionalization but genuinely internationalisation.

## Discussion: Shaping the future of higher education

Having examined the four major issues facing Hong Kong universities, this section turns to discuss the trends shaping the future of higher education. It argues that the role of the government in higher education development in Hong Kong since 1997 has become more important, especially in the making of world-class universities and the transformation of Hong Kong as a regional education hub.

Hong Kong universities are under constant pressure to be more relevant and responsive to market needs. While institutional autonomy in making decisions on academic matters and resource allocation entitled to universities is largely respected, there has been stronger emphasis on the importance of external scrutiny in the forms of quality assurance and audits to be institutionalised in the higher education sector in line with such prevailing ideas as "value for money" and "fitness for purpose". Teaching, research and management have been regularly subject to the external scrutiny. The allocation of resources, especially those on research activities, is pegged with the results of external audits as a means to stimulate better performance delivered by the publicly-funded universities. While more prudent use and distribution of limited resources in universities is appreciated, universities have been encouraged to look for alternative sources of revenues other than the government as a means to "decentralise" the financial responsibilities of higher education, which has long been shouldered by the government. While the government takes a step back from financing higher education with an excuse of economic slowdown or depression, it has strengthened its role through the UGC to scrutinise and evaluate the performance and quality of public universities.

The universities are at the crossroads between competition and collaboration. It is undeniable that universities are constantly competing with each other for "star" or outstanding professors, best students, research funds, international reputation and also social donations in the higher education market. Although the higher education market is not a totally free market, for it is partly subsidised by the government, intra- and inter-institutional competitions are becoming more obvious with key performance indicators have been put in place. While competition among universities is encouraged to stimulate institutional improvement, institutional collaboration is of equal importance to prevent unnecessary wastage of resources by eliminating and avoiding duplication of teaching and research efforts. Competition and collaboration are not mutually exclusive, but they are complementary to each other to ensure a healthy development of higher education. A two-pronged strategy of competition and collaboration among the universities should be adopted to ensure continuous self-improvement and more effective use of limited resources simultaneously.

In the face of heightened pressure on competing teaching and research resources, as what can be seen from the imposition of more stringent criteria on research performance assessment and the open bidding of a certain proportion of undergraduate and research postgraduate places to be reallocated among UGC-funded institutions, there have been more critics from academics against the marketization and commercialization of higher education, leading to the alienation between university management and academics, who tend to pay more attention on how to uphold core values such as academic freedom and institutional autonomy and to achieve the goals of creating knowledge in the long run rather than just competing for financial resources in the short run. Academics in Hong Kong are aware of the negligence of research outputs on local issues, especially those which are written in Chinese, for they cannot be published in international journals (Tse, 2013). The "publish or perish" phenomenon still affects profoundly the work of academics as they need to spend more time on research at the expense of teaching quality (Yeung, 2000). Furthermore, the more recent controversy over the delayed appointment of a HKU pro-vice-chancellor, for the only candidate having close ties to a co-founder of Occupy Central Movement in 2014, triggered widespread concerns over whether the government was interfering in university affairs and thus threatening academic freedom (Cheung, 2015). These are the unresolved issues that need to be addressed so as to reflect on how higher education development should move on in Hong Kong. While it is important for Hong Kong universities to pursue "excellence", which should not be only about international rankings, it is also important to preserve the "soul" of university by upholding its core values, achieving its long-term goals, and serving the needs of society.

## Conclusion

Wang Gungwu, former HKU's vice-chancellor and renowned sinologist, points out that there has been a general decline in the confidence of Asian universities for the past three decades (Wang, 1992). In the past, many believed it was due to the lack of funding and facilities which prevented universities for doing an excellent job. However, the focus has shifted to the inadequacies of university structures and on how to reform them in order to make sure of more efficient use of funds and facilities in order to make distinctive contributions and thus justify their existence. Although most universities aim at international excellence and reputation, they have met with frustration and have attributed this to the shortage of resources and also the lack of appreciation by their communities. In spite of these drawbacks facing most Asian universities, with no exception for the ones in Hong Kong, they are very much eager to strive for a world-class status as revealed from a series of international university rankings (Altbach, 2003). Clark (1998, 2004) suggests that the future of universities denotes the transformation towards the direction of "entrepreneurial universities". The meaning of "entrepreneurial" in the context of higher education indicates "the attitudes and procedures that most dependably lead to the modern self-reliant, self-steering university" (Clark, 2004, 7).

When most countries put a strong emphasis on the development of quality assurance system, the changing university-government relationship and the policy and strategies of internationalisation, these issues have also prevailed in Hong Kong over the past two decades since massification took place in the 1990s. While Hong Kong is striving to be a regional education hub, it is not immune from global practices adopted from the process of policy borrowing and learning. As Currie (2004) addresses, if universities are going to be a model of institutions for the society, it is necessary to shore up democratic collegiality against the rush to managerialize the decision-making processes in universities. Moreover, there is a need for caution against picking up the latest management fad blindly without consideration about the unique context and nature of higher education. It is more important to uphold the core values of scholarly integrity and professional autonomy amidst greater pressure for public accountability.

## References

Altbach, P. (2003). The cost and benefits of world-class universities. *International Higher Education, 33*, 5–8.
Apple, M. (2001). *Educating the 'right' way*. New York: RoutledgeFalmer.
Barnett, R. (1990). *The idea of higher education*. Buckingham: The Society for Research into Higher Education & Open University Press.
Barnett, R. (1997). *Realizing the university*. London: Institute of Education, University of London.
Barnett, R. (2000a). *Realizing the university in an age of supercomplexity*. Buckingham: The Society for Research into Higher Education & Open University Press.
Barnett, R. (2000b). Reconfiguring the university. In P. Scott (Ed.). *Higher education re-formed* (pp. 114–129). New York: Falmer Press.
Bok, D. (2003). *Universities in the market place: The commercialization of higher education*. Princeton: Princeton University Press.
Bottery, M. (2000). *Education, policy and ethics*. London: Continuum.

Carnoy, M. (2000). Globalization and education reform. In N. Stromquist & K. Monkman (Eds.), *Globalization and education: Integration and contestation across cultures* (pp. 43–61). Lanham: Rowan & Littlefield Publishers.

Cheng, K. (2002). The quest for quality education: The quality assurance movement in Hong Kong. In J. Mok & D. Chan (Eds.), *Globalization and education: The quest for quality education in Hong Kong* (pp. 41–65). Hong Kong: Hong Kong University Press.

Cheung, T. (2015, August 25). 'Academic freedom is under threat': 300 Hong Kong academics petition over delay in HKU's pro-democracy appointment. *South China Morning Post*.

Clark, B. (1998). *Creating entrepreneurial universities: Organizational pathways of transformation*. Oxford: Pergamon.

Clark, B. (2004). *Sustaining change in universities: Continuities in case studies and concepts*. Buckingham: Society for Research into Higher Education & Open University Press.

Cunich, P. (2012). *A history of the University of Hong Kong* (Volume 1, 1911–1945). Hong Kong: Hong Kong University Press.

Currie, J. (2004). The neo-liberal paradigm and higher education: A critique. In F. Odin & P. Manicas (Eds.), *Globalization and higher education* (pp. 42–62). Honolulu: University of Hawaii Press.

Currie, J., & Newson, J. (1998). Globalizing practices: Corporate managerialism, accountability, and privatization. In J. Currie & J. Newson (Eds.), *Universities and globalization: Critical perspectives* (pp. 141–152). Thousand Oaks: Sage Publications.

Currie, J., Petersen, C., & Mok, K. (2006). *Academic freedom in Hong Kong*. Lanham, MD: Lexington Books.

De Wit. (2002). *Internationalization of higher education in the United States of America and Europe: A historical, comparative, and conceptual analysis*. Westport: Greenwood Press.

Education Commission. (2000). *Reform of the education system in Hong Kong: Learning for life, learning through life*. Hong Kong: Government Printer.

Education and Manpower Bureau. (2005). *The new academic structure for senior secondary education and higher education: Action plan for investing in the future of Hong Kong*. Hong Kong: Education and Manpower Bureau.

French, N. (1999). *The University Grants Committee's approach to quality assurance in higher education in Hong Kong*. Paper presented at a meeting of the Higher Education Research and Development Society of Australasia (HERDSA) Hong Kong Branch on 29 January. Hong Kong: University Grants Committee.

Hong Kong Government. (1978). *The development of senior secondary and tertiary education*. Hong Kong: Government Printer.

Information Services Department. (2015). *Hong Kong 2014*. Hong Kong: Government Logistics Department.

Kember, D. (2010). Opening up the road to nowhere: problems with the path to mass higher education in Hong Kong. *Higher Education, 59*, 167–179.

Kennedy, D. (1997). *Academic duty*. Cambridge: Harvard University Press.

Kerr, C. (2001). *The uses of the university* (Fifth edition). Cambridge: Harvard University Press.

Knight, J. (2004). New rationales driving internationalization. *International Higher Education, 34*, 3–5.

Leung, A. (2003). *The budget 2003–04*. Hong Kong: Printing Department, HKSAR Government.

Lin, A. (2002).The founding of the University of Hong Kong: British imperial ideals and Chinese practical common sense. In K. Chan-Lau & P. Cunich (Eds.), *An impossible dream: Hong Kong University from foundation to re-establishment, 1910–1950* (pp. 1–22). Oxford: Oxford University Press.

Lucas, C. (1996). *Crisis in the academy: Rethinking higher education in America*. New York: St. Martin's Press.

Marginson, S., & Considine, M. (2000). *The enterprise university: Power, governance and reinvention in Australia*. Cambridge: Cambridge University Press.

National People's Congress. (1990). *The basic law of the Hong Kong Special Administrative Region of the People's Republic of China*. Beijing: Standing Committee of the National People's Congress, The People's Republic of China.

Newman, J. (1996). *The idea of a university*. New Heaven: Yale University Press.

Peters, M., Marshall, J., & Fitzsimons, P. (2000). Managerialism and educational policy in a global context: Foucault, neoliberalism, and the doctrine of self-management. In N. Burbules & C. Torres (Eds.), *Globalization and education: Critical perspectives* (pp. 109–132). New York: Routledge.

Postiglione, G. (1996). The future of the Hong Kong academic profession in a period of profound change. In P. Altbach (Ed.), *The international academic profession: Portraits of fourteen centuries* (pp. 191–227). Princeton: The Carnegie Foundation for the Advancement of Teaching.

Postiglione, G. (1997). Hong Kong's universities within the global academy. In G. Postiglione & J. Tang (Eds.), *Hong Kong's reunion with China: Global dimensions* (pp. 239–268). Hong Kong: Hong Kong University Press.

Postiglione, G. (2002). The transformation of academic autonomy in Hong Kong. In M. Chan & A. So (Eds.), *Crisis and transformation in China's Hong Kong* (pp. 307–321). Hong Kong: Hong Kong University Press & M.E. Sharpe.

Quacquarelli Symonds (QS). (2014). *QS World University Rankings 2014–15*. London: QS.

Quality Assurance Council. (c. 2007). *Quality Assurance Council audit manual* (First audit cycle). Hong Kong: University Grants Committee.

Quality Assurance Council. (c. 2011). *Quality Assurance Council audit manual* (Second audit cycle). Hong Kong: University Grants Committee.

Readings, B. (1998). *The university in ruins*. Cambridge: Harvard University Press.

Schugurensky, D. (2003). Higher education restructuring in the era of globalization: Toward a heteronomous model? In R. Arnove & C. Torres (Eds.), *Comparative education: The dialectic of the global and the local* (Second edition) (pp. 292–312). Lanham: Rowan & Littlefield Publishers.

Shive, G. (1992). Educational expansion and the labour force. In G. Postiglione (Ed.), *Education and society in Hong Kong: Toward one country and two systems* (pp. 215–231). Hong Kong: Hong Kong University Press.

Sporn, B. (1999). *Adaptive university structures: An analysis of adaptation to socioeconomic environments of US and European universities*. London: Jessica Kingsley Publishers.

Stromquist, N. (2003). *Education in a globalized world: The connectivity of economic power, technology, and knowledge*. Lanham: Rowan & Littlefield Publishers.

Stromquist, N., & Monkman, K. (2000). Defining globalization. In N. Stromquist & K. Monkman (Eds.), *Globalization and education: Integration contestation across cultures* (pp. 3–25). Lanham: Rowan & Littlefield Publishers.

Sweeting, A. (2001). *Education in Hong Kong, 1941 to 2001: Visions and revisions.* Hong Kong: Hong Kong University Press.
Taylor, S., Rizvi, F., Lingard, B., & Henry, M. (1997). *Educational policy and the politics of change.* London: Routledge.
The Times Higher Education Supplement. (2015). *World University Rankings 2014–15.* London: The Times Higher Education Supplement.
Trade Development Council. (2005). *Exporting higher education services to the Chinese mainland: The Hong Kong advantages.* Hong Kong: Trade Development Council.
Tsang, D. (2009). *Chief Executive's policy address 2009.* Hong Kong: Government Logistics Department.
Tse, T. (2002). A critical review of the quality education movement in Hong Kong. In J. Mok & D. Chan (Eds.), *Globalization and education: The quest for quality education in Hong Kong* (pp. 143–169). Hong Kong: Hong Kong University Press.
Tse, T. (2013). Endless controversies over education reforms. In K. Law & J. Cheng (Eds.), *On the chessboard: Donald Tsang's legacy for C.Y. Leung* (pp. 163–193). Hong Kong: City University of Hong Kong Press [in Chinese].
Tung, C. (2001). *Chief Executive's policy address 2001.* Hong Kong: Government Printer.
Tung, C. (2004). *Chief Executive's policy address 2004.* Hong Kong: Government Logistics Department.
University Grants Committee. (1996). *Higher education in Hong Kong: A report by the University Grants Committee.* Hong Kong: University Grants Committee.
University Grants Committee. (1999). *University Grants Committee of Hong Kong China: Report for July 1995 to June 1998.* Hong Kong: Government Printer.
University Grants Committee. (2002). *Higher education in Hong Kong: Report of the University Grants Committee.* Hong Kong: University Grants Committee.
University Grants Committee. (2004). *Hong Kong higher education: Integration matters.* Hong Kong: University Grants Committee.
University Grants Committee. (2010). *Aspirations for the higher education system in Hong Kong.* Hong Kong: University Grants Committee.
University Grants Committee. (2013). *University Grants Committee annual report 2012–13.* Hong Kong: University Grants Committee.
University Grants Committee. (2015). *Non-local student enrolment (headcount) of UGC-funded programmes by institutions, level of study, place of origin and mode of study, 2013–14 to 2014–15.* Hong Kong: University Grants Committee.
University of Hong Kong. (2003). *Fit for purpose: The review of governance and management structures at the University of Hong Kong.* Hong Kong: University of Hong Kong.
Wang, G. (1992). Universities in transition in Asia. *Oxford Review of Education, 18*(1), 17–27.
Whitty, G., Power, S., & Halpin, D. (1998). *Devolution and choice in education: The school, the state and the market.* Buckingham: Open University Press.
Yeung, C., & Lee, J. (2007). *Report of the Commission of Inquiry on allegations relating to the Hong Kong institute of education.* Hong Kong: Government Logistics Department.
Yeung, L. (2000, July 16). Under pressure to 'publish or perish'. *South China Morning Post.*
Yung, A. (2002). Community college: A new born baby of the Hong Kong education system for the new millennium. *Hong Kong Teachers' Centre Journal, 1,* 32–44.

# Index

Note: Information in figures and tables is indicated by page numbers in *italics*.

accountability 14, 152–4, 161, 189–91; *see also* reporting, public
advisory boards: language policy and 63–4
Anti-National Education Movement 131–3
autocracy, in schools 184–5

basic education 5–6, 9–10; colonial legacy and 74–5; quality in 75–82, *76–8*, *80*, *81*
Basic Law 129
biliterate/ trilingual policy (BTP) 9, 61–3; as compromise 64–5
BTP *see* biliterate/ trilingual policy (BTP)

Canada 78, *81*, *86*, *87*, *88*
capital 47–8, 84–5
case study: Direct Subsidy Scheme 44–7
CBS *see* cross-boundary students (CBS)
centralisation 66–7
Cheng, K. M. 113
China, mainland: gender differences in student achievement in *81*; mathematical literacy in *78*; migration from 11; in PISA *76*
Chinese as medium of instruction (CMI) policy 42–3; colonial legacy and 55–6; compulsory 59–61; *see also* language policy
Chinese immigrant students (CIS) 201, 202, 206–9; *see also* immigrant students
Chinese University (CUHK) 217, 222
choice: background on 40–1; capital and 47–8; class differentiation and 47–8; Direct Subsidy Scheme and 41–4; early childhood education vouchers and 27–8; Medium of Instruction policy and 42–3; private sector and 49; social closure and 49; social implications of 47–9
CHSC *see* Committee on Home-School Co-Operation (CHSC)
CIS *see* Chinese immigrant students (CIS)
civic education: and anti-national education movement 131–3; civic identity and 136, 139; civil disobedience and 135–6; colonial legacy and 129–30; defined 129; depoliticisation and 130–1; development of 133–7; empowerment and 136–7; in Hong Kong context 128–31; liberal studies and 131, 134–5; Moral and National Education and 132; morality and 135, 138; Occupy Movement and 133–7; policy recommendations 137–40; political action and 135, 138–9; political literacy and 134–5; politicisation and 130
civic identity 136, 139
civil disobedience 135–6
class *see* socioeconomic status
clients, parents as 189–91
closure, social 49
collaboration, in home-school partnerships 186–9
colonial legacy: in basic education 74–5; civic education and 129–30; early childhood education and 21–2; language policy and 55–7
Committee on Home-School Co-Operation (CHSC) 188
cross-boundary students (CBS) 201, 203; *see also* immigrant students

## Index

CUHK *see* The Chinese University (CUHK)
culture 82
curriculum issues, with immigrant students 205–6
curriculum reform 5–8, 14–15; causes of high level of implementation of 118–20; costs of 120–1; culture and 122; epistemological shifts and 115, *115*; forces leading to 116; globalisation and 116; level of implementation of *117*, 117–18; nature of 113–15, *115*; neo-liberalism and 119–20; outcomes of *117*, 117–18; scale of 112, 113–15, *115*; teachers and 120–1; whole-person development and 113–14

decentralisation 66, 148–9, 150–1, 192, 226–7
demographics 11, 74, 201–3
Direct Subsidy Scheme (DSS) 10, 13, 15; background on 40–1; case study on 44–7; choice and 41–4; and English as medium of instruction 51, 67–8; exclusivity and 46–7; fee-remission and 50; objectives of 50; parents and 44–7; private sector and 49; quality and 46; social implications of 47–9; socioeconomic status and 50–1; tuition and 43, 48, 50
disadvantaged groups: Direct Subsidy Scheme and 46–7; and early education voucher scheme 26–7; *see also* immigrant students
disempowerment 136–7
doubly non-permanent resident (DNR) parents 201
DSS *see* Direct Subsidy Scheme (DSS)

early childhood education 5–6; colonial legacy and 21–2; fee-remission scheme in 25–6; free 32–3; half-day operation in 25, 27–8; neo-liberalism and 22–3, 33; quality in 33–4; vouchers in 21–34
economic, social, and cultural status (ESCS) 85, *86*, *88*, 88–9; *see also* socioeconomic status (SES)
educational market *see* market, educational
educational reforms: consequences of 15–17; implications of 17–18; neo-liberalism and 147–9; overview of 4–9, 5–8; responses to 11–15;

shadow education and 99–100; *see also* curriculum reform
Education Bureau (EDB) 153, 181
EDB *see* Education Bureau
Education Manpower Bureau (EMB) 153–4, 156, 181
Education Ordinance 107
Education University of Hong Kong (EdUHK) 216
EdUHK *see* The Education University of Hong Kong
EMB *see* Education Manpower Bureau (EMB)
EMI *see* English as medium of instruction (EMI)
employment: shadow education and 104
empowerment 136–7
English, in shadow education 98
English as medium of instruction (EMI): choice and 42–3; colonial legacy and 55–6; Direct Subsidy Scheme and 51, 67–8; public reporting and 171; unintended consequences of 67–8; *see also* language policy
equality: context of education in search of 74–5; development of concept 73; education's influence on social 73–4; of immigrant students 82–4, *83*, *84*; shadow education and 105–6; socioeconomic status and 84–91, *86–90*
equity: early childhood education vouchers and 26–7; language policy and 67–8
ESCS *see* economic, social, and cultural status (ESCS)
ESR *see* External School Review (ESR)
exclusivity: Direct Subsidy Scheme and 46–7
External School Review (ESR) 153–4, 163, 168, 174; *see also* reporting, public

family *see* home-school partnerships; parents
family resource hypothesis 84–5
fee-remission scheme 25–6, 50
fertility rate 11
Finland 78, 79, *81*, *86*, *87*, *88*
funding 3, 119, 219–20; *see also* Direct Subsidy Scheme (DSS)

gender disparity, in academic achievement 79–82, *80*, *81*
girls *see* gender disparity, in academic achievement

## Index

globalisation 10–11, 116, 127, 145–7, 156–7, 218–19; *see also* neo-liberalism
government spending *see* spending
*Guidelines 2012* 132–3

higher education 7–8, 9; decentralisation in 226–7; funding in 219–20; future of 226–7; globalisation and 218–19; government-university relationship in 221–3; immigrant students and 202; institutions 215–16; internationalisation and 224–6; issues facing 220–6; massification of 100–1; past and present of 215–18; policy context of 218–20; private 223–4; quality in, institutionalization of 220–1; University Grants Committee and 215–16, 220–1, 223
HKDSE *see* Hong Kong Diploma of Secondary Education (HKDSE)
HKIEd *see* Hong Kong Institute of Education (HKIEd)
HKU *see* University of Hong Kong (HKU)
HKUST *see* Hong Kong University of Science and Technology (HKUST)
home-school partnerships: accountability and 189–91; benefits of 181; collaboration in 186–9; committee on 187–8; decentralisation and 192; Education Ordinance on 180–1, 191–2; frameworks for 182; growing confidence stage in 182; immigrant students and 209; parental role in 183–93; parent involvement and 181–3; parents as clients in 189–91; parents as school governors in 191–3; parents as unwelcome guests in 183–6; parents as volunteers in 186–9; Parent-Teachers Associations and 188–9; as policy rhetoric 193–5; power relations in 183; professional uncertainty stage in 182; quality and 190–1; School Management Initiative and 186–7; self-contained stage of 182, 185–6; tensions with 182–3
Hong Kong Academy of Performing Arts 216
Hong Kong Advanced Level Examination 120
Hong Kong Certificate of Education Examination 120

Hong Kong Diploma of Secondary Education (HKDSE) 100, 114, 120
Hu Jintao 131

identity: civic 136, 139; of migrant students 203–5
IMC *see* incorporated management committee (IMC)
immigrant students 16, 74, 82–4, *83*, *84*, 92, 201–9
implementation theory 12
incorporated management committee (IMC) 152
Institute of Education (HKIEd) 216, 217, 222–3
internationalisation: in higher education 224–6

Japan 76, 78, 79, 81, 86, 87, 88
junior secondary education 5–6

key learning areas (KLAs) 114
key performance measures (KPM) 163, 167
KLAs *see* key learning areas (KLAs)
Korea 76, 78, 79, 81, 86, 87, 88
KPM *see* key performance measures (KPM)

language policy: and acquisition 9, 16; advisory bodies and 63–4; after 1997 58–9; biliterate/trilingual 9, 61–3; colonial legacy and 55–7; dilemma of 63–7; equity and 67–8; governance and 66–7; history of 54–63; immigrant students and 208; language enhancement and 57; language landscape and 58–9; medium of instruction and 42–3, 51; politics and 66; recommendations 68–9; shadow education and 102; unintended consequences of 67–8; *see also* Chinese as medium of instruction (CMI) policy; English as medium of instruction (EMI)
leadership 154–6
Li, Arthur 222
Liberal Studies (LS) 131, 134–5
Liechtenstein 76
literacy 76, 77, *77*, 80, *80*, 81, 83, 84, 86, 89, *117*, 117–18
LS *see* Liberal Studies (LS)

Macao 76, 78, 79, 81, 86, 87, 88
mainland *see* China, mainland

management, school-based 150–2
Management Review (MR), in higher education 221
market, educational 10; background on 40–1; neo-liberalism and 149; voucher scheme and 30–2
massification, of post-secondary education 100–1
Mathematics 76, 77, 77, 78, 79–80, 80, 81, 83, 84, 86, 88, 88–9, 90, 117, 117–18
means-tested fee-remission scheme 25–6
media: school reporting and 169–71
medium of instruction *see* Chinese as medium of instruction (CMI) policy; English as medium of instruction (EMI)
Medium of Instruction (MOI) policy 42–3, 54, 55–7; *see also* language policy
migration 11, 74; *see also* immigrant students
minority students 16; Direct Subsidy Scheme and 46–7; vouchers and 32; *see also* disadvantaged groups; immigrant students
MNE *see* Moral and National Education (MNE)
MOI *see* Medium of Instruction (MOI) policy
Moral and National Education (MNE) 11, 12–13, 132
morality, political action and 135
Morris, Paul 222
MR *see* Management Review (MR)

NCS *see* non-Chinese speaking students (NCS)
neo-liberalism 10, 13, 16; curriculum reform and 119–20; decentralisation and 148–9; defined 147; early childhood education and 22–3, 33; educational reform and 147–9; values of 147–8; vouchers and 22–3, 23–4, 31–2; *see also* globalisation
Netherlands 76
New Right 149; *see also* neo-liberalism
news media: school reporting and 169–71
*1985 Guidelines* 130
*1996 Guidelines* 130
nine-year basic education *see* basic education

non-Chinese speaking students (NCS) 201, 202, 204, 206, 207–8; *see also* immigrant students

Occupy Movement 133–7, 227
"One Country, Two Systems" 128–9, 137, 138

parents: accountability orientation and 14; as clients 189–91; Direct Subsidy Scheme and 44–7; doubly non-permanent resident 201; early childhood education vouchers and 23, 28–9; exclusion of 183–4, 183–5; immigrant students and 209; involvement of 181–3; as school governors 191–3; tensions with 182–3; as unwelcome guests 183–9; as volunteers 186–9; work-family balance and 32; *see also* choice; home-school partnerships
Parent-Teachers Associations (PTAs) 188–9
PIRLS *see* Progress in International Reading Literacy Study (PIRLS)
PISA *see* Programme for International Student Assessment (PISA)
placement systems 45
POA *see* Primary One Admission (POA)
political action, morality and 135
political literacy 134–5
population: demography 11, 74, 201–3; size 3, 4
post-secondary education *see* higher education
primary education 5–6
Primary One Admission (POA) 45
principals 154–6
private higher education 223–4; *see also* higher education
private tutoring 15–16, 16–17; *see also* shadow education
professional development 154–6
Programme for International Student Assessment (PISA) 2, 74, 75, 76, 77, 79–80, 80, 82, 83, 85, 86–7, 89, 90, 91, 117, 117–18
Progress in International Reading Literacy Study (PIRLS) 74
PSE (post-secondary education) *see* higher education
PTAs *see* Parent-Teachers Associations (PTAs)
public reporting *see* reporting, public
Putonghua language 58, 61–2, 62–3

QAC *see* Quality Assurance Council (QAC)
QAI *see* Quality Assurance Inspectorate (QAI)
quality: accountability and 152–4; in basic education 75–82, *76–8, 80, 81*; context of education in search of 74–5; Direct Subsidy Scheme and 46; in early childhood education 33–4; in higher education, institutionalization of 220–1; home-school partnerships and 190–1; in non-profit *vs.* for-profit 31; and vouchers for early childhood education 24, 28–30, 33
Quality Assurance Council (QAC) 221
Quality Assurance Inspectorate (QAI) 152–3, 162, 168, 170; *see also* reporting, public

RAE *see* Research Assessments Exercise (RAE)
reading *76, 77, 77, 80, 80, 81, 83, 84, 86, 89, 117,* 117–18
recentralisation 66
reforms, educational: consequences of 15–17; implications of 17–18; neo-liberalism and 147–9; overview of 4–9, *5–8*; responses to 11–15; shadow education and 99–100; *see also* curriculum reform
reporting, public 14; consequences of 171–2; demand for 161; development of 162–4; disputes over 164–72; and English as medium of instruction 171; generation of information for 165–7; implications of 172–5; information disclosure in 167–9; media and 169–71; origins of 162–4; teachers and 164–5; uses of 161, 163–4; work required for 167; *see also* accountability
Research Assessments Exercise (RAE) 219
role modeling 104–5

St. Stephen's Girls' College (SSGC) 49–50
SBA *see* School-Based Assessment (SBA)
SBM *see* school-based management (SBM)
SBS *see* School-Based Support Scheme (SBS)
School-Based Assessment (SBA) 100
school-based management (SBM) 150–2, 180

School-Based Support Scheme (SBS) 206–7
school district *see* school net
School Management Committee (SMC) 191–2
School Management Initiative (SMI) 119, 150–1, 186–7
school net 41
school placement systems 45
schools: defined 107n1; number of 3, *4*
School Self-Evaluation (SSE) 153–4, 162
science *76, 77, 77, 80, 80, 81, 84, 87, 117,* 117–18
SCOLAR *see* Standing Committee on Language Education and Research (SCOLAR)
secondary education: junior *5–6*; senior *7–8*
Secondary School Places Allocation (SSPA) 45, 51n1, 79
segregation, social *89,* 89–91, *90*
SES *see* socioeconomic status (SES)
shadow education 16–17; academic subjects in 96, 98; advice and 104–5; and backwash on regular schooling 106–7; competition and 101; defined 95–6; domestic support and 104–5; education reform and 99–100; employment and 104; expansion of 99–103; features of 96–9, *97*; implications of expansion of 103–7; intensity of 98; language in 98; language policy and 102; modes 98–9; participation rates in *97*; post-secondary education and 100–1; privateness in 96; regulatory framework and 102–3; role modeling and 104–5; scale of 96–7, *97*; social stratification and 105–6; supplementation in 96; *see also* private tutoring
Singapore *76, 78, 81, 86, 87,* 116
SMC *see* School Management Committee (SMC)
SMI *see* School Management Initiative (SMI)
social closure 49
social equality 73–4; *see also* equality
social media 136
social mobility 15
social segregation *89,* 89–91, *90*
socioeconomic status (SES) 15–16; Direct Subsidy Scheme and 47–8, 50–1; equality and 84–91, *86–90*; shadow education and 105–6

South Asian students 207–8
spending 3–4, *4*; early childhood education vouchers and 30–1
SSE *see* School Self-Evaluation (SSE)
SSGC *see* St. Stephen's Girls' College (SSGC)
SSPA *see* Secondary School Places Allocation (SSPA)
Standing Committee on Language Education and Research (SCOLAR) 62, 64
status attainment 73–4
student(s): Chinese immigrant 201, 202, 206–9; cross-boundary 201, 203; demographic shifts in 201–3; of doubly non-permanent resident parents 201; enrollment numbers 3, *4*; immigrant 16, 74, 82–4, *83*, *84*, 92, 201–2, 201–9; minority 16; non-Chinese speaking 201, 202, 204, 206, 207–8; South Asian 207–8; variation of performance of 77–9, *78*
subsidies *see* Direct Subsidy Scheme (DSS)
Sweden 78, *81*, *86*, *87*
Switzerland 76

Taipei 76, *81*, *86*, *87*, 88
Target Oriented Curriculum (TOC) 115, 119
teachers: public reporting and 164–5; workload of 120–1
Teaching and Learning Quality Process Reviews (TLQPR) 220
TIMSS *see* Trends in International Mathematics and Science Study (TIMSS)
TLQPR *see* Teaching and Learning Quality Process Reviews (TLQPR)
TOC *see* Target Oriented Curriculum (TOC)
Trends in International Mathematics and Science Study (TIMSS) 2, 74, 82

Tsang, Donald 12, 25, 131–2, 223
tuition: Direct Subsidy Scheme and 43, 48, 50
Tung Chee-Hwa 200
tutorial centres 97; *see also* shadow education
tutoring, private 15–16, 16–17; *see also* shadow education

UGC *see* University Grants Committee (UGC)
United Kingdom 78, *81*, *86*, *87*
United States 78, 82, *86*, *87*
university *see* higher education
University Grants Committee (UGC) 215–16, 220–1, 223
University of Hong Kong (HKU) 217, 222
University of Science and Technology (HKUST) 216, 217, 222

volunteers, parents as 186–9
vouchers, in early childhood education 21–34; affordability and 26–7; choice and 27–8; costs and 26; disadvantaged groups 26–7; as distributive policy 24; effectiveness of 23; equity and 26–7; fee-remission scheme and 25–6; half-day operation and 25, 27–8; impact of 25–30; introduction of 22; issues of 30–2; market and 30–2; neo-liberalism and 22–3, 23–4, 31–2; parents and 23, 28–9; as policy tool 22–5; quality and 24, 28–30, 33; spending and 30–1; technocratic measures of 24–5; tensions with 25–30

Wang Gungwu 227–8
women *see* gender disparity, in academic achievement
work-family balance 32

Zimbabwe 183